ASPEN COLLEGE SERIES

Elder Law for Paralegals

Laurel A. Vietzen

Professor Emeritus
Elgin Community College

Wolters Kluwer
Law & Business

AUSTIN   BOSTON   CHICAGO   NEW YORK   THE NETHERLANDS

Aspen Publishers
Attn: Permissions Department
76 Ninth Avenue, 7th Floor
New York, NY 10011-5201

To contact Customer Care, e-mail customer.service@aspenpublishers.com, call
1-800-234-1660, fax 1-800-901-9075, or mail correspondence to:

Aspen Publishers
Attn: Order Department
PO Box 990
Frederick, MD 21705

Printed in the United States of America.

1 2 3 4 5 6 7 8 9 0

ISBN 978-0-7355-0867-5

Library of Congress Cataloging-in-Publication Data

Vietzen, Laurel A.
    Elder law for paralegals / Laurel A. Vietzen.
        p. cm. — (Aspen college series)
    Includes index.
    ISBN-13: 978-0-7355-0867-5
    ISBN-10: 0-7355-0867-4
    1. Older people — Legal status, laws, etc. — United States 2. Legal
assistants — United States — Handbooks, manuals, etc. 3. Older
people — Legal status, laws, etc. I. Title.
KF390.A4V54 2011
346.7301'3 — dc22
                                                                2011004315

About Wolters Kluwer Law & Business

Wolters Kluwer Law & Business is a leading provider of research information and workflow solutions in key specialty areas. The strengths of the individual brands of Aspen Publishers, CCH, Kluwer Law International, and Loislaw are aligned within Wolters Kluwer Law & Business to provide comprehensive, in-depth solutions, and expert-authored content for the legal, professional, and education markets.

CCH was founded in 1913 and has served more than four generations of business professionals and their clients. The CCH products in the Wolters Kluwer Law & Business group are highly regarded electronic and print resources for legal, securities, antitrust and trade regulation, government contracting, banking, pension, payroll, employment and labor, and healthcare reimbursement and compliance professionals.

Aspen Publishers is a leading information provider for attorneys, business professionals, and law students. Written by preeminent authorities, Aspen products offer analytical and practical information in a range of specialty practice areas from securities law and intellectual property to mergers and acquisitions and pension/benefits. Aspen's trusted legal education resources provide professors and students with high-quality, up-to-date, and effective resources for successful instruction and study in all areas of the law.

Kluwer Law International supplies the global business community with comprehensive English-language international legal information. Legal practitioners, corporate counsel, and business executives around the world rely on the Kluwer Law International journals, loose-leafs, books, and electronic products for authoritative information in many areas of international legal practice.

Loislaw is a premier provider of digitized legal content to small law firm practitioners of various specializations. Loislaw provides attorneys with the ability to quickly and efficiently find the necessary legal information they need, when and where they need it, by facilitating access to primary law as well as state-specific law, records, forms, and treatises.

Wolters Kluwer Law & Business, a unit of Wolters Kluwer, is headquartered in New York and Riverwoods, Illinois. Wolters Kluwer is a leading multinational publisher and information services company.

Summary of Contents

Contents

1
♦ ♦ ♦

The Practice of Elder Law

2
♦ ♦ ♦

Advance Directives

3

◆ ◆ ◆

Guardianship/Conservatorship

4

◆ ◆ ◆

Social Security

5

◆ ◆ ◆

Medical Matters

6
◆ ◆ ◆

Medicare

7
◆ ◆ ◆

Medicaid

8
◆ ◆ ◆

Estate Planning

9
◆ ◆ ◆

Housing

10
◆ ◆ ◆

Abuse, Neglect, and Financial Exploitation

11
◆ ◆ ◆

Financial Matters

12
◆ ◆ ◆

End-of-Life Issues

13
◆ ◆ ◆

Family Matters

14
◆ ◆ ◆

Discrimination

Preface

My experience with elder law began about 30 years ago, when my in-laws (who lived several states away) visited a law firm for the first time in their lives and were persuaded to sign estate planning documents that they did not understand and that were not appropriate to their situation. The attorney, who did not have a paralegal and charged an outrageous fee, did not listen to their concerns and showed them no respect. When I graduated from law school the following year and began practicing estate planning and probate, I promised myself I would do a better job. A big part of doing a better job involves use of paralegals to keep costs down and communication up. I was fortunate that my paralegals had excellent communication skills as well as substantive knowledge.

Later, as the coordinator of a paralegal program, I had a request for a course in Elder Law. I knew it was more than estate planning and I began exploring the topic. I was again fortunate: There were program graduates working in the field even though we had not offered the class. My preparation to teach the class involved learning a lot of substantive law and spending time in law firms to pick up the "culture" of dealing with these clients. A book on this subject could be huge, if it covered that substantive law in detail as well as the "soft skills" required for ethical practice and good client communication. I think I've found the right balance: giving students the terminology and legal framework they need to be effective without overwhelming them with detail and, at the same time, keeping the content client-focused, as this area of practice must be.

I would like to thank the busy professionals who were so generous in providing information for the profiles: Noel Anschutz, Rev. Amity Carrubba, LaShonda Dillard, Greg Duncan, Heather Finn, Pete Flowers, Dr. Ron Hirsch, Eric Matusewich, Tina McHorney, Kathy Motley, Kimberly Murphy, Jennifer Poulin, Lisa Wagman, and, particularly, the people at Law ElderLaw, LLP, Aurora, IL.

Laurel A. Vietzen
February 2011

Elder Law for Paralegals

1

◆ ◆ ◆

The Practice of Elder Law

◆ ◆ ◆

Objectives

When you complete this chapter, you will:

- Understand the ethical issues and rules particularly important when representing older clients.
- Recognize the factors relevant to assessing a client's decision-making capacity.
- Be aware of the emotional, physical, and cultural barriers to communication between an older client and a legal professional.
- Know how to search for family and financial information for a client.

What Is Elder Law?

According to the U.S. Department of Health and Human Services Administration on Aging,[1] the older population—persons 65 years or older—numbered 38.9 million in 2008 (the latest year for which data is available). They represented 12.8 percent of the U.S. population, about one in every eight Americans. By 2030, there will be about 72.1 million older persons, representing about 19 percent of the population. The people in the "older" category are living longer, expecting more independence, and engaging in more active lives than their predecessors, thereby creating more potential for legal issues.

This demographic change presents challenges at all levels from the international, as shown in Exhibit 1.1, to the local. In testimony before the Senate Finance Committee on February 10, 2010, Michael J. Burgess, director of the New York State Office for the Aging, said:

> These are difficult economic times across the country and here in New York State. Older New Yorkers, their families and their caregivers are feeling the impact of the economic downturn, as it affects their income (since this year there is no federal cost-of-living adjustment for Social Security recipients), their investments, and their standard of living. The impact on standard of living is particularly problematic for those who are already living close to poverty levels; many older New Yorkers rely on the services funded through the state, federal and local budgets for assistance with food, shelter, and tasks of daily living. Counties continue to report escalating costs and diminishing revenue while needs are growing, in part due to the State's changing demographics. From 2000 to 2015, all but four counties in New York will experience increases in the proportion of their residents who are over age sixty-five. Governor Paterson's budget ensures that the New York State Office for the Aging (NYSOFA) will be able to preserve the local infrastructure of the service network for older adults and the home and community-based services they and their families need to support independent living. This is a network that has been very successful in leveraging local dollars, including significant contributions from the program participants themselves. The network of Area Agencies on Aging (AAAs) and community-based service providers is the first line of support when an older adult needs assistance following an illness or hospitalization.

> Excerpted from *http://www.aging.ny.gov/News/2010/NYSOFADirectors2010 Budget Testimony.pdf*

EXHIBIT 1.1
International Perspective on the Aging Population

In almost every country, the proportion of people age 60 years and older is growing faster than any other age group, as a result of both longer life expectancy and declining fertility rates, according to the World Health Organization (WHO), which regards the aging population as a success story for health policies and socioeconomic development. While this trend presents challenges for the developed world, 70

---

[1] *http://www.aoa.gov/aoaroot/aging_statistics*

EXHIBIT 1.1 **(continued)**

percent of all older people now live in low- or middle-income countries. In developing countries, this demographic change, coupled with traditions based on people living shorter lives and having several children, can be devastating. For example, as the first generation of people born under China's 1979 One-Child policy reaches adulthood, people without siblings are finding the burden of caring for aging parents overwhelming. Institutional care is not readily available and, because of cultural traditions, most people do not trust nursing homes and hired caregivers.

The United Nations Population Division, Department of Economic and Social Affairs, indicates that:

- One out of every ten persons is now 60 years or older; by 2050, one out of five will be 60 years or older; and by 2150, one out of three persons will be 60 years or older.
- The oldest members of this group (those 80 years or older) is the fastest growing segment of the older population. They currently make up 13 percent of the over-60 age group and will grow to 20 percent by 2050. The number of centenarians is projected to increase fourteen-fold by 2050.
- The majority of older persons (55 percent) are women. Among the oldest, 64 percent are women.
- Striking differences exist between regions. One out of five Europeans is 60 years or older, compared with one out of twenty Africans.
- As the tempo of aging in developing countries is more rapid, developing countries will have less time than developed countries to adapt to the consequences of population aging.
- On average, about 70 percent of older persons in more developed countries, and only 38 percent in the least developed countries, are urban dwellers.
- The impact of population aging is increasingly evident in the old-age dependency ratio — the number of working-age persons (15 to 64 years) per older person (65 years or older) — that is used as an indicator of the "dependency burden" on potential workers. Between 2005 and 2050, the old-age dependency ratio will almost double in more developed regions and almost triple in less developed regions.

The term "dependency burden" provides some insight into the need for the specialty area of "elder law." While elders were traditionally seen as possessing essential knowledge and experience, many segments of society now view them as an economic and physical burden. Economic downturns often aggravate this perception and make the reality more difficult. Older people may be at greater risk of losing their jobs and less likely to be retrained and reemployed, increasing their economic and physical vulnerability. Where public health care is lacking, families may forgo health care for older adults to allocate their scarce resources toward food or education for younger family members.

Of course, the change is also felt in private lives. Any legal issue faced by one of these people is likely to have repercussions for family members, often working from a distance, so elder law issues affect a very large segment of the population. In addition, a young person can face "elder issues," such as diagnosis (personally, or of a spouse or child) with a chronic, life-changing medical condition. That does not mean that elder law is simply general practice marketed to a specific segment of the population. Most general-practice lawyers know little about navigating Social Security benefits or preserving assets while applying for Medicaid. A truly ethical lawyer knows when she is not competent to handle a particular problem and finds someone who can handle it.

In identifying the topics for this book, I had to do the very thing I repeatedly ask students not to do: Make assumptions. While older clients may have any type of legal problem, including arrest for criminal behavior, I had to assume that certain problems are less likely to be of concern to the young and more likely to be of concern to older people in order to keep this book at a reasonable length. In order to identify those topics, I consulted the Web site of the American Association of Retired Persons **AARP**, which conducts surveys to assess the concerns and views of its members with respect to legal (and other) issues.[2]

AARP
Nonprofit organization with a mission of improving the lives of people age 50 and older

Regardless of the area of law, dealing with older clients and others facing elder issues does implicate certain ethical and practical concerns. This chapter provides an overview of those concerns, many of which are discussed in detail in later chapters.

Of course, it's not only the legal professions that face ethical challenges as a result of the demographic trend. In October 2009, the television news show *60 Minutes* reported that Medicare fraud had pushed aside cocaine as the number one criminal enterprise in South Florida. Improper Medicare payments may involve a mistake or intentional fraud by medical professionals. Because the cost is so great, Congress has enacted laws, such as the Improper Payments Information Act of 2002[3] (IPIA) and the Physician Self-Referral (Stark) Act[4] to monitor and reduce losses. Exhibit 1.2 is a chart from the 2009 report by the Centers for Medicare and Medicaid Services. According to the Kaiser Family Foundation,[5] Medicare Spending was expected to account for 12 percent of all federal spending in 2010, a total of $504 billion, making the 7.8 percent improper payment rate extremely significant to the economy.

Examples

Examining a client's explanation of Medicare benefits, you see that a payment was made for surgery and say, "Mrs. Lopez, I didn't know you had surgery," to which she replies, "I didn't, that is just the goofy way those doctors talk—they just cleaned the cut on my hand and bandaged it." Or maybe she responds, "I got a free toaster oven just for going into that clinic and filling out some forms in case I ever decide to use them." What may be going on in these situations?

For more information, see *http://www.medicare.gov/fraudabuse/overview.asp.*

---

[2]*http://www.aarp.org/research/*
[3]31 USC 3321
[4]42 USC 1395nn
[5]*http://www.kff.org/medicare/upload/7615-03.pdf*

EXHIBIT 1.2
National Error Rates by Year (dollars in billions)[6]

Year	Total paid	Over-payments	Over payment rate	Under-payments	Under payment Rate	Total Improper Payments	Total Improper Payment Rate
1996	$168.1	$23.5	14.0%	$0.3	0.2%	$23.8	14.2%
1997	$177.9	$20.6	11.6%	$0.3	0.2%	$20.9	11.8%
1998	$177.0	$13.8	7.8%	$1.2	0.6%	$14.9	8.4%
1999	$168.9	$14.0	8.3%	$0.5	0.3%	$14.5	8.6%
2000	$174.6	$14.1	8.1%	$2.3	1.3%	$16.4	9.4%
2001	$191.3	$14.4	7.5%	$2.4	1.3%	$16.8	8.8%
2002	$212.8	$15.2	7.1%	$1.9	0.9%	$17.1	8.0%
2003	$199.1	$20.5	10.3%	$0.9	0.5%	$12.7	6.4%
2004	$213.5	$20.8	9.7%	$0.9	0.4%	$21.7	10.1%
2005	$234.1	$11.2	4.8%	$0.9	0.4%	$12.1	5.2%
2006	$246.8	$9.8	4.0%	$1.0	0.4%	$10.8	4.4%
2007	$276.2	$9.8	3.6%	$1.0	0.4%	$10.8	3.9%
2008	$288.2	$9.5	3.3%	$0.9	0.3%	$10.4	3.6%
2009	$308.4	$23.0	7.5%	$1.1	0.4%	$24.1	7.8%

Ethical Issues

Many of the ethical issues that arise in dealing with older clients arise from a good thing: family involvement. The client may visit the law office accompanied by a relative or a close friend; the relative or friend may feel "entitled" to information about the client's legal matters and even entitled to control the process. The legal professional must assess the situation using the ethical rules for the relevant jurisdiction.

Familiarize yourself with those rules. The American Bar Association publishes Model Rules (*http://www.abanet.org/cpr/mrpc/mrpc_toc.html*), but each state enacts its own rules, which may not be the same as the Model Rules. Starting at *http://www.abanet.org/cpr/links.html#States*, find the Web sites that contain the rules of professional conduct and ethics opinions for your state. Visit the Web site and examine the rules, paying particular attention to sections dealing with conflicts of interests, confidentiality, loyalty, and professional independence. Refer to those sections to analyze the following.

---

[6]*http://www3.cms.gov/CERT/Downloads/CERT_Report.pdf*

Who Is the Client?

Scenario 1. Chris, the owner of Chris Construction, has been a client of the firm for many years, for both personal and business matters. Chris's mother, Pat, is a widow, 70 years old, with no business experience. Pat has never used a lawyer. Chris makes an appointment for Pat to visit the firm. Does it make a difference whether Pat is writing a will, asking advice about a contract she entered into, or asking about obtaining visitation rights with respect to the children of her deceased son, Mike? Mike's widow resists involvement with her late husband's family.

Let's take it a step further. Pat is seeking visitation with Mike's children and Chris is whole-heartedly behind the effort. Pat is on a fixed income, so Chris paid the retainer and has been paying the bills for the firm's representation of Pat. Last weekend, however, Chris got some disturbing news about Mike's oldest son, Sam, age 16. Sam was arrested for beating his mother. Chris found out that Sam also has a history of shoplifting and petty theft. Chris is afraid that Sam will victimize Pat if there is contact between the two. Chris comes in to tell the firm to quietly "let the matter die."

Scenario 2. Jack and Jill, married for 42 years, come to the firm for wills. During the interview, Jill does most of the talking. She says that they each want a will that leaves everything to the other and that after the second of the two dies, the estate should be split equally between their two children. Jack nods and seems generally agreeable. The next day, Jack calls and asks to speak in confidence. He admits that he has an out-of-wedlock child (Jordan) from an affair he had with his secretary 15 years ago. Jill does not know, and he is adamant that she must not find out. Jack wants his will to include a substantial gift for Jordan. Is there a problem?

Conflict of Interests
Ethical problem in which loyalty is divided between competing interests

Each of these situations involves a possible **conflict of interests** that the lawyer should have recognized and addressed in advance. The ethical rules of many states allow a lawyer to handle a case, despite a possible conflict, if the lawyer believes he will be able to provide competent representation to each party and that each party gives informed consent, which may have to be in writing.

Confidentiality and Communication

Confidentiality
Ethical obligation of legal professionals to protect client information

Privilege
Legal protection against forced disclosure of communications between client and certain professionals, such as lawyers

The situations described above also implicate **confidentiality**. Speaking to the client in the presence of another person may not only destroy **privilege**, it may mean that the client is not speaking freely.

With limited exceptions, "attorney-client communications in the presence of a third party who is not the agent of either are generally not protected by the privilege." Weatherford v. Bursey, 429 U.S. 545, 554 n. 4 (1977).

Examine Exhibit 1.3, Rule 1.6 from the ABA Model Rules, and consider what you would do in these circumstances:

1. In helping an older client straighten out his financial affairs, you become aware that Medicare has paid for expensive medical equipment

the client did not receive. The client tells you that he does not care because the doctor is his cousin's son and, after all, this is "free."

2. A client visits the office to sign her will and seems light-headed. You ask her whether she feels well enough to go through with the signing. The client admits that she has not been taking her medications because she does not like the side effects and tells you that she does not care if it shortens her life.

3. A client visits the office to sign her will and seems light-headed. You ask her whether she feels well enough to go through with the signing. The client admits that she did not sleep last night because her son, Jack, slapped her. He has done it before, sometimes knocking her to the floor. She says that because of this, she intends to leave him no inheritance. She begs you not to tell anyone because she cannot live alone and would rather die than go to an institution. Jack has also been a client of the firm, in connection with writing his own will.

4. Client Bill comes in to discuss writing a new will. He is accompanied by his new girlfriend, Angie, who is at least 40 years younger than him. Bill wants Angie to sit in on the meeting. Bill casually mentions that Angie is attending a local college and that he is helping her by paying her rent, tuition, car payment, and charge account bills. You are uneasy because you know that Bill has limited funds and will likely require nursing home care soon. You also know that Bill's children are not aware of the situation.

Also consider whether the lawyer is able to meet communications obligations with respect to these clients. Model Rule 1.4 (and equivalent state rules) requires that a lawyer promptly inform the client of any decision or circumstance that will require the client's informed consent and reasonably consult with the client about how the client's objectives will be accomplished.

Is the Client Capable of Making Decisions?

The situations described above involve the possibility that the client is being controlled by another person. A lawyer or paralegal can often make that determination by simply talking to the client outside the presence of that other person. What if the client appears confused or determined to make decisions not in her own best interest? Model Rule 1.14 addresses clients with diminished **capacity**; find the equivalent rule for your state. In general, the lawyer should, as far as reasonably possible, maintain a normal client-lawyer relationship with the client. If the lawyer believes that the client is at risk of substantial harm (physical, financial, or emotional) and cannot adequately protect her own interests, the lawyer may take protective action, including seeking appointment of a **Guardian** or **conservator** (these procedures are discussed in depth in Chapter **3**) to manage the affairs of the **ward**. In taking such action, the lawyer has a limited exemption from confidentiality requirements.

Capacity
Competency, ability to make reasonable decisions

Guardian
Person responsible for the care or management of another person or property

Conservator
Person appointed to protect and manage assets

Ward
Person under the protection of another

EXHIBIT 1.3
Rule 1.6: Confidentiality of Information

(a) A lawyer shall not reveal information relating to the representation of a client unless the client gives informed consent, the disclosure is impliedly authorized in order to carry out the representation or the disclosure is permitted by paragraph (b).

(b) A lawyer may reveal information relating to the representation of a client to the extent the lawyer reasonably believes necessary:

(1) to prevent reasonably certain death or substantial bodily harm;

(2) to prevent the client from committing a crime or fraud that is reasonably certain to result in substantial injury to the financial interests or property of another and in furtherance of which the client has used or is using the lawyer's services;

(3) to prevent, mitigate or rectify substantial injury to the financial interests or property of another that is reasonably certain to result or has resulted from the client's commission of a crime or fraud in furtherance of which the client has used the lawyer's services;

(4) to secure legal advice about the lawyer's compliance with these Rules;

(5) to establish a claim or defense on behalf of the lawyer in a controversy between the lawyer and the client, to establish a defense to a criminal charge or civil claim against the lawyer based upon conduct in which the client was involved, or to respond to allegations in any proceeding concerning the lawyer's representation of the client; or

(6) to comply with other law or a court order.

The comments to the Model Rules mention consultation with family members or health care providers among the actions the lawyer might take. The possibility that such a consultation might be necessary makes avoidance of conflicts of interest especially important!

Unfortunately, the Rules do not include objective guidelines for determining whether a client is competent. A person may have a good grasp of reality but be intent on making a decision that others would label as "wrong." For example, a client with a solid understanding of his financial situation and of his family situation may be determined to give his money to a "girlfriend" he has known for only a few days. A client who understands that her health is failing and that she cannot take care of herself may be determined to stay in her own home.

Psychosis
Mental disorder in which, reality is highly distorted

Dementia
Mental deterioration

Be careful not to confuse the physical signs of aging with indicators of competence. Many older people suffer tremors, hearing and vision loss, and even difficulty speaking; do not confuse those symptoms with **psychosis** or **dementia**. They may be on medication or have emotional issues stemming from grief or anxiety that make them appear confused, disengaged, or inattentive. Consider emotional and cultural issues, described in the next section.

The Comments to the Model Rules suggest consideration of:

- The client's ability to explain her reasoning in making a decision,
- Consistency of state of mind,
- Ability to appreciate the consequences of a decision,
- Substantive fairness of a decision, and
- Consistency of a decision with known long-term commitments and values of the client.

According to the Mayo Clinic (*http://www.mayoclinic.com/health/dementia/ DS01131*):

Dementia isn't a specific disease. Instead, it describes a group of symptoms affecting intellectual and social abilities severely enough to interfere with daily functioning. It's caused by conditions or changes in the brain. Different types of dementia exist, depending on the cause. Alzheimer's disease is the most common type.
Memory loss generally occurs in dementia, but memory loss alone doesn't mean you have dementia. Dementia indicates problems with at least two brain functions, such as memory loss along with impaired judgment or language. Dementia can make you confused and unable to remember people and names. You may also experience changes in personality and social behavior. However, some causes of dementia are treatable and even reversible.

Emotional/Cultural Issues

Even in the best of circumstances, communication with an older client can present a challenge to a much younger legal professional. The client may appear to be unwilling or unable to focus on the relevant issue, unable to see the need for prompt action, or even hostile to those trying to help. In his book, *How to Say It to Seniors,* David Solis suggests that communication can improve when the younger person understands the needs of the older person to maintain control and to establish his legacy.

Taking a moment to consider the wording of a request can often make a difference. Consider the control implications of "Mr. Mao, these are the documents you need to sign today," versus "Mr. Mao, do you have any questions about these documents before you sign?" Adapt your own pace to the pace of the client. That pace may be slower than you prefer because of the client's need to explain herself, her history, and her legacy. Patient communication between a client and a legal professional can be a two-way street, as demonstrated in Exhibit 1.4.

To build a connection with the client, start with open-ended questions and statements, such as "How can we help you today?" or "Tell me about your family." Starting with specific questions, aimed at getting information relevant to your assumptions about the client's goals, such as "Who do you want to name on your power of attorney?" make the client feel rushed and controlled. Take the time to explore the client's needs and goals rather than relying on the client's conclusions about the best way to achieve his goals. A client may come in and say, "I need to transfer my house to my son," thinking that that is a way to become eligible for Medicaid, when, in fact, such a transfer could have disastrous consequences. Force yourself to really listen to what is being said, instead of thinking about what you will say next. Having a standard intake form that flows logically from topic to topic will make it easier for you to stay focused on the client.

To make communication even more challenging, an older client may be seen for the first time in an emergency situation. He may be facing life-threatening surgery; she may have lost her husband suddenly and not know what to do. In these situations a client will often focus on matters that may seem secondary to the legal professional: *Who will take care of the dog? I don't know how the title to the house is held. Where did he put his will?* These are natural reactions and should not, alone, be interpreted as signs of incompetence. The important thing is to reassure the client that you can and will help, despite missing documents or other issues.

EXHIBIT 1.4
Using Technology to Improve Communication

Cary Client calls with a simple question about whether certain documents have arrived. The file has been handled by Lawyer Lynn and Paralegal Paul, but both are out of the office today. Do you:

- Take the time to go to the file room, dig through the file, and call Cary back;
- Leave a message for Paul and hope he is back in the office tomorrow and has time to take care of this; or
- In under 60 seconds, pull up the following spreadsheet on your computer and find that the documents have been scanned and linked to the spreadsheet so that you can look at them by simply clicking the link?

Attorney-client	Correspondence	Work Product	Docs from Client	Court
Intake 6/7	Letter to Manor Care 6/14	Outline of plan for Medicaid eligibility, 6/28	Spouse death certificate 8/2/95	Petition for guardianship 11fd2130
Fee agreement signed 6/14	E-mail from Manor Care, 6/22	Notes from Lynn Lawyer's call to Soc. Sec. 6/16	Will, 1990, prepared by Fletcher firm	
Notes from client meeting 6/30		Research memo: status of disabled child, Paralegal Paul, 8/10	Client birth certificate rcvd 6/30	

Working with older clients often involves contact with intense personal grief and loss. Clients may exhibit anger, depression, denial, and refusal to cooperate. It can be painful to witness clients in distress, but a legal professional must put the client's needs first and concentrate on listening and understanding. Determining the client's needs may require patience while listening to lengthy stories that appear to have nothing to do with the law. Even if the client's needs are not revealed in those stories, listening builds trust. In addition to focused listening, the legal professional can:

- Ascertain whether the anxiety has a basis in fact (recent death, medical diagnosis); chronic anxiety or grief that is not tied to an event may mean the client needs medical help;
- Discourage clients from making irrevocable decisions during times of intense grief;
- Protect the client from outsiders who would take advantage of intense grief; and
- Assist the client in obtaining non-legal help.

Assessing competency and determining whether there is a conflict of interests may require assessment of family dynamics. If the firm has previously represented members of the family, it may be possible to identify changes in relationships. Education levels, social class, race, religion, and culture may also be important factors in how the client and family communicate and make decisions. For example, various studies[7] indicate different attitudes among ethnic groups about whether patients should be informed of a diagnosis of an incurable disease. Similar studies have found differences in how families make purchasing decisions[8] and decisions about medical care.[9] Some cultures consider the topic of mental illness as "off limits"; some regard direct eye contact as rude.

Don't forget that your own cultural characteristics may influence how you perceive the client and the family! How would you react to a client with a thick accent, a client who uses poor grammar, a client who has had a stroke and is partially paralyzed, or a client who will not shake hands?

The Geriatric Mental Health Foundation, *http://www.gmhfonline.org*, has resources for those dealing with mental health issues in the elderly.

How can you assist the client with non-legal issues? Be aware of all the resources available online and in your community. Later chapters will direct you to some of those resources and, as a paralegal, you should maintain a file or database of resources for transportation, independent living and home care, and similar issues as you find them. A good starting point is *http://www.aarp.org/internetresources/*.

---

[7]See, e.g., *http://www.ncbi.nlm.nih.gov/pubmed/11035693* and *http://www.libraryindex.com/pages/3104/End-Life-Ethical-Considerations-PATIENT-AUTONOMY.html*.
[8]*http://www.acrwebsite.org/volumes/display.asp?id=6360*
[9]*http://www.jstor.org/pss/585399*

Physical Limitations

The physical environment in which a client is interviewed is always important for preserving confidentiality and creating a comfortable atmosphere, but it is especially important in serving older clients, who may have physical limitations. Consider:

ADA
Americans with Disabilities Act, requires reasonable accommodation of disabilities

- Is the office **ADA** compliant?[10] Will the client be able to get to the exterior door, from that door to the interview room, and from the interview room to a restroom without encountering obstacles such as stairs, long walks, or poor lighting?
- Is the temperature comfortable? Older people are often uncomfortable in offices kept very cool in the warmer months.
- Is your office or conference room equipped with sturdy chairs so that the client can get up without help and free of tripping hazards?
- Can you minimize background noise, sit closer, or use amplifiers to accommodate hearing loss?
- Can you reduce glare and adjust lighting to accommodate vision problems?
- Can you visit the client at home if necessary?

To learn more about guidelines for accommodation of disabilities in various situations, visit *http://www.ada.gov*.

You can also adapt your own behavior to accommodate the physical limitations of age:

- Look at the client while speaking; speak in a low tone and do not shout.
- Shake hands gently, and walk slowly when leading the way to the office or conference room.
- Slow down, repeat or summarize as necessary, and take breaks as needed.
- Use larger fonts for print material.
- Convey information and ask questions in smaller bits; do not change topics without transition.

Cultural/Generational Issues

In your personal life you may be an interesting, unique individual and you may express that in your style of dress and grooming. You may take pride in your casual, easygoing attitude. You may even feel as though you can help people overcome stereotypes and become more open-minded. On the job, however, it's all about the client. Your role is to make the client comfortable, not to change or challenge the client. Many older people are uncomfortable with the social climate that prevails among younger people, so it is important that you know which specific actions may be a distraction from a comfortable professional relationship. See Exhibit 1.5.

---

[10]The Americans With Disabilities Act, "ADA," 42 U.S.C. §12101, requires that places of "public accommodation," such as law firms, provide reasonable accommodations to make their premises accessible. For more information, visit *http://www.ada.gov*.

EXHIBIT 1.5
Lorraine Says

- Do not call me by my first name until I ask you to do so.
- If there is someone else in the room, do not talk around or over me.
- Do not use demeaning terms, such as "sweetie," "young lady," or "dear."
- Be aware that I may be offended by "you guys," slang, and even mild cursing.
- I may find it very difficult to discuss family matters — divorce, adoption, mental health issues. Approach these issues with a businesslike tone and be patient about my response.
- I consider financial information personal and do not like revealing details to a younger person.
- My perception of you, as a professional, may be lowered by the sight of piercings, tattoos, bare torso flesh, cleavage, a short skirt, too much makeup, or any extreme fashion statement.
- I especially dislike seeing a man wearing a hat indoors.

Lorraine is 84 years old and, as a result of recent health problems, has had to use the services of a law office on several occasions. Her issues were serious: management of a trust, sale of a home, and a power of attorney. Because some of the individuals with whom she dealt did not understand her perceptions, Lorraine felt like her concerns were not taken seriously.

The Paralegal's Role

An older client might be involved in any kind of litigation, transactional, or administrative matter, so a paralegal's role might encompass any of the duties common to the particular area of law involved. There is, however, one common responsibility beyond the unique communications and ethical concerns: information gathering. An older client may have physical or mental limitations that prevent her from providing the law office with needed information and documents. A recently deceased spouse may have taken total responsibility for finances or record keeping.

The first step, of course, is to determine what is needed and to ask the client or the client's family for the necessary information. Firm patience is key, as noted by paralegal Jennifer Poulin in Exhibit 1.6. A thorough client intake sheet, readily accessible to everyone who will work on the file, is essential. Have you ever had to answer the same question for several different people during an appointment with a professional? Imagine having answered that question four times, watching people take notes, then being asked for the same information when you call with a follow-up question a few days later. Clients do not like to think that their information is being misplaced or that their stories are not important enough to remember.

EXHIBIT 1.6
Jennifer Says

Jennifer Poulin is a freelance paralegal, working with attorneys in and around Springfield, Massachusetts, in the fields of estate planning, Medicaid planning, and personal injury. After earning a BA in paralegal studies from Elms College in Chicopee, Massachusetts, Ms. Poulin worked as a paralegal at law firms in Hartford, Connecticut, and, later, in Springfield.

Jennifer says, "After working in the fast-paced and demanding field of personal injury for several years, I decided to take a job as an estate planning and elder law paralegal for a change of pace. My concentration of work was the preparation of Medicaid applications for the elder law clients. I would like to say this area of law is like being a financial detective, as preparing these applications requires a great deal of attention to the details of the applicant's financial background.

Typically, the client/applicant is residing in a nursing home, so the attorney and I will often meet with his or her spouse or child to discuss their Medicaid eligibility. This is typically an emotional time as their loved one usually is quite ill and being told he or she will not be returning home. I work with the spouse or the child to gather together all the necessary financial documentation to apply for Medicaid benefits. It takes a great deal of hand-holding during this time, because the spouse or the child of the applicant is typically not in the frame of mind to be sorting through financial documents. Once I compile all the requested paperwork, I will prepare and complete the application, often dedicating a day or two to do so depending on what other work assignments I have.

For those interested in pursuing this area of law, it is important to be patient with the applicant's family by both lending an ear and gently but firmly working with them to gather together the necessary documentation to file in a timely manner. It is also crucial that you pay close attention to details, as you will be responsible for reviewing your client's financial documents, which can be quite voluminous. They are certainly skills necessary for success as a paralegal in this area of law."

Tip

Rather than giving a client a list of needed documents (which creates a risk that the client will return with a big cardboard box full of 20 years' worth of documents), create a list of the documents needed for every type of matter your firm handles (e.g., birth certificate, existing will, army discharge papers) and print labels. Affix each of the labels to a clasp-type envelope and put the envelopes into a file folder or bag with your firm's contact information. The client can put a document in each envelope, know when she has everything, and bring it back in an organized way.

EXHIBIT 1.7
Sources of Client Information

Need	*Possible source*
Legal documents: wills, powers of attorney, etc.	• Ask about in-home safe or safety deposit box. • Talk to client's previous lawyer. • Ask about in-home safe or safety deposit box.
Financial, banking, insurance records	• Contact client's accountant or tax professional. • Obtain copies of previous year tax filings from *http://www.irs.gov/taxtopics/tc156.html*, form 4506, to look for information about investment income. • Search state unclaimed property index at *http://www.unclaimed.org*. • Contact former employers concerning insurance. • Use the Medical Information Bureau to search for policies: *http://www.mib.com/html/lost-life-insurance.html*.
Real estate	Search county recorder's offices in counties in which client lived or frequently visited.
Debts	Conduct a **UCC**[11] **lien** search through Secretary of State—quick link available through *http://www.nass.org*
Family information	For birth, adoption, marriage, divorce, and death records, start at the state department of health. The Association of State and Territorial Health Officials, *http://www.astho.org*, provides links to those departments.

UCC
Uniform Commercial Code, laws governing commercial transactions

Lien
Legal claim against an asset to secure repayment of a loan

In some cases it may be necessary to go through the client's accumulated papers and question caregivers, neighbors, and friends about where the client has worked and lived and which businesses the client used. The chart shown in Exhibit 1.7, while not exhaustive, may provide some useful starting points. Of course, it's not just paralegals who must be aware of the unique needs of elder clients. If a firm practices elder law, everyone must be on board. Some elder law firms regard the receptionist as one of the most important members of the team. That person's attitude and skills set the tone for the client's visit. Everyone should be aware that the firm's clients may be experiencing emotional turmoil, may have physical limitations that they are embarrassed to reveal, and may need assistance in ways that other clients do not. No one should think, "That's not my job." All members of the firm should adapt how they work—from answering the phone with a welcoming tone to offering assistance if they see a client alone in the reception area.

Assignments

Imputation
Attribution of a
characteristic to another

Notary Public
Person authorized to
administer oaths, witness
signatures, certify
authenticity of documents

Escheat
Reversion of property to
state, absent heir

1. Reconsider the situation in which a husband and wife come together to the firm to write wills. Suppose Jack and Jill's lawyer is one of five lawyers in a firm. Would the situation change if different lawyers interviewed Jack and Jill? Find your state's rule concerning **Imputation** of Conflict of Interest.

2. A longtime client is in the office with her son, in order to sign a deed transferring her house to the son. She is acting as if she is not sure what is going on. You have been asked to notarize the deed. Should you do so? Visit the **Notary Public** Code of Professional Responsibility for some insight: *http://www.nationalnotary.org/UserImages/Notary_Code.pdf.*

3. Search your state's unclaimed property database for property belonging to members of your family — forgotten bank accounts, etc. Unclaimed property is often transferred to the state under a principle known as **escheat.**

4. Find the Web site for your county recorder. Write a short summary of how you could search for real estate records. Does the site include a UCC search function? What other documents are available through this office?

5. Find the Web site for your state's Secretary of State and write a short summary about how you would conduct a UCC search and what types of liens you could find.

6. Use the online ADA Guide for Small Businesses (*http://www.ada.gov/smbusgd.pdf*) and describe the priorities for removing barriers to accessibility.

7. In 2005 the American Psychological Association and the American Bar Association Commission on Law and Aging published *Assessment of Older Adults with Diminished Capacity: A Handbook for Lawyers* (*http://www.apa.org/pi/aging/resources/guides/diminished-capacity. pdf*). Review that publication and answer the following questions:
   a. What are the three legal standards of diminished capacity?
   b. What are the "red flags" of diminished capacity?
   c. What are the pros and cons of seeking input from a medical professional?
   d. What are the "mitigating factors"?
   e. Does the publication recommend that legal professionals use a formal assessment tool?
   f. Using the checklist in the handbook, identify factors relevant to assessing capacity in this situation:
   Sarah Gold was born in Poland in 1934 to Leo and Helen Warshawsky; the immediate family emigrated to the United States in 1936, leaving grandparents, aunts, uncles, and cousins behind. Sarah is a devout Jew.

---

[11]UCC refers to the Uniform Commercial Code, which provides (Article 9) for filing of certain security interests.

Her husband, Dr. Leopold Gold (died 5 years ago), son of David and Ruth, was a surgeon and the couple accumulated substantial wealth during their long marriage. Sarah has two children, Helen and David. Both are college-educated, hard-working, and married. David has a three-year-old son, Cody. Helen has a four-year-old daughter, Madison, and is expecting another baby. Sarah has been increasingly distant from her children since the birth of the first grandchild. There have been the usual disagreements about appropriate feeding and training for babies, and people in your office believe that Sarah is a bit jealous of the attention her children focus on the babies. Things came to a crisis when, at a family gathering a few weeks ago, Helen announced that she had learned that her baby will be a girl and that they have chosen the name Riley. The next day Sarah called to make an appointment to change her will (she does this regularly). Because she is angry about the baby's name, she wants to leave her children nothing. Anger is not new to Sarah; she manifested her grief over the death of her husband by threatening to sue his doctors, the hospital, and even the funeral home. Sarah has done research on the Internet and, based on her findings, intends to leave her entire fortune to the Holocaust Museum in Skokie, Illinois.

8. Do an Internet search of client intake forms used by attorneys and develop an intake form for an elder law firm.

9. Visit a local law firm. Identify the ways in which its physical layout is "senior friendly" and/or difficult for older clients.

10. Use a search engine to find news articles concerning the attorney and paralegal for Huguette Clark and identify all of the ethical issues you can find.

11. Do some online research and write a short summary of how Medicare fraud occurs and what people can do to prevent it.

12. **Critical Thinking:** At the end of this chapter, you will find an abstracted version of a case, *In Re: Mid-America Living Trust Associates, Inc.*, which is the basis of the discussion questions that follow. Because the full-length opinion includes extensive analysis of opinions from other states, you may prefer to read the entire case. In later chapters, this book will generally refer you to cases that you can find online (or in bound reporters, if you prefer) so that you can have the benefit of the full opinion, without the additional cost of adding them to the book. Your school may have a subscription to a computer-assisted legal research service, or **CALR,** such as Lexis, Loislaw, or Westlaw, or you can use free Web sites such as *http://www.findlaw.com/casecode* or *http://law.lexisnexis.com/webcenters/lexisone*. Finding the cases will also improve your online research skills.

CALR
Computer-assisted legal research

Mid-America Case: Questions for Discussion

◆ Is the practice of law regulated by the state supreme court in your state? Is there an administrative agency that conducts investigations, publishes rules, etc.?

◆ Does your state have a definition of "practice of law"?

◆ Even if the activities described in the case did not constitute unauthorized practice of law, they could be considered predatory toward senior citizens. Why? Which marketing techniques might make seniors particularly vulnerable?

◆ Can you think of any reason that this company might prefer senior citizens as clients, rather than younger people? Consider both "cultural" differences between older and younger people and the reality of life expectancy.

◆ Some people believe that the public would benefit from more competition and that allowing non-lawyers to provide legal services would result in lower fees. Discuss the pros and cons of allowing the client to choose a non-lawyer to provide legal services.

◆ Identify the interests that create a conflict of interests for the review attorneys. Might there be other interests involved? For example, might the trust company make a profit, in addition to the initial fee, if the "forms" typically name a particular financial institution to administer the clients' assets?

◆ Discuss the risks to client confidentiality inherent to the Mid-America business model.

◆ Does the Mid-America business model provide any reliable way of assessing client competency?

◆ Does this case in any way reduce the role of "traditional" paralegals, working under the supervision of a lawyer who is working directly for a client? Might legalizing non-lawyer practice actually minimize the role of traditional paralegals?

Review Questions

1. Identify and discuss the three most common ethical concerns for legal professionals in the practice of elder law.
2. Identify and discuss three barriers to effective communications that are of particular concern in dealing with the elderly.
3. What are the social and economic implications of an aging society?
4. Describe how you would find and organize important documents for a client who cannot provide you with needed information.
5. What are the physical characteristics of an office in which an elder client would feel most comfortable?
6. What is AARP? Do you think that senior citizens have an unfair amount of political power in this country? Why?

In Re: MID-AMERICA LIVING TRUST ASSOCIATES, INC.

927 S.W.2d 855 (Mo., 1996)

This action was brought by the Chief Disciplinary Counsel (CDC) against respondents Mid-America Living Trust Associates, Inc., and Robert Dillie. The CDC seeks a declaration that respondents have engaged in the unauthorized practice of law and injunctive relief. The CDC has alleged, in particular, that respondents have: 1) rendered legal advice to individuals concerning the need for and advisability of various types of living trusts; 2) gathered information from individuals for use in determining what type of trust is appropriate and in preparing trust documents; 3) prepared trust documents for individuals; 4) prepared other legal documents including wills and durable powers of attorneys for individuals; and 5) that Mid-America charged and collected fees for these services. [The circuit judge enjoined the described activities.]

Mid-America works through trust associates that it defines as "independent contractors" to obtain clients . . . usually individuals with a financial planning business, insurance business, or stock brokerage business who have learned of Mid-America through education programs sponsored by Mid-America or advertising in trade publications. Trust associates may attend "Estate-Planning School," a training seminar put on by Mid-America, and all have signed a standard contract agreement [that] includes a clause instructing the contractor to "not give any tax or legal advice to clients; make, alter or discharge any wills or trusts, incur any liability on behalf of Mid-America Living Trust Associates."

The "trust associate" who recommends and sells a living trust also gathers personal and financial information from the client by completing a workbook provided by Mid-America. Clients may choose their own attorney or an attorney recommended by Mid-America who has agreed to review trust documents. If a Mid-America review attorney is selected by the client, the trust associate directs the client to make out two checks: one to Mid-America and one to the review attorney. The workbook and the checks are mailed to Mid-America.

Mid-America paralegals contact the client and verify the information. The paralegals, based on input from in-house counsel, the review attorney, or personal experience, decide which form of trust would be most appropriate and draft initial documents from blank prototypes. The prototypes include forms for single and married persons in community and noncommunity property states. The marital trust prototype includes joint marital trust documents and separate trust documents. There are documents for estates having tax consequences and forms for pour-over wills, durable and general powers of attorney, health care declarations, and health care powers of attorney. The trust documents, workbook, and attorney check are then mailed to the review attorney. The review attorney sometimes communicates directly with the client, but not always. The paralegal makes changes if directed to by the attorney. The documents are then mailed to the trust associate, who delivers the documents for execution by the client. Mid-America also provides assistance in retitling assets and preparing quitclaim deeds. . . . Mid-America has utilized three Missouri attorneys as review attorneys. The review attorneys have charged clients fees ranging from $100 to $250. The clients typically pay between $595 and $1,995 for Mid-America's services. Mid-America pays the trust associates a commission for each trust they recommend to Mid-America in accordance with a written schedule.

In the first page of the Training and Procedures Manual provided to all trust associates, Mr. Dillie "welcomes" Mid-America's trust associates to "our 'Family' of Associates" and encourages them "in [their] new business adventure—great success in the living trust industry." The manual and a training video alone, according to the manual, explain what a trust is, why trusts are beneficial, how to complete the estate plan, and, particularly, "how to make a successful sales presentation and close a sale." The manual explains how to fill out the workbook and gives a brief synopsis of the legal issues the client should be aware of when selecting a trustee, personal representative, conservator, guardian, or the person to designate as a durable power of attorney. The manual explains different ways to distribute property or exclude relatives from the trust, as well as other important information. Significant differences between state laws are also highlighted.

The manual tells associates to encourage clients to choose one of Mid-America's review attorneys:

Have your clients list the attorney of their choice—for obvious reasons we hope they choose our recommended attorney—on the line provided. "In the bizarre instance where the clients want their own attorney, explain that the trust will have to be sent to that attorney for review and they will be responsible for that attorney's fees, which could be substantially more than $100. If they persist, understand that this trust, if sent to their attorney, will very likely be canceled—since their attorney will probably offer to do the trust for them." The manual also instructs the trust associates not to share the name of the review attorney with the client unless they specifically request it, to avoid "any unlawful solicitation on behalf of the attorney." According to one of the trust associates, the clients are instructed to make their checks out to "Review Attorney" [and] instructed to sign an "Attorney Representation" form stating that the client recognizes "[a] potential conflict of interest between the Corporate Attorney's preparation of my/our estate documents and his representation of Mid-America exists and I/we consent thereto." The clients also sign a "Disclosure and Compliance" form which states that "I/We understand that the representative is not an attorney or certified tax authority, and I have been advised to consult an attorney and/or tax accountant for tax or legal advice."

The consequences of incompetent representation are especially dangerous because they are often invisible for many years, but then cause great hardship and expense, such as when a deed, will, or trust is found to be ineffective or not to achieve the results originally intended. Accordingly, we seek to allow only those who have been found by investigation and examination to be properly prepared and skilled to practice law and who demonstrate that they conform to higher standards of ethical conduct necessary in fiduciary and confidential relationships.

The "practice of law" is defined [by Missouri statute] as: "the appearance as an advocate in a representative capacity or the drawing of papers, pleadings or documents or the performance of any act in such capacity in connection with proceedings pending or prospective before any court of record, commissioner, referee or any body, board, committee or commission constituted by law or having authority to settle controversies." The "law business" is defined as: "the advising or counseling for a valuable consideration of any person, firm, association, or corporation as to any secular law or the drawing or the procuring of or assisting in the drawing for a valuable consideration of any paper, document or instrument affecting or relating to secular rights or the doing of any act for a valuable consideration in a representative capacity, obtaining or tending to obtain or securing or tending to secure for any person, firm, association, or corporation any property or property rights whatsoever." Although the "practice of law" includes acts done both in and out of court, "law business" in particular implies that a non-lawyer has "held himself out" in a business "by repeated acts" or "by the exaction of a consideration" in which he acts in the same capacity as a lawyer. These statutes are "primarily intended to protect the public from the rendition of certain services, deemed to require special fitness and training on the part of those performing the same, by persons not lawfully held to possess the requisite qualifications."

This Court has attempted to maintain a "workable balance" in these matters between the public's protection and the desired efficiency and economic benefits that result from a competitive marketplace. We allow non-attorneys to perform routine services, ancillary to other valid activities and without compensation, such as the filling in of blanks in approved form real estate documents. Also, non-attorneys may sell generalized legal publications and "kits," so long as no "personal advice as to the legal remedies or consequences flowing therefrom" is given. The need for public protection demands the strictest scrutiny when the exercise of judgment and discretion is applied to the particular legal needs of an individual.

The marketing and drafting of living trusts and related legal instruments by non-lawyers is not unique to Missouri. It has been the subject of substantial criticism by groups appearing before the Senate Special Committee on Aging (Sept. 24, 1992) [and] the subject of criticism by legal commentators. Trust marketing schemes have been rejected repeatedly by court decisions and state ethic opinions as the unauthorized practice of law. Generally, critics argue three types of harm develop from trust marketing schemes by non-lawyers. First, unregulated solicitation by non-lawyers allows for abusive marketing practices, particularly aimed at the elderly. Second, there is no assurance of competency by non-lawyers. Third, a conflict of interest exists between those who benefit from the sale of a particular legal instrument and the client for whom that legal instrument may not be appropriate.

Legal commentators have noted high-pressure tactics and exaggerated benefits used to promote living trusts. Lori A. Stiegal et al., On Guard Against Living Trusts Scams, NBA Nat'l B. Ass'n Mag., January/February 1994. Representatives solicit customers "by telephone, mail, newspaper advertisements, door-to-door, and in 'seminars' presented in hotels and restaurants." Charles F. Gibbs, The Marketing of Living Trusts by Non-Attorney Promoters, 20 ACTEC. "The public, particularly senior citizens, are told that the living trust is a cure-all for the problems entailed in asset management and wealth transfer, a claim with no more validity than the curative claim for snake oil." . . . "The non-lawyer who sold the trust told the couple it would cost their sons $65,000 to settle their estate through probate and the courts." . . . Trust company recommended "that 'everyone' with an estate over $50,000 should have a living trust."

The competency of non-lawyers to draft estate documents was questioned by Barlow F. Christensen in his article, The Unauthorized Practice of Law: Do Good Fences Really Make Good Neighbors — Or Even Good Sense?, 1980 Am. B. Found. Res.J. 159 (1980). Although generally opposed to heavy regulation of the legal practice, Christensen acknowledged that "proficiency in the field of estate planning requires knowledge of difficult and technical fields of law —

estates, trusts, wills, and tax law—that may not be at the command of the average insurance agent. . . . [M]ost insurance agents have not had extensive further training, and as a general matter the competency of insurance agents in the drafting of estate plans would seem to be questionable at best."

Courts [in several states] have held that trust marketing companies and their employees practice law by advising and counseling clients that a specific of estate plan or trust is needed and by preparing and drafting the necessary trust documents. Courts have found that attorneys participating in such schemes violate their ethical duties not to assist in the unauthorized practice of law and to avoid conflicts of interest [and] have noted actual harm to trust clients and the substantial fees charged. All courts that have addressed the issue have held that non-lawyer trust salespeople render legal advice and engage in the unauthorized practice of law when they recommend living trusts to specific individuals. . . . Even if the advice is termed as a "suggestion" or the client is encouraged to consult his own attorney, courts have still found that financial planners or insurance salespeople cannot advise a client as to his or her specific need for a particular form of disposition without practicing law illegally.

Referral attorneys, as well as in-house attorneys, have also been found to suffer from a conflict of interest. Obviously, an attorney's interests are divided by simultaneously working for a trust marketing company and attempting to represent the company's clients. . . . However, attorneys who regularly receive referrals from trust marketing companies, without being directly employed by them, also have been found to suffer from a conflict of interest. An attorney's advice may be tainted by his desire to continue receiving referrals.

Mid-America notes that the paralegals drafting the trusts are directly supervised by in-house counsel. However, the in-house counsel is employed by Mid-America, not the client, and has a direct conflict of interest. . . . Likewise, the review attorney cannot "cure" Mid-America's unauthorized practice of law for three reasons. First . . . the review attorney enters the picture too late. Mid-America's non-lawyer trust associate has already given legal advice . . . , recommended and sold a trust instrument, and received valuable consideration. Mid-America has also drafted a custom document tailored to the client's particular needs, prior to the participation of the review attorney. Second, participation by review attorneys in Mid-America's trust marketing businesses violates rules of conduct . . . and cannot cure the unauthorized practice of law. See Rule 4-5.4(c); Rule 4-5.5(b) . . . [A]ttorneys reviewing or drafting legal documents recommended or drafted by non-attorneys are aiding in the unauthorized practice of law or working with a conflict of interest. Finally, although Mid-America claims to welcome independent review, it actually instructs trust associates to avoid review by truly independent attorneys, and to encourage clients to choose an attorney from Mid-America's approved referral list. . . . Mid-America appears to discourage individualized contact between the client and recommended attorneys as well. . . . The manual states that "we do not give them the name of the attorney unless THEY request it," purportedly to avoid attorney solicitation. One trust associate interviewed indicated that "the instructions from Mid-America were to make the attorney check payable to 'Review Attorney,'" and not directly to the attorney chosen. Mid-America further stipulated that "review attorneys sometimes, but not always, communicate directly with the clients."

A brief review of the testimony of one of Mid-America's review attorneys, Griesedieck, reveals the inadequacy of Mid-America's review scheme. Ms. Griesedieck reviewed six cases referred to her, five of which she advised to seek a refund from Mid-America. . . . It is significant that five of the six trusts that Mid-America's trust associates recommended, gathered information on, and accepted payment for, were not appropriate for the individual client.

The potential for harm and the actual harm caused by unlicensed persons advising individuals regarding their legal decisions and drafting living trusts outweighs any savings or additional service to the public. . . . Accordingly, we modify the recommendations of the Master and order that:

1. Mid-America and its non-lawyer agents, servants, employees, and trust associates cease soliciting, counseling, recommending, and selling trusts, wills, and all other legal instruments, for valuable consideration, to Missouri residents;

2. Mid-America and its non-lawyer agents, servants, employees and trust associates cease drawing, preparing, or assisting in the preparation of trust workbooks, trusts, wills, and powers of attorney, for valuable consideration, for Missouri residents without the direct supervision of an independent licensed attorney selected by and representing those individuals . . . .

www.CrosswordWeaver.com

ACROSS

1. obligation to protect secrecy of client information
5. mental disorder, reality is distorted
8. UCC, Uniform _____ Code
11. conflict of _____ , divided loyalties
14. initials, law that concerns people with disabilities
15. nonprofit organization, works to improve lives of older people
16. mental deterioration
17. reponsible for incompetent person

DOWN

1. reponsible for assets of incompetent
2. _____ public, witnesses signatures
3. ability to make sound decisions
4. federal law requires responsable _____ of disabilities
6. protection against forced disclosure of client communications
7. legal claim against property to secure payment
9. property reverts to state
10. attribution of a characteristic to another
12. the "c" in CALR
13. protected person

2

◆ ◆ ◆
_____

Advance Directives
_____
◆ ◆ ◆

Objectives

When you complete this chapter, you will:

- Know the options available for various types of advance directives.
- Identify the factors relevant to choosing the best advance directive for a particular client.
- Recognize the considerations relevant to drafting an advance directive.
- Draft a power of attorney.

Overview: Options Available for Advance Directives

There are many legal tools available for dealing with competency issues. The choice of the appropriate tool depends on a number of factors. Keep in mind that physical frailty is not the same as incompetency, and that incompetency raises two separate problems: decisions about the person's care and decisions about the person's property.

For property decisions, the options include:

Representative Payee
Person designated to receive payments, such as social security

- Power of attorney for property, also called a financial power of attorney.
- Trust, an arrangement under which a trustee manages property for the benefit of a beneficiary. Trusts are explored, in detail, in Chapters 7 and 8.
- Use of a **representative payee** to manage the individual's income.

This chapter will focus primarily on care decisions. For care decisions, the options include:

- Advance directives, such as a living will or health care power of attorney, which may be temporary or may become effective only at the happening of a future event. Advance directives are generally considered the best way of dealing with competency issues, but are possible only while the client is competent.
- Conservatorship or guardianship, a legal process for appointment of a person or entity to make decisions with respect to the person and/or property of the incapacitated person (discussed in the Chapter 3). This is generally considered the last option.

As you read about these options, focus on function. What is called a "living will" in one state may be called an "advance health care directive" in another, but the functions are the same.

Surrogate Decision Making Without Advance Directives

Default Surrogate Decision-Making Laws
Laws identifying who may make decisions for incompetent individual, absent instructions from that individual

Many people believe that if they become unable to make decisions, those decisions can automatically be made by a spouse or an adult child. Spouses and adult children sometimes attempt to make medical decisions on behalf of their spouses or parents without any legal basis for doing so. In fact, some states have **default surrogate decision-making laws**, but other states do not. In a state without such a law, the family of an individual without an advance directive might have to obtain a guardianship, an expensive and time-consuming process described in Chapter 3.

Tip

Find out where your state stands: *http://new.abanet.org/aging/Pages/StateLawCharts.aspx*

Even if a state does have a law identifying surrogate decision makers, it might not be consistent with the client's wishes, it might not grant the surrogate the level of authority needed, it might cause a family conflict, or it may designate, as a surrogate, an individual who is unavailable or unable to make a decision. By executing an advance directive, a client can either state preferences in advance of need or identify an individual to make decisions about her care and property in the event of incapacity. The authority of surrogates and guardians acting without written direction from the patient has been the subject of several very controversial court decisions. The decisions at issue were matters of life and death, and the courts had to confront conflicting values and beliefs.

The most recent case, *Schiavo*,[1] demonstrates the pitfalls of relying on surrogate decision-making laws. The case involved a conflict between the husband of a woman in a vegetative state and the woman's parents. State law gave the husband surrogate decision-making authority. A state court had entered an order allowing removal of a feeding tube, based on "clear and convincing evidence that Theresa Schiavo was in a persistent vegetative state and that Theresa would elect to cease life-prolonging procedures if she were competent to make her own decision."[2] The case nonetheless proceeded to involve enactment of a special law, extensive media coverage and political pressure, and, ultimately, the federal courts. A federal appeals court refused to enter a restraining order to require restoration of a feeding tube. The Supreme Court refused to stay the decision.

The "clear and convincing evidence" standard was established in *Cruzan v. Director, Missouri Dept. of Health*,[3] in which the parents of a young woman in a persistent vegetative state wanted to remove life support. The woman had no written advance directive, but had stated that "if sick or injured she would not wish to continue her life unless she could live at least halfway normally." The state court held that, absent clear and convincing evidence of her wishes, she should remain on life support. The Supreme Court affirmed. Years earlier, in *Quinlan*,[4] the New Jersey Supreme Court had permitted removal of a respirator under similar circumstances, basing its decision on the patient's right to privacy, her guardian's right to assert that interest, and medical evidence that the patient would never recover.

In those cases, the courts, families, and medical professionals were faced with trying to determine what a patient would have wanted given a choice between death and life in a vegetative state—a choice that even the patient would not

---

[1] 403 F.3d 1223 (11th Cir. 2005)
[2] 780 So. 2d 176 (Fla. App. 2001)
[3] 497 U.S. 261 (1990)
[4] 355 A.2d 647 (N.J. 1976)

have made easily. They were faced with evidence about religious beliefs, medical miracles, financial motives, and much more. Even in cases that involve less serious issues and do not gain notoriety, families can be torn apart by disagreements among siblings, concerns about privacy, and patients resisting treatment. Proper documentation of the patient's wishes can avoid the stress, loss of privacy, and expense the families endured in those cases.

End-of-life issues, right to refuse treatment, and assisted suicide are discussed in detail in Chapter 12.

Advance Directives

By executing an advance designation of a surrogate to act in the event of incapacity, the client could solve part of the problem without giving instructions or expressing wishes. Doing so would, however, put the surrogate in a very difficult position and possibly open the door to legal challenges. The client can also express wishes without identifying a surrogate to act. With the number of options available, there are endless opportunities for confusion and contradiction. As a paralegal, you must determine whether your client has any existing advance directives and make sure that the client does not have or create directives that might result in a conflict.

Anatomical Giving
Organ donation or giving body to scientific research

Some advance directives indicate the client's wishes without identifying an individual responsible for making decisions not covered by those wishes. If those wishes are not likely to be controversial, such a document may be adequate to handle a particular issue. For example, a client might sign an organ donation card, also called a directive for **anatomical giving**.

In order to promote anatomical giving and strengthen the respect given organ donations, most states have adopted the Uniform Anatomical Gifts Act promulgated by the National Conference of Commissioners on Uniform State Laws. The Uniform Act simplifies procedures and imposes duties on hospitals and government agencies. Find out what your state is doing at *http://www.anatomicalgiftact.org/DesktopDefault.aspx?tabindex2&tabid72* and *http://organdonor.gov/research/acotapp6.htm*.

Living Will
Document containing instructions about health care

DNR
Medical order — do not resuscitate

Similarly, a **living will** medical directive describes a patient's wishes with respect to health care in the event that he is unable to make decisions. It typically does not identify a decision maker and is directed at health care providers. A **DNR** order, based on an agreement between a doctor and a competent terminally ill patient or the authorized representatives of a terminally ill patient, is similar in that it states a specific request with respect to medical care and is directed at caregivers without identifying a surrogate decision maker.

A **health care proxy**, on the other hand, identifies a person to make health care decisions on behalf of the patient. A health care proxy is sometimes called a power of attorney for health care and can serve both purposes—naming a decision maker and describing the patient's wishes. In executing a **power of attorney** (POA), the **principal** appoints an **agent**[5] to make decisions and take actions. The agency relationship is a matter of "getting things done." It generally does not involve transfer of ownership, create support obligations, or change the tax status of the individuals.

Every state has its own law governing advance directives. Find your state's law concerning living wills at *http://estate.findlaw.com/estate-planning/living-wills/estate-planning-law-state-living-wills.html*. To find the power of attorney statute for your jurisdiction, visit *http://www.abanet.org/aging/about/pdfs/power_of_attorney_laws_citations_by_state.pdf* or *http://www.abanet.org/rppt/cmtes/pt/e1/pte1_state_statutes.html* or *http://law.findlaw.com/state-laws/durable-power-of-attorney*.

Because discussion of each state's individual laws would be impossible, much of the discussion that follows is based on the Uniform Health-Care Decisions Act and the Uniform Power of Attorney Act, promulgated by the National Conference of Commissioners on Uniform State Laws. A NCCUSL uniform law is not law until it is adopted by a particular state, but many states have laws that mirror the Uniform Acts. It is essential that you understand what the laws of your state require.

Living Wills

A living will, or medical directive, is directed to health care providers and instructs the doctors and hospitals about the patient's wishes in specific situations. Some states limit their use to situations involving **terminal** illness, permanent loss of consciousness, or other advanced illness. The current trend is to use a more flexible definition, as demonstrated by the Michigan definition reproduced in Exhibit 2.1. Of course, these directives are valid only in situations involving a patient unable to make her own decisions. A patient who is able to make and communicate decisions can direct her own care, regardless of having previously executed a medical directive. Because the client does not know in advance what her end-of-life circumstances will be, living wills tend to be general, rather than specific, and can leave gaps.

Another disadvantage of a living will is that it is effective only if the hospital or doctor is aware of it. The patient's doctor and neighborhood hospital may have copies of his living will, but they will do no good if the patient is rushed to a hospital, unconscious, while on vacation in another state. To minimize the likelihood that a living will might be overlooked or lost, the client should carry a card stating that he has a living will, and may want to register the will so it can be available to medical providers at any location. The U.S. Living Will Registry provides such a service: *http://www.uslivingwillregistry.com*. Several states have similar registries.

Health Care Proxy
Identifies person to make health care decisions

Power of Attorney
Document in which principal appoints agent to act on her behalf

Principal
Person who appoints and is affected by actions of agent

Agent
One who acts on behalf of a principal

Terminal
Describing an illness likely to result in death

---

[5]The term *attorney-in-fact* is synonymous with *agent*, but is not used in this text to avoid confusion with *attorney at law*.

EXHIBIT 2.1
Terminology

Michigan amended its Dignified Death Act to include the following definition and eliminate an earlier definition of *terminal* as describing a patient having a life expectancy of less than six months. This definition gives both doctors and patients more flexibility in determining appropriate treatment.

333.5653 Definitions

(1) As used in this part:

(a) "Advanced illness," except as otherwise provided in this subdivision, means a medical or surgical condition with significant functional impairment that is not reversible by curative therapies and that is anticipated to progress toward death despite attempts at curative therapies or modulation, the time course of which may or may not be determinable through reasonable medical prognostication. For purposes of section 5655(b) only, "advanced illness" has the same general meaning as "terminal illness" has in the medical community.

Other medical terms commonly used in connection with end-of-life decisions:

- *Artificial Sustenance: fluids and nutrition provided by a feeding tube or intravenous means*
- *Brain Death: irreversible loss of brain function and activity, including involuntary activity necessary to sustain other organs*
- *Chronic: persistent or recurring*
- *CPR: cardiopulmonary resuscitation: an emergency procedure consisting of external cardiac massage and artificial respiration*
- *DNR: a medical order: do not attempt resuscitation in case of cardiac or respiratory arrest*
- *Hospice Care: care provided to patients with terminal conditions; includes palliative care*
- *Palliative Care: care that provides relief of the pain, stress, and other debilitating symptoms of serious illness, regardless of whether the illness itself is treatable or curable*
- *Persistent Vegetative State: severely impaired consciousness in which patient is incapable of voluntary motion or communication*
- *Unconscious: without awareness or sensory perception*

PSDA
Patient Self-Determination
Act, a federal law

The Patient Self-Determination Act, or **PSDA**, reproduced in Exhibit 2.2, requires that health care providers have policies and provide patients with certain information concerning advance directives, including living wills. The best way to

EXHIBIT 2.2
42 U.S.C. 1395cc: Patient Self-Determination Act (PSDA)

(f) Maintenance of written policies and procedures

(1) For purposes of subsection (a)(1)(Q) of this section and sections 1395i–3 (c)(2)(E), 1395l (s), 1395w–25 (i), 1395mm (c)(8), and 1395bbb (a)(6) of this title, the requirement of this subsection is that a provider of services, Medicare+Choice organization, or prepaid or eligible organization (as the case may be) maintain written policies and procedures with respect to all adult individuals receiving medical care by or through the provider or organization —

(A) to provide written information to each such individual concerning —

(i) an individual's rights under State law (whether statutory or as recognized by the courts of the State) to make decisions concerning such medical care, including the right to accept or refuse medical or surgical treatment and the right to formulate advance directives (as defined in paragraph (3)), and

(ii) the written policies of the provider or organization respecting the implementation of such rights;

(B) to document in a prominent part of the individual's current medical record whether or not the individual has executed an advance directive;

(C) not to condition the provision of care or otherwise discriminate against an individual based on whether or not the individual has executed an advance directive;

(D) to ensure compliance with requirements of State law (whether statutory or as recognized by the courts of the State) respecting advance directives at facilities of the provider or organization; and

(E) to provide (individually or with others) for education for staff and the community on issues concerning advance directives.

Subparagraph (C) shall not be construed as requiring the provision of care which conflicts with an advance directive.

(2) The written information described in paragraph (1)(A) shall be provided to an adult individual —

(A) in the case of a hospital, at the time of the individual's admission as an inpatient;

(B) in the case of a skilled nursing facility, at the time of the individual's admission as a resident;

(C) in the case of a home health agency, in advance of the individual coming under the care of the agency;

(D) in the case of a hospice program, at the time of initial receipt of hospice care by the individual from the program; and

(E) in the case of an eligible organization (as defined in section 1395mm (b) of this title) or an organization provided payments under section 1395l (a)(1)(A) of this title or a Medicare+Choice organization, at the time of enrollment of the individual with the organization.

Duplicate Originals
Multiple copies of a document with original (not copied) signatures

avoid refusal to honor a living will is to provide **duplicate originals** to the client's health care professionals and facilities (nursing home, hospital) and to a trusted family member or close friend before it is needed, so that any objections can be raised immediately. The firm should also keep a duplicate original. If the client has a home in another state, make sure that she has a living will that complies with the laws of that state and that the health care providers in that location have copies. The patient should be told to discuss her wishes with her doctors and family members as soon as possible. The topic of death is difficult, but having this discussion is essential in order to avoid conflict during a time of crisis for the client. See Exhibit 2.3.

EXHIBIT 2.3
Doctor Ron Says: The Importance of the Hard Conversation

Aging inevitably brings changes in health. While some diseases occur as a result of lifestyle, such as lung disease and various forms of cancer from smoking or liver disease from excess alcohol consumption, many diseases, such as hypertension, arthritis, and dementia, are natural consequences of aging. It is impossible to predict when illness will strike or how serious it will be, so people must be prepared.

Dr. Ronald Hirsch is a Board-Certified Internal Medicine Specialist. He is Chairman of the Board of Health for his city, Elgin, IL, where he spearheaded a drive to ban smoking, and Medical Director for Case Management at Sherman Hospital.

Medicare spent $50 billion in 2008 on care provided to patients in the last two months of their lives. Much of this care was provided in costly intensive care units with state-of-the-art technology that can prolong life indefinitely. Many of the patients never talked to their families about end-of-life wishes. A living will provides some guidance, but the wording limits its use to situations where it is clear to everyone that survival is unlikely. A power of attorney for health care designates a family member to make those hard decisions, but without knowing what the patient would want, loved ones often defer to "doing everything," hoping for a miracle.

While a physician's duty is to provide accurate medical information to a patient, failure to inform can also have financial consequences. In *Arato v. Avedon*, a physician was sued for not disclosing to a patient his life expectancy from pancreatic cancer. He died without having made proper financial preparations, resulting in substantial losses for his heirs, so it is incumbent on physicians to provide realistic estimates of life expectancy and advise patients to plan both medically and financially for death. It is important for patients to realize that death is not optional and will arrive sooner or later, perhaps even suddenly, and failure to prepare can have devastating consequences, both emotional and financial, for heirs.

EXHIBIT 2.3
(continued)

Arato v. Avedon, Supreme Court of California, 858 P.2d 598 (1993) [summary]
The family of a deceased cancer patient sued the treating physicians, alleging that
the doctors failed to inform the decedent fully about the illness prior to treatment. They claimed that if the decedent had known of his low statistical life
expectancy, he would have forgone treatment and tended to his financial affairs,
and that, as a result of the failure to disclose, they suffered business, real estate,
and tax losses. The Court of Appeal reversed a defense verdict, holding that
defendants had breached a duty to obtain **informed consent** by failing to disclose information material to the decision whether to undergo treatment, and
that the jury instructions were misleading as to that duty.

Informed Consent
Consent given voluntarily,
after disclosure of adequate
information

    The Supreme Court reversed and remanded with directions to affirm the trial
court. The Court of Appeal erred in determining that defendants had breached a
duty. Although a physician has a duty to disclose all information material to the
decision to undergo a course of treatment, it is for the jury to determine whether
there is a duty to make a particular disclosure; it is not a matter of law that
statistical life expectancy information is material. The jury instructions adequately
conveyed the legal standard governing evaluation of the sufficiency of disclosures. The doctrine of informed consent does not impose a duty upon physicians to disclose information material to a patient's nonmedical interests. Since
the propriety of disclosing statistical life expectancy information to a cancer patient depends on the standard of practice within the medical community, expert
testimony was properly admitted at trial for the limited purpose of illustrating
community practice.

Tip

Helping the Client: The American Bar Association has an online toolkit
with excellent suggestions for the conversations clients should have with
their agents, family members, and health care providers, as well as questions
they should ask themselves: *http://www.abanet.org/aging/toolkit.*

What You Need to Know

The law differs from state to state. Examine the Arizona law, reproduced in Exhibit 2.4, which is fairly typical. It:

- Includes a standard form, but does not require use of that form.
- Grants health care professionals immunity from liability for actions taken in good faith.
- Requires language that clearly indicates the intent of the patient.
- Requires that the form be dated and signed or marked by the patient, or, if the patient is unable to sign or mark the document, a notary or witness can verify the patient's wishes.
- Requires that the document be notarized or witnessed in writing by at least one adult who affirms that the notary or witness was present and that the person appeared to be of sound mind and free from duress at the time.
- Requires that the notary or witness not be a person designated to make medical decisions on the principal's behalf or a person directly involved with the provision of health care to the principal at the time the health care power of attorney is executed.
- Requires that if the directive is witnessed by only one person, that person may not be related to the principal and may not be entitled to any part of the principal's estate.

Find your state statute and write a summary of its requirements for a living will. How does the statute address the requirements of the PSDA? What is required of a health care provider that does not want to honor a living will?

EXHIBIT 2.4
Arizona Statute[7]

36-3261. Living will; verification; liability

A. An adult may prepare a written statement known as a living will to control the health care treatment decisions that can be made on that person's behalf. The person may use the living will as part of or instead of a health care power of attorney or to disqualify a surrogate.

B. If the living will is not part of a health care power of attorney, the person shall verify his living will in the same manner as prescribed by section 36-3221.

C. A health care provider who makes good faith health care decisions based on the provisions of an apparently genuine living will is immune from criminal and civil liability for those decisions to the same extent and under the same conditions as prescribed in section 36-3205.

---

[7] *http://www.azleg.gov/ArizonaRevisedStatutes.asp*

EXHIBIT 2.4
(continued)

36-3262. Sample living will

Any writing that meets the requirements of this article may be used to create a living will. A person may write and use a living will without writing a health care power of attorney or may attach a living will to the person's health care power of attorney. If a person has a health care power of attorney, the agent must make health care decisions that are consistent with the person's known desires and that are medically reasonable and appropriate. A person can, but is not required to, state the person's desires in a living will. The following form is offered as a sample only and does not prevent a person from using other language or another form:

Living Will

(Some general statements concerning your health care options are outlined below. If you agree with one of the statements, you should initial that statement. Read all of these statements carefully before you initial your selection. You can also write your own statement concerning life-sustaining treatment and other matters relating to your health care. You may initial any combination of paragraphs 1, 2, 3 and 4 but if you initial paragraph 5 the others should not be initialed.)

_____ 1. If I have a terminal condition I do not want my life to be prolonged and I do not want life-sustaining treatment, beyond comfort care, that would serve only to artificially delay the moment of my death.

_____ 2. If I am in a terminal condition or an irreversible coma or a persistent vegetative state that my doctors reasonably feel to be irreversible or incurable, I do want the medical treatment necessary to provide care that would keep me comfortable, but I do not want the following:

_____ (a) Cardiopulmonary resuscitation, for example, the use of drugs, electric shock and artificial breathing.

_____ (b) Artificially administered food and fluids.

_____ (c) To be taken to a hospital if at all avoidable.

_____ 3. Notwithstanding my other directions, if I am known to be pregnant, I do not want life-sustaining treatment withheld or withdrawn if it is possible that the embryo/fetus will develop to the point of live birth with the continued application of life-sustaining treatment.

_____ 4. Notwithstanding my other directions, I do want the use of all medical care necessary to treat my condition until my doctors reasonably conclude that my condition is terminal or is irreversible and incurable or I am in a persistent vegetative state.

_____ 5. I want my life to be prolonged to the greatest extent possible.

**EXHIBIT 2.4
(continued)**

Other or Additional Statements of Desires

I have ___ I have not ___ attached additional special provisions or limitations to this document to be honored in the absence of my being able to give health care directions.

36-3221. Health care power of attorney; scope; requirements; limitations; fiduciaries

A. A person who is an adult may designate another adult individual or other adult individuals to make health care decisions on that person's behalf or to provide funeral and disposition arrangements in the event of the person's death by executing a written health care power of attorney that meets all of the following requirements:

1. Contains language that clearly indicates that the person intends to create a health care power of attorney.

2. Except as provided under subsection B of this section, is dated and signed or marked by the person who is the subject of the health care power of attorney.

3. Is notarized or is witnessed in writing by at least one adult who affirms that the notary or witness was present when the person dated and signed or marked the health care power of attorney, except as provided under subsection B, and that the person appeared to be of sound mind and free from duress at the time of execution of the health care power of attorney.

B. If a person is physically unable to sign or mark a health care power of attorney, the notary or each witness shall verify on the document that the person directly indicated to the notary or witness that the power of attorney expressed the person's wishes and that the person intended to adopt the power of attorney at that time.

C. A notary or witness shall not be any of the following:

1. A person designated to make medical decisions on the principal's behalf.

2. A person directly involved with the provision of health care to the principal at the time the health care power of attorney is executed.

D. If a health care power of attorney is witnessed by only one person, that person may not be related to the principal by blood, marriage or adoption and may not be entitled to any part of the principal's estate by will or by operation of law at the time that the power of attorney is executed.

E. A person whose license as a fiduciary has been suspended or revoked pursuant to section 14-5651 may not serve as an agent under a power of attorney in any capacity unless the person is related to the principal by blood, adoption or marriage. This prohibition does not apply if the person's license has been reinstated and is in good standing.

Powers of Attorney

A power of attorney or proxy can be used to authorize an agent to act with respect to either health care or property decisions (or, in some states, both) and generally provides more flexibility. With that flexibility, there are choices. A power of attorney can be immediately effective or it can be a **springing power**, which will come into effect at a future time (e.g., "when my doctor certifies in writing that I am unable to handle my own affairs"). A **durable power** continues after its signer becomes incompetent, which, of course, is usually the intent of the principal, particularly with respect to health care decisions. It can be a **special or limited power**, limited to a particular transaction, such as the sale of a house, or it can be limited to certain categories of actions and decisions, such as health care or property. A power of attorney that delegates all possible authority is referred to as **universal**. The power of attorney can give the agent broad **discretion** or it might include specific instructions.

Be sure to learn the law in your state. Does the law require special language to make the power durable or does it presume durability? Can you combine a health care power of attorney with a power for property, or must they be separate? Is a separate form required for medical records? While some states have statutory forms of power of attorney (like the Texas forms shown in Exhibit 2.5), the form should never be used until the client is fully informed about the options, has talked to her doctor and/or family members, and has made a decision.

Springing Power
Power that becomes effective in the future

Durable Power
Power that remains valid despite incompetence of principal

Special or Limited Power
Power of attorney for specific transactions

Universal
Describing a power of attorney granting all authority permitted by law

Discretion
Freedom to make decisions based on one's own judgment

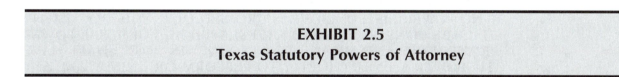

EXHIBIT 2.5
Texas Statutory Powers of Attorney

[TEXAS] STATUTORY DURABLE POWER OF ATTORNEY[8]

NOTICE: THE POWERS GRANTED BY THIS DOCUMENT ARE BROAD AND SWEEPING. THEY ARE EXPLAINED IN THE DURABLE POWER OF ATTORNEY ACT, CHAPTER XII, TEXAS PROBATE CODE. IF YOU HAVE ANY QUESTIONS ABOUT THESE POWERS, OBTAIN COMPETENT LEGAL ADVICE. THIS DOCUMENT DOES NOT AUTHORIZE ANYONE TO MAKE MEDICAL AND OTHER HEALTH CARE DECISIONS FOR YOU. YOU MAY REVOKE THIS POWER OF ATTORNEY IF YOU LATER WISH TO DO SO.

I, _____(insert your name and address), appoint _____ (insert the name and address of the person appointed) as my agent (attorney-in-fact) to act for me in any lawful way with respect to all of the following powers except for a power that I have crossed out below.

---

[8]*http://www.statutes.legis.state.tx.us/Docs/PB/htm/PB.XII.htm*

EXHIBIT 2.5
(continued)

TO WITHHOLD A POWER, YOU MUST CROSS OUT EACH POWER WITHHELD.

> Real property transactions;
> Tangible personal property transactions;
> Stock and bond transactions;
> Commodity and option transactions;
> Banking and other financial institution transactions;
> Business operating transactions;
> Insurance and annuity transactions;
> Estate, trust, and other beneficiary transactions;
> Claims and litigation;
> Personal and family maintenance;
> Benefits from social security, Medicare, Medicaid, or other governmental programs or civil or military service;
> Retirement plan transactions;
> Tax matters.

IF NO POWER LISTED ABOVE IS CROSSED OUT, THIS DOCUMENT SHALL BE CONSTRUED AND INTERPRETED AS A GENERAL POWER OF ATTORNEY AND MY AGENT (ATTORNEY-IN-FACT) SHALL HAVE THE POWER AND AUTHORITY TO PERFORM OR UNDERTAKE ANY ACTION I COULD PERFORM OR UNDERTAKE IF I WERE PERSON-ALLY PRESENT.

SPECIAL INSTRUCTIONS:

Special instructions applicable to gifts (initial in front of the following sentence to have it apply):

I grant my agent (attorney-in-fact) the power to apply my property to make gifts, except that the amount of a gift to an individual may not exceed the amount of annual exclusions allowed from the federal gift tax for the calendar year of the gift.
ON THE FOLLOWING LINES YOU MAY GIVE SPECIAL INSTRUC-TIONS LIMITING OR EXTENDING THE POWERS GRANTED TO YOUR AGENT.

_____

UNLESS YOU DIRECT OTHERWISE ABOVE, THIS POWER OF AT-TORNEY IS EFFECTIVE IMMEDIATELY AND WILL CONTINUE UNTIL IT IS REVOKED.

**EXHIBIT 2.5
(continued)**

CHOOSE ONE OF THE FOLLOWING ALTERNATIVES BY CROSSING OUT THE ALTERNATIVE NOT CHOSEN:

(A) This power of attorney is not affected by my subsequent disability or incapacity.
(B) This power of attorney becomes effective upon my disability or incapacity. YOU SHOULD CHOOSE ALTERNATIVE (A) IF THIS POWER OF ATTORNEY IS TO BECOME EFFECTIVE ON THE DATE IT IS EXECUTED. IF NEITHER (A) NOR (B) IS CROSSED OUT, IT WILL BE ASSUMED THAT YOU CHOSE ALTERNATIVE (A).

If Alternative (B) is chosen and a definition of my disability or incapacity is not contained in this power of attorney, I shall be considered disabled or incapacitated for purposes of this power of attorney if a physician certifies in writing at a date later than the date this power of attorney is executed that, based on the physician's medical examination of me, I am mentally incapable of managing my financial affairs. I authorize the physician who examines me for this purpose to disclose my physical or mental condition to another person for purposes of this power of attorney. A third party who accepts this power of attorney is fully protected from any action taken under this power of attorney that is based on the determination made by a physician of my disability or incapacity.

I agree that any third party who receives a copy of this document may act under it. Revocation of the durable power of attorney is not effective as to a third party until the third party receives actual notice of the revocation. I agree to indemnify the third party for any claims that arise against the third party because of reliance on this power of attorney.
If any agent named by me dies, becomes legally disabled, resigns, or refuses to act, I name the following (each to act alone and successively, in the order named) as successor(s) to that agent:

_____.

Signed this _____ day of _____, __.   _____
                                           (your signature)

State of _____
County of _____

This document was acknowledged before me on _____(date)
by _____ (name of principal).

EXHIBIT 2.5
(continued)

_____
(signature of notarial officer)

(seal, if any, of notary)

_____

(printed name)   My commission expires: _____

THE ATTORNEY IN FACT OR AGENT, BY ACCEPTING OR ACTING UNDER THE APPOINTMENT, ASSUMES THE FIDUCIARY AND OTHER LEGAL RESPONSIBILITIES OF AN AGENT.

MEDICAL POWER OF ATTORNEY DESIGNATION OF HEALTH CARE AGENT[9]

I, __ (insert your name) appoint:

Name: _____

Address: _____ Phone: _____

as my agent to make any and all health care decisions for me, except to the extent I state otherwise in this document. This medical power of attorney takes effect if I become unable to make my own health care decisions and this fact is certified in writing by my physician.

LIMITATIONS ON THE DECISION-MAKING AUTHORITY OF MY AGENT ARE AS FOLLOWS: _____

DESIGNATION OF ALTERNATE AGENT.
(You are not required to designate an alternate agent but you may do so. An alternate agent may make the same health care decisions as the designated agent if the designated agent is unable or unwilling to act as your agent. If the agent designated is your spouse, the designation is automatically revoked by law if your marriage is dissolved.)
If the person designated as my agent is unable or unwilling to make health care decisions for me, I designate the following persons to serve as my agent to make health care decisions for me as authorized by this document, who serve in the following order:

_____

[9]http://www.statutes.legis.state.tx.us/Docs/HS/htm/HS.166.htm#166.164

**EXHIBIT 2.5
(continued)**

A. First Alternate Agent

    Name: _____

    Address: _____ Phone: _____

B. Second Alternate Agent (name and address lines)

    The original of this document is kept at:_____

The following individuals or institutions have signed copies:

    Name: _____ Address: _____

DURATION.

I understand that this power of attorney exists indefinitely from the date I execute this document unless I establish a shorter time or revoke the power of attorney. If I am unable to make health care decisions for myself when this power of attorney expires, the authority I have granted my agent continues to exist until the time I become able to make health care decisions for myself.

(IF APPLICABLE) This power of attorney ends on the following date: _____

PRIOR DESIGNATIONS REVOKED.
I revoke any prior medical power of attorney.

ACKNOWLEDGMENT OF DISCLOSURE STATEMENT.
I have been provided with a disclosure statement explaining the effect of this document. I have read and understand that information contained in the disclosure statement.

(YOU MUST DATE AND SIGN THIS POWER OF ATTORNEY.)
I sign my name to this medical power of attorney on _____ day of _____ (month, year) at_____
(City and State)

_____

              (Signature)

          _____
              (Print Name)

STATEMENT OF FIRST WITNESS.

EXHIBIT 2.5
(continued)

I am not the person appointed as agent by this document. I am not related to the principal by blood or marriage. I would not be entitled to any portion of the principal's estate on the principal's death. I am not the attending physician of the principal or an employee of the attending physician. I have no claim against any portion of the principal's estate on the principal's death. Furthermore, if I am an employee of a health care facility in which the principal is a patient, I am not involved in providing direct patient care to the principal and am not an officer, director, partner, or business office employee of the health care facility or of any parent organization of the health care facility.

Signature: _____

Print Name: _____ Date: _____

Address: _____

SIGNATURE OF SECOND WITNESS.

Signature: _____

Print Name: _____ Date: _____

Address: _____

Effective Dates

Although outsiders (such as banks) may be reluctant to act on a springing power of attorney if they are not certain whether the power has "sprung" into effect, some clients are reluctant to sign a power of attorney for property that is immediately effective because they fear giving up control. The concern does not normally arise with respect to health care POAs because a springing power is generally triggered by a determination by the doctor who will direct care under the POA. A common resolution of this concern, with respect to property POAs, is to have the client sign a power of attorney, effective upon signing, but not give the agent possession of the document until it is needed. Having an agent for property while competent can have advantages. For example, a principal planning extended travel can instruct her agent to deposit checks and pay her bills during her absence.

Even if the agent has the document, the principal retains authority to direct the agent and to revoke the power as long as the principal is competent. Remember: A durable power continues in effect after the principal becomes incompetent. The parties are in a **fiduciary relationship** and the agent has legal obligations to the principal, including the obligation to obey the lawful instructions of a competent principal.

When a competent principal revokes a power of attorney, it is essential that the agent and all third parties be notified immediately, in writing. The revocation may have to comply with statutory formalities, such as notarization or witnessing, and should be delivered personally or by certified mail, with a receipt request. Third parties can be made more comfortable in dealing with agents if the power of attorney specifically indicates how they will be notified of revocation. In some states, principals induce third parties to act on powers of attorney by declaring that revocation will be recorded.

All powers of attorney terminate automatically upon the death of the principal, so third parties often require the agent to affirm that the principal is alive before honoring the power. Third parties are also reluctant to honor an "old" document, so the client may want to re-execute his directives every few years, even if his needs or wishes do not change. State law may also automatically terminate the agency of a spouse in the event of a divorce.

Fiduciary Relationship
Relationship imposing legal duties of trust and disclosure

Choosing an Agent

The nature of an agency relationship, requiring trust and disclosure, makes it especially important that the client choose the right people. Unlike a guardian, an agent normally operates without court supervision or a surety. The client should choose a primary agent and at least one backup or standby agent. Sometimes clients may want to appoint multiple primary agents to avoid "hurt feelings," but this should be avoided unless the client is willing to give detailed instructions for resolving conflict. Having multiple agents can also mean that multiple approvals are required for any action—resulting in great inconvenience. Considerations in choosing an agent include:

- Agent's willingness and ability to make difficult decisions.
- Agent's availability (time and location).
- Agent's understanding of client's goals and wishes and ability to communicate to family members and health care providers who may oppose those wishes.
- Agent's eligibility under state law (age, competency, involvement in patient's medical care, relationship, financial interest).

While it is possible to obtain the services of a professional to act as agent, it can be expensive, and such agents will generally insist on use of their own documents, which contain powers they are comfortable with and disclaimers to their benefit.

Powers Given the Agent

A client considering a power of attorney for health care must consider whether she wants:

- To give strict instructions or give her agent flexibility to make decisions based on circumstances.
- To specify a particular type of care environment, such as hospice care.
- To authorize the agent to change doctors, care facilities, etc.
- To allow or refuse life-sustaining treatments of various types, such as artificial nutrition or hydration.
- To continue treatment in particular circumstances (for example, a permanent vegetative state).
- To be an organ donor, participate in medical research, or donate her body to science.

Tip

The ABA has links to state-specific advance directives for health care: *http://new.abanet.org/aging/Pages/default.aspx.*

A client considering a power of attorney for property must consider whether he wants to give his agent various powers. Remember, any of these powers can be eliminated or restricted. For example, the principal might want to limit the authority to make gifts to gifts of $10,000 per year to each of his children. The principal should consider whether he wants the agent to be able to:

- Make gifts, which can be an important part of estate planning for gift tax purposes and an extremely important part of Medicaid planning (discussed in Chapters 7 and 8).
- Manage and/or sell real estate—this may require that the power be recorded.
- Manage, buy, or sell **personal property**.[6]
- Deal with banks, investment brokers, and other financial institutions.
- Deal with government agencies.
- Make loans or provide for the support of another.
- File tax returns.
- Pursue and settle claims.
- Change insurance designations.

Personal Property
Physical, moveable items, also known as chattel

---

[6]Property is categorized as real (land and buildings), personal—also called chattel (moveable items), and intangible (financial instruments, patent rights, etc.).

- Hire and fire — this can include hiring a family member as a caregiver, which can be an important step in Medicaid planning.
- Operate the client's business.
- Create, amend, or revoke a trust.
- Delegate to another.
- Compensate herself.

Of course, every client has unique circumstances that must be considered in deciding which powers to grant and which to withhold.

Drafting

Most attorneys prefer to draft their clients' powers of attorneys. A statutory or other form specific to your state is a good starting point because it will generally comply with state law concerning formalities addressing witnessing and notarization, but you should never use a form without carefully considering whether it meets the client's needs and then modifying it as necessary. State laws make different assumptions about the powers of an agent, in the absence of a statement to the contrary, and it is important to draft documents with a clear understanding of those assumptions. Pay particular attention to formalities required by state law if the power is to be recorded; for example, if the power can be used to buy and sell real estate.

The power of attorney must include clear language about its effective dates, whether it is a durable power, and how it can be revoked. A power may include a release of liability to encourage third parties to be willing to deal with the agent. Some powers include a section for the agent to sign, accepting the delegation, or for the principal to acknowledge the agent's signature. Some include an affidavit, which the agent must sign and have notarized in order to act. The agent must affirm that the principal is alive, that the attached power of attorney is a true copy, that the agent has no knowledge of revocation or termination of the power, and that the power of attorney is in full force and effect.

Many banks and financial institutions are willing to act only on their own "in-house" forms, so the paralegal must first determine where the client has accounts, contact those institutions, and obtain required forms to be executed simultaneously with the power drafted by the attorney. In addition, some governmental agencies are not willing to accept powers of attorney that may be valid under the laws of the particular state in which they were executed. Always determine, in advance, what is required:

- For information about using a power of attorney before the Internal Revenue Service, see *http://www.irs.gov/publications/p947/ar02.html*.
- For information about dealing with Social Security issues on behalf of another, see *http://www.socialsecurity.gov/phila/PDF/nh-current.pdf* and *http://www.socialsecurity.gov/pubs/10076.html*.
- To determine whether your state Medicaid agency requires a particular form, see *http://www.nasmd.org/links/state_medicaid_links.asp*.
- To download the Medicare form for permission to access health care information, see *http://www.medicare.gov/MedicareOnlineForms*.

- To access information about your state department of revenue, see *http://www.aicpa.org/Research/ExternalLinks/Pages/TaxesStatesDepartmentsofRevenue.aspx.*

After the supervising attorney has approved a final draft, prepare multiple copies of each document for execution. Many parties dealing with an agent (for example, the client's stockbroker) insist on keeping an original. Arrange for witnesses and a notary public, as required by state law. Have the client initial each page and any alterations.

Agent Obligations

The law office representing the principal must be very cautious in dealing with the agent, to avoid a possible conflict of interest. If the agent contacts the firm with respect to the power of attorney, the firm should remind the agent that privilege does not apply and may even ask the agent to sign a disclaimer.

Example

A law firm represents the principal, but has also represented the agent in a number of unrelated legal matters. During a routine visit by the principal and agent, in connection with the sale of some property, the paralegal becomes suspicious that the agent may have used some of the principal's money to pay his own debts and that the principal seems afraid of the agent. The paralegal thinks the agent might have even physically abused the principal. What can the paralegal do?

To limit contact with the agent, a firm may wish to refer the agent to outside educational materials, such as those provided by the Colorado Bar Association: *http://www.cobar.org/index.cfm/ID/21280.*

Generally, the agent must be told to:

- Read the documents.
- Understand the limits on her power (for example, that she cannot make loans).
- Keep careful records and never **commingle** the principal's money and accounts with her own.
- Make her role clear by signing, for example, "Michelle Obama, as attorney-in-fact for Barack Obama."
- Communicate regularly with the principal.
- Be represented by independent counsel, who can address matters such as whether state law requires the agent to follow the principal's wishes and state fiduciary standards — for example, can the agent do what is best for the family if it is not what the principal might want or what might be best for the principal? This is particularly important in situations involving large amounts of property or money or complicated family situations.

Commingle
To combine funds or properties

Step-by-Step Guidelines

1. Advise the client about options available and decisions that must be made; have the client consult family, trusted friends, and health care professionals. Find out whether the client has existing directives and/or might need documents effective in other states.
2. Determine which financial institutions, government agencies, and health care institutions the client deals with; find out what those institutions require and obtain needed forms.
3. Based on the client's wishes, the attorney will determine which advance directives are best.
4. Draft documents, carefully checking for required formalities, inconsistencies between documents, and consistency with client wishes.
5. After the attorney reviews and approves the documents, make multiple copies and arrange for execution with necessary witnesses and a notary present.
6. After execution of the documents, record if required, provide copies to institutions (hospital, doctor, bank, broker) as needed, and ensure that the firm has a duplicate original of each, stored in a safe place.
7. Determine whether the agent needs to be educated about his duties, how to use the power of attorney, and required accounting.

Assignments

---

1. Visit the Living Will Registry (*http://www.uslivingwillregistry.com*) and determine:
   a. Which states have their own registries?
   b. Does the service cover organ donations?
   c. Does the client/patient have to re-register periodically?
   d. Does a care provider have to be registered with the service to obtain client information?
2. Find your state statute concerning DNRs and write a short summary.
3. Critical Thinking: Compare the two Texas POA forms in Exhibit 2.5:
   a. Identify the language in each that makes it "durable."
   b. Can you imagine a situation in which a client would not want the power to be durable?
   c. Why is the witness provision on the health POA so specific about who can witness?
   d. Why is the property POA so specific, listing specific tasks that the agent might perform, while the health POA is more concerned with identifying the people involved and, instead of specifying what the agent might do, allows the principal to specify what the agent

cannot do? Why might it be a good idea for the principal to be very specific about her wishes?

4. Ruth Zia is an intelligent 76-year-old woman in good health. Ruth is a widow and would like to designate her daughter, Miranda Mboya, to handle her medical and financial affairs in the event of disability. Ruth trusts Miranda totally. She also trusts her other daughter, Janna Andrusz, age 43, but feels that Janna might not be as emotionally able to handle the responsibility, particularly decisions that would concern Janna's own child, Bryant. Bryant is an irresponsible alcoholic and Ruth does not want any of her money used to enable his behavior. She has written a will that addresses the situation. Ruth is wealthy enough to worry about estate taxes, so she has had the habit of giving each of her daughters $10,000 as a gift each year, but she has given Janna her gift by paying $10,000 toward Janna's mortgage, to prevent Janna from giving Bryant cash. An issue of concern to Ruth is that Miranda works for an international charity and spends about half of her time in Africa; she has a home there and is married to a citizen of the country in which she has a home. Miranda is 49 years old and has no children. Ruth has only one other close relative — her brother, Mathew. Mat is 81 and in poor physical health, but mentally alert. Ruth would trust Mat to make her financial decisions, but she would not want either Mat or Janna to make health decisions. She feels that they are "soft-hearted" and would try to prolong her life at all costs. Ruth is adamant that she would not want artificial nutrition or hydration and does not want to be kept alive in a vegetative state. Unless she has a reasonable chance of recovery to a good quality of life, Ruth wants medical care to be limited to pain control.

Working with a classmate, determine which advance directives would be best for Ruth. Draft those documents in a form that meets your state's requirements. If you need additional factual information, your instructor may supply it.

5. Critical/Ethical Thinking:
   a. The client executed a power of attorney for health care but did not execute a power of attorney for property. She is now incompetent, and her daughter, her attorney-in-fact under the POA, wants to place the client in a nursing home. Does the POA authorize the daughter to sign the nursing home contract, or is that a matter of property? *See Owens v. Nat'l Health Corp.*, 263 S.W.3d 876 (Tenn., 2007); *cert. den.* 129 S. Ct. 59, 172 L. Ed. 2d (2008).
   b. An agent may act on behalf of the principal, but what if the agent does not act? Suppose the attorney-in-fact for an incompetent person fails to file a lawsuit within the limitations period. Is the claim barred? *See Sullivan ex rel. Wrongful Death Beneficiaries of Sullivan v. Chattanooga Med. Investors*, 221 S.W.3d 506 (Tenn. 2007).
   c. Suppose that the attorney-in-fact retains an attorney to assist in matters relating to the POA. Could this possibly create an attorney-

client relationship between the lawyer and the person who created the POA (who may be incompetent)? *See Estate of Keatinge v. Biddle,*789 A.2d 1271 (Me., 2002).

Review Questions

1. What formalities does your state require for a living will? What are the obligations of a medical professional who does not want to honor the directive? Is the use of a living will limited to specific medical situations?
2. Does your state have a default surrogate decision-making law?
3. What formalities does your state require for execution of a power of attorney?
4. Discuss the advantages and disadvantages of a springing power of attorney as opposed to a power effective immediately.
5. Why might a health care proxy or a power of attorney be a better option than a living will?
6. Why might a client be better served by a power of attorney rather than simply designating a person to act as guardian in the event of incapacity?
7. What can be done to make third parties, such as banks, more likely to honor a client's power of attorney?
8. Read the summary of the *Aradon* case included in Exhibit 2.3. Why do you think a doctor might not want to tell a patient the "hard truth"? Can you think of circumstances in which the family might feel the doctor caused them a loss by giving a bad prognosis? Do you think that patients ever know the truth, but are not candid with their loved ones? Do you think the court's decision addresses these situations? Do you think a "bright line" can be drawn to describe a doctor's obligations in such a situation?

www.CrosswordWeaver.com

ACROSS

1. Also called a limited POA
4. Appoints an agent
9. Agent will need duplicate _____ of POA
10. Broad authority to make decisions
12. Some states have _____ surrogate decision-making laws
13. Initials, federal law concerning advance directives
14. Illness likely to result in death
20. Required if POA will be used in connection with real estate
21. Financial instruments are _____ property
23. To mix accounts
24. Nature of principal-agent relationship

DOWN

2. Another term for personal property
3. _____ will, describes patient's wishes with respect to care
5. _____ property, land and buildings
6. Can revoke agency while competent
7. Corporate or professional agent requires
8. Health care _____, aka power of attorney
11. Acts on behalf of another
15. POA, survives incompetence
16. _____ giving, organ donation
17. POA effective in future
18. POA that delegates all possible authority
19. Required in some states when advance directive is executed
22. Always terminates POA

3

◆ ◆ ◆

Guardianship/Conservatorship

◆ ◆ ◆

Objectives

When you complete this chapter, you will:

- Know the options available for various types of guardianships and conservatorships.
- Identify the due process concerns relevant to guardianship.

- Know the process for appointment of a guardian in your state and your state's rules concerning jurisdiction, priority of appointment, duties of a guardian, and court supervision.
- Draft a petition for guardianship.

Guardianship Defined

When a client's needs cannot be met by means of an advance directive or trust, either because an outside party refuses to act on the authority of the power of attorney or because the client failed to execute advance directives while competent, guardianship or conservatorship may be the only means of protecting the client. Guardianship has serious legal implications and is not readily available in all circumstances. Contrary to what some believe, a relative cannot readily "take over" when a senior family member begins acting in a way that "raises red flags."

In many states guardianship refers to the judicial appointment of a guardian to be a legal representative, responsible for the physical well-being and/or financial matters of an incompetent individual, the ward, while conservatorship refers to management of property owned by a conservatee. In a few places, guardianship is used to refer to an involuntary process, while conservatorship refers to an appointment not contested by the ward. Some people use the terms interchangeably, but this book uses the term *conservatorship* to refer to management of property only. It is important to know how the terms are used in your area; Louisiana law uses the term *interdiction*.

Adjudication
Judicial review and determination

Because either type of appointment may strip a person of legal rights, it should not be sought without consideration of alternatives, and courts do not grant it lightly. A guardianship is available only if there is an **adjudication** of incapacity, generally after it is too late to establish powers of attorney or trusts. A guardianship may be necessary even if the individual has executed advance directives, but outsiders refuse to honor those directives without a court order. Proceedings are costly, emotionally difficult, and time-consuming. Contrary to popular belief, close relatives cannot easily obtain a guardianship or "put away" an older relative.

Law Governing Appointment

UGPPA
Uniform Guardianship and Protective Proceedings Act

The process of obtaining a guardianship is a matter of state law. Those laws include different rules about jurisdiction, transfer, and other matters, which can lead to conflict. Because of the potential for conflict, the Uniform Law Commission has published, and about 20 states have adopted, the Uniform Guardianship and Protective Proceedings Act (**UGPPA**). The American Bar Association Commission on Law and Aging (*http://new.abanet.org/aging/Pages/guardianshipjurisdiction.aspx*) promotes adoption of uniform law in this field. To determine whether UGPPA has been enacted in your state, visit *http://www.nccusl.org/Update/DesktopDefault.aspx?tabindex=2&tabid=60*. If your state has not adopted the uniform law, you may be able to find your state law by visiting *http://new.abanet.org/aging/Pages/StateLawCharts.aspx*, by using a search engine such as Google to search "state name Guardianship law," or by starting at *http://www.law.cornell.edu/statutes.html* to navigate to your state code.

Types of Guardianship

Courts prefer to use the least restrictive option that will adequately protect the **alleged incompetent person (AIP)**. Some courts describe the AIP as the "individual at risk," the conservatee, or the ward; in guardianship proceedings the AIP is sometimes called the **respondent**. This chapter will generally refer to the "individual." Options available under state law may include:

- **Guardian at Litem:** a guardian appointed by the court to protect the individual's rights during litigation.
- **Co-Guardians**: guardians acting at the same time. They may serve separate functions, such as a **guardian of the person** (responsible for the physical well-being of the ward) and a **conservator of the estate** (responsible for property). If they serve the same function, consider whether one can act independently of the other(s).
- **Emergency Guardian** (sometimes called a *special medical guardian*): a guardian typically appointed to consent to medical treatment for the individual. This is a temporary appointment.
- **Limited or Partial Guardianship: a** guardianship that covers specific functions (less than plenary guardianship).
- **Plenary Guardianship:** a guardianship that covers all matters.
- **Stand-by Guardian:** a guardian who is not currently authorized to act; typically named by a spouse or parent currently acting as guardian, to act if current guardian does not.
- **Successor Guardian:** after adjudication an individual without capacity cannot be left without a guardian—a successor guardian will act if guardian cannot or does not act.
- **Temporary Guardianship:** guardianship that may be available in emergency situations, without a full hearing—for example, if the individual needs immediate medical decisions or is otherwise at risk.

Preliminary Concerns

Jurisdiction and Venue

Jurisdiction refers to the power of a court to make an enforceable ruling in a case. Once the court system with jurisdiction is identified, **venue** can be determined to identify the proper court within that system. Many states will exercise jurisdiction in a guardianship case if the disabled individual is **domiciled** or is physically present in that state. Most states will exercise jurisdiction to appoint a

Alleged Incompetent Person (AIP)
Person for whom guardianship is proposed

Respondent
Person being sued or responding to law suit

Co-Guardians
Guardians acting at the same time

Guardian of the Person
Person responsible for the physical well-being of the ward

Conservator of the Estate
Person responsible for property

Jurisdiction
Power of court to hear a particular case

Venue
Location of trial within proper court system

Domiciled
Where a person lives

conservator if the individual is domiciled or has property in the state. Conflicts can arise if the individual is physically located in a state other than his domicile—or if there is uncertainty about domicile, perhaps because the individual owns property in more than one state.

The UGPPA's objective is to assure that an appointment is made in only one state, except in cases of emergency, or if multiple appointments are required because the individual owns property located in different states. The act provides that the individual's "home state" has primary jurisdiction and defines "home state" as the state in which the individual was physically present, including periods of temporary absence, for at least six consecutive months immediately before the filing of a petition for a protective order or appointment of a guardian. If the individual was not physically present in a single state for the six months immediately preceding the filing of the petition, the home state is the place where the individual was last physically present for at least six months, as long as that presence ended within the six months prior to the filing of the petition. The home state's ability to act continues for up to six months following the individual's physical relocation to another state.

A "significant connection state" refers to the state in which the individual has a significant connection other than physical presence, and in which substantial evidence concerning the individual is available. An individual may have several significant connection states, but only one home state. Factors that may be considered in determining significant connection include:

- Location of family and others required to be notified of the proceeding.
- Length of time the individual was at any time physically present in the state and duration of absences.
- Location of the individual's property.
- Extent to which the individual has other ties to the state such as voting registration, state or local tax returns, vehicle registration, driver's license, social relationships, and receipt of services.

The UGPPA provides that a significant connection state can make an appointment or issue another type of protective order under specific circumstances, if there is no home state or if the home state has failed to act.

Priorities for Appointment

If an individual has made an advance designation of a guardian, courts will generally honor the person's wishes unless the appointment is not in the best interests of the individual (note the second section of the Illinois statute in Exhibit 3.1). If there is no advance directive or if the designated guardian cannot serve, the court will look to the statutory qualifications for appointment and priorities for appointment.

Note the Illinois statute's qualifications. Find your state's qualifications and priorities and compare them. Does your state have similar language concerning people convicted of felonies? Is there a similar prohibition on guardianship by an agency providing residential services? What is the purpose of such a prohibition?

The UGPPA lists the priorities as follows:

EXHIBIT 3.1
Illinois Statute

---

755 ILCS 5/11a-5. Who may act as guardian

(a) A person is qualified to act as guardian of the person and as guardian of the estate of a disabled person if the court finds that the proposed guardian is capable of providing an active and suitable program of guardianship for the disabled person and that the proposed guardian:

(1) has attained the age of 18 years;

(2) is a resident of the United States;

(3) is not of unsound mind;

(4) is not an adjudged disabled person as defined in this Act; and

(5) has not been convicted of a felony, unless the court finds appointment of the person convicted of a felony to be in the disabled person's best interests, and as part of the best interest determination, the court has considered the nature of the offense, the date of offense, and the evidence of the proposed guardian's rehabilitation. No person shall be appointed who has been convicted of a felony involving harm or threat to an elderly or disabled person, including a felony sexual offense.

(b) Any public agency, or not-for-profit corporation found capable by the court of providing an active and suitable program of guardianship for the disabled person, taking into consideration the nature of such person's disability and the nature of such organization's services, may be appointed guardian of the person or of the estate, or both, of the disabled person. The court shall not appoint as guardian an agency which is directly providing residential services to the ward. One person or agency may be appointed guardian of the person and another person or agency appointed guardian of the estate.

(c) Any corporation qualified to accept and execute trusts in this State may be appointed guardian of the estate of a disabled person.

Sec. 11a-6. Designation of Guardian.

A person, while of sound mind and memory, may designate in writing a person, corporation or public agency qualified to act under Section 11a-5 [755 ILCS 5/11a-5], to be appointed as guardian or as successor guardian of his person or of his estate or both, in the event he is adjudged to be a disabled person. The designation may be proved by any competent evidence, but if it is executed and attested in the same manner as a will, it shall have prima facie validity. If the court finds that the appointment of the one designated will serve the best interests and welfare of the ward, it shall make the appointment in accordance with the designation. The selection of the guardian shall be in the discretion of the court whether or not a designation is made.

(1) A guardian, other than a temporary or emergency guardian, currently acting for the individual;

(2) A person nominated as guardian by the ward, if at the time of the nomination, the ward had sufficient capacity to express a preference;

(3) An agent appointed a durable power of attorney for health care;

(4) Spouse or a person nominated by will or other signed writing of a deceased spouse [an example of a stand-by guardian];

(5) An adult child;

(6) A parent, or an individual nominated by will or other signed writing of a deceased parent; and

(7) An adult with whom the ward has resided for more than six months before the filing of the petition.

(b) With respect to persons having equal priority, the court shall select the one it considers best qualified. The court, acting in the best interest of the ward, may decline to appoint a person having priority and appoint a person having a lower priority or no priority.

(c) An owner, operator, or employee of a long-term-care institution at which the respondent is receiving care may not be appointed as guardian unless related to the respondent by blood, marriage, or adoption.

As you can see, a guardian may be a family member or an unrelated individual. Some states authorize corporations to act as guardians, as shown in the Illinois statute. A guardian may be compensated or may be a volunteer. Many states and counties have public guardians. If there is no such office, the judge may appoint an attorney or other individual. If the ward has assets, those assets may be used to compensate a public guardian; if the ward is **indigent**, the public absorbs the cost. A state may allow a **foreign guardian**, but appointment of a foreign guardian may result in inconvenience.

At least one state, Florida, requires training for nonprofessional guardians and has an exam. The National Guardianship Association (*http://www.guardianship. org*) provides resources for guardians, including a center for guardianship certification. Certification is a means by which a guardian can establish to a court that she is qualified for appointment and is familiar with and agrees to abide by guardianship laws and ethical standards. The Association is open to both professional and family guardians. Many states and bar associations have additional information online because guardianships are often sought by family members, acting **pro se**. Find out what is available for your state by using a search engine, such as Google, and entering the name of your state and the word *guardianship*.

Indigent
Without funds

Foreign Guardian
A guardian from another state or country

Pro Se
Acting on one's own behalf

Petition

The process begins with the filing of a petition in compliance with statutory requirements. Examine the Colorado statute in Exhibit 3.2 and the sample petition in Exhibit 3.3 to see what is typically required. Take particular notice of the reference to a physician's report; this is required in some states. In other states, the court initially orders an evaluation (described below); evidence about the AIP's condition and whether a guardianship is the least restrictive alternative are considered at a subsequent hearing.

Examine the sample California Declaration of Capacity, to be completed by the health care provider, at *http://www.courtinfo.ca.gov/forms/fillable/gc335.pdf.*

EXHIBIT 3.2
Colorado Statute

The Colorado statute is fairly typical in describing the required contents of a petition.

15-14-304. Judicial appointment of guardian petition.

(1) An individual or a person interested in the individual's welfare may petition for a determination of incapacity, in whole or in part, and for the appointment of a limited or unlimited guardian for the individual.

(2) The petition must set forth the petitioner's name, residence, current address if different, relationship to the respondent, and interest in the appointment and, to the extent known, state or contain the following with respect to the respondent and the relief requested:

(a) The respondent's name, age, principal residence, current street address, and, if different, the address of the dwelling in which it is proposed that the respondent will reside if the appointment is made;

(b) (I) The name and address of the respondent's:

(A) Spouse, or if the respondent has none, an adult with whom the respondent has resided for more than six months within one year before the filing of the petition; and

(B) Adult children and parents; or

(II) If the respondent has neither spouse, adult child, nor parent, at least one of the adults nearest in kinship to the respondent who can be found with reasonable efforts;

(c) The name and address of each person responsible for care or custody of the respondent, including the respondent's treating physician;

(d) The name and address of each legal representative of the respondent;

(e) The name and address of each person nominated as guardian by the respondent;

(f) The name and address of each proposed guardian and the reason why the proposed guardian should be selected;

(g) The reason why guardianship is necessary, including a brief description of the nature and extent of the respondent's alleged incapacity;

(h) If an unlimited guardianship is requested, the reason why limited guardianship is inappropriate and, if a limited guardianship is requested, the powers to be granted to the limited guardian; and

(i) A general statement of the respondent's property with an estimate of its value, including any insurance or pension, and the source and amount of any other anticipated income or receipts.

EXHIBIT 3.3
Sample of a Petition Compliant with Illinois Law

IN THE _____ COURT FOR ____

_____ COUNTY, STATE *insert correct title for court*

In the Matter of the Guardianship of:)

)

Ward name _____,   ) No.____ _____

) *docket number, will be assigned*
               by clerk

Alleged Disabled Person.   ) *when petition is filed*

PETITION FOR APPOINTMENT OF A GUARDIAN

Petitioner, *name & address; check state law, need petitioner be a resident?*, alleges as follows:

1. Petitioner, _____ is *relationship to the ward* _____.
2. The alleged disabled person, _____, was born _____ and *his or her* current residence is *address* _____.
3. *Ward name* currently has no guardian and has no agent under the *cite relevant state law; if AIP has an advance directive, describe.*
4. The names and addresses of the nearest relatives of *ward name* are, in statutory order *(cite your state's priority statute)*:
5. *Ward name's* property, with the estimated value of $_____.*List of real and significant personal property*
6. Current and anticipated receipts consist of: *identify ward's income*
7. A plenary guardianship is necessary because *ward* has been diagnosed by physician *name and address* as suffering from *diagnosis* more fully stated in the report of said physician, which has left *ward* without sufficient understanding or capacity to make or communicate responsible decisions concerning the care of *his or her personal and/or financial affairs.*
8. The physician's report has been submitted with this Petition in a sealed envelope to the Clerk of the Court consistent with section XX of the *name of state law* Act and is incorporated herein by reference and made a part hereof.
9. A limited guardianship will not provide sufficient protection for *ward name*
10. The proposed guardian, ____, is qualified to be appointed the guardian of the *person or estate* of *ward name* in that *petitioner name* is not of unsound mind, is not an adjudged disabled person, *has not been convicted of a felony — check state law* and meets all other requirements of §xx of the Act.

**EXHIBIT 3.3
(continued)**

WHEREFORE, Petitioner, prays that an order be entered adjudicating *ward name* to be a disabled adult within the meaning of the Probate Act and appointing and naming *petitioner name* as plenary guardian of the *person or estate* of *ward name.*

Dated this day_____ of _____, 20_____.

_____
Petitioner

VERIFICATION BY CERTIFICATION

_____, respectfully states that _____ is the Petitioner herein, and that _____ has read the foregoing Petition for Appointment of Guardian and under penalties as provided by law pursuant to Section XX of the Code ofXX, the undersigned certifies that the statements set forth in this petition are true and correct except as to matters therein stated to be on information and belief and as to such matters the undersigned certifies as aforesaid that _____ believes that same to be true.

_____
Petitioner

The petitioner is not always the proposed guardian. For example, a concerned friend or neighbor who is unqualified or unable to act as guardian might want to get help. A common situation involves an older person who is taken to the hospital and is ready for discharge, but is unable to care for himself and unable to consent to or obtain benefits to pay for residential care. If no friend or relative is available, the hospital might petition for appointment of a temporary guardian to serve those functions.

The paralegal must gather information and documents before preparing a petition:

- Information about family, for notice to interested persons.
- Information about the individual's income and assets.
- Any advance directives, wills, or trusts executed by the individual.
- Information about the individual's living situation, abilities, and health.
- Information about how a guardianship would benefit the individual—some states require this information or a plan as part of the petition.

Critical Thinking: Who Is Going to Pay for This?

Petitioners and guardians, particularly those who are not related to the ward, do not have to spend their own money or work as volunteers. Most states have a statute similar to the Florida law shown in Exhibit 3.4. Note the requirement for an itemized statement and review by the court. Why? Note also the reference to fees for work done by legal assistants. How does that serve the same purpose as the itemized statement?

Due Process Protections

Parens Patriae
State's power to protect individuals

In the past, guardianship proceedings were often seen as non-adversarial. Courts focused on the state's inherent **parens patriae** power to protect individuals and did not adhere to procedures employed in adversarial changes. There was often an assumption that the petitioner and guardian were acting and would continue to act in the best interest of the individual. Guardianship proceedings were often uncontested because the individual did not have the ability to object. That began to change in the 1970s, because of media attention, congressional hearings, and studies that revealed abuse. Most statutes now include standards and definitions designed to prevent such abuse.

What society thinks is in the best interest of an individual may not be what that person wants. An older person may want to stay in her own home, even though her abilities to care for herself and to manage her money are severely limited by forgetfulness and physical weakness. Her children and her doctor may want her to move to a care facility. Should the court rule in favor of protection or of **self-determination**? Might there be alternatives? Because of the due process implications of confining a person to an institution or using medications to restrain an individual, California, for example, has different procedures for "probate" conservatorships and mental health conservatorships.

Self-determination
Right to make one's own decisions

Notice is an essential component of due process, and the UGPPA requires that the AIP be given written notice at least 14 days before the hearing. The notice may be delivered in a number of ways. Other **interested parties** are also entitled to notice. Examine the Indiana statute and form of notice (Exhibit 3.5), which are typical.

Interested Parties
Persons entitled to notice of guardianship proceedings

How does your state compare to others with respect to notice requirements? See *http://www.abanet.org/aging/legislativeupdates/pdfs/Chart_Notice_6-08.pdf*.

Most courts prefer that the AIP appear at the hearing; some courts appoint a guardian ad litem, a visitor, investigator, or evaluators (courts use different terms, but the function is the same) to investigate and report on the situation, regardless

---

EXHIBIT 3.4
Florida Fee Statute

Fla. Stat. §744.108. Guardians and attorneys fees and expenses

(1) A guardian, or an attorney who has rendered services to the ward or to the guardian on the ward's behalf, is entitled to a reasonable fee for services rendered and reimbursement for costs incurred on behalf of the ward.

(2) When fees for a guardian or an attorney are submitted to the court for determination, the court shall consider the following criteria:

(a) The time and labor required;

(b) The novelty and difficulty of the questions involved and the skill required to perform the services properly;

(c) The likelihood that the acceptance of the particular employment will preclude other employment of the person;

(d) The fee customarily charged in the locality for similar services;

(e) The nature and value of the incapacitated person's property, the amount of income earned by the estate, and the responsibilities and potential liabilities assumed by the person;

(f) The results obtained;

(g) The time limits imposed by the circumstances;

(h) The nature and length of the relationship with the incapacitated person; and

(i) The experience, reputation, diligence, and ability of the person performing the service.

(3) In awarding fees to attorney guardians, the court must clearly distinguish between fees and expenses for legal services and fees and expenses for guardian services and must have determined that no conflict of interest exists.

(4) Fees for legal services may include customary and reasonable charges for work performed by legal assistants employed by and working under the direction of the attorney.

(5) All petitions for guardian's and attorney's fees and expenses must be accompanied by an itemized description of the services performed for the fees and expenses sought to be recovered.

(6) A petition for fees or expenses may not be approved without prior notice to the guardian and to the ward, unless the ward is a minor or is totally incapacitated.

(7) A petition for fees shall include the period covered and the total amount of all prior fees paid or costs awarded to the petitioner in the guardianship proceeding currently before the court.

(8) When court proceedings are instituted to review or determine a guardian's or an attorney's fees under subsection (2), such proceedings are part of the guardianship administration process and the costs, including fees for the guardian's attorney, shall be determined by the court and paid from the assets of the guardianship estate unless the court finds the requested compensation under subsection (2) to be substantially unreasonable.

EXHIBIT 3.5
Indiana Statute

IC 29-3-6-1 Sec. 1.

(a) When a petition for appointment of a guardian or for the issuance of a protective order is filed with the court, notice of the petition and the hearing on the petition shall be given by first class postage prepaid mail as follows:

(1) If the petition is for the appointment of a successor guardian, notice shall be given unless the court, for good cause shown, orders that notice is not necessary.

(2) If the petition is for the appointment of a temporary guardian, notice shall be given as required by IC 29-3-3-4(a).

(3) If the subject of the petition is a minor, notice of the petition and the hearing on the petition shall be given to the following persons whose whereabouts can be determined upon reasonable inquiry:

(A) The minor, if at least fourteen (14) years of age, unless the minor has signed the petition.

(B) Any living parent of the minor, unless parental rights have been terminated by a court order.

(C) Any person alleged to have had the principal care and custody of the minor during the sixty (60) days preceding the filing of the petition.

(D) Any other person that the court directs.

(4) If it is alleged that the person is an incapacitated person, notice of the petition and the hearing on the petition shall be given to the following persons whose whereabouts can be determined upon reasonable inquiry:

(A) The alleged incapacitated person, the alleged incapacitated person's spouse, and the alleged incapacitated person's adult children, or if none, the alleged incapacitated person's parents.

(B) Any person who is serving as a guardian for, or who has the care and custody of, the alleged incapacitated person.

(C) In case no person other than the incapacitated person is notified under clause (A), at least one (1) of the persons most closely related by blood or marriage to the alleged incapacitated person.

(D) Any person known to the petitioner to be serving as the alleged incapacitated person's attorney-in-fact under a durable power of attorney.

(E) Any other person that the court directs.

Notice is not required under this subdivision if the person to be notified waives notice or appears at the hearing on the petition.

(b) Whenever a petition (other than one for the appointment of a guardian or for the issuance of a protective order) is filed with the court, notice of the petition and the hearing on the petition shall be given to the following persons, unless they appear or waive notice:

(1) The guardian.

(2) Any other persons that the court directs, including the following:

(A) Any department, bureau, agency, or political subdivision of the United States or of this state that makes or awards compensation, pension, insurance, or other allowance for the benefit of an alleged incapacitated person.

**EXHIBIT 3.5
(continued)**

(B) Any department, bureau, agency, or political subdivision of this state that may be charged with the supervision, control, or custody of an alleged incapacitated person.

IC 29-3-6-2 Sec. 2. A copy of the petition shall be attached to the notice, and the notice must be in substantially the following form:

NOTICE

TO: (name and address of person receiving notice)

On (date of hearing) at (time of hearing) in (place of hearing) at (city), Indiana, the (name and address of court) will hold a hearing to determine whether a guardian should be appointed for (name of alleged incapacitated person or minor). A copy of the petition requesting appointment of a guardian is attached to this notice.

At the hearing the court will determine whether (name of alleged incapacitated person or minor) is an incapacitated person or minor under Indiana law. This proceeding may substantially affect the rights of (name of alleged incapacitated person or minor).

If the court finds that (name of alleged incapacitated person or minor) is an incapacitated person or minor, the court at the hearing shall also consider whether (name of proposed guardian, if any) should be appointed as guardian of (name of alleged incapacitated person or minor). The court may, in its discretion, appoint some other qualified person as guardian. The court may also, in its discretion, limit the powers and duties of the guardian to allow (name of alleged incapacitated person or minor) to retain control over certain property and activities. The court may also determine whether a protective order should be entered on behalf of (name of alleged incapacitated person or minor).

(Name of alleged incapacitated person) may attend the hearing and be represented by an attorney. The petition may be heard and determined in the absence of (name of alleged incapacitated person) if the court determines that the presence of (name of alleged incapacitated person) is not required. If (name of alleged incapacitated person) attends the hearing, opposes the petition, and is not represented by an attorney, the court may appoint an attorney to represent (name of alleged incapacitated person). The court may, where required, appoint a guardian ad litem to represent (name of alleged incapacitated person or minor) at the hearing.

The court may, on its own motion or on request of any interested person, postpone the hearing to another date and time.

_____

(signature of clerk of the court)

of whether the AIP appears. Some judges will even visit the AIP at home or in the hospital or care facility if the AIP is unable to attend the hearing or waives appearance. The AIP may want to contest the proceedings and to obtain or request appointment of her own attorney to advocate her position, because a guardian at litem is not bound by confidentiality and is required to look at the AIP's best interests, which are not always the same as the AIP's wishes.

Although the law often refers to "least restrictive means," which must be determined on a case-by-case basis, the practical realities may dictate the decision. For example, an individual may not have the ability to handle investments, checking accounts, credit cards, etc., but might be able to handle small cash transactions, such as going to the grocery store with $50. How might a court structure a conservatorship? What would be the difficulties, from the conservator's point of view, that might make the "least restrictive" arrangement unduly burdensome?

Determination of Competency

Functional
Focused on abilities

Status-oriented
Focused on diagnosis

Least Restrictive
Guardianship standard, designed to give protected individual greatest possible autonomy

Dementia
Mental deterioration of physical origin

Psychotropic Drugs
Drugs that alter mental function or emotions

Required Findings
Court's conclusions justifying decision

Letters of Office
Order authorizing guardian to act

Surety Bond
Insurance to protect ward from financial loss due to guardian's actions

The UGPPA defines "incapacitated" to mean that an individual is "unable to receive and evaluate information or make or communicate decisions to such an extent that the individual lacks the ability to meet essential requirements for physical health, safety, or self-care, even with appropriate technological assistance." Note that the definition is **functional**—it focuses on the individual's abilities—rather than **status-oriented**. Being old or having a physical or even a mental illness does not necessarily equate with lack of capacity. Some states use the term *decisional incapacity* to clarify that physical problems are not determinative. Note also the word *essential*; should an individual be considered incapacitated because, for example, her manner of dress and grooming is unacceptable to her family? Note also that the focus is on whether the individual has the ability to make competent decisions, not whether his decisions are actually good decisions. People have the right to make "bad" decisions that displease their families. Some state definitions refer to the "necessity" of appointment. This is an acknowledgement of the goal of using the **least restrictive** means of assisting the individual.

States have their own definitions, and the burden is on the petitioner to prove, usually by "clear and convincing evidence," that the AIP falls within the definition. All adults are presumed competent. A medical professional may not know the elements of the statutory definition and may be unaware of the need to address those elements. A diagnosis, even of a serious mental condition, such as **dementia** or use of **psychotropic drugs**, may not be enough.

If the court is able to make **required findings** based on the evidence, it will issue an order, sometimes called **letters of office**, appointing a guardian. The order will typically include the duration of the guardianship, a description of the guardian's authority, a provision concerning compensation of the guardian, and requirements for reporting. Depending on the circumstances, the court may require a **surety bond**. The record of proceedings on competency will be sealed to protect the privacy of the individual.

Obligations of Guardian

The obligations and authority of the guardian depend on the type of guardianship: guardianship of the person or conservatorship of property; plenary or limited. The obligations also depend on state law. Guardianship is a fiduciary relationship, and, at the very least, the guardian is required to put the ward's interests ahead of her own and investigate for possible abuse of the ward. For this reason, a person cannot be forced to act as a guardian against her will.

In general, a guardian is not required to provide for a ward out of her own funds, to provide actual physical custody of the ward, to be liable for a ward's actions, or to be liable for harm to a ward caused by a caregiver selected by the guardian.

Accounting

The court retains jurisdiction, and the guardian may be required to file periodic reports. For example, a conservator may be required to submit a financial plan, an inventory, and periodic accountings. The Florida statute, reproduced in Exhibit 3.6, is typical. A paralegal is often responsible for assisting the guardian in setting up a system to track income and expenses and in producing the annual report in compliance with statutory requirements.

To see samples of guardianship annual accounting forms, use a search engine, such as Google, to search for "sample guardian accounting," or visit *http://www.courtinfo.ca.gov/programs/equalaccess/guard.htm*.

EXHIBIT 3.6
FLORIDA STATUTES CHAPTER XVIII, Domestic Relations 744.3678
Annual Accounting

(1) Each guardian of the property must file an annual accounting with the court.

(2) The annual accounting must include:

(a) A full and correct account of the receipts and disbursements of all of the ward's property over which the guardian has control and a statement of the ward's property on hand at the end of the accounting period. This paragraph does not apply to any property or any trust of which the ward is a beneficiary but which is not under the control or administration of the guardian.

EXHIBIT 3.6
(continued)

(b) A copy of the annual or year-end statement of all of the ward's cash accounts from each of the institutions where the cash is deposited.

(3) The guardian must obtain a receipt, canceled check, or other proof of payment for all expenditures and disbursements made on behalf of the ward. The guardian must preserve all evidence of payment, along with other substantiating papers, for a period of 3 years after his or her discharge. The receipts, proofs of payment, and substantiating papers need not be filed with the court but shall be made available for inspection and review at the time and place and before the persons as the court may order.

(4) The guardian shall pay from the ward's estate to the clerk of the circuit court a fee based upon the following graduated fee schedule, upon the filing of the annual financial return, for the auditing of the return:

(a) For estates with a value of $25,000 or less the clerk of the court may charge a fee of up to $20.

(b) For estates with a value of more than $25,000 up to and including $100,000 the clerk of the court may charge a fee of up to $85.

(c) For estates with a value of more than $100,000 up to and including $500,000 the clerk of the court may charge a fee of up to $170.

(d) For estates with a value in excess of $500,000 the clerk of the court may charge a fee of up to $250.

Upon petition by the guardian, the court may waive the auditing fee upon a showing of insufficient funds in the ward's estate. Any guardian unable to pay the auditing fee may petition the court for a waiver of the fee. The court may waive the fee after it has reviewed the documentation filed by the guardian in support of the waiver.

(5) This section does not apply if the court determines that the ward receives income only from social security benefits and the guardian is the ward's representative payee for the benefits

A guardian of the person may be required to submit periodic reports on the ward's physical, social, and emotional conditions, living arrangements, and professional services provided to the ward (such as medical care). The guardian may be required to obtain court permission for making certain changes.

Of course, there are things that a guardian typically cannot do for the individual, including consent to marriage or divorce, or casting a vote. Many states require court approval for major decisions, such as:

- Administering medications and other extremely restrictive medical measures, such as confinement to a ward or shock therapy.
- Changing housing arrangements or legal domicile.
- Making gifts.
- Releasing interests.
- Establishing a trust.
- Selling real estate.
- Entering a contract on behalf of the ward.
- Exercising rights under an insurance or employee benefits plan.

Exercise of Substituted Judgment

What standard is applied to the guardian's exercise of **substituted judgment**? Many states require that the guardian make decisions by conforming as closely as possible to what the ward, if competent, would have done or intended under the circumstances. The guardian must take into account her knowledge of the ward's personal, philosophical, religious, and moral beliefs and values. In some cases, such as where the ward has serious dementia, it may be impossible to determine what the ward would have wanted under the circumstances and the guardian must use the "best interest" standard of decision making. This means that in reaching a decision, the guardian should act in the manner of a **reasonably prudent** person (or investor, if a conservatorship). In reaching a decision, the guardian should weigh the benefits, the possible risks and consequences, and the possible alternatives, and should then select the best option available. In making medical decisions, the guardian must adhere to the informed consent standard. When appropriate, the guardian may also have to consider the "least restrictive" standard. Of course, the guardian's choices are limited by financial concerns. For example, the individual's income and public benefits may be inadequate to pay for the housing that would be "best" for the individual. Financial concerns are a major factor when a public guardian is required, as discussed in Exhibit 3.7.

The National Guardianship Association has promulgated a model code of ethics (*http://www.guardianship.org/pdf/codeEthics.pdf*) that emphasizes the duties of loyalty and trust. The guardian must not make decisions based on his own best interests and must not withhold information.

Guardianship can be limited to a specific time period, after which the court must determine whether to renew the appointment. Guardianship can be terminated if the ward regains competence, and, of course, guardianship terminates upon the death of the ward. In most states, a petition for termination of guardianship puts the burden of proof on the party claiming that the individual is still incapacitated. Any termination will normally require a final report to the court.

Substituted Judgment
Judgment exercised on behalf of another guardian cannot or does not act

Reasonably Prudent
Standard for actions of guardian

EXHIBIT 3.7
Dealing with Cuts in Funding

Kimberly Murphy received her law degree from the University of Iowa College of Law. In addition to serving as Associate Director of the National Health Law and Policy Resource Center (NHLP), Ms. Murphy maintains a private law practice specializing in elder law, probate law, and health law. She is an active member of the Iowa State Bar Association and serves on the Guardianship/Conservatorship Committee of the Probate Section of the Iowa Bar Association. She also is a member of the Iowa Committee on Probate Procedure and Forms, which was established by the Iowa Supreme Court. Based on her demonstrated expertise regarding guardianships, Ms. Murphy has received national guardianship certification from the National Guardianship Association, which establishes and promotes a nationally recognized standard of excellence in guardianship.

The NHLP was founded in 1981. Its mission is to promote laws and public policies that foster and facilitate accessible, affordable, and quality health services and related services for all Americans, particularly vulnerable and disadvantaged populations. It furnishes a nonpartisan forum for informed dialogue, based on the best available data and information, between academics, practitioners, and public policy makers on important health law and policy issues. The NHLP Web site (*http://www.uiowa.edu/law-nhlp/about.shtml*) is a wealth of resources for those serving vulnerable clients.

Ms. Murphy understands the need for such resources. From 2007 to 2009, she was Administrator of the Iowa Office of Substitute Decision Maker in the Iowa Department of Elder Affairs. The Office of Substitute Decision Maker was established to assure that Iowans had access to resources and information regarding substitute decision making, to provide statewide education to individuals routinely addressing substitute decision-making issues, and to investigate and intervene in problematic guardianships and conservatorships. In her capacity as Administrator, she served as a member of the Iowa Substitute Decision Maker Task Force and Iowa Substitute Decision Maker Curriculum Committee, and she was responsible for developing a statewide curriculum on substitute decision makers and a statewide training program utilizing that curriculum. Unfortunately, many of the resources previously available under the state program have fallen victim to budget cuts common to all states.

With respect to dealing with budget cuts and doing more for your clients with less from the government, Ms. Murphy says, "The economic crisis and corresponding budget cuts have made it difficult for clients to obtain traditional assistance from government programs. Many necessary programs have been cut and some eliminated. It is more important than ever to look for creative solutions when assisting clients. Look for nontraditional resources that exist outside of government. In Iowa, for example, the National Health Law and Policy Resource Center has dedicated itself to filling the gap of public education left by the elimination of the Office of Substitute Decision Maker. Other organizations and nonprofit associations that may be able to provide guidance include local law school clinics and legal aid organizations, nonprofit entities dealing with disability or aging issues, and organizations dealing with specific and related causes, such as the Alzheimer's Association."

Assignments

---

1. Visit *http://new.abanet.org/aging/Pages/guardianshipjurisdiction.aspx*; scroll to the resource that includes cases involving jurisdiction issues. Find, read, and summarize a case from your jurisdiction.

2. Critical Thinking: Read the short Florida cases at the end of this chapter.
   a. Why might the judge in the Fernandez case have not followed normal trial procedure?
   b. There is a reference in the *Magill* case to an award of fees to the guardian ad litem. Where will the money come from?
   c. In *Magill*, do you think that appointment of all three daughters as guardian was a good idea? What would the court have had to find in order to reject the declaration?

3. Find your state law requiring an accounting by a guardian. Your firm's client, Ali Iqbal, has just been appointed as guardian for his father, Mohammed Iqbal. Write a letter, describing to Ali how he will be required to account for his father's finances. Mr. Iqbal is a person of average intelligence, so do not write in "legalese."

4. Use Google or a similar search engine to find samples of guardianship questionnaires. Using what you find as a starting point, put together an intake form to be used for questioning a client who wants to seek guardianship of an older relative.

5. Locate your state's law pertaining to guardianship proceedings and determine:
   a. What are the priorities for appointment?
   b. Who is entitled to notice of a petition? How and when must that notice take place?
   c. Does the statute include a "least restrictive" or "least intrusive" standard?
   d. How does the statute define incapacity? How would a physician's report address the requirements of the statute?
   e. What does the statute say about awards of costs and fees? Can the petitioner be reimbursed for seeking guardianship

6. Based on the statutory requirements and/or forms you find online, prepare a guardianship petition, to be filed in your local state trial court, for this situation. Adeline Andrews was born May 21, 1929. She is a widow and lives with her only child, daughter Darlene Hendry, at 350 River Bluff Road, in your town, your state. Darlene would like to be her mother's legal guardian so that she can make medical decisions and deal with financial institutions. Adeline has no advance directives and has never had a guardian or conservator. Darlene is a competent adult, has never been convicted of a felony, and is also a widow. Adeline's physician, Elise Warski, MD, has provided a written report indicating that Adeline has dementia with Lewy bodies. She suffers tremors and other

physical manifestations. She is not able to understand her diagnosis or answer questions about her treatment preferences. She does not remember where she has bank accounts, or where she lives. Her assets consist of $240,000 in savings and income of $1,800 per month. If you need additional information, your instructor can provide it.

Review Questions

1. What protections does your state have in place for individuals who wish to challenge a guardianship petition identifying them as incapacitated?
2. What protections does your state have in place to prevent an appointed guardian from taking advantage of or neglecting responsibilities to a ward?
3. Does your state restrict the actions that may be taken by a guardian without court approval?
4. How do courts in your state determine competency?
5. Does your state or county have a public guardian?
6. What are the requirements for a petition for guardianship in your state?

FERNANDEZ V. FERNANDEZ

36 So. 3d 175 (Fla. App. 2010)

This is an appeal of an order denying a verified petition to determine incapacity. We remand for a new trial.

Nancy Fernandez, the daughter, filed a verified petition to determine incapacity of her mother, Elsa Maria Fernandez. The court appointed an examining committee. Two members of the examining committee recommended a limited guardianship and the third member concluded that no guardianship was necessary.

The matter came before the trial court for an evidentiary hearing. The mother and daughter were present and each was represented by counsel. Other witnesses were also present and testified. The trial court denied the petition and the daughter has appealed.

The daughter contends that the trial court failed to follow proper trial procedure. We conclude that the daughter's argument is well taken.

We surmise that the trial court, acting from the best of motives, decided that the hearing would proceed more expeditiously if the trial court conducted the examination of witnesses instead of allowing counsel to do so. The trial court swore the witnesses and denied the daughter's request to invoke the rule of exclusion of witnesses. The court called and questioned the witnesses, affording almost no opportunity for examination or cross-examination by the parties. There were no opening or closing statements.

Respectfully, this was not proper procedure. The Florida Probate Rules provide that in adversary proceedings, "the proceedings, as nearly as practicable, shall be conducted similar to suits of a civil nature and the Florida Rules of Civil Procedure shall govern. . . . " Fla. Prob. R. 5.025(d)(2). "The adjudicatory hearing must be conducted at the time and place specified in the notice of hearing and in a manner consistent with due process." §744.331(5)(a), Fla. Stat. (2008).

As this was an evidentiary hearing in a contested proceeding, the matter should have been tried as is customary in a bench trial. The parties should have been given an opportunity to make opening and closing statements. Each party should have been given an opportunity to present evidence, call and question witnesses, and cross-examine the other side's witnesses. When the guardian ad litem gave her report, cross-examination by the parties should have been allowed.

At the start of the hearing, the daughter invoked the rule of exclusion of witnesses. The trial court denied that request. The request should have been granted. The Evidence Code provides:

90.616 Exclusion of witnesses.

(1) At the request of a party the court shall order, or upon its own motion the court may order, witnesses excluded from a proceeding so that they cannot hear the testimony of other witnesses except as provided in subsection (2).

(2) A witness may not be excluded if the witness is:

(a) A party who is a natural person.

(b) In a civil case, an officer or employee of a party that is not a natural person. The party's attorney shall designate the officer or employee who shall be the party's representative.

(c) A person whose presence is shown by the party's attorney to be essential to the presentation of the party's cause.

(d) In a criminal case, the victim of the crime, the victim's next of kin, the parent or guardian of a minor child victim, or a lawful representative of such person, unless, upon motion, the court determines such person's presence to be prejudicial. §90.616, Fla. Stat. (2008)

The parties, of course, were not subject to exclusion. *Id.* §90.616(2)(a). The other fact witnesses were all relatives of the parties. Because the daughter timely invoked the rule, the relatives should have been excluded. The daughter does not complain about the fact that the guardian ad litem was allowed to remain. For the stated reasons, we reverse the order now before us and remand for a new trial. We express no opinion on the merits of the petition.

MAGILL V. DRESNER

2010 Fla. App. LEXIS 11268 (2010)

The appellants, Marianne Magill Acuna and Marilyn Magill, appeal an order of the probate court appointing the appellee, Jack Dresner, as plenary guardian for their mother. They also appeal an order granting attorney's fees to the attorney *ad litem*, appellee Hung V. Nguyen, and an order denying a motion for disqualification of the trial judge. We affirm both the order granting attorney's fees to Nguyen and the order denying the motion for disqualification. However, because there was insufficient evidence to rebut the statutory presumption that the designated preneed guardian is entitled to serve as guardian, we reverse the order appointing Dresner plenary guardian.

1. Concerning the appellants' claim that the trial court erred when it awarded attorney's fees to Nguyen, we find that the appellants lack standing to challenge the order. . . .

The ward, Shirley Magill, has three daughters: the appellants, Marianne Magill Acuna and Marilyn Magill, and Maureen Tew. Maureen is married to the petitioner below, Jeffrey Tew. On June 23, 2006, Shirley executed a Declaration Naming Preneed Guardian, which stated in relevant part:

> If I am determined at any time to be incapacitated, as that term is defined in the Florida Guardianship Law as it now exists or may hereafter be amended, I declare that my three (3) children MARIANNE ACUNA, MARILYN MAGILL, AND MAUREEN TEW, together, or the survivor thereof, are to serve as guardian of my person and property, to exercise all delegable legal rights and powers and to perform all the tasks necessary to care for me and my property. If none of my children are able or willing to serve as Guardian of my person and property, for any reason, then I appoint my son-in-law, JEFFREY TEW, to act as Guardian of my person and property.

Subsequently, on May 12, 2009, Tew filed a petition to determine incapacity seeking the appointment of a guardian of the property of Shirley. Tew later filed a motion to amend, seeking the determination of Shirley's total incapacity and the appointment of a plenary guardian.

At the hearing on the petition, the probate court heard testimony from the examining committee concerning Shirley's mental capacity. Additionally, Tew presented evidence that the appellants and Maureen were in disagreement as to Shirley's living arrangement: the appellants sought to rotate caring for their mother in each of the daughters' homes, while Maureen believed that Shirley should remain in her home and be cared for by medical aides. At the conclusion of the hearing, the probate court found Shirley to be incapacitated and, at the suggestion of Tew, appointed Dresner, Shirley's long-time accountant, as her plenary guardian. The probate court appointed Dresner, rather than Shirley's daughters, because it was under the impression that the Declaration required them to be in agreement in order to serve as guardian. Specifically, the probate court found that the Declaration "named the three daughters to act in unison" and ruled that "[t]he three daughters being in deadlock, they cannot be appointed as co-guardians. The assets of Shirley Magill will dissipate very quickly if the three daughters have to come to court on most issues to be resolved." The probate court was under the impression that the Declaration required the three daughters to act in unison because of representations made by Tew concerning the contents of the Declaration. It is undisputed that at the time of the hearing neither Tew nor Nguyen had filed the Declaration with the probate court. The appellants appeal from the order appointing Dresner as plenary guardian, arguing that the probate court erred in disregarding Shirley's Declaration that her daughters serve as her guardian.

2. Dresner, who had been acting as the emergency temporary guardian of Shirley's property, expressed reservations about being the guardian of Shirley's person. . . . The trial court instructed Dresner to refer to the appellants and Maureen and to try to act in a way with which all of the sisters would agree, or to hire a case manager.

As this Court has previously stated, "[w]here a ward's preference as to the appointment of a guardian is capable of being known, that intent is the polestar to guide probate judges in the appointment of their guardians." Florida's preneed guardian statute, section 744.3045, Florida Statutes (2009), provides for a statutory rebuttable presumption in favor of the designated preneed guardian serving as guardian. That statute states in relevant part:

4) Production of the declaration in a proceeding for incapacity shall constitute a rebuttable presumption that the preneed guardian is entitled to serve as guardian. The court shall not be bound to appoint the preneed guardian if the preneed guardian is found to be unqualified to serve as guardian.

The probate court is not bound to appoint the designated preneed guardian as guardian when that preneed guardian is found to be unqualified to serve. §744.3045(4). . . . An appellate court reviews a probate court's appointment of a guardian under an abuse of discretion standard. . . . Accordingly, where the ward has designated a preneed guardian in a written declaration, as Shirley did in this case, the rebuttable presumption in favor of that designated preneed guardian serving as guardian may only be overcome by substantial, competent evidence. . . .

We find that the probate court abused its discretion in appointing Dresner as Shirley's plenary guardian. First, the probate court failed to properly consider the Declaration prior to appointing Dresner. It is undisputed that the Declaration was not filed with the probate court until June 24, 2009, eight days after the hearing on the petition. Therefore, the probate court did not have the Declaration before it when it concluded that the Declaration required all three daughters to act in unison as guardian. Instead, the probate court based its conclusion on representations made by Tew concerning the Declaration as well as other testamentary documents Shirley executed. This was error.

Second, contrary to the probate court's belief, the Declaration is clear that it is Shirley's wish that in the event of her incapacitation her three daughters are to serve as her guardian. The probate court did not make a factual finding that any of the daughters was unqualified, unwilling, or unable to serve as guardian. Rather, the probate court based its conclusion on a belief that the Declaration required them to act in unison, and that because one of the sisters, Maureen, was not in agreement with the appellants concerning their mother's living arrangement, she could not appoint all three to serve as guardian. Because the Declaration does not require unanimity among the daughters in order to be appointed or serve as guardian, this conclusion was also erroneous.

Finally, there was no evidence that the appointment of the daughters as guardian would not be in Shirley's best interest. The record reveals simply that the appellants and Maureen are in disagreement concerning one aspect of their mother's life — her living arrangement. As already explained, the Declaration does not require that they be in agreement on all aspects of their mother's life or care. Because Dresner and Nguyen agreed with Maureen's proposal for her mother's living arrangement and the probate court ultimately appointed Dresner as plenary guardian, the probate court's ruling has the effect of allowing the minority of the designated preneed guardians to control the majority. This result, however, is contrary to the plain language of the Declaration, which clearly allows for decisions concerning guardianship matters to be made by majority rule rather than minority. Additionally, the probate court's finding that Shirley's assets will "dissipate very quickly" because the appellants and Maureen cannot agree on this one aspect of their mother's life has no basis in fact in the record.

For the above reasons, the record lacks substantial competent evidence to overcome the statutory presumption that the designated preneed guardians, as set forth in Shirley's Declaration, are entitled to serve as her plenary guardian. Accordingly, we reverse the order on appeal appointing Dresner the plenary guardian and reverse with directions to the probate court to appoint all three daughters, the appellants and Maureen, as the plenary guardian of their mother, Shirley.

Affirmed in part, reversed in part, and remanded with directions.

www.CrosswordWeaver.com

ACROSS

2. Judicial determination
3. Letters of _____
8. Covers all matters
9. Guardian to act if named guardian does not
11. Determination based on diagnosis alone
12. _____ patriae, state power to protect
13. Guardianship for specific purpose or transaction

14. Court makes these to justify decision
20. Individual for whom guardianship proceedings are pending
23. Initials sometimes used to describe individual for whom guardianship is proposed
24. A diagnosis indicating mental deterioration of physical origin
25. Ward's interest in self-_____ must be balanced against need for protection
26. _____ bond
27. A drug with impact on mind, emotions, or behavior
28. Most states look for the least _____ means of protection
29. Guardian in another state

DOWN

1. Responsible for property
4. Determination that focuses on person's abilities
5. Ward's property, income, assets
6. _____ judgment
7. _____ investor rule
10. Pro _____, acting for self
15. Home
16. Guardianship available in emergency situations
17. Without funds
18. Guardian of _____, responsible for physical well-being
19. Power of court to hear case
21. Location of trial within proper court system
22. _____ parties, entitled to notice

4

◆ ◆ ◆

Social Security

◆ ◆ ◆

Objectives

When you complete this chapter, you will:

- Understand the differences between the major U.S. Social Security programs.
- Know who is eligible for benefits under the major programs.
- Describe how social security retirement and disability benefits are calculated.
- Understand the appeals process for Social Security Administration determinations.

- Know how to resolve common problems with the Social Security Administration.

Overview of OASDI

OASDI
Old-Age, Survivors, and Disability Insurance

Totalization Agreements
Agreements with other countries, concerning people who have worked in two or more countries

The United States social security system, sometimes called **OASDI** (Old-Age, Survivors, and Disability Insurance), originated as part of the New Deal during the Great Depression of the 1930s. Many other countries have similar systems and treaties called **totalization agreements** that address the situation of people who have moved from one country to another.

The U.S. system includes several programs, including the larger OASDI programs for:

- Retirement benefits for contributing workers and spouses (and some divorced former spouses) and disabled[1] dependent children.
- Survivor benefits, available to spouses (including some divorced spouses) and dependents (children and dependent parents) of deceased workers.
- Disability insurance, available to disabled workers, spouses age 62 or older (including some divorced spouses), dependent or disabled children of workers, and spouses of workers if the spouse is caring for the worker's disabled child or child younger than age 16.
- Health Insurance for Aged and Disabled (**Medicare**) (discussed in Chapter 6).
- Grants to States for Medical Assistance Programs (**Medicaid**) (discussed in Chapter 7).

Medicare
Health insurance for aged and disabled

Medicaid
Grants to states for medical assistance programs

These "social security" programs are social insurance, not retirement or pension plans. Unlike most private plans, social security is "portable" — that is, a worker can change employers many times and generally will continue to contribute to and be entitled to payments from the same system. A private pension is not universal — it does not necessarily cover all individuals in a particular workplace or the dependents of those who are covered. Social Security covers the majority of American workers and does make payments to people who have not contributed, based on their relationship to a contributor (**derivative benefits**). On the other hand, these programs are funded by contributors and are not "welfare."

Derivative Benefits
Benefits paid to people other than the worker who contributed

A private system accumulates money paid into it, invests the funds, and eventually uses that money to pay pensions to the workers who contributed to the fund. Social Security is a "pay as you go" system because benefits have historically been paid almost entirely by using revenue from current payroll taxes. FICA contributions from current workers are used to pay benefits to retired workers. It is projected that payroll tax revenue will be insufficient to cover Social Security benefits within the next 25 years and that the system will begin to withdraw money from the Social Security Trust Fund. There is significant

---

[1]A disabled child can be any age, but the disability must have begun before the child reached age 22 and, with some exceptions, married children are not eligible for benefits.

political controversy about the Trust Fund, because its assets are Treasury Bonds; the actual "funds" are on loan to the federal government.

Social security was originally intended as one of three parts of a person's retirement, along with a private pension and investments. Increasingly, workers do not have private pensions or investments, and a surprising percentage try to make ends meet with only a social security check—an average of slightly more than $1,000 per month in 2010.

Clients may confuse the various benefits administered by the government—they may refer to all benefits programs as "social security." They may have no knowledge of other programs from which they could benefit. To fully serve clients, paralegals should be aware of several programs that are not part of OASDI and that are beyond the scope of this book:

- Unemployment benefits, a joint federal-state program financed through employer payroll taxes.
- Temporary Assistance for Needy Families (**TANF**), a federally funded, state-administered program, administered by the Administration for Children and Families within the U.S. Department of Health and Human Services. This program may assist elder clients who are caring for grandchildren and experiencing financial need.

  TANF
  Temporary Assistance for Needy Families

- Supplemental Security Income (**SSI**), assistance for the elderly, blind, and disabled with minimal income and assets. Unlike retirement and disability benefits, which are based on contributions to the system, SSI is based on the recipient's resources. Although it is administered by the Social Security Administration, it is not funded by the same source. As of January 2010, 26.4 percent of SSI recipients were age 65 or older.

  SSI
  Supplemental Security Income

- Two other federal system parallel, but are separate from, traditional "social security." Until 1984, employment by the federal government was covered under the Civil Service Retirement System (CSRS) and not by Social Security. In 1984, the Federal Employees Retirement System (**FERS**) was established to cover new federal workers. Some workers who had been covered by the CSRS program chose to switch to the FERS program. Work under FERS is covered by Social Security. In addition, there is a separate **Railroad Retirement System** (*http://www.rrb.gov*) that provides monthly benefits to retired and disabled workers and their dependents and to survivors of deceased railroad workers. The number of people covered by the railroad workers system has declined.

  FERS
  Federal Employees Retirement System

  Railroad Retirement System
  Not part of social security system

Participation

Almost all Americans, even those who have never worked or paid into the system, are eligible for at least some social security benefits. As shown in Exhibit 4.1, a substantial percentage of people are currently receiving benefits. That number is expected to grow, and the change in the ratio of current recipients to current contributors is also expected to change. The various programs identified in the exhibit have different eligibility requirements, discussed in the sections that follow.

EXHIBIT 4.1
Social Security Benefits[2]

In 2010, nearly 53 million Americans will receive $703 billion in Social Security benefits. That is about 17 percent of the population, or 310,067,246, as of this writing.[3]

Group	Number	Payments
Retired workers	34 million	$40 billion
Dependents	2.9 million	$1.7 billion
Disabled workers	8 million	$8.5 billion
Dependents	1.9 million	$0.6 billion
Survivors	6.4 million	$6.3 billion

Social Security is the major source of income for most of the elderly:

- Nine out of ten individuals age 65 and older receive Social Security benefits.
- Social Security benefits represent about 40 percent of the income of the elderly.
- Among elderly Social Security beneficiaries, 52 percent of married couples and 72 percent of unmarried persons receive 50 percent or more of their income from Social Security.
- Among elderly Social Security beneficiaries, 20 percent of married couples and about 41 percent of unmarried persons rely on Social Security for 90 percent or more of their income.

Social Security provides more than just retirement benefits:

- Retired workers and their dependents account for 69 percent of total benefits paid.
- Disabled workers and their dependents account for 19 percent of total benefits paid.
  - About 91 percent of workers age 21 to 64 in covered employment and their families have protection in the event of a long-term disability.
  - Almost one in four of today's 20-year-olds will become disabled before reaching age 67.
  - 69 percent of the private sector workforce has no long-term disability insurance.

[2] http://www.ssa.gov/pressoffice/basicfact.htm
[3] http://www.census.gov

EXHIBIT 4.1
(continued)

Survivors of deceased workers account for about 13 percent of total benefits paid:

- About one in eight of today's 20-year-olds will die before reaching age 67.
- About 97 percent of persons age 20 to 49 who worked in covered employment in 2010 have survivors insurance protection for their young children and a surviving spouse caring for the children.

An estimated 156 million workers, 93 percent of all workers, are covered under Social Security:

- 52 percent of the workforce has no private pension coverage.
- 31 percent of the workforce has no savings set aside specifically for retirement.

Can the System Survive?   In 1935, the remaining life expectancy of a 65-year-old was 12.5 years; today it's 18 years. By 2035, there will be almost twice as many older Americans as today—up from 40.7 million today to 76.3 million. There are currently 2.9 workers for each Social Security beneficiary. By 2035, there will be 2.1 workers for each beneficiary.

Funding

OASDI and Medicare benefits are funded by payroll taxes on employers and employees called **FICA (Federal Insurance Contributions Act)** contributions, which are deposited into dedicated funds. If a worker is self-employed, the worker pays the entire tax; otherwise the employer and employee each pay half of the FICA amount—see Exhibit 4.2. Many state and federal workers, student workers, members of religious communities, and a few others do not pay FICA. These workers may still be eligible for benefits if they have a sufficient history of contributing through other employment, but their benefit amounts are affected, as described later in this chapter.

FICA (Federal Insurance Contributions Act)
Payroll taxes that fund social security benefits

EXHIBIT 4.2
Internal Revenue Service Form W-2

You are probably familiar with IRS Form W-2. Note that boxes 3 through 7 require the employer to identify the employee's income that was subject to FICA and how much was actually withheld (based on the percentages shown below) and submitted to FICA.

22222	Void ☐	a Employee's social security number	For Official Use Only ▶ OMB No. 1545-0008		
b Employer identification number (EIN)				1 Wages, tips, other compensation	2 Federal income tax withheld
c Employer's name, address, and ZIP code				3 Social security wages	4 Social security tax withheld
				5 Medicare wages and tips	6 Medicare tax withheld
				7 Social security tips	8 Allocated tips
d Control number				9 Advance EIC payment	10 Dependent care benefits
e Employee's first name and initial	Last name		Suff.	11 Nonqualified plans	12a See instructions for box 12
				13 Statutory employee ☐ Retirement plan ☐ Third-party sick pay ☐	12b
				14 Other	12c
					12d
f Employee's address and ZIP code					
15 State Employer's state ID number	16 State wages, tips, etc.	17 State income tax	18 Local wages, tips, etc.	19 Local income tax	20 Locality name

Form **W-2** Wage and Tax Statement **2010** Department of the Treasury—Internal Revenue Service For Privacy Act and Paperwork Reduction Act Notice, see back of Copy D.

Tax Rates as a Percentage of Taxable Earnings[4]

Rate for Employees and Employers, Each	Medicare HI*	Total	Self-Employed	Self-Employed HI	Total
6.20%	1.45%	7.65%	12.40%	2.90%	15.30%

*Hospital Insurance

[4]Tax rates are set by the Internal Revenue Code.

Are You a FICA Contributor?

FICA (Social Security and Medicare) taxes do not apply to service performed by students employed by a school, college, or university where the student is pursuing a course of study. Whether the organization is a school, college, or university depends on the organization's primary function. In addition, whether employees are students for this purpose requires examining the individual's employment relationship with the employer to determine whether employment or education is predominant in the relationship. See *http://www.irs.gov/charities/article/0,,id=120663,00.html* for more information.

There is a limit on the amount subject to FICA each year, known as the **contribution and benefit base**. In 2010, that amount was $106,800.

Throughout a worker's career, the **Social Security Administration (SSA)** keeps track of her earnings. Monthly retirement benefits depend upon earnings record and the age at which the retiree chooses to begin receiving benefits.

Entitlement to and Calculation of Retirement Benefits

Eligibility for retirement benefits depends on a "credit" system. By meeting a minimum income threshold ($1,120 per credit in 2010), workers can earn up to four credits per year toward retirement benefits. Anyone born in 1929 or later needs 10 years of work (40 credits) to be eligible for retirement benefits. People born before 1929 need fewer years of work.

A worker's retirement income benefit is based on his **Primary Insurance Amount (PIA)**, which is a percentage of the highest 35 years of the worker's covered earnings (before deduction for FICA), limited by the contribution and benefit base. If the worker has fewer than 35 years of covered earnings, zeros are used to bring the total number of years of earnings up to 35. Wages are indexed to account for inflation, using the **average wage index (AWI)**. The PIA is adjusted annually by automatic cost-of-living adjustments. Low-income workers receive a higher percentage of average lifetime earnings than those in the upper income brackets. A worker with average earnings can expect a retirement benefit that replaces about 40 percent of his average lifetime earnings.

The earliest age at which (reduced) retirement payments are payable is currently 62. Full retirement benefits depend on a retiree's year of birth:

Contribution and Benefit Base
Limit on wages subject to FICA

Social Security Administration (SSA)
Administers social security programs

Primary Insurance Amount (PIA)
Average of highest 35 years of earnings

Average Wage Index (AWI)
Adjusts contributions for inflation

Year of Birth	Full Retirement Age
1937 or earlier	65
1938	65 and 2 months
1939	65 and 4 months
1940	65 and 6 months
1941	65 and 8 months
1942	65 and 10 months
1943–1954	66
1955	66 and 2 months
1956	66 and 4 months
1957	66 and 6 months
1958	66 and 8 months
1959	66 and 10 months
1960 and later	67

A worker who starts benefits before normal retirement age has her benefit reduced based on the number of months between the start of benefits and normal retirement age. A worker might also continue working beyond full retirement age, which can increase future benefits in two ways. Each additional year of work adds another year of earnings to the mix in calculating PIA. In addition, benefits increase automatically by a certain percentage from the time the worker reaches full retirement age until she starts receiving benefits or until she reaches age 70. The percentage varies depending on year of birth. For example, for a worker born in 1943 or later, 8 percent per year is added to the benefit for each year beyond full retirement age in which the worker does not seek benefits.

Under the Senior Citizens' Freedom to Work Act of 2000, *42 U.S.C. 403*, a worker who has reached full retirement age can work and earn any amount with no reduction in benefits. If a recipient, younger than full retirement age, earns more than a certain amount, benefits are reduced, but not truly lost. Benefits are increased at full retirement age to account for benefits withheld due to earlier earnings. There are special rules for the first year after retirement; see *http://www. socialsecurity.gov/pubs/10069.html.*

The retirement age rules and the calculation of benefits are different for those claiming benefits as:

- Unmarried children — under age 18, or 18 to 19 years old and a full-time student (up to grade 12), or over 18 and disabled — who have a parent who is disabled or retired and entitled to benefits or have a deceased parent who paid enough into the system.
- Surviving or current spouses, qualified by age (a spouse may not have worked or may have contributed less to the system and, therefore, may obtain better benefits applying under other spouse's work record).
- Divorced, unmarried former spouses, qualified by age (generally eligible if the marriage lasted for at least 10 years), of a retired or deceased worker.
- Surviving parents, of qualifying age, who received at least half of their support from a deceased worker.

Same-Sex Couples

Although at least one federal court challenge is pending, as of this writing, claiming benefits under the history of a same-sex partner was precluded by 1 U.S.C. 7, the 1996 Defense of Marriage Act, which states: "In determining the meaning of any Act of Congress, or of any ruling, regulation, or interpretation of the various administrative bureaus and agencies of the United States, the word 'marriage' means only a legal union between one man and one woman as husband and wife, and the word 'spouse' refers only to a person of the opposite sex who is a husband or a wife."

Common-Law Marriage

A "common-law marriage" is one in which neither a religious nor civil ceremony was held. In some states, a common-law marriage exists if a man and a woman agree to be married for the rest of their lives. Most states (even those in which a man and woman cannot enter into a valid common-law marriage) generally recognize a common-law marriage that has been validly entered into in another state. The SSA will recognize a common-law marriage with adequate proof. The SSA has a form to allow the parties, or the survivor, and relatives (or others) to answer questions; other relevant evidence can include bank and insurance records, rent receipts, or other documentation of transactions entered into as a couple.

Benefits may also be reduced under the Government Pension Offset (**GPO**) if the applicant, spouse, widow or widower (remember, a worker's spouse may have had a job, but apply for spousal social security benefits) receives a pension from a federal, state, or local government job at which she did not pay Social Security taxes. Under the Windfall Elimination Provision (**WEP**) a worker who is eligible for a pension from any governmental agency or nonprofit organization, or who worked in another country and did not pay into U.S. social security on those earnings, may also have benefits decreased but not totally eliminated. These provisions, said to prevent "double dipping," can result in hardship for workers who have spent part of their careers in the private sector, contributing to the system, and part of their careers in the public sector. Their benefits are reduced, according to a calculation table.

GPO
Government Pension Offset

WEP
Windfall Elimination Provision

Given the complexity of these calculations and the likelihood of change, there is no reason to memorize the rules. The SSA makes access to the rules and calculation of benefits relatively easy: *http://www.socialsecurity.gov/pgm/links_-retirement.htm*

Applying for and Receiving Retirement Benefits

The SSA recommends application for benefits about three months prior to retirement. The process can be handled online (*http://www.socialsecurity.gov/pubs/10523.html*), although the SSA may request documentation, such as a birth, death, or marriage certificate, depending on the benefits being claimed. It is possible to claim benefits but suspend receipt of those benefits if, for example, the worker does not currently need the income but wants to enable a spouse to claim benefits.

Beginning in March 2011, the SSA requires that beneficiaries receive their monthly benefits by direct deposit or direct express. About one-third of recipients have to pay income taxes on a percentage of their benefits, based on combined income from various sources. The SSA mails a benefit statement (Form SSA-1099) showing the amount of benefits received. Recipients with tax liability on their benefits may opt to have federal taxes withheld, or may make quarterly estimated tax payments.

COLA
Cost-of-living adjustment

To prevent erosion of benefits by inflation, there is an annual cost-of-living adjustment (**COLA**). The COLA is based on the percentage increase in the Consumer Price Index. If there is no increase, there is no COLA.

Entitlement to and Calculation of Disability Benefits

The program known as Social Security Disability Insurance (SSDI) pays benefits to people who are younger than retirement age and cannot work because of a medical condition. Benefits are based on work history; Supplemental Security Income (SSI) is available to disabled individuals with limited or no work history. The federal definition is very strict and requires that the disability be expected to last at least one year, result from a listed condition, or be expected to result in death. SSDI does not cover partial disability or short-term disability, although individuals who have such conditions (or who are otherwise ineligible under the disability program, such as young children who have become disabled) may be eligible for SSI. For adults, 18 and older, the medical criteria for SSI and SSDI are the same. The worker must be unable to continue in his or her previous job and unable to adjust to other work, with age, education, and work experience taken into account.

Application for SSDI should be made as soon as the disability occurs because the process will take at least several months. Initial applications are often rejected, so the applicant must appeal and even seek a hearing. Benefits begin in the sixth full month after the disability began but are paid in arrears. This means that an individual must be disabled for at least six months before receiving benefits. So, if a person's disability is determined to have begun on January 15, her first disability benefit will be paid *for* the month of July and be received in August. Medicare coverage starts automatically after a person has been on disability for two years. When a person receiving disability benefits reaches retirement age, the benefits remain the same but become retirement benefits.

Once the SSA determines that the individual qualifies under tests described in Exhibit 4.3, the applicant will be referred to her state's Disability Determination Services office. That office will gather information from medical providers and may require and pay for a special examination. Based on whether the applicant is working, what kind of work the applicant has done or can do, the severity of the condition as described in medical records and whether it is on the list of impairments (there are special rules for blind people), the office will make a decision and send a letter detailing that decision. Benefits can be granted immediately if the claimant's impairment meets all the qualifications of severity as described in the "Listing of Impairments." If the listing specifications are not met, the SSA reviews the case in more detail to determine whether the claimant is disabled and unable to work, considering not only from past work, but from all work, even the most sedentary. If the applicant disagrees with the decision, she may pursue an appeal as described later in this chapter.

The amount of the SSDI benefit is based on average lifetime earnings and, like retirement benefits, may be affected by the individual's entitlement to a government pension. Benefits are not available to workers who are confined because of commission of a serious crime, which includes confinement to a medical facility based on a finding of not guilty by reason of insanity or incompetence to stand trial; workers who have violated a condition of parole or probation; and workers who have outstanding warrants for serious crimes. In some cases, family members of such workers may be entitled to benefits.

Individuals receiving disability are encouraged to try working again. Special work incentives and employment support programs allow them to keep benefits and Medicare coverage while they "test the waters." In addition, under the "ticket to work" program, disabled individuals can obtain training and other services to help them get back to work.

Working with SSA

Common Problems

As described in Exhibit 4.4, paralegals are often on the frontlines of dealing with the SSA on behalf of clients. Efficient delegation to paralegals is essential to keeping the cost of legal services reasonable. Some problems are common and can be resolved easily:

Common Problem	*Solution*
Wages or other information reported incorrectly	Workers age 25 and older receive annual statements, which must be checked for inaccurate information. Worker has three years to report inaccuracies, but there is no time limit on correcting failure to report. Worker needs W-2, pay stub, or evidence from the employer (if self-employed, tax return and proof of timely filing) and form OAR 7008: *http://www.ssa.gov/online/ssa-7008.pdf* and *http://www.socialsecurity.gov/pubs/10081.html*
Derivative benefits may be higher than worker's	Determine whether entitled to benefits as widow(er) or divorced former spouse: *http://www.socialsecurity.gov/retire2/applying6.htm*
Applicant not competent	Obtain designation of a representative payee to deal with SSA and manage benefits: *http://www.socialsecurity.gov/payee/faqrep.htm*

Common Problem	Solution
Client receives notice of overpayment	Appeal (described below) or request a waiver of recovery of overpayment: *http://www. socialsecurity.gov/OP_Home/handbook/ handbook.19/handbook-1914.html*

Other times, the SSA makes a determination adverse to the applicant, and appeal is appropriate. Some SSA decisions are not considered "initial determinations" and are not subject to administrative or judicial review. Examples include withholding part of a monthly benefit to recover an overpayment, authorizing fees for representation, and denying a request to extend the time period to request review of a determination or decision.

Appeals Process

The SSA mails a written notice of the initial determination (except in cases involving termination of benefits due to death), which, in the context of retirement or disability benefits, might typically involve:

- Entitlement, continuing entitlement, or re-entitlement to, or termination of benefits.
- Amount of benefits or recomputation of benefits.
- Revision of earnings records.
- Deduction from benefits because of work.
- Establishment or termination of a period of disability.
- Whether benefits should be paid to another person on the applicant's account.
- Who will act as **representative payee**.
- Overpayment or underpayment of benefits, and whether overpaid benefits must be repaid.
- How underpayment of benefits due a deceased person will be paid.
- Deduction from disability benefits because of refusal to accept rehabilitation services.
- Whether vocational rehabilitation will significantly increase the likelihood that the person will not have to return to disability benefits so that benefits may be continued even though the person is not now disabled.
- Reduction in disability benefits because of receipt of benefits for workers' compensation.
- Penalties imposed because of failure to report certain events.
- Nonpayment of benefits because of confinement for more than 30 continuous days in a correctional institution for conviction of a crime or in a medical facility because a court found the individual was not guilty for reason of insanity, that he was unable to stand trial due to mental defect, or that he was sexually dangerous.
- Nonpayment because a person has not furnished satisfactory proof of eligibility or Social Security number.
- Nonpayment of benefits because the recipient has an unsatisfied warrant for more than 30 continuous days for certain crimes and parole/probation conditions.

Representative Payee
Person who acts on behalf of benefit recipient

EXHIBIT 4.3
Who Can Receive Benefits under SSDI?

- Disabled works who qualify under the "recent work" and "duration of work" tests.
- Certain blind workers who meet the "duration of work" test.
- Certain family members of a disabled worker.
- Spouse (may include ex-spouse if married to worker 10 years and not remarried) age 62 or older.
- Spouse, any age, if caring for a child of the worker—younger than 16 or disabled.
- Unmarried child (includes an adopted child and, in some cases, a stepchild or grandchild) under age 18 or under age 19 if in elementary or secondary school full time.
- Unmarried child, with a disability that started before age 22.

SSA limits the amount that can be received by a family if several members are eligible for benefits.

Partial Sample of Duration of Work Test Chart

Age at Which Worker Became Disabled	Duration of Work Generally Required
Before age 28	1.5 years
30	2 years
34	3 years
38	4 years
42	5 years

Recent Work Test

Worker Became Disabled	Generally Needs
In or before the quarter of 24th birthday	1.5 years of work during 3-year period ending with the quarter disability began
In the quarter after 24th birthday but before the quarter of 31st birthday	Work during half the time for the period beginning with the quarter after 21st birthday and ending with the quarter disability began
In the quarter of 31st birthday or later	Work during five years out of the 10-year period ending with the quarter disability began

---

EXHIBIT 4.4
Noel Says

Noel S. Anschutz, Disability Claims Director at the Richard Harris Firm in Las Vegas, obtained an AAS in Paralegal Studies from the ABA-approved program at Pima Community College, followed by a BS in Business Administration. Noel is proud to be an aggressive advocate for the rights of the injured and disabled. She has a strong litigation background and worked in legal aid before becoming a Professional Social Security Representative. She is the first non-attorney in Nevada operating under the SSA's non-attorney direct-pay project. This means she has taken a competency exam administered by the SSA, carries malpractice insurance, and must meet minimum yearly continuing legal education requirements. Ms. Anschutz is a member of the National Organization of Social Security Representatives, a Board Member of the Community College of Southern Nevada Paralegal Program Advisory Board, a member of the National Federation of Paralegal Associations, Past President of the Paralegal Association of Southern Nevada, and a member of the State Bar of Nevada Ethics Committee.

Describing her career path, Noel says:

All of the jobs I have had in the past are a complete culmination of skills and experiences that help me do my job today. Working at Legal Aid was particularly instrumental. I took that job specifically to learn Social Security disability law as it is a very small area of law where it is hard to gain experience. Hosting and coordinating a national paralegal convention was also instrumental. I gained skills related to organization, leading a team, project management, and stress management.

[In my current job I make] independent decision about client acceptance, handle the case from initial client interview to administrative hearings, manage two staff members, and report to the owner of the firm.

[To succeed in this field:] Do the internship! Try working for a temp agency. You will get a feel for different law firms and different areas of law without committing. Temp. jobs sometimes lead to permanent employment. Establish your reputation. Reputation is everything as legal communities are typically very small. Don't burn your bridges, *ever*. You are the commodity; sell yourself: What skills do you have that will benefit the employer, not how can the employer benefit you. Get a Web site with your resume information on it, make business cards, buy personalized thank-you cards.

Actively participate in your local paralegal association. Work for quality lawyers and law firms. The attorney you work for makes a difference. Take initiative but be careful not to go too far. You don't know what you don't know — ask questions, even if you think you are right. However, don't go to the attorney with problems. Go with the problems and a few solutions. It shows initiative and doesn't put more stress on the attorney. This is what you were hired for, to relieve some of the stress, not add to it. Case management skills make you invaluable. Try to learn this on the job — it's a difficult skill to teach in a classroom. Paying attention to detail is a *must*, as are the ability to focus for long periods of time, tenacity, and having some compulsive traits.

There will be attorneys who are difficult to work with. If you are working for a difficult but good attorney, learn all you can and get out. Sometimes the difficulty is related to the attorney's stress level, trust level, or personal problems; whatever you do, don't take it personally. Grow a thick skin and respectfully stand up for yourself when necessary. Humor also can go a long way to facilitate stress relief. Abuse should never be tolerated, and is never worth it, no matter how much money you are making.

The notice will state the reasons for the determination, the effect of the determination, and information concerning the right to reconsideration or a hearing. If an applicant is dissatisfied with SSA's initial determination, she may have to pursue administrative review. All requests made in this process should be made in writing; the SSA has forms available for most requests. The requests can be filed with any SSA office or office of the Railroad Retirement Board, if appropriate. In general, each request must be filed within 60 days of the determination that triggered the request. A longer period may be allowed for good cause, if the applicant requests an extension before the decision becomes final; otherwise failure to timely file a request makes the decision permanent.

The process starts with a written request for reconsideration, which can include an opportunity to submit additional evidence. In some kinds of cases reconsideration is called a case review, a disability hearing, an informal conference, or a formal conference. Reconsideration is the SSA's means of self-monitoring and is conducted by a reviewer who was not involved in the initial decision. Some states have pilot programs under which an applicant can skip the reconsideration step and go directly to the next step. In addition, an expedited appeals process is available, allowing the case to go directly to a federal district court at this point, if the only issue is the constitutionality of a provision of the Social Security Act.

If reconsideration does not produce a satisfactory result, the applicant should make a written request for a hearing before an Administrative Law Judge (**ALJ**) of the Office of Disability Adjudication and Review (**ODAR**). It may take several months to get a hearing. Under certain circumstances, an ALJ can make a decision without an oral hearing. If there is a hearing, the applicant will be sent notice of the time and place at least 20 days in advance and may appear in person or by video teleconference. The applicant may appear alone or with a representative, who need not be an attorney. The representative must be designated in writing (SSA-1696-U4: *http://www.socialsecurity.gov/online/ssa-1696.pdf*). If the representative is not an attorney, he must also sign the SSA-1696-U4 or submit a written acceptance. It is not necessary for an attorney to accept an appointment in writing. The representative may not sign or testify on behalf of the applicant, but he may submit and examine evidence, make statements, and perform other functions. New evidence and testimony may be presented; the applicant may examine evidence and question witnesses. Under limited circumstances, the applicant and necessary witnesses may receive an allowance for travel expenses. The ALJ has authority to call pre-conferences, post-conferences, and to issue **subpoenas.** The ALJ may also have experts, such as doctors, to act as advisors.

After the ALJ makes a determination, the applicant may request review by the Appeals Council of the Office of Disability Adjudication and Review (or the Council may request review on its own motion). The Appeals Council, which is located in Virginia, does not hold hearings; it accepts written briefs, and response time can be very slow. Review of an Appeals Council decision goes to a federal district court. Federal district court decisions can be reviewed by federal circuit courts of appeal; the Supreme Court may review decisions by circuit court.

A decision that has become final within the SSA may be reopened and revised, on request by the applicant or on SSA's own motion:

   A. Within 12 months from the date of the notice of the initial determination for any reason;

ALJ
Administrative Law Judge

ODAR
Office of Disability Adjudication and Review

Subpoenas
Used to obtain evidence and testimony

B. Within four years (two years in the SSI program) from the date of the notice of the initial determination, if there is good cause for reopening it. "Good cause" can be found to exist if:

  1. New and material evidence is submitted;

  2. A clerical error was made; or

  3. The evidence that was considered in making the determination or decision clearly shows that an error was made.[5]

C. At any time if the determination or decision was based on fraud or similar fault.

A decision to not reopen is not an initial determination and is not subject to appeal.

Assignments

1. Using the Social Security Web site, determine:
   A. What information is required to complete a basic application for disability benefits and which other forms are required.
   B. Whether a worker's retirement benefits are reduced when that worker's divorced former spouse seeks benefits based on the worker's contributions.
   C. How the SSA is normally notified of a death, and what is the one-time payment that may be made to a spouse at the time of a worker's death.
2. Use a search engine to find the Disability Determination Services office for your state; does it describe the "five-step process"?
3. Use the SSA Web site (*http://www.ssa.gov/disability/professionals/bluebook/AdultListings.htm*) to determine under what circumstances HIV infection is listed as an impairment for an adult and for a child.
4. Determine whether the United States has a totalization agreement with Mexico.
5. Critical Thinking: Jack, a high-earning lawyer, born in 1948, spent 20 years in the Army JAG Corps, followed by 20 years in private practice, and is ready to retire. Jack was married to Chris for 12 years. Chris was born in 1959, but has not worked since 1985, when their child, Pat, was born. Pat was born prematurely and has extensive disabilities. Pat has never worked and will never be able to work. Jack's current spouse, Lyn, was born in 1962, and currently works full-time. They have a child, Jordan, born in 2004. Lyn would like to retire as soon as possible. Jack's mother, born in 1929, relies on Jack for more than half of her support. Identify all of the possible benefits available and all of the factors that will be relevant to the calculation of benefits.

---

[5] *http://www.socialsecurity.gov/OP_Home/handbook/handbook.20/handbook-toc20.html*

6. Critical Thinking: Read the *Antonson* case at the end of the chapter.
   A. Draft a timeline of events, focusing on the procedural history of the case. Assuming that the plaintiff is genuinely unable to work, do you think the timeframe is reasonable?
   B. Note that the plaintiff was accompanied at the hearing by a paralegal. What do you think about that?
   C. What does the court mean by *de novo* review? Explain how the standard of review operates in a case like this.
   D. Describe, in your own words, what the ALJ could have done to avoid remand in this case and to enter the same decision, so that it would be upheld on appeal.
7. Identify and discuss at least two proposals for "saving" social security from the shortfall predicted to result from increased life expectancy, the change in the ratio of contributors to recipients, and the federal government's borrowing from the fund.
8. Use the online calculator at *http://www.ssa.gov/planners/benefitcalculators.htm* to estimate your own social security benefits or those of a friend or family member.

Review Questions

1. What is meant by the expression "pay as you go" system?
2. Explain the PIA and AWI calculations.
3. How does part-time work after retirement affect benefits?
4. What should be done if a client is not competent to deal with the SSA?
5. Why might a worker, eligible for retirement benefits, "claim and suspend"?
6. Identify outside factors that may reduce a person's retirement or disability benefits.
7. What are the basic requirements for disability benefits?
8. Can a paralegal represent a client at a social security hearing? Are there any special requirements?

ANTONSON V. ASTRUE

2009 U.S. Dist. LEXIS 125482 (U.S. District Court, D. N.Y.)

In June 2003, Plaintiff filed applications for disability, disability insurance, and Supplemental Security Income benefits. Plaintiff alleges that he was disabled and unable to work during the period between November 13, 2002 and March 1, 2004, primarily due to pain and depressive disorder. Plaintiff's applications were denied by the Commissioner of Social Security. Plaintiff, through his attorney, commenced this action on June 3, 2008, by filing a Complaint in the United States District Court for the Northern District of New York. Plaintiff seeks judicial review of the Commissioner's denial of benefits. [B]ecause of deficiencies in the record, the Court recommends that this case be remanded.

In June of 2003, Plaintiff applied for disability, disability insurance, and SSI benefits, alleging that he had been unable to work since February 26, 1999. The Commissioner initially denied the applications on February 10, 2004. Plaintiff timely requested a hearing before an Administrative Law Judge ("ALJ"). On July 27, 2006, Plaintiff appeared with a paralegal from his attorney's office at a hearing before ALJ Tyminski in Utica, New York. At the hearing, Plaintiff amended his alleged disability period, claiming disability only during a closed period between November 13, 2002, and March 1, 2004. On September 5, 2006, the ALJ issued a written decision denying Plaintiff's applications for benefits. The ALJ's decision became the Commissioner's final decision on April 24, 2008, when the Social Security Administration's Appeals Council denied Plaintiff's request for review. Plaintiff commenced this action by filing a Complaint on June 3, 2008.

A court reviewing a denial of disability benefits may not determine de novo whether an individual is disabled. See 42 U.S.C. §§405(g), 1383(c)(3). [T]he Commissioner's determination will only be reversed if the correct legal standards were not applied, or it was not supported by substantial evidence. "Substantial evidence" is . . . "such relevant evidence as a reasonable mind might accept as adequate to support a conclusion." Where evidence is deemed susceptible to more than one rational interpretation, the Commissioner's conclusion must be upheld. If supported by substantial evidence, the Commissioner's finding must be sustained "even where substantial evidence may support the plaintiff's position and despite that the court's independent analysis of the evidence may differ from the [Commissioner's]." In other words, this Court must afford the Commissioner's determination considerable deference, and may not substitute "its own judgment for that of the [Commissioner], even if it might justifiably have reached a different result upon a de novo review."

The Commissioner has established a five-step sequential evaluation process to determine whether an individual is disabled as defined under the Social Security Act. The Supreme Court recognized this analysis in *Bowen v. Yuckert,* 482

U.S. 137 (1987), and it remains the proper approach for analyzing whether a claimant is disabled.[3]

While the claimant has the burden of proof as to the first four steps, the Commissioner has the burden of proof on the fifth and final step. The final step of the inquiry is divided into two parts. First, the Commissioner must assess the claimant's job qualifications by considering physical ability, age, education, and work experience. Second, the Commissioner must determine whether jobs exist in the national economy that a person having the claimant's qualifications could perform. See 42 U.S.C. §423(d)(2)(A); 20 C.F.R. §§416.920(g); 404.1520(g).

The ALJ concluded that Plaintiff met the insured status requirements of the Social Security Act . . . had not engaged in substantial gainful activity between November 13, 2002 and March 1, 2004 . . . had not established any medically determinable severe impairments that would prevent substantial gainful activity for a continuous twelve months. After reviewing the medical evidence, the ALJ concluded that there was "no competent and acceptable clinical evidence of record evincing the existence of any impairment or combination of impairments, mental and/or physical, that has precluded [Plaintiff] from engaging in past relevant work for not less than 12 continuous months, let alone the alleged closed period of disability." Therefore, the ALJ determined that Plaintiff was not under a "disability," as defined under the Act. As noted above, the ALJ's decision became the Commissioner's final decision on October 26, 2007, when the Appeals Council denied Plaintiff's request for review.

Plaintiff contends that the decision should be reversed. He offers three (3) principal arguments in support. First, Plaintiff asserts that the ALJ's decision was not supported by substantial evidence and was contrary to the opinions of Plaintiff's treating medical providers. Second, Plaintiff argues that the ALJ did not properly credit his allegations of disabling pain. Third, Plaintiff contends that the ALJ did not give sufficient consideration to the effect of Plaintiff's mental impairments.

Under the "treating physician's rule," the ALJ must give controlling weight to the treating physician's opinion when the opinion is well-supported by

---

[3]This five-step process is detailed as follows:

> First, the [Commissioner] considers whether the claimant is currently engaged in substantial gainful activity.

> If he is not, the [Commissioner] next considers whether the claimant has a "severe impairment" which significantly limits his physical or mental ability to do basic work activities.

> If the claimant has such an impairment, the third inquiry is whether, based solely on medical evidence, the claimant has an impairment which is listed in Appendix 1 of the regulations.

> If the claimant has such an impairment, the [Commissioner] will consider him disabled without considering vocational factors such as age, education, and work experience; the [Commissioner] presumes that a claimant who is afflicted with a "listed" impairment is unable to perform substantial gainful activity.

> Assuming the claimant does not have a listed impairment, the fourth inquiry is whether, despite the claimant's severe impairment, he has the residual functional capacity to perform his past work.

Finally, if the claimant is unable to perform his past work, the [Commissioner] then determines whether there is other work which the claimant could perform.

medically acceptable clinical and laboratory diagnostic techniques and is not inconsistent with the other substantial evidence. 20 C.F.R. §404.1527(d)(2).[4]

Even if a treating physician's opinion is deemed not to be deserving of controlling weight, an ALJ may nonetheless give it "extra weight" under certain circumstances. . . . ALJ should consider the following factors when determining the proper weight to afford the treating physician's opinion . . . : (1) length of the treatment relationship and the frequency of examination, (2) nature and extent of the treatment relationship, (3) supportability of opinion, (4) consistency, (5) specialization of the treating physician, and (6) other factors that are brought to the attention of the court. C.F.R. §404.1527(d)(1)-(6).

Plaintiff argues that . . . the following statement by Dr. Masten, an orthopedic and pain management doctor: "I have stated that he can do his activities of daily living. By that I mean brushing his teeth, combing his hair so he is not totally disabled. But he is severely disabled. He cannot lift more than five pounds at a time if he goes grocery shopping. He is very limited in what he can do. He cannot bend well, he cannot lift, he cannot lift a basket of laundry." Dr. Masten diagnosed Plaintiff as suffering from "ongoing thoracic and cervical referred pain" and opined that his prognosis was "guarded for full recovery" and "good for partial recovery." Plaintiff's physical therapist, Wick, noted that he complained "of being constantly fatigued and when he does any activity after a couple of days he fatigues to the point where he needs five days to rest to recover." Plaintiff also points to records from a visit to Rome Memorial Hospital's Urgent Care Center, including a visit wherein Plaintiff complained of "chronic chest pain" caused by an injury to his chest. Plaintiff received physical therapy for his pain and was examined by Bryla, a chiropractor. Bryla diagnosed Plaintiff as suffering from a "mild thoracic strain/ sprain," which he indicated was caused by a February 1999 work injury.

ALJ concluded that Plaintiff had not established any medically determinable severe impairments that would prevent substantial gainful activity for a continuous 12 months. With regard to Dr. Masten's assessment that Plaintiff was "severely disabled," ALJ noted that Dr. Masten "refused" to complete a residual functional capacity assessment. ALJ also referenced Dr. Masten's statement that Plaintiff could perform his activities of daily living. This Court finds that the ALJ failed to adequately develop the record. The ALJ concluded that Plaintiff had not established any medically determinable "severe" impairments." Thus, the ALJ stopped his analysis at Step Two of the sequential process.

"An impairment or combination of impairments is found 'not severe' and a finding of 'not disabled' is made at this step when medical evidence establishes only a slight abnormality or a combination of slight abnormalities which would have no more than a minimal effect on an individual's ability to work even if the individual's age, education, or work experience were specifically considered (i.e., the person's impairment(s) has no more than a minimal effect on his or her physical or mental ability(ies) to perform basic work activities)." The remaining analysis set forth in Steps Three through Five must be undertaken where the claim is more than de minimis.

In July 2003, well within the period of alleged disability, Dr. Masten, Plaintiff's treating physician, opined that Plaintiff was "severely disabled," "very

---

[4]"The 'treating physician's rule' is a series of regulations set forth by the Commissioner detailing the weight to be accorded a treating physician's opinion."

limited" in what he could do, and unable to lift five pounds. Contrary to the ALJ's indication, it is not clear that Dr. Masten "refused" to perform a residual functional capacity assessment. Rather, the doctor simply noted that a functional capacity evaluation was "not done." This does not permit a conclusion that the doctor "refused" to complete a RFC. Moreover, these assessments from Plaintiff's treating physician certainly indicated that his condition was more than de minimis. Further, although Dr. Masten stated that Plaintiff was able to perform his activities of daily living, he qualified this statement by explaining that he meant that Plaintiff could brush his teeth and comb his hair, making it clear that he nevertheless considered Plaintiff "severely disabled." It is well-settled that "[s]uch activities do not by themselves contradict allegations of disability," as people should not be penalized for enduring the pain of their disability in order to care for themselves. "We have stated on numerous occasions that 'a claimant need not be an invalid to be found disabled' under the Social Security Act."

The ALJ indicated that "[p]ain is a symptom, not a medical diagnosis," apparently suggesting that Dr. Masten had not provided a sufficient medical diagnosis regarding Plaintiff's medical condition. However, there is no indication that the ALJ re-contacted Dr. Masten to request clarification or additional information regarding the diagnosis. The ALJ has an "affirmative duty to develop the record and seek additional information from the treating physician, sua sponte, even if plaintiff is represented by counsel" to determine upon what information the treating source was basing his opinions. 20 C.F.R. §§404.1512(e)(1), 416.912(e)(1). Failure to re-contact is error.

Here, the ALJ screened out Plaintiff's claim at Step Two in the face of an opinion from his treating physician that he was "severally disabled" and "very limited." At a minimum, to the extent that the ALJ determined that Dr. Masten's assessment was insufficiently supported by clinical findings or undermined by other evidence of record, the ALJ was obligated to re-contact Dr. Masten to request further information and clarification. This Court finds that a remand is warranted and that, on remand, the ALJ should re-contact Dr. Masten and request that he (1) provide further clarification regarding his diagnosis during the relevant period, and (2) either provide a residual functional capacity assessment with respect to the relevant period or explain why he chose not to perform such an assessment in the first instance. The ALJ should then re-evaluate whether Plaintiff satisfied the Step Two analysis in light of any additional information provided by Dr. Masten.

"It is well settled that 'a claimant's subjective evidence of pain is entitled to great weight' where . . . it is supported by objective medical evidence." Where, as here, an ALJ rejects subjective testimony concerning pain and other symptoms, the ALJ "must do so explicitly and with sufficient specificity to enable the Court to decide whether there are legitimate reasons for the ALJ's disbelief and whether his determination is supported by substantial evidence." In this case, Plaintiff testified that, during the period of alleged disability, he spent most of his time "laying down" because it would become difficult and painful to hold his head up after a small amount of exertion. He was able to perform very basic activities of daily living, but did not perform any household chores. Plaintiff testified that he was only able to lift light objects and needed help grocery shopping. He indicated that he was able to sit or stand for an hour and that any physical exertion increased his pain.

The ALJ discounted Plaintiff's testimony, noting that one of his previous treating physician's indicated the possibility that Plaintiff was "doctor shopping" and that his complaints might contain "an element of malingering." However, Plaintiff's testimony is certainly consistent with Dr. Masten's assessment that he was "severally disabled." Further, the State Agency review doctor noted that Plaintiff had indicated an ability to walk only one mile before needing a rest and stated that he experienced pain upon lifting more than ten pounds or standing more than thirty minutes. The State Agency doctor opined that, based upon the totality of the evidence, "those statements are . . . credible." On remand, the ALJ should revisit his credibility assessment in light of the information obtained upon re-contacting Plaintiff's treating medical providers.

Dr. Tabrizi, Plaintiff's treating psychiatrist, opined that Plaintiff had an "[e]xtended impairment in functioning due to mental illness" and diagnosed an Axis I 296.33 mental illness (Major Depressive Disorder, Recurrent) and generalized anxiety disorder. The ALJ concluded that Plaintiff's mental impairment was not severe, noting that Dr. Tabrizi's assessment was (1) not supported by clinical notes or findings and (2) contradicted by the assessment of the consultative psychiatric examiner.

However, " . . . an ALJ cannot simply discount a treating physician's opinion based on a lack of clinical findings that accompany that opinion." "[A] treating physician's failure to include objective support for the findings in his report does not mean that such support does not exist; he might not have provided this information in the report because he did not know that the ALJ would consider it critical to the disposition of the case." Under the circumstances, the ALJ had an obligation to re-contact Dr. Tabrizi to request further information regarding the clinical basis for his diagnosis. Second, although Dr. Shapiro opined that the results of her consultative examination "do not appear to be consistent with any psychiatric problems that would significantly interfere with [Plaintiff's] ability to function on a daily basis," she was not a treating source. Before accepting the assessment of a consultative examiner over that of Plaintiff's treating provider, the ALJ had an affirmative obligation to more fully develop the record. On remand, the ALJ should re-contact Dr. Tabrizi and request any clinical notes or findings related to the period of alleged disability and/or a further explanation from Dr. Tabrisi regarding his diagnosis.

"Section 405 (g) provides district courts with the authority to affirm, reverse, or modify a decision of the Commissioner 'with or without remanding the case for a rehearing.'" Remand is "appropriate where, due to inconsistencies in the medical evidence and/or significant gaps in the record, further findings would . . . plainly help to assure the proper disposition of [a] claim." Given the deficiencies in the record . . . it is recommended that the case be remanded.

Crossword Puzzle

www.CrosswordWeaver.com

ACROSS

4. Issued to obtain evidence or testimony
5. Benefits may be reduced because of receipt of government _____
7. WEP = Windfall _____ Provision
8. Relevant to retirement and disability
10. Workers have a separate program, not administered by SSA
12. Health insurance for aged and disabled
13. Initials, sometimes used to describe social security system
14. Initials, ALJ is from this office
15. Determines eligibility for disability benefits _____ of work
16. _____ court hears social security appeals
21. Usual first step to challenge initial determination
22. ALJ = _____ Law Judge

DOWN

1. _____ work test, relevant to eligibility for disability benefits
2. Agreement with another country
3. Appeals _____, located in Virginia
6. SSI = _____ Security Income
9. SSA = Social _____ Administration
11. Initials, payroll tax
12. Grants to states for medical assistance programs
17. Initials, program that provides benefits without regard to contribution
18. Initials, since 1984 covers federal workers
19. AWI = Average _____ Index
20. Initials, average of highest 35 years

5

◆ ◆ ◆

Medical Matters

◆ ◆ ◆

Objectives

When you complete this chapter, you will:

- Understand how the practice of geriatric medicine differs from the practice of general medicine.
- Know the effects of recent health law reforms on senior clients.
- Identify the medical issues most problematic for seniors and know the terminology associated with those issues.

As discussed in Chapter 1, the communication necessary to be a good advocate for a senior client requires understanding of the client's physical condition and the unique risks and challenges faced by the client. A paralegal working on behalf of seniors may have to communicate with medical caregivers and must have some knowledge of the issues and terminology that are part of that role. A thorough discussion of medical issues is beyond the scope of this book, and this information is intended only as a starting point.

What Is Geriatric Medicine?

Geriatrics
Medical specialty concerned with problems of aging

Most elder patients receive primary care from internists or family practitioners and are referred to specialists as needed, but most members of these medical teams have no special training in **geriatrics,** the study of diseases and conditions related to aging. While many senior citizens thrive with that care and do not have major problems particularly associated with aging, others have problems that require specialized care. Many medical schools now offer specialties in geriatrics (see Exhibit 5.1).

EXHIBIT 5.1
Medical Specialty Rankings, 2010: Geriatrics[1]

---

1   **Johns Hopkins University**
     Baltimore, MD
2   **Mount Sinai School of Medicine**
     New York, NY
3   **University of California Los Angeles (Geffen)**
     Los Angeles, CA
4   **Duke University**
     Durham, NC
5   **University of Michigan Ann Arbor**
     Ann Arbor, MI
6   **University of Washington**
     Seattle, WA
7   **Harvard University**
     Boston, MA
8   **University of Pittsburgh**
     Pittsburgh, PA
9   **Yale University**
     New Haven, CT
10   **University of California San Francisco**
     San Francisco, CA

---

[1] *http://grad-schools.usnews.rankingsandreviews.com/best-graduate-schools/top-medical-schools/geriatrics*

At these schools, doctors learn about the social, housing, and emotional issues associated with aging, in addition to the medical conditions to which older people are especially susceptible. For example, the Mayo Clinic Geriatrics Fellowship within the Department of Internal Medicine is described as follows:

> The first year will have the traditional strong clinical emphasis. Longitudinal clinical experiences include a weekly geriatric continuity clinic, bi-weekly skilled nursing facility visits, and a monthly home visit program performing physician referred geriatric consultations and county social service referred comprehensive geriatric assessments. Hospital-based rotations include physical medicine and rehabilitation, geropsychiatry, geriatric medical orthopedics, geriatric acute care, hospice and palliative care, primary care internal medicine and geriatrics, and subacute care. Outpatient rotations include clinics in physical medicine and rehabilitation, urogynecology, wound care, dementia, Parkinson's and movement disorders, Dementia Behaviors Assessment and Response Team, congestive heart failure, and podiatry. Electives are available in sleep disorders, endocrine diseases, GI motility, and others.

HIPAA

A client or caregiver may provide information about the client's health status and concerns, but if you need to obtain medical records, you need to understand the privacy protections that limit access to those records. The privacy rule, implemented under the Health Insurance Portability and Accountability Act (**HIPAA**), 42 U.S.C. §1320d, protects certain information against disclosure by health care providers, health care organizations, and insurance plans. Protected information includes anything that identifies the individual and relates to the individual's past, present, or future physical or mental health or condition; provision of health care to the individual; or past, present, or future payment for the provision of health care to the individual. The rule is complex and contains various exceptions, including an exception to allow disclosure to the authorized representative of the individual, which makes written designation of a health care proxy essential. The rule is enforced by the Office of Civil Rights, within the U.S. Department of Health and Human Services, and more information is available at *http://www.hhs.gov/ocr/privacy/hipaa/understanding/summary/privacysummary.pdf*.

HIPAA
Health Insurance Portability and Accountability Act, contains privacy law

Medical Team

A team approach to senior health care can involve a wide range of professional and nonprofessional workers. The members of the team differ in education, level of contact with the patient, and levels and areas of responsibility. Effective communication requires understanding. Of course, the list that follows is far from comprehensive and does not include important team members who often work behind the scenes, such as lab workers, medical imaging specialists, and phlebotomists. It also does not include people such as social workers and hospital discharge counselors, who are not trained in medicine but are essential to quality care. The American Medical Association lists information about more than 80 health care careers.

Chiropractor   A chiropractor, also known as a doctor of chiropractic or chiropractic physician, can diagnose and treat patients with health problems of the musculoskeletal system and treat the effects of those problems on the nervous system and on general health. Most state licensing boards require at least two years of undergraduate education, but an increasing number are requiring a bachelor's degree. All boards require the completion of a four-year program at an accredited chiropractic college leading to the Doctor of Chiropractic degree.

Community Health Worker/Health Educator   These terms are used to describe a variety of individuals who play a role in solving health care problems by providing information, advocacy, and education. For example, a community health worker might educate underserved minority community members about the importance of health screenings, such as mammograms. The role is not defined by any particular education or license.

Dentist   A general dentist (DMD or DDS) is licensed by the state as a primary care professional for patients in all age groups; there is no recognized geriatric dental specialty, although a number of dental problems are associated with aging. Despite a strong link between dental health and general health and even emotional health, many senior citizens do not get the dental care they need. The reason is often cost—it is estimated that only about 20 percent of older people have dental insurance.[2]

Mental Health Professionals   Training and regulation of individuals who provide mental health services varies widely. Psychiatrists are physicians (medical doctors) who complete a residency in psychiatry. Clinical psychologists are not medical doctors but have advanced degrees in clinical psychology and have served clinical internships. Individual states also set standards for licensed clinical social workers, psychiatric nurse specialists, and other licensed counselors, such as substance abuse counselors, marital and family counselors, and pastoral counselors. Whether individuals in each category can write prescriptions is a matter of state law.

Nurses   An Advanced Practice Nurse (APN) is an RN (described below) with a post-baccalaureate education, and may be authorized by state law to perform additional functions independent of a physician, such as writing prescriptions. An APN may be a nurse practitioner (NP), clinical nurse specialist (CNS), certified nurse-midwife (CNM), or certified registered nurse anesthetist (CRNA).

Registered nurses (RN) may be educated at the diploma (hospital-based), associate, or bachelor's degree level. Today, most RNs are prepared through associate and baccalaureate degree programs. Upon graduation, all nurses must

---

[2]*http://www.kronkosky.org/research/Research_Briefs/Dental%20Care%20and%20the%20Elderly%20March%202009.pdf*

pass a national licensing examination, known as the National Council Licensing Examination, to obtain a state license.

Vocational or licensed practical nurses (LPN) usually receive up to 12 months of basic nursing skills training and practice under the supervision of a registered nurse or physician. As indicated by the title, an LPN must take a test and obtain a state license.

Nutritionist   A Registered Dietitian (RD) or nutritionist is trained in nutrition science and generally has a minimum of a bachelor's degree in food and nutrition from an accredited university. Most states regulate the profession by requiring a license or certification.

Pharmacists   Pharmacists dispense drugs and medications prescribed by physicians, physician assistants, nurse practitioners, and dentists and advise health care professionals and patients on the use and proper dosage of medications, as well as expected side effects and interactions with other prescription and nonprescription medicines. All states license pharmacists and require at least a bachelor's degree from an accredited school of pharmacy.

Physician (MD)   Physicians obtain their MD (medical doctor) degrees by attending medical school, typically for four years, after obtaining a bachelor's degree. After graduation from medical school, physicians enroll in intensive postgraduate residency training in a particular specialty, which lasts at least three years. Licensure to practice medicine is regulated by each state. Board certification in a specialty is an elective process that requires a minimum number of years of residency in the specialty and successful completion of oral and/or written examinations.

Physician Assistant (PA)   Physician Assistants should not be confused with other medical office assistants, who may perform clerical work or routine clinical tasks. A PA practices medicine with the supervision of a licensed physician and may even write prescriptions. A typical PA has a bachelor's degree and more than four years of health care experience prior to admission to a two-year PA program. After graduation, PAs must pass a national certifying examination and are licensed by the states in which they practice. Board certification examinations are available in Primary Care and Surgery.

Podiatrist   Podiatrists, specialists in foot care, must be licensed, which requires three to four years of undergraduate education, completion of a four-year podiatric college program, and passing scores on national and state examinations.

Therapists   Physical therapists, occupational therapists, speech and language therapists, art or music therapists, and even pet therapists can contribute to the well-being of an older patient. All states regulate the practice of physical therapy and the practice of occupational therapy, usually requiring a post-baccalaureate degree from an accredited program and a passing score on an examination.

Physical therapists provide care to people of all ages who have functional problems resulting from, for example, back and neck injuries, sprains/strains and fractures, arthritis, burns, amputations, stroke, multiple sclerosis, conditions such as cerebral palsy and spina bifida, and injuries related to work and sports. Physical therapist assistants work under the direction and supervision of a physical therapist. Physical therapists evaluate and diagnose movement dysfunction and use interventions to treat patients. Interventions may include therapeutic exercise, functional training, manual therapy techniques, assistive and adaptive devices and equipment, and physical agents and electrotherapeutic modalities.

Occupational therapists help patients improve their ability to perform tasks in living and working environments. They work with individuals who suffer from a mentally, physically, developmentally, or emotionally disabling condition. Occupational therapists help clients to perform all types of activities, from using a computer to caring for daily needs such as dressing, cooking, and eating. Physical exercises may be used to increase strength and dexterity, while other activities may be chosen to improve visual acuity or the ability to discern patterns. For example, a client with short-term memory loss might be encouraged to make lists to aid recall, and a person with coordination problems might be assigned exercises to improve hand-eye coordination. Occupational therapists also use computer programs to help clients improve decision-making, abstract-reasoning, problem-solving, and perceptual skills, as well as memory, sequencing, and coordination—all of which are important for independent living.

Recreational, music, art, and pet therapists are not regulated in most states, and they use a variety of techniques, including arts and crafts, animals, sports, games, dance and movement, drama, music, and community outings, to improve and maintain the physical, mental, and emotional well-being of their clients. Therapists help individuals reduce depression, stress, and anxiety; recover basic motor functioning and reasoning abilities; build confidence; and socialize effectively so that they can enjoy greater independence and reduce or eliminate the effects of their illness or disability. In addition, therapists help people with disabilities integrate into the community by teaching them how to use community resources and recreational activities.

Vision Optometrists, also known as doctors of optometry, or ODs, are the main providers of vision care. They examine people's eyes to diagnose vision problems, such as nearsightedness and farsightedness, and they test patients' depth and color perception and ability to focus and coordinate the eyes. Optometrists may prescribe eyeglasses or contact lenses, or they may provide other treatments, such as vision therapy or low-vision rehabilitation. Ophthalmologists are physicians who perform eye surgery, as well as diagnose and treat eye diseases and injuries. Like optometrists, they also examine eyes and prescribe eyeglasses and contact lenses. Dispensing opticians fit and adjust eyeglasses and, in some states, may fit contact lenses according to prescriptions written by ophthalmologists or optometrists.

Effects of Recent Changes in Health Law on Senior Clients

As a student you are probably aware that the 2010 health reform law provides an option for young adults to stay on their parents' health plans, requires most people to buy insurance, and provides subsidies for those who cannot afford coverage, and calls for states to establish insurance pools (called "exchanges") for people with pre-existing medical conditions, the unemployed, and others who otherwise cannot obtain insurance. But several lesser-known provisions may have an impact on elder clients. The full text of the law (more than 900 pages), the Patient Protection and Affordable Care Act, has not been codified as of this writing and can be found at *http://thomas.loc.gov.*

While benefits available under traditional Medicare (discussed in Chapter 6) are not cut, the law does phase in cuts in payments to Medicare Advantage programs, which may result in elimination of some of the additional benefits seniors have gotten through those programs. The law also schedules reductions in payments for home health care and to hospitals. On the other hand, Medicare will begin to pay for annual wellness benefits, and the existing prescription drug program has been overhauled to eliminate a gap in coverage that has been known as the "donut hole."

The legislation establishes an Independent Payment Advisory Board to submit legislative proposals to reduce Medicare spending if that spending grows in excess of the growth rate under Consumer Price Index measures for a five-year period that ends in 2013. The law prohibits the board from submitting any idea that would ration care, raise taxes, or change benefits. The Department of Health and Human Services is to establish a new office to coordinate the care of "dual eligibles"—individuals who qualify for both Medicare and Medicaid, many of whom are poor elderly.

The law creates a program to help employers handle the cost of health care for retirees age 55 and older who are not eligible for Medicare. The reimbursements will cover 80 percent of medical claims between $15,000 and $90,000 for retirees, their spouses, and dependents until the state insurance exchanges are in place in 2014.

The new law makes a number of changes that will have an impact on people of all ages. Most of these are intended to change the way we approach medicine, and encourage prevention rather than repeated treatment after the fact. Some of these changes will take time to implement and even longer to produce results.

- A new federal Patient-Centered Outcomes Research Institute will provide funding for studies to help doctors make more-informed decisions to eliminate unnecessary medical care and tests and provide care that has been shown to be effective.
- The law promotes "team care" that may include nurse practitioners, care managers, and nutritionists, depending on individual health needs.
- The law promotes preventative care and encourages screening. It eliminates copayments and deductibles on certain preventative services, such as immunizations, mammograms, and cholesterol testing, and provides doctors and care teams with financial incentives to keep people well.

- The law promotes efficient use of technology. Doctors will be expected to exchange paper charts for electronic medical records, to improve the accuracy of information in those records, and to make sure the records are accessible to the patient and the professionals participating in the patient's care.
- The Food and Drug Administration is authorized to approve lower-cost versions of biologic drugs, also called biosimilars or follow-on biologics—after drugmakers have 12 years of market exclusivity.
- Insurers will have to justify premium increases to the federal government and state insurance commissioners.
- In 2014, Medicaid, the state-federal program for the poor, will expand to include everyone who makes less than 133 percent of the poverty line ($14,400 in 2010 for individuals). Currently, most poor people without children aren't covered; states can expand their Medicaid programs to cover these people immediately and get federal aid to do so until the state insurance exchanges are in place in 2014.

Senior Citizen Medical Issues

In their book, *Taking Charge: Good Medical Care for the Elderly and How to Get It*,[3] attorney Jeanne Hannah and Dr. Joseph Friedman, MD, identify several common, preventable medical problems for the elderly: delirium, medication errors and adverse drug reactions, dehydration and malnutrition, and falls. This book discusses these issues as conditions of the mind, medical treatment issues, and care issues, including falls and other accidents.

All of these problems can arise in the home, where well-intentioned caregivers fail to recognize potential problems or fail to act on them. Unfortunately, they can also arise in even the most expensive professional care settings. According to the *New York Times*,[4] in 2008:

> More than 90 percent of nursing homes were cited for violations of federal health and safety standards last year, and for-profit homes were more likely to have problems than other types of nursing homes, federal investigators say in a report issued on Monday. About 17 percent of nursing homes had deficiencies that caused "actual harm or immediate jeopardy" to patients, said the report, by Daniel R. Levinson, the inspector general of the Department of Health and Human Services. Problems included infected bedsores, medication mix-ups, poor nutrition, and abuse and neglect of patients. Inspectors received 37,150 complaints about conditions in nursing homes last year, and they substantiated 39 percent of them, the report said. About one-fifth of the complaints verified by federal and state authorities involved the abuse or neglect of patients. About two-thirds of nursing homes are owned by for-profit companies, while 27 percent are owned by nonprofit organizations and 6 percent by government entities, the report said. The inspector general said 94 percent of for-profit nursing homes were cited for deficiencies last year, compared with 88 percent of nonprofit homes and 91 percent of government homes.

---

[3] 2006, Old Mission Press
[4] Robert Pear, Sept. 30, 2008

Conditions of the Mind

A patient's medical care may suffer because the patient is unable to communicate symptoms due to a condition of the mind, or a condition of the mind may be a symptom of another medical problem that remains undiagnosed. **Dementia,** also discussed in Chapter 1, is an illness that itself causes loss of mental function. Alzheimer's Disease is a form of dementia. **Delirium,** on the other hand, is a condition in which the patient suffers confusion or hallucinations as the result of another condition, such as dehydration, a metabolic disorder, or a urinary tract infection. Delirium may have a sudden onset, while dementia progresses at a slower pace. Unfortunately, delirium may result in death because a health care professional, unfamiliar with the patient's normal behavior, mistakes the condition for dementia or for **psychosis.** According to a study conducted by the Vanderbilt University Medical Center, emergency physicians missed delirium in 76 percent of cases.[5]

Delerium itself escalates risk. According to the *New York Times*, elderly patients experiencing delirium were hospitalized six days longer and placed in nursing homes 75 percent of the time, five times as often as those without delirium. Nearly one-tenth died within a month. Experts say delirium can contribute to death by weakening patients or leading to complications like pneumonia or blood clots.[6]

Dementia
Condition causing mental impairment, loss of memory, and confusion

Delirium
Confusion or hallucinations caused by another medical condition

Psychosis
Mental illness

Medical Treatment Issues

Medical **malpractice** is negligence, the failure to exercise reasonable care, by a professional health care provider: doctor, nurse, dentist, technician, hospital, or nursing facility. A health care provider fails to exercise reasonable care when it departs from a standard of practice of those with similar training and experience in performing its duties, resulting in harm to a patient. Although large awards sometimes make news, in reality few plaintiffs obtain such results. While we all want the best possible care for ourselves and our families, the law does not require the best care, only care that meets the standard of practice. The goal of a medical malpractice lawsuit is to compensate the injured patient, not to "punish" the provider.

Malpractice
Professional's failure to exercise reasonable care

Fear of malpractice can create an ethical dilemma for health care providers, who may feel that they should order every possible test and treatment to document their exercise of care. Of course, this increases the cost of treatment, sometimes with little corresponding benefit. It may also be contrary to the wishes of a terminal patient.

Many malpractice problems are the result of understaffing at senior care facilities, discussed in Chapter 9, or of miscommunication between members of the medical team, discussed earlier in this chapter.

Medications While modern medicines have tremendous benefits for older patients, they also create problems. Some of the most common medication-related problems (**MRPs**) are difficulty in remembering to take medications and

MRPs
Medication-related problem

---

[5]*http://www.ncbi.nlm.nih.gov/pubmed/19154565*, accessed August 31, 2010
[6]*http://www.nytimes.com/2010/06/21/science/21delirium.html*, accessed August 31, 2010

remembering whether medications have been taken; difficulty in reading labels or in hearing instructions; difficulty in opening bottles, breaking tablets, or handling injections and applications; improper storage of medications; incorrect dosage, sometimes because of changes in weight or other physical characteristics; failure to consider the possible serious impacts of "natural" or over-the-counter drugs; dealing with medications that must be taken under specific conditions (with or without food, not at the same time as another medicine); "polypharmacy," the use of too many medications; interactions between drugs; inadequate medication because symptoms are disregarded as "just part of getting older"; sharing medicine or using expired medicine to save money; and not getting prescriptions filled when needed, because of financial or transportation issues. Caregivers must be aware that pharmacists can help with most of these problems, if informed of the difficulty. Caregivers must also keep accurate records of everything the patient takes, both prescription and over-the-counter, and when it is taken, and provide that information to every medical professional dealing with the patient. Caregivers (and legal professionals dealing with elder patients) should recognize the symptoms of MRPs:

- excessive drowsiness
- confusion
- depression
- delirium
- insomnia
- Parkinson's-like symptoms
- incontinence
- muscle weakness
- loss of appetite
- falls and fractures
- changes in speech and memory

Care Issues

Dehydration and Malnutrition

All human beings need to eat, so why are malnutrition and dehydration particular problems for seniors? Elderly persons do not feel thirsty as quickly as young people do and do not drink water and other liquids as often. Some of the medicine they take can also lead to water loss. Depression and physical changes, such as decline in smell and taste, dental problems, and difficulty in chewing, can affect the desire to eat and nutritional intake. Older people may have difficulty swallowing because of a variety of medical problems. Limitations on sight, hearing, and mobility may make shopping and cooking and even eating in a restaurant difficult. As a matter of convenience, a senior citizen may eat the same foods over and over, not getting the needed variety of foods.

Problems related to hydration and nutrition can be even worse among nursing home residents, particularly those with dementia or limited mobility, necessitating regulations like those shown in Exhibit 5.2. As with other quality-of-care issues, facilities vary and inadequate staffing can result in conditions that fall far short of standards.

EXHIBIT 5.2
Federal Regulation of Nutrition and Hydration in Skilled Nursing Facilities

Federal regulations state the following:

(i) Nutrition. Based on a resident's comprehensive assessment, the facility must ensure that a resident:

(1) Maintains acceptable parameters of nutritional status, such as body weight and protein levels, unless the resident's clinical condition demonstrates that this is not possible; and

(2) Receives a therapeutic diet when there is a nutritional problem.

(j) Hydration. The facility must provide each resident with sufficient fluid intake to maintain proper hydration and health. (42 CFR 483.25)

42 CFR 483.35 provides additional details:

The facility must provide each resident with a nourishing, palatable, well-balanced diet that meets the daily nutritional and special dietary needs of each resident.

(a) *Staffing*. The facility must employ a qualified dietitian either full-time, part-time, or on a consultant basis.

(1) If a qualified dietitian is not employed full-time, the facility must designate a person to serve as the director of food service who receives frequently scheduled consultation from a qualified dietitian.

(2) A qualified dietitian is one who is qualified based upon either registration by the Commission on Dietetic Registration of the American Dietetic Association, or on the basis of education, training, or experience in identification of dietary needs, planning, and implementation of dietary programs.

(b) *Sufficient staff*. The facility must employ sufficient support personnel competent to carry out the functions of the dietary service.

(c) *Menus and nutritional adequacy*. Menus must:

(1) Meet the nutritional needs of residents in accordance with the recommended dietary allowances of the Food and Nutrition Board of the National Research Council, National Academy of Sciences;

(2) Be prepared in advance; and

(3) Be followed.

(d) *Food*. Each resident receives and the facility provides:

(1) Food prepared by methods that conserve nutritive value, flavor, and appearance;

(2) Food that is palatable, attractive, and at the proper temperature;

(3) Food prepared in a form designed to meet individual needs; and

(4) Substitutes offered of similar nutritive value to residents who refuse food served.

(e) *Therapeutic diets*. Therapeutic diets must be prescribed by the attending physician.

(f) *Frequency of meals*.

(1) Each resident receives and the facility provides at least three meals daily, at regular times comparable to normal mealtimes in the community.

(2) There must be no more than 14 hours between a substantial evening meal and breakfast the following day, except as provided in (4) below.

EXHIBIT 5.2
(continued)

(3) The facility must offer snacks at bedtime daily.

(4) When a nourishing snack is provided at bedtime, up to 16 hours may elapse between a substantial evening meal and breakfast the following day if a resident group agrees to this meal span, and a nourishing snack is served.

(g) *Assistive devices.* The facility must provide special eating equipment and utensils for residents who need them.

(h) *Paid feeding assistants:*

(1) *State-approved training course.* A facility may use a paid feeding assistant, as defined in §488.301 of this chapter, if:

(i) The feeding assistant has successfully completed a State-approved training course that meets the requirements of §483.160 before feeding residents; and

(ii) The use of feeding assistants is consistent with State law.

(2) *Supervision.*

(i) A feeding assistant must work under the supervision of a registered nurse (RN) or licensed practical nurse (LPN).

(ii) In an emergency, a feeding assistant must call a supervisory nurse for help on the resident call system.

(3) *Resident selection criteria.*

(i) A facility must ensure that a feeding assistant feeds only residents who have no complicated feeding problems.

(ii) Complicated feeding problems include, but are not limited to, difficulty swallowing, recurrent lung aspirations, and tube or parenteral/IV feedings.

(iii) The facility must base resident selection on the charge nurse's assessment and the resident's latest assessment and plan of care.

(i) *Sanitary conditions.* The facility must . . . .

To read more regulations, visit *http://edocket.access.gpo.gov/cfr_2009/octqtr/pdf/42cfr483.35.pdf.*

Falls

CDC
Centers for Disease Control, a federal agency

As shown in Exhibit 5.3, falls are both a common occurrence and a serious problem for older patients. The problem is especially severe among nursing home residents. The Centers for Disease Control (**CDC**) reports[7]:

[7]Information from *http://www.cdc.gov/ncipc/factsheets/nursing.htm*

- Each year, an average nursing home with 100 beds reports 100 to 200 falls. About 1,800 older adults living in nursing homes die each year from fall-related injuries.
- Muscle weakness and walking or gait problems are the most common causes of falls among nursing home residents. These problems account for about 24 percent of the falls in nursing homes.
- Environmental hazards in nursing homes cause 16 percent to 27 percent of falls among residents. Such hazards include wet floors, poor lighting, incorrect bed height, and improperly fitted or maintained wheelchairs.
- Medications can increase the risk of falls and fall-related injuries. Drugs that affect the central nervous system, such as sedatives and anti-anxiety drugs, are of particular concern.
- Other causes of falls include difficulty in moving, for example, from the bed to a chair, poor foot care, poorly fitting shoes, and improper or incorrect use of walking aids.

Driving The physical effects of aging can impair a senior citizen's ability to drive safely. Relatives and caregivers may decide that the senior should stop driving, but driving is such a key factor in independence that seniors may resist. Laws differ from state to state; some states have initiatives to educate and assist senior drivers, and some have vision and testing requirements that may result in loss of license. The Insurance Institute for Highway Safety reports that senior drivers are not causing more crashes than in the past and are not dying more often in crashes, even though they hold on to their licenses longer. In fact, the rate of fatal crashes per licensed driver 70 and older declined from 1997 to 2008. Rates of less severe crashes reported to police officers also declined.[8]

For links to more information, visit *http://www.seniordrivers.org*. To help a senior client who wants to keep driving but needs to make changes, visit *http://helpguide.org/elder/senior_citizen_driving.htm*.

Wandering Wandering refers to a cognitively impaired person moving within her home freely, without an appreciation of safety risks. **Elopement** means that the person has left home unsupervised and is unable to protect herself because she does not have the instinct to ask for help or respond to offers of help. While wandering and elopement are serious problems for impaired elders in a home setting, they are no less problematic for nursing care facilities. Historically, patients were often physically restrained or medicated to prevent wandering and elopement. Studies[9] have indicated that restraints are not an effective way of protecting patients. Federal law now provides the following:

Elopement
Impaired individual leaves home, unsupervised

---

[8] *http://www.iihs.org/externaldata/srdata/docs/sr4506.pdf*, visited August 31, 2010
[9] *http://www.alz.org/national/documents/Fallsrestraints_litereview_II.pdf*, visited August 31, 2010

EXHIBIT 5.3
Falls[10]

How big is the problem?

- More than one-third of adults 65 and older fall each year in the United States.
- Among older adults, falls are the leading cause of injury deaths. They are also the most common cause of nonfatal injuries and hospital admissions for trauma.
- In 2005, 15,800 people 65 and older died from injuries related to unintentional falls; about 1.8 million people 65 and older were treated in emergency departments for nonfatal injuries from falls, and more than 433,000 of these patients were hospitalized.
- The rates of fall-related deaths among older adults rose significantly over the past decade.

What outcomes are linked to falls?

- 20 percent to 30 percent of people who fall suffer moderate to severe injuries such as bruises, hip fractures, or head traumas. These injuries can make it hard to get around and limit independent living. They also can increase the risk of early death.
- Falls are the most common cause of traumatic brain injuries, or TBI. In 2000, TBI accounted for 46 percent of fatal falls among older adults.
- Most fractures among older adults are caused by falls.
- The most common fractures are of the spine, hip, forearm, leg, ankle, pelvis, upper arm, and hand.
- Many people who fall, even those who are not injured, develop a fear of falling. This fear may cause them to limit their activities, leading to reduced mobility and physical fitness, and increasing their actual risk of falling.
- In 2000, direct medical costs totaled $179 million for fatal falls and $19 billion for nonfatal fall injuries.

Who is at risk?

- Men are more likely to die from a fall. After adjusting for age, the fall fatality rate in 2004 was 49 percent higher for men than for women.
- Women are 67 percent more likely than men to have a nonfatal fall injury.
- Rates of fall-related fractures among older adults are more than twice as high for women as for men.
- In 2003, about 72 percent of older adults admitted to the hospital for hip fractures were women.

---

[10]*http://www.cdc.gov/HomeandRecreationalSafety/Falls/adultfalls.html* (internal references and citations omitted)

**EXHIBIT 5.3
(continued)**

- The risk of being seriously injured in a fall increases with age. In 2001, the rates of fall injuries for adults 85 and older were four to five times that of adults 65 to 74.
- Nearly 85 percent of deaths from falls in 2004 were among people 75 and older.
- People 75 and older who fall are four to five times more likely to be admitted to a long-term care facility for a year or longer.
- There is little difference in fatal fall rates between whites and blacks, ages 65 to 74.
- After age 75, white men have the highest fatality rates, followed by white women, black men, and black women.
- White women have significantly higher rates of fall-related hip fractures than black women.
- Among older adults, non-Hispanics have higher fatal fall rates than Hispanics.

Older adults can take several steps to protect their independence and reduce their risk of falling:

- Exercise regularly; exercise programs like tai chi that increase strength and improve balance are especially good.
- Ask their doctor or pharmacist to review their medicines — both prescription and over-the-counter — to reduce side effects and interactions.
- Have their eyes checked by an eye doctor at least once a year.
- Improve the lighting in their home.
- Reduce hazards in their home that can lead to falls.

§483.13 Resident behavior and facility practices.

(a) *Restraints.* The resident has the right to be free from any physical or chemical restraints imposed for purposes of discipline or convenience, and not required to treat the resident's medical symptoms.

Nursing homes can protect residents by assessing patients regularly, hiring and training staff adequate to the supervision needs of the residents, installing alarms and safety devices, and responding promptly to alarms. Individual caregivers can educate themselves on reducing wandering and elopement using various resources, including the Mayo Clinic Web site (*http://www.mayoclinic.com/health/alzheimers/HQ00218*). The Alzheimer's Association also has a 24-hour assistance program (*http://www.alz.org/safetycenter/we_can_help_safety_medicalert_safereturn.asp*).

Glossary of Medical Terminology

Activities of Daily Living (ADLs): Walking, getting in and out of bed, bathing, dressing, eating, toileting, self-administration of medications, etc. Used for assessing functional status.

Acute Care: Medical care intended to treat or cure disease or injury within a limited time period. Acute care usually refers to physician or hospital services of less than three months' duration.

Administrator: A person licensed to run a nursing home; has training in fiscal, legal, social, and medical aspects of running an institution.

Adult Day Care: Daytime supervision alternative between home care and institutional care.

Allied Health Professionals: Persons with training in fields related to medicine, such as medical social work and physical or occupational therapy.

Alzheimers Disease: A progressive, irreversible form of dementia.

Ambulatory: Able to walk; **Ambulatory with Assistance:** Able to walk with the aid of a cane, crutch, brace, wheelchair, or walker.

Analgesics: Drugs used to reduce pain, such as aspirin, Tylenol, Darvon, codeine, Demerol, and Dilaudid.

Ancillary Services: Not provided by a nursing home, such as podiatry, dentistry, etc.

Anti-Anxiety Medications: Drugs that have a calming or soothing, quieting or pacifying effect without depressing, such as Valium and Librium.

Anti-Depressants: Drugs that regulate mood, such as Elavil, Desyrel, Prozac, and Tofranil.

Anti-Hypertensives: Drugs that lower blood pressure.

Anti-Inflammatory Medications: Drugs used to treat inflammation conditions like arthritis, including aspirin, Butazolidin, Indocin, and Motrin/ibuprofen.

Anti-Psychotics: Tranquilizing drugs more powerful than anti-anxiety drugs, to reduce psychotic behaviors, including Thorazine, Haldol, Mellaril, and Navane.

Approved Amount: Amount Medicare determines to be reasonable for a service under Part B—may be less than the actual amount charged.

Arteriosclerosis/Atherosclerosis: Fatty deposits in artery walls causing a decrease in size and flexibility of artery; can affect brain and heart.

Assignment: Medicare provider bills Medicare directly and agrees to accept Medicare's allowed charge as payment in full. Medicare pays the provider directly. The provider can then bill the beneficiary for deductibles and coinsurance.

Benefit Maximum: Limit health insurance policy will pay for a loss or covered service; can be expressed as a length of time (e.g., 90 days), a dollar amount, or a percentage of Medicare-approved amount and may refer to a specific illness, time frame, or the life of the policy.

Carcinoma: Malignant tumor—cancer.

Carriers: Private insurance organizations under contract with the federal government to handle claims for services covered by Medicare Part B.

Categorically Needy Medicaid Program: Individuals eligible for all medical services under Medicaid due to financial need.

Catheter: Tube into bladder to drain urine, also called Foley catheter or indwelling catheter.

Charge Nurse: Licensed Practical Nurse (LPN) or Registered Nurse (RN) responsible for supervising aides on a unit, dispensing medication, and providing patient care.

Chemical Restraint: Drugs that depress the central nervous system.

Chuks: Trade name for disposable pad used under incontinent persons or under draining areas.

Coinsurance: Amount, usually 20 percent of allowed charges, not reimbursed by Medicare.

Continent: Able to control the passage of urine and feces.

Continuum of Care: Includes: (1) community support services such as senior centers; (2) in-home care, such as meal delivery, homemaker, shopping, and chore services, home health services, personal care, and visitors, (3) community-based services such as adult day care; (4) non-institutional housing such as congregate housing, shared housing, and board and care homes; and (5) nursing homes and subacute and acute facilities as necessary.

Contractures: Shortening of muscles producing distortions or deformities or limitations on movement of the joints.

CPR: Cardiopulmonary resuscitation.

Custodial Care: Attempts to maintain a person at existing level—does not involve skilled rehabilitation or nursing services.

Decubitus Ulcer: A sore caused by lack of blood circulating to an area of the body—often results from sitting or lying in one position too long, also called bedsores and pressure sores.

Deductible: Annual payment responsibility of patient under Medicare or other insurance carrier.

Dehydration: Lack of adequate fluid in the body.

Denial of Payment: Can be used by government to sanction a facility with serious deficiencies.

Diabetes: Caused by failure of the pancreas to secrete insulin, among older people a common cause of poor circulation and poor eyesight. Medications include insulin, Orinase, and Diabinase.

Diagnostic Related Group (DRG): Groups into which all illnesses are classified to determine Medicare payment.

Disorientation: Loss of familiarity with surroundings or loss of bearings with respect to time, place, and person.

Diuretics: Drugs given to help eliminate excess fluid; often needed for heart disease.

Do Not Resuscitate Order (DNR): A code or order, usually in a patient's medical record, indicating that no intervention should be undertaken if heart or breathing stops. Death occurs undisturbed. Other care (pain medications, antibiotics) continues. May supplement other advance directives.

Double Effect: Medication intended for pain relief that has effect of hastening death.

Durable Medical Equipment (DME): As defined by Medicare, equipment that (1) can withstand repeated use, (2) is primarily used for a medical purpose, (3) is generally not useful absent an illness or injury, and (4) is appropriate for home use. Examples include oxygen and wheelchairs.

Edema: Collection of fluids in tissues, resulting in swelling.

Emphysema: A condition in which the lungs become distended or ruptured.

Explanation of Medicare Benefits (EOMB) Form: Statement sent to beneficiary to show what action has been taken in processing Medicare claims for a period. If payment is to beneficiary, a check will be attached. Most Medigap policies pay claims based on an EOMB.

Fiscal Intermediaries: Private insurance companies under contract with federal government to handle Medicare Part A claims from hospitals, skilled nursing facilities, and home health agencies.

Five Wishes: Document including living will and power of attorney and expressing patient wishes about treatment, comfort, funeral, last thoughts, etc. If properly signed/witnessed, constitutes a lawful advance directive in most states.

Gastrointestinal Disease: Disease of the stomach, colon, bowels, or rectum; such as stomach ulcer, colitis, diverticulitis. Medications include Tagamet and Donnatal.

Geri-Chair: A wheelchair that cannot be self-propelled; must be pushed, has a high back, foot ledge, and removable tray.

Glasgow Coma Scale: Used for assessing level of consciousness.

Glaucoma: Disease of the eye. Early sign of glaucoma: lights appear to have a halo.

Grab Bar: Bar or railing around tub, shower, toilet.

Health Insurance Information Counseling Assistance Program (HIICAP): Peer-counseling program to assist and answer questions for Medicare beneficiaries.

Health Maintenance Organization (HMO): An organization that, for a pre-paid fee, provides comprehensive health maintenance and treatment services.

Heart Medications: Include Digoxin, Lanoxin, and Digitalis.

Home Health Agency (HHA): Certified by Medicare to provide skilled nurses, homemakers, home health aides, and therapeutic services, such as physical therapy in patient's home.

Hospice: Care that addresses physical, spiritual, emotional, social, financial, and legal needs of dying patient and family — can be given in the home, a hospice facility, or a combination of both.

Hypertension: High blood pressure or elevated pressure in the arteries.

I and O: Intake (of food and liquids) and output (of urine and feces).

IMR: Intermediate Care Facility for the Mentally Retarded.

Informed Consent: Consent to proposed medical procedure after receiving relevant information.

Life Care Arrangement or Contract: Contract between resident and nursing home — resident assigns all assets in return for guaranteed lifetime care.

Lucid: Capable of understanding, not impaired.

Managed Care: In general, indicates some management of health care other than by caregiver and patient, in order to control cost. Generally involves "gate-keeper," usually a primary care physician, who "opens the door" to specialty providers and coordinates care. Managing care is not the same as providing treatment.

Medical Director: Physician who formulates and directs medical policy for nursing home.

Mini Mental State Exam (MMSE): Test for cognitive impairment

Nasal Gastric (NG) Tube: Tube for liquid feeding (gastric feeding).

Obtunded: Mentally "dull."

Occupational Therapist (OT): Conducts therapy to maintain, restore, or teach manual dexterity and hand-eye coordination.

Ombudsman: "Citizen's representative" in a nursing home, protects patients' rights through advocacy and education.

Organic Brain Syndrome (OBS): May be acute (rapid onset, short and severe) or chronic; reversible or irreversible — resulting in impaired mental function.

Orientation x1, 2, or 3: Describes patient's level of awareness.

Osteoporosis: Causes decrease in bone strength.

Paraplegia: Paralysis of legs and other muscles up to mid-chest, from damage to spine.

Parkinsons Disease: Shaking palsy caused by a neurological disorder.

Participating Provider: Certified or licensed institution, facility, agency, or health professional in participation agreement with Medicaid agency.

Patient Care Plan: Formulated by Registered Nurse in conjunction with physician for ongoing care and rehabilitation of nursing home resident.

Patient Copayment: Amount of allowed charges for which Medicaid recipient must pay.

Peer Review Organization (PRO): Physician group or other professional medical organization that reviews quality and appropriateness of services covered by Medicare and Medicaid. PROs must review SNF care when a hospitalized patient is discharged to the SNF and is readmitted to the hospital within 30 days, or a Medicare beneficiary complains about an SNF's quality of care.

Personal Needs Allowance (PNA): Money protected from Medicaid for nursing home resident's personal use.

Presbycusis: Impaired hearing due to old age.

PRN: Abbreviation — indicates that medication is given or treatment performed only as needed.

Proprietary Facility: Privately owned and operated for the purpose of making a profit.

Psychopathy: Any mental disease, especially characterized by defective character or personality.

Psychotropic Medications: Used to treat and control mental illness.

Reasonable Charges: Allowable charges, of which Medicare will cover a percentage–published annually, based on actual charges by physicians and suppliers in the area during the previous year.

Reserve Days: Every Medicare patient has a lifetime reserve of 60 days; if patient has been in the hospital for 90 days (for which Medicare will pay a percentage), patient can use reserve days to remain in the hospital on doctor's orders. If patient does not wish to use reserve days she must inform the hospital in writing in advance.

Residents Council: Organization of nursing home residents, to improve quality of life, care, and communication within institution.

Respite: Substitute care to give home caregiver a rest.

Room Occupancy Fee: Basic room rental fee for nursing home.

Sedatives: Provide calming of nervous excitement — includes Noctec, Nembutal, Seconal, chloral hydrate, and phenobarbital.

Skilled Care: Institutional care less intensive than hospital care, but including procedures requiring skills of an RN. Medicare and Medicaid reimburse for care at the skilled level if provided in a facility certified as meeting Skilled Nursing Facility (SNF) standards.

Skilled Nursing Facility (SNF): Facility certified by Medicare or Medicaid to provide skilled care.

Social Services: Assistance, by social workers—housing, transportation, meals, recreation, etc.

Social Worker: Trained to identify social and emotional needs of nursing home residents and provide services. Full-time social workers are not required in nursing homes, although facilities must provide social services. Social worker is often responsible for admissions and discharges.

Spend Down: To establish Medicaid eligibility by incurring medical expenses until income (after medical expenses) meets Medicaid requirements.

Stroke: Blood supply to a part of the brain tissue is cut off and nerve cells cannot function. Effects may be severe or slight, temporary or permanent.

Subacute Care: Provided to patients sufficiently stable to no longer require acute care—too complex for conventional nursing center—typically for medically complex patients who require extensive physiological monitoring, intravenous therapy or pre- or postoperative care.

Suppliers: Persons or companies other than doctors and health care facilities that provide equipment or services covered by Part B—ambulance, laboratories, etc.

Third-Party Payment: Made by other than patient or family (Medicare or private insurance).

TPR: Abbreviation for measurement of temperature, pulse, and respiration.

Turn Q2H: Turn every two hours. A nursing home resident who is unable to move must be turned frequently to prevent skin breakdown and other physical problems.

Urinary Tract Infection (UTI): Infection common in patients with catheters.

Utilization Review: Requires hospital or nursing home to evaluate the appropriateness of Medicare and Medicaid patients' admission to and continued stay in the institution—conducted by a committee composed of health professionals.

Vital Signs: Temperature, pulse, respiration, and blood pressure.

EXHIBIT 5.4
Attorney Flowers Says

Illinois medical malpractice attorney Peter J. Flowers has received many honors over the years. He's been named an Illinois Super Lawyer in the area of medical malpractice, and recognized as a Leading Lawyer by his peers, a distinction awarded to fewer than 5 percent of attorneys in Illinois. In addition, he is a member of both the elite Verdict Club society, which includes top attorneys from around the United States and of the Million Dollar Forum, having resolved many cases in excess of $1,000,000. Mr. Flowers served as president of the 2,300-member Illinois Trial Lawyers Association from 2009 to 2010, during which time he created legislative initiatives and strategic communications programs.

Mr. Flowers uses paralegals in his practice, and advises people on how to avoid malpractice and obtain the best medical care. When asked what medically vulnerable clients can do to protect themselves, Mr. Flowers set out the following recommendations:

EXHIBIT 5.4
(continued)

---

1. **Obtain copies of medical records.** The patient is entitled to these records and it is worth the small copying fee you may be charged. Reviewing the records can help prevent miscommunications between the patient and the doctor, and among the various health care providers working with the patient.

2. **Communicate with health care workers efficiently and effectively.** Misdiagnosis is often the result of improper communication. Put it in writing; don't hesitate to provide a list of concerns and symptoms, and to ask that a copy of the list be put in your chart. Be sure to keep a copy.

3. **Work hard to find the best possible primary care doctor.** If your internist or family doctor is not proactive, or if you are not comfortable with the doctor for any reason, find a new doctor.

4. **Be safe, sensible, and skeptical about drugs.** Two million Americans are hurt by adverse reactions to drugs every year, and about 100,000 of the reactions are fatal. The Food and Drug Administration does not independently study the safety of the drugs it approves, but relies on studies performed by manufacturers, which can be self-serving. Some doctors prescribe new medications because they have received "perks" from the pharmaceutical companies. Several respected scholars suggest avoiding new prescription drugs until they have been on the market at least two years.

5. **Understand that no medical test is perfect.** Seek a second or even a third opinion at every major crossroads. Some people obtain a second opinion only when considering elective surgery, but it is important and appropriate to seek another opinion for any significant medical condition.

6. **Research specialists.** Is the surgeon or other specialist board certified? Does she have significant experience with the condition at issue? If she takes offense at these questions, find a new doctor.

7. **Have an advocate present.** Every patient should have an advocate present at every health care encounter, especially in the hospital. Bring a friend or family member with you to ensure your concerns are properly communicated.

8. **Find a hospital with high safety and satisfaction ratings.** Using a Web site, such as *http://www.hospitalcompare.hhs.gov*, *http://www.planetree.org*, *http://www.qualitycheck.org*, or *http://www.leapfroggroup.org* will help you research a particular hospital.

9. **Educate yourself if you have a chronic condition.** Learn how to audit your care to make sure you get it. For some of the most common serious medical conditions, some organizations have developed checklists that can be used to audit the quality of care.

**EXHIBIT 5.4
(continued)**

---

10. **In summary:** Take personal responsibility for your own health by proactively communicating with your primary doctor, and researching your doctors and your own illness to make sure you receive the best medical care possible, while also avoiding the worst.

Assignments

---

1. Visit *http://www.hhs.gov/ocr/privacy/hipaa/faq/index.html* and determine whether a facsimile (fax) version of a HIPAA authorization is valid under the privacy rule. Does an authorization require a witness?
2. Visit a local urgent care or hospital facility and obtain an HIPAA authorization form. These may also be available on the facility's Web site. What does the form say about authorization? Does the form give the patient the right to limit the information to be released or is it a general release?
3. At the time of this writing, the 2010 law was new and most of it had not been implemented. Many of its provisions are ambitious and may be difficult to implement. Conduct some online research and summarize some of the problems that have been encountered or are anticipated in meeting the goals of the Act.
4. Visit the CDC Web site and identify the steps a nursing home can take to reduce falls.
5. **Critical Thinking:** Using your school's CALR subscription, Lexisone, Findlaw.com, or bound case reporters, find and read *Noland Health Servs. v. Wright*, 971 So. 2d 681 (Ala. 2007).

◆ Why are the parties arguing about this? Does it make a difference whether they resolve the underlying question of malpractice in a courtroom or in binding arbitration? Why might the nursing home prefer arbitration?
◆ Daughter-in-law Vicky argued that she did not sign away Dorothy's (the patient) right to bring suit when she signed admission papers containing an arbitration clause as a "responsible party" rather than as a "representative." Why does the "label" placed on the signature matter?

◆ The court found that the agreement had no relevance to the medical malpractice claims in any event. Why? Can you see any public policy reasons for making this distinction between tort law and contract law?

◆ Many people might be more interested in finding out why Dorothy fell, whether she received prompt care, whether she died or recovered, and what kinds of conditions existed at the nursing home. It is unlikely that those matters will ever be reported in a case available through conventional legal resource materials. Why?

Review Questions

1. Explain the difference between delirium and dementia.
2. Under what circumstances might a patient need a geriatric specialist?
3. Discuss the conflict faced by health care providers caring for elder patients and fearing malpractice liability.
4. Identify preventable causes of medical problems among the elderly.
5. Why do we care about medical privacy? Do you see any aspects of the 2010 law that might raise privacy concerns?
6. What responsibilities does a nursing care facility have with respect to wandering and elopement?

www.CrosswordWeaver.com

ACROSS

2. Eye doctor
4. Consent given after full disclosure
7. Lack of adequate fluid in body
11. CPR, _____ pulmonary resuscitation
12. Initials, privacy law
15. Deals with problems of the feet
17. Able to walk
19. _____ signs, pulse, respiration
20. _____ wishes, includes living will
21. Health care provider fails to exercise reasonable care
23. Represents patients in nursing care
24. Specialty concerned with medical problems of aging
25. Financial responsibility of the patient

DOWN

1. HMO, health _____ organization
3. Fluids collect in body, causing swelling
5. Errors, a major concern for elders
6. Initials, nurse, less than RN
8. _____ therapist might help stroke victim relearn eating and bathing
9. Cares for dying patient
10. Care of limited duration
13. Advanced _____ nurse has a post-bac degree
14. Mental health professional, is an MD
16. DNR, do not _____
18. Capable of understanding, not mentally impaired
22. _____ care, involves gatekeeper

6

◆ ◆ ◆

Medicare

◆ ◆ ◆

Objectives

When you complete this chapter, you will:

- Be able to describe what is covered by Medicare Parts A, B, C, and D.
- Know the features available with Medigap insurance.
- Have a basic understanding of Medicare patients' rights and the procedures for appeal.

Overview

Medicare, a program enacted (42 U.S.C. §1395), along with Medicaid, in 1965, is a federally funded health insurance program that does not depend on wealth or income and is available to eligible people whether they are working or retired. The program covers:

- People age 65 or older.
- People under age 65 with certain disabilities eligible for social security.
- People of all ages with end-stage renal disease (permanent kidney failure requiring dialysis or a kidney transplant).

The "parts" of the Medicare program are discussed in the following sections. Because almost all seniors rely on Medicare, elder law paralegals must know the basics of working with the system, as described in Exhibits 6.1 and 6.3.

Part A: Hospital Insurance

Most people do not pay a premium for Part A because they or a spouse already paid for it through their payroll taxes while working. Medicare Part A (Hospital Insurance) helps cover inpatient care in hospitals, including critical-access hospitals, and skilled nursing facilities (not custodial or long-term care). It also helps cover hospice care and some home health care. Beneficiaries must meet certain conditions to get those benefits.

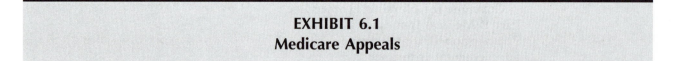

EXHIBIT 6.1
Medicare Appeals

The federal Center for Medicare Services (CMS), *http://www.medicare.gov*, is part of the Department of Health and Human Services. The Web site explanation of how to appeal a denial of Medicare benefits appears below. There are, of course, time limits for pursuing an appeal, and an appeal can be expedited under certain circumstances. In some situations, a patient may receive an Advance Notice that a proposed service is likely not covered. The appeals process can ultimately lead to litigation in a federal trial court; the relevant statute contains a provision for attorneys' fees.

The Medicare Summary Notice (MSN) that you receive from the company that handles claims for Medicare will tell you if Medicare has paid your medical claim or denied it. If your medical claim is denied and you believe Medicare should have covered it, you can request a redetermination (first-level appeal). The MSN will explain how to file an appeal.

If you disagree with the redetermination decision, you have the right to ask for a second level appeal, called a reconsideration. You should read the redetermination decision carefully because it will explain how to ask for a reconsideration. A Qualified Independent Contractor (QIC) that didn't take part in the

EXHIBIT 6.1
(continued)

first appeal makes the reconsideration decision. You can also write a letter. Your written request must include the following information:

- Your name.
- Your Medicare Health Insurance Claim (HIC) number on your red, white, and blue Medicare card.
- The specific service and/or items for which a redetermination is being requested.
- The date(s) of service.
- Your signature or the signature of your authorized or appointed representative.

To request a reconsideration with the appropriate QIC, follow the instructions on your Medicare Redetermination Notice. If you need help, call 1-800-MEDICARE (1-800-633-4227).

A request for reconsideration may be made on a standard CMS form. This form will be mailed with the Medicare Redetermination Notice. If the form is not used, the request must contain at least all of the following information:

- The beneficiary's name.
- The beneficiary's Medicare HIC number.
- The specific service(s) and item(s) for which the reconsideration is requested, and the specific date(s) of service.
- The name and signature of the party or representative of the party.
- The name of the contractor that made the redetermination.

The Medicare Reconsideration Request form can be found at *http://www.cms. hhs.gov/cmsforms/downloads/CMS20033.pdf.*

Appeals of Medicare Advantage Plan and Part D decisions follow a similar process, also described on the Web site.

Coverage for Hospital Care

There is a "gap" in coverage for hospital care. As of 2010, the patient must pay:

- A total of $1,100 for a hospital stay of 1–60 days.
- $275 per day for days 61–90 of a hospital stay.

- $550 per day for days 91–150 of a hospital stay unless the patient applies some of her 60 "lifetime reserve days."[1]
- All costs for each day beyond 150 days.

Because a hospital is paid a flat rate by Medicare, depending on the diagnosis and procedures, hospitals have a financial incentive to discharge Medicare patients as soon as possible. Patients and families often believe the patient is being discharged from the hospital too soon. During a hospital stay, patients must be given two notices, each labeled "Important Message from Medicare," one upon or near the time of admission and the other no more than two days before the planned discharge. The notices contain information about the appeals process, which generally involves the hospital's **PRO**, or peer review organization. Examine Exhibit 6.2, which contains the regulation requiring the notices. The patient is required to sign receipt of the first notice. What can the hospital do if the patient refuses?

PRO
Hospital's peer review organization

EXHIBIT 6.2
42 CFR 405.1205

Sec. 405.1205: Notifying beneficiaries of hospital discharge appeal rights.
  (a) Applicability and scope.
    (1) For purposes of Sec. Sec. 405.1204, 405.1205, 405.1206, and 405.1208, the term "hospital" is defined as any facility providing care at the inpatient hospital level, whether that care is short term or long term, acute or non acute, paid through a prospective payment system or other reimbursement basis, limited to specialty care or providing a broader spectrum of services. This definition includes critical access hospitals.
    (2) For purposes of Sec. Sec. 405.1204, 405.1205, 405.1206, and 405.1208, a discharge is a formal release of a beneficiary from an inpatient hospital.
    (b) Advance written notice of hospital discharge rights. For all Medicare beneficiaries, hospitals must deliver valid, written notice of a beneficiary's rights as a hospital inpatient, including discharge appeal rights. The hospital must use a standardized notice, as specified by CMS, in accordance with the following procedures:
    (1) Timing of notice. The hospital must provide the notice at or near admission, but no later than 2 calendar days following the beneficiary's admission to the hospital.
    (2) Content of the notice. The notice must include the following information:

---

[1]Each recipient has 60 "lifetime reserve days" that can be used after the 90th day of hospital stay.

EXHIBIT 6.2
(continued)

(i) The beneficiary's rights as a hospital inpatient including the right to benefits for inpatient services and for post-hospital services in accordance with 1866(a)(1)(M) of the Act.

(ii) The beneficiary's right to request an expedited determination of the discharge decision including a description of the process under Sec. 405.1206, and the availability of other appeals processes if the beneficiary fails to meet the deadline for an expedited determination.

(iii) The circumstances under which a beneficiary will or will not be liable for charges for continued stay in the hospital in accordance with 1866(a)(1)(M) of the Act.

(iv) A beneficiary's right to receive additional detailed information in accordance with Sec. 405.1206(e).

(v) Any other information required by CMS.

(3) When delivery of the notice is valid. Delivery of the written notice of rights described in this section is valid if:

(i) The beneficiary (or the beneficiary's representative) has signed and dated the notice to indicate that he or she has received the notice and can comprehend its contents, except as provided in paragraph (b)(4) of this section; and

(ii) The notice is delivered in accordance with paragraph (b)(1) of this section and contains all the elements described in paragraph (b)(2) of this section.

(4) If a beneficiary refuses to sign the notice. The hospital may annotate its notice to indicate the refusal, and the date of refusal is considered the date of receipt of the notice.

(c) Follow up notification.

(1) The hospital must present a copy of the signed notice described in paragraph (b)(2) of this section to the beneficiary (or beneficiary's representative) prior to discharge. The notice should be given as far in advance of discharge as possible, but not more than 2 calendar days before discharge.

(2) Follow up notification is not required if the notice required under Sec. 405.1205(b) is delivered within 2 calendar days of discharge.

Coverage for Nursing Home Care

As discussed further in Chapter 7, Medicare covers medical *treatment*; it does not cover **custodial care** if it is the only kind of care needed. Custodial care is care that helps with usual daily activities, such as getting in and out of bed, eating, bathing, dressing, and using the bathroom. It may also include care that most people do themselves, like using eyedrops, oxygen, and taking care of colostomy or bladder catheters. Custodial care is often given in a nursing facility.

Medicare will cover **skilled care** only if *all* of the following are true:

Skilled Care
Involves medical care, some Medicare coverage

1. The patient has Medicare Part A Hospital Insurance and days left in the benefit period (discussed later) available to use.
2. The patient had a qualifying in-patient hospital stay of three consecutive days or more, not including the day the patient leaves the hospital.
3. The patient entered into a skilled nursing facility (SNF) within a short period of time (generally 30 days) of leaving the hospital.
4. The patient's doctor has ordered SNF services, which require the skills of professional personnel such as registered nurses, licensed practical nurses, physical therapists, occupational therapists, speech-language pathologists, or audiologists, and are furnished by, or under the supervision of, these skilled personnel.
5. The patient requires skilled care on a daily basis and the services, as a practical matter, can be provided only in an SNF on an inpatient basis. If the patient is in an SNF for skilled rehabilitation services only, care is considered daily care even if the therapy services are offered just five or six days a week.
6. The skilled services are reasonable and necessary for a medical condition that was treated during the qualifying hospital stay.
7. The SNF is Medicare-certified.

After leaving the SNF, a patient who re-enters the same or another SNF within 30 days may not need another three-day qualifying hospital stay to get additional SNF benefits. This is also true if the patient stops getting skilled care while in the SNF and then starts getting skilled care again within 30 days. A benefit period begins on the day the patient starts using hospital or SNF benefits under Part A. A patient can have as many as 100 days of SNF coverage in a benefit period. However, there is a gap: During days 21 through 100 of SNF care, the patient may have to pay up to $137.50 per day (2010 co-pay). After 100 days, Medicare pays nothing until a new benefit period begins and the patient re-qualifies for SNF care.

The benefit period ends when the patient has not been in an SNF or a hospital for at least 60 days in a row or, if in an SNF, has not received skilled care there for at least 60 days in a row. There is no limit to the number of benefit periods a patient can have.

Part B: Medical Insurance

Most people pay a monthly premium for Part B. The premium can vary with income and whether the recipient has the premium directly deducted from her social security check. In 2010 it was generally $96 to $110 per month. If a person chooses not to pay for Part B during the Initial Enrollment Period (**IEP**), a seven-month period beginning three months before and ending three months

IEP
Initial Enrollment Period

after the month in which she turns age 65, perhaps because she is still working, her future premiums may be higher. If the IEP is missed, there is no "redo," but an individual may be able to enroll during an eight-month Special Enrollment Period (**SEP**), generally if she had, but lost, group health insurance coverage other than by expiration of a COBRA continuation period. Otherwise the individual may be able to enroll during the General Enrollment Period (**GEP**), January 1 through March 31 each year, with coverage beginning on July 1. These limited enrollment periods can create serious problems for seniors, including coverage gaps and extra costs, as demonstrated in the case at the end of the chapter.

SEP
Special Enrollment Period

GEP
General Enrollment Period

Part B helps cover doctors' services and outpatient care. It also covers some other medical services that Part A does not cover, such as some of the services of physical and occupational therapists, and some home health care, when medically necessary.

Medicare sets amounts for procedures, and some doctors do not "accept assignment" of the approved amount as payment in full. In 2008, Medicare paid doctors on average 78 percent of what private insurers paid. A doctor can charge up to 15 percent more than Medicare's approved amount. Because of the low reimbursement rate, some doctors "opt out" of Medicare altogether. Many people are concerned about access to service as the first wave of the "baby boomer" generation becomes eligible for Medicare, particularly with respect to primary care physicians, an area already facing a shortage. The American Medical Association says that 17 percent of the more than 9,000 doctors surveyed restrict the number of Medicare patients in their practice. Among primary care physicians, the rate is 31 percent.[2]

The gap in Part B consists of a deductible ($155 per year in 2010) plus 20 percent of the Medicare-approved amount for services after meeting the $155 deductible. Medigap policies, described below, can cover part of this gap as well as the amount charged above the Medicare-approved amount. As of 2010, Medicare will pay for an annual checkup, and deductibles and co-pays will be eliminated for some preventative services and screenings.

Prescription Drug Coverage

Medicare Prescription Drug Coverage, also known as **Part D**, is insurance through private companies. Everyone with Medicare can get this relatively new coverage that may help lower prescription drug costs and help protect against higher costs in the future. Beneficiaries choose the drug plan and pay a monthly premium. According to the Kaiser Family Foundation, the national average for premiums in 2009 ranged from $10.30 to $136.80 per month, depending on the program chosen.[3] As with some other insurance plans, if a beneficiary decides not to enroll in a drug plan when they are first eligible, they may pay a penalty if they choose to join later. Beneficiaries may make changes to their coverage only during an annual election period (AEP).

Medicare Prescription Drug Coverage
A federal program to subsidize the costs of prescription drugs for Medicare beneficiaries

Part D
Insurance for prescription drug coverage

---

[2]*http://www.usatoday.com/news/washington/2010-06-20-medicare_N.htm*, visited September 18, 2010
[3]*http://www.kff.org/medicare/upload/7835.pdf*

The so-called "donut hole" of drug coverage refers to the difference between the initial coverage limit and the catastrophic coverage threshold. For example, in 2009, the gap opened after the cost of prescription drugs, including a patient's deductibles and co-pays, reached $2,700. The patient was then responsible for paying the next $3,453.75 until total drug costs reached $6,153.75. At that point, catastrophic coverage would set in and Medicare would again begin covering costs. The donut hole is gradually being eliminated by the use of rebates and price discounts subsidized by the pharmaceutical industry beginning in January 2011, the premium subsidy that higher-income Part D enrollees receive will be limited so that they will pay a higher portion of their plan premiums.

Supplemental Insurance

Under the original Medicare plan, patients can go to any doctor or hospital that accepts Medicare, but, as mentioned above, there are gaps in coverage. Many people obtain Medigap insurance, described below, to cover the gaps, co-pays, and deductibles.

Medicare Advantage Plans
Coverage, through private companies, to fill the gaps in Medicare

Part C
Prescription drug coverage

As an alternative, a Medicare beneficiary may choose from **Medicare Advantage Plans**, also known as **Part C,** which are operated by private companies and available in many areas. With one of these plans, which essentially combine Parts A and B and are available only to recipients who have both parts, there is no need for (or benefit to) a Medigap policy. Original Medicare beneficiaries are allowed to switch to Part C during an enrollment period each year. These plans include:

- Health Maintenance Organizations (HMOs)
- Preferred Provider Organizations (PPOs)
- Private Fee-for-Service Plans
- Medicare Special Needs Plans
- Medicare Medical Savings Account Plans (MSAs)

These plans may cover more services (such as dental care, vision care, and wellness programs) and have lower out-of-pocket costs than the Original Medicare Plan. Some plans even cover prescription drugs. Some plans, such as HMOs, limit the patient to certain doctors and certain hospitals to get covered services. The case at the end of the chapter demonstrates a problem that can arise with respect to limitations on patient choice.

Medigap insurance is sold by private insurance companies. By law, companies can offer only 12 standard Medigap insurance plans — plans referred to by the letters A through L. All plans with the same letter in the same state cover the same benefits, but the premiums can vary. All 12 Medigap policies cover basic benefits, but each has additional benefits that vary according to the plan. For example, all of the plans cover hospital days 61 through 150. Beyond the basics, each plan has a different set of benefits and/or deductibles. Plan A is the most basic plan. Plans B through L offer everything in Plan A and give even more coverage. Some cover part of skilled nursing home care. Medicare "Select" policies, available in some states, can be less expensive but limit the patient's choice of doctors and hospitals.

None of the standard Medigap plans cover the following services:

- Long-term care to help with daily functions, such as bathing, dressing, eating, or using the bathroom.
- Vision or dental care.
- Hearing aids.
- Private-duty nursing.
- Prescription drugs.

Medicare does not cover any health care costs incurred outside of the United States, but some Medigap plans cover emergency care outside the United States. Some plans cover certain at-home help if the patient is already receiving skilled home health care that is covered by Medicare. These plans cover at-home help for up to eight weeks after a patient no longer needs skilled care. Some plans offer limited preventative care benefits. Once a Medicare recipient obtains a Medigap plan, the insurance company must keep renewing it. As of 2010, substantial cuts in government subsidies for Medigap plans may mean higher premiums or reduced benefits for some 10 million participants. For more information on Medigap policies, see *http://www.medicare.gov/medigap/default.asp*.

EXHIBIT 6.3
Lisa Says

Lisa S. Wagman, CP, has been a practicing paralegal in New Jersey since 1980 and has extensive litigation expertise in the areas of product liability, medical negligence, personal injury, class actions, mass torts, and wrongful death, having represented both plaintiffs and defendants throughout this period. She earned an Associate's Degree in Legal Technology in 1983 (the first ever ABA-approved college degree program in New Jersey), and earned the designation of Certified Paralegal (CP) in 1985 through the National Association of Legal Assistants.

In January 2004, Lisa founded Social Security Disability Benefit Consultants in Cherry Hill, New Jersey. Since 2004, she has helped hundreds of claimants throughout the country win their disability claims before the Social Security Administration. She represents claimants at hearings before Administrative Law Judges, as permitted by the Code of Federal Regulations, and has maintained a 99.8 percent success rate on all of her clients' claims to date. She also gives lectures to paralegals concerning Social Security disability law, and authors educational e-newsletters to help the public understand the ins and outs of the disability claims process. She is a member of the National Association of Disability Representatives (NADR) and National Organization of Social Security Claimants Representatives (NOSSCR).

Ms. Wagman enjoys helping individuals win their disability claims and gain the financial security and health insurance benefits they so desperately need. She feels that it is the most rewarding work that she has ever done during her long career as a paralegal.

Assignments

1. The numbers in this book may no longer be accurate. Use the Medicare Web site to find the current Part A, Part B, and skilled nursing care deductibles and co-pays.

2. Use the same Web site to determine which diabetic services are covered by Medicare and the circumstances under which Medicare will pay for clinical trials.

3. Use the Medicare Web site to locate a female physician who practices geriatric care and participates in Medicare near your home.

4. Critical Thinking: Read the case summary at the end of the chapter, *Frazier v. Johnson*.

   - Why was the plaintiff acting pro se?
   - The plaintiff was apparently enrolled in a Medicare Advantage (MA) program. The regulation at issue provides:

   MA organization must meet the following requirements: . . .

   (3) Specialty care. Provide or arrange for necessary specialty care, and in particular give women enrollees the option of direct access to a women's health specialist within the network for women's routine and preventive health care services provided as basic benefits (as defined in Sec. 422.2). The MA organization arranges for specialty care outside of the plan provider network when network providers are unavailable or inadequate to meet an enrollee's medical needs.

   - What does this section mean, in the context of the number of providers "opting out" of Medicare?
   - What does the reference to "emergent care" mean? Examine the CFR restriction: *http://edocket.access.gpo.gov/cfr_2009/octqtr/ 42cfr422.112.htm.* What would happen if no MA network provider was available and the situation was critical, such as a burst appendix?
   - Why do you think the plaintiff went to an out-of-plan provider?

5. Critical Thinking: Read the case summary at the end of the chapter, *Bolognese v. Leavitt*.

   - Why do you think plaintiffs, like the plaintiff in this case, are often represented by paralegals at administrative hearings?
   - Why do you think the plaintiff failed to enroll in time to avoid the surcharge?
   - Do you think that people are often unaware of the need to enroll in Medicare during the enrollment period, particularly if they are still working and covered by employer insurance or if they retired early and are receiving social security and think that enrollment at 65 is automatic?
   - Why is there no mention of a surcharge for Part A coverage?
   - Why might an individual be reluctant to enroll in Part B?

- Do you think the surcharge is too harsh? Do you think the plaintiff should have obtained an equitable remedy?
- About how much would the surcharge have been if the premium was $100 per month?

Review Questions

1. Identify the groups that qualify for Medicare.
2. Define what is covered by Parts A, B, C, and D.
3. What is meant by the letter designations on Medigap policies?
4. Describe the differences between custodial care and skilled care.
5. If a patient has no Medigap coverage and spends 97 days in the hospital, what additional information do you need to determine her financial responsibility?
6. Why might a doctor not accept Medicare patients?
7. Which parts of Medicare generally require payment of a premium?
8. Explain the importance of enrollment periods.

Bolognese v. Leavitt

2008 U.S. Dist. LEXIS 49966 (W.D., N.Y., 2008)

Gerald Bolognese ("Plaintiff") brings this action pursuant to 42 U.S.C. §§405(g) and 1395ff(b), seeking review of a final decision of the Secretary of the United States Department of Health and Human Services ("Secretary") denying his request for a waiver of a surcharge imposed on his monthly Medicare Part B premiums. Specifically, Plaintiff alleges that the decision of Administrative Law Judge ("ALJ") Dombeck denying his request for a waiver was erroneous and not supported by substantial evidence contained in the record and was not supported by the applicable law.

Plaintiff seeks reversal of the Secretary's ruling. The Secretary moves for judgment on the pleadings on the grounds that ALJ Dombeck's decision was supported by substantial evidence contained in the record. Plaintiff cross-moves for judgment on the pleadings on the grounds that the ALJ's decision was contrary to law, was not supported by substantial evidence, and resulted from bias.

Plaintiff, born on January 20, 1943, was employed as a tire builder for Dunlop Tires, Inc. from 1967 to 1991. As a result of a back injury sustained by Plaintiff in the late 1980s, Dunlop Tires placed him on disability retirement effective February 1, 1991. Upon his retirement, under the terms of the Goodyear Dunlop Tires North America Ltd. 1950 Pension Plan, Plaintiff became entitled to a basic pension benefit and a Temporary Disability Supplement. Plaintiff also was entitled to continued ealth insurance coverage under the Dunlop Plan. However, the Dunlop Plan provided that once a retired employee became eligible for Medicare coverage, the plan would pay secondary to Medicare, thereby covering only the portions of medical bills not covered by Medicare. Once the Dunlop Plan became the secondary provider, it would pay the Medicare-eligible participant a "Special Medicare Benefit" in order to partially reimburse the participant for his or her Medicare Part B premiums.

Plaintiff applied for Social Security disability benefits in 1991. In 1992, following denial by the Social Security Administration and subsequent appeal, an ALJ awarded disability benefits retroactive to August 1991. When Dunlop Plan learned that Plaintiff had become eligible for Social Security disability benefits, it terminated his Temporary Disability Supplement, effective February 1, 1993.

Under the Social Security Act, individuals under the age of 65, such as Plaintiff at the time he was awarded Social Security benefits, are eligible to enroll in Medicare Part A hospital insurance benefits once they have been entitled to Social Security disability benefits for 25 months. Individuals entitled to enroll in Part A may also enroll in the Part B program. 42 C.F.R. §407.10. Plaintiff became entitled to Medicare Part A and Part B supplemental medical insurance in August 1993. He enrolled in Part A during his initial enrollment period (May 1, 1993, through November 30, 1993). He would have been automatically enrolled in Part B at that time, but he opted to decline enrollment in Part B. The Dunlop Plan continued to pay on a primary basis for medical services provided to Plaintiff until 2002.

Upon declining Part B coverage during the initial enrollment period, an individual may subsequently enroll during the "general enrollment period," *see* 42 C.F.R. §407.15(a), from January 1 through March 31 of each calendar year.

By failing to enroll for Part B coverage after expiration of the initial enrollment period, the [SSA] may require a Medicare applicant to pay a surcharge on the monthly Medicare premiums. This surcharge is calculated by increasing the monthly premium by ten percent for each full twelve-month period between the close of the individual's initial enrollment period and the close of the enrollment period in which he enrolled. *Id.* §§408.22, 408.24(a).

Plaintiff enrolled in the Part B program on January 15, 2003, and his Part B coverage became effective on July 1, 2003. [T]he Social Security Administration determined that because Plaintiff had delayed his enrollment by a total of 112 months (from November 30, 1993, the last day of his initial enrollment period, through March 31, 2003, the last day of the general enrollment period for 2003), his monthly premium would be increased by a 90 percent surcharge-ten percent for each period of twelve months of the delayed enrollment.

Plaintiff requested reconsideration and an administrative hearing on the imposition of the surcharge. Plaintiff appeared and was represented by a paralegal at an administrative hearing before ALJ Dombeck on September 28, 2004. In a comprehensive and well-reasoned decision dated December 6, 2004, the ALJ denied Plaintiff's request for waiver of the surcharge. Plaintiff made a timely request for review to the Medicare Appeals Council. The ALJ's decision became the final decision of the Secretary when the Appeals Council denied Plaintiff's request for review of the ALJ's decision on May 31, 2006. On July 26, 2006, Plaintiff filed this action appealing the Secretary's decision.

In order to waive the 90 percent surcharge . . . , Plaintiff would have to show that he qualifies for a special enrollment period, or that he is entitled to equitable relief under the applicable statute or regulations. Because Plaintiff failed to demonstrate eligibility for either, I affirm the ALJ's decision denying Plaintiff's request for a waiver. A special enrollment period is available to disabled individuals under the age of 65 if, at the time of their initial enrollment period, they were covered by a large group health plan, such as Dunlop Plan, by means of their "current employment status." 42 U.S.C. §1395p(i)(1); 42 C.F.R. §407.20. At the time of his initial enrollment period, Plaintiff was covered under the Dunlop Plan as a retiree, not as a current employee. Therefore, the ALJ's determination that Plaintiff does not qualify for a special enrollment period under 42 U.S.C. §1395p(i)(1) or 42 C.F.R. §407.20 is in accordance with applicable law.

Equitable relief, including establishment of a special initial enrollment period or a special general enrollment period, as well as adjustment of premiums, is available to a Medicare Part B applicant if the applicant meets the statutory or regulatory requirements for such relief. See 42 U.S.C. §1395p(h); 42 C.F.R. §407.32. Under the Social Security Act, equitable relief is available for a claimant whose "nonenrollment in [Medicare Part B] is unintentional, inadvertent, or erroneous and is the result of the error, misrepresentation, or inaction of an officer, employee, or agent of the Federal Government, or its instrumentalities . . . ." ALJ Dombeck correctly determined that Plaintiff's delayed enrollment in Medicare Part B was not attributable to any error, misrepresentation, or inaction of an officer, employee, or agent of the Federal Government or its instrumentalities. I find that there is substantial evidence in the record to support the ALJ's determination on this matter.

The Program Operations Manual System ("POMS") is an internal interpretative guideline issued by the Social Security Administration. POMS provides guidelines for instances when the Social Security Administration might provide equitable relief to a Medicare Part B applicant, such as granting a special enrollment period or waiving or reducing a premium surcharge. See POMS §HI 00805.320. Plaintiff claims to qualify for equitable relief under §HI 00805.320 of POMS which provides: A disabled beneficiary may allege he/she was misinformed about whether [a large group health plan (such as Dunlop Plan)] was the primary payer of benefits. If . . . the information alleged was given by an employee or agent of the Federal Government . . . the employer, or by the [large group health plan], equitable relief may be granted to correct the results of the incorrect information. However, even if Plaintiff met the requirements for equitable relief set forth in the POMS, the POMS provisions lack the force of law and create no judicially-enforceable rights, *See Schweiker v. Hansen*, 450 U.S. 785 (1981) (finding that a handbook for internal use by Social Security Administration employees "has no legal force, and . . . does not bind the [Social Security Administration]") . . . . . . See also Social Security Administration, POMS Disclaimer, *https://secure.ssa.gov/apps10/poms.nsf/aboutpoms* (June 24, 2008) ("[t]he POMS states only internal SSA guidance. It is not intended to, does not, and may not be relied upon to create any rights enforceable at law by any party in a civil or criminal action."). Accordingly, the POMS does not aid Plaintiff in establishing a claim for equitable relief. As ALJ Dombeck noted, the Social Security Act and the corresponding regulations do not extend equitable relief to a claimant whose delay in enrolling for Medicare Part B resulted from the error, misinformation, or inaction of a private sector, non-governmental source, such as Dunlop Tires or the Dunlop Plan. See 42 U.S.C. §1395p(h); 42 C.F.R. §407.32. There is substantial evidence in the record to support the ALJ's finding that neither Dunlop Tires nor the Dunlop Plan insurance providers are an instrumentality of the Federal Government. Therefore, even if those entities did provide Plaintiff with incorrect information, their representatives cannot bind the Secretary.

[T]here is substantial evidence to support the ALJ's finding that Plaintiff's delayed enrollment was not attributable to misinformation from Dunlop Tire, Dunlop Plan, or any of either entities' agents or employees. Plaintiff contends that Dunlop Plan administrators misled and misinformed him by failing to inform him that he should have enrolled in Medicare Part B in August 1993, and that Plan continued to pay as primary insurer when it should have paid as a secondary insurer, thereby causing him to delay enrollment. Plaintiff's claim that Dunlop Plan, under provisions of its health benefits plan, was responsible for informing him of his need to enroll in Medicare Part B is not borne out by the evidence. Plaintiff has failed to provide any evidence establishing that Dunlop took on the affirmative duty to notify plan participants as to when they were required to apply for governmental benefits. At the conclusion of the hearing, the ALJ afforded Plaintiff extra time to supplement the record with the contract, which Plaintiff claimed established the Dunlop Plan's responsibility for informing Plan participants as to when they were required to apply for governmental benefits. Plaintiff, however, did not produce the contract, or any other evidence that would support his claim.

Plaintiff, at the administrative hearing, introduced the written notice that he received from the [SSA] indicating that his Disability benefits had been granted on appeal. Plaintiff claims that this document established that Dunlop knew of the successful Social Security appeal, and that Dunlop should have known that plaintiff eventually would become eligible for Medicare SMI thereafter. The ALJ found (and it was not disputed) that Dunlop acknowledged receipt of the notification issued in December 1992, but also found that plaintiff did not comply with Dunlop's request in 1993 for a copy of the award notice, thus preventing Dunlop from determining when its obligation to act as a primary payer ceased. The ALJ concluded that Dunlop continued to act as a primary payer "due in substantial part to failure to provide the Plan with necessary information that had been requested." Although plaintiff was notified that he was being awarded Social Security Disability benefits in late 1992, he failed to provide Dunlop with the information it requested, and yet insisted that Dunlop should have notified him of his obligation to enroll for Medicare Part B. [G]iven the lack of evidence that would support Plaintiff's claim that the Dunlop Plan had a responsibility to notify him when he should enroll in Medicare Part B, I find that the ALJ's denial of equitable relief is supported by substantial evidence in the record and is in accordance with applicable law.

In Plaintiff's cross-motion, he alleges biased decision making on behalf of the ALJ. Plaintiff failed to raise the claim during the hearing or in his request for review before the Appeals Council. Failure to raise a bias claim at the administrative level constitutes a waiver of the right to object to conduct of the ALJ. Therefore, I find that Plaintiff waived his bias claim by failing to raise it at the administrative level. I conclude that the ALJ's decision is supported by substantial evidence in the record and is in accordance with applicable law . . . , I grant the Secretary's motion for judgment on the pleadings, and deny Plaintiff's cross-motion. Plaintiff's Complaint is dismissed with prejudice.

Frazier v. Johnson
312 Fed. Appx. 879 (9th Cir. 2009)

Frazier, an enrollee in a qualified Medicare plan, appeals pro se the district court's summary judgment upholding the Secretary's denial of reimbursement for the cost of surgery performed by a doctor outside of the plan. Although our review is de novo, we will not reverse the Secretary's decision unless it is "arbitrary, capricious, an abuse of discretion, not in accordance with the law, or unsupported by substantial evidence on the record taken as a whole." Applying that standard, we affirm.

Frazier contends his out-of-plan surgery was medically necessary and superior to what his plan offered. The record indicates, however, that his Medicare health provider, Kaiser Foundation Health Plan, offered similar, if not essentially the same, treatment that Frazier received from the out-of-plan physician. [A]n independent review board, the Center for Health Dispute Resolution (CHDR), rejected Frazier's request for the out-of-plan surgery, reasoning that Kaiser offered "a medically appropriate treatment plan" and there was no evidence that the out-of-plan treatment was either "medically superior" or "medically preferable" for Frazier. An administrative law judge (ALJ) also denied Frazier's request for reimbursement, finding that Frazier "did not have an emergent medical condition or other reason for going to an out-of-plan specialist" and noting that Kaiser "did not refuse medical treatment, but instead, offered [Frazier] . . . medical services that met the standard of reasonable medical care."

[S]ubstantial evidence supports the administrative determination that Kaiser offered a surgical procedure adequate to meet Frazier's medical needs, such that out-of-plan specialty care was not necessary. Kaiser's treatment was medically adequate to treat Frazier's condition and Kaiser's doctors were qualified to perform the procedure. Moreover, there is no basis to conclude that Kaiser's proposed procedure did not adequately address Frazier's concerns regarding potential side-effects. Thus, Frazier did not demonstrate that he required "specialty care . . . outside of the plan" or that his provider's services were "unavailable or inadequate" to meet his needs. 42 C.F.R. §422.112(a)(3) . . . .

Frazier raises various constitutional claims, but only his due process claim warrants discussion. "Due process protects against the deprivation of life, liberty, or property." Assuming the denial of Medicare benefits implicates such interests, Frazier was entitled to adequate notice and "opportunity to be heard at a meaningful time and in a meaningful manner." Although Frazier had ample opportunity to present his case, including two internal reviews by Kaiser, an independent review by CHDR, an evidentiary hearing before an ALJ, appeal to the Medicare Appeals Council, and a hearing in federal district court, he argues he was denied due process because he was precluded from making "a full presentation of the case." He cites the ALJ's rejections of his requests for subpoenas, the admission of hearsay evidence, the ALJ's alleged bias, and the district court's . . . summary judgment. None of these events denied Frazier due process of law. The ALJ did not abuse his discretion in denying the subpoenas because there was no showing that other witnesses were necessary given the parties' submission of documentary evidence in the administrative record. As we previously indicated, hearsay is generally admissible in administrative proceedings. Moreover, there is no indication the ALJ was biased. AFFIRMED.

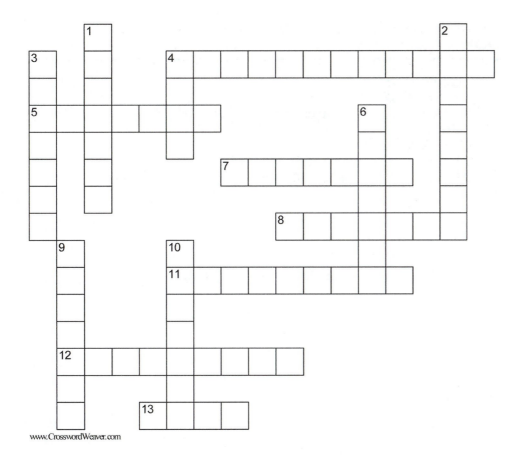

www.CrosswordWeaver.com

ACROSS

4. Part D covers _____ drugs
5. Care covered by Medicare
7. MSN, Medicare _____ notice
8. Part B is _____ insurance
11. Also known at Part C, Medicare _____ plans
12. Care not covered by Medicare
13. Medicare pays a _____ rate, giving hospitals incentive to discharge early

DOWN

1. Sold by private companies
2. Covered by Part A
3. Lifetime _____ days can be used after 90 hospital days
4. PRO, _____ review
6. SNF, skilled _____ facility
9. Must be given near admission and discharge
10. Most people have paid for Medicare by _____ taxes

7

◆ ◆ ◆

Medicaid

◆ ◆ ◆

Overview
Long-Term Care
Protecting the Community Spouse
Transfers, Trusts, "Look-Backs," and Estate Recovery
Treatment of Income
    Step-by-Step Medicaid Preparation

Objectives

When you complete this chapter, you will:

- Know your state guidelines for Medicaid eligibility for long-term care
- Understand financial protection available to a patient's non-institution-alized spouse
- Be aware of the look-back rules and the potential hazards of gifting
- Identify the types of trusts that may be used to provide for family members

Overview

At the time of this writing, Medicaid was the largest single health program in the United States. According to the Kaiser Foundation, Medicaid is responsible for payment of roughly one in five health care dollars and one-half of nursing home dollars. Helping clients navigate the Medicaid maze is a huge part of the practice of elder law, but it is also the most difficult part because the law differs from state to state and because the law changed drastically with the enactment of the Deficit Reduction Act of 2005 (**DRA**), 42 U.S.C. 1396 p.

Medicaid is a state-administered program, partially funded by the federal government, that is available to certain individuals and families who meet guidelines relating to income, assets, and resources. Because it is state administered, some states have names for their programs other than "Medicaid." For example, California has MediCal and Massachusetts has MassHealth. Medicaid makes payments directly to eligible providers. Patients are restricted in their choice of providers, and, because Medicaid does not fully reimburse providers, many providers limit the number of Medicaid patients they serve.

Not all low-income people qualify, but a person is not automatically disqualified from receiving Medicaid simply because of age, employment, or even citizenship (legal aliens may qualify). Medicaid recipients do not necessarily obtain any other form of benefits (such as SSI or welfare). A state may require that the applicant be a resident of the state. States have some discretion in determining criteria for Medicaid eligibility and co-payment requirements. In general, the criteria for eligibility are structured to provide benefits to pregnant women, children, and people with specific medical conditions. This chapter will focus on program characteristics most relevant to elder clients, rather than those related to children and pregnant women. Keep in mind, however, that Medicaid, and particularly the **CHIP** programs, might be relevant to a grandparent raising grandchildren.

The 2010 Patient Protection and Affordable Care Act requires gradual elimination of "categories" and calls for expansion of coverage to all adults under age 65 with incomes below 133 percent of the Federal Poverty Level by 2014. To offset a requirement that all individuals have health insurance, the law also creates "exchanges," or insurance markets, which individuals can use to purchase coverage from private health insurance plans. Low-income individuals will qualify for subsidies to make coverage provided in the exchange more affordable. This will enable a significant number of people who are currently uninsured, many of whom are age 55 to 65, to obtain coverage. States are required to operate their programs in a manner that ensures that beneficiaries will actually receive promised services, not simply be reimbursed if they manage to acquire services on their own. This does not mean that states have to directly provide medical services by employing providers, but simply confirms that states must administer plans in a way that ensures that services and care are actually available in accordance with statutory requirements.

Services and benefits available in addition to traditional long-term Medicaid for nursing home care differ from state to state. The trend is moving away from institutional nursing home care to home- and community-based care. Most states offer home and community options under the "waiver and demonstration" project authority that is in the statute to allow states flexibility in operating Medicaid programs. For example, Illinois has a Community Care Program under which an aged, disabled, or blind individual who meets income and assets requirements can obtain a card for medical services on a monthly basis. Unlike

DRA
Deficit Reduction Act of 2005

CHIP
Children's Health Insurance Program

long-term Medicaid, the program does not consider asset transfers to determine eligibility. The program has provisions for emergency medical care for non-citizens who are not eligible for long-term Medicaid and in-home care in a variety of circumstances. In addition, Illinois is one of a few states that offer coverage for supportive living facilities.

Tip

Find out which demonstration or waiver programs are offered in your state at *http://www.cms.gov/MedicaidStWaivProgDemoPGI/08_WavMap.asp.*

Medicare beneficiaries who meet their state's income and assets requirements may obtain Medicaid benefits to cover costs, deductibles, and co-payments not covered by Medicare. People who receive both Medicare and Medicaid are called **"dual eligibles."** Most significant to elder law practitioners is the fact that Medicaid can pay for nursing home care that is not covered by Medicare or private insurance and is beyond the means of the patient. A new law requires the Centers for Medicare and Medicaid Services (CMS) to establish a Federal Co-ordinated Health Care Office that is tasked with leading efforts to improve integration of Medicare and Medicaid benefits for dual eligibles.

"Dual Eligibles"
Receives both Medicare and Medicaid

Long-Term Care

The October 2010 MetLife Market Survey of Nursing Home, Assisted Living, Adult Day Services, and Home Care Costs studied costs at licensed facilities throughout the country and revealed that average rates for a private room increased by 4.6 percent, from $219 daily or $79,935 annually in 2009, to $229 daily or $83,585 annually in 2010. National average rates for a semi-private room increased by 3.5 percent from $198 daily or $72,270 annually in 2009 to $205 daily or $74,825 annually in 2010.[1] This kind of expense can rapidly deplete the lifetime savings of elderly couples, even if they have planned and saved. When the money runs out, nursing home residents turn to Medicaid, but some nursing facilities take only private-pay patients, and others require that the patient be able to pay for a certain amount of time in order to be admitted. Some facilities allocate a specific number of "Medicaid beds," creating a risk that a private-pay patient's funds will run out at a time when no Medicaid beds are available. Federal law generally prohibits a facility from evicting a non-paying resident unless another facility is willing to accept that individual, and many elder law experts worry that under new rules (described below), nursing care facilities will become bankrupt and close.

---

[1]From *http://www.metlife.com/assets/cao/mmi/publications/studies/2010/mmi-2010-market-survey-long-term-care-costs.pdf*

In general, a client should apply for Medicaid if her income is low, she has a health care need, and she appears to fit into one of the categories. A state caseworker will then assess eligibility. Coverage may start retroactive to any or all of the three months prior to application, if the individual would have been eligible during the retroactive period. However, people sometimes make serious mistakes in attempting to deplete their resources so that they can get Medicaid while still "leaving something" for their families. Careful questioning is essential.

Determining Medicaid eligibility is extremely complicated and, as described in Exhibit 7.3, requires a great deal of sensitivity to the client's needs and desires. The starting point is assessment of the client's resources. Existing resources determine whether the client is eligible. Applicants sign a waiver to enable the state to verify assets by looking at credit reports and tax records. Misrepresentation is a crime.

States differ with respect to whether they consider income as an asset in this determination. Assets that are generally not considered in determining eligibility include the following:

- Personal possessions, such as clothing, furniture, and jewelry.
- One motor vehicle, regardless of value, used for transportation of the applicant or a household member — check state law concerning exclusion of vehicles.
- The applicant's principal residence in the same state in which the individual is applying for coverage. The residence includes surrounding land, which is especially important to farm families. Some states require proof of a reasonable likelihood of being able to return home, or assume "abandonment" after a specified period (such as 120 days), but the residence may be exempt under other circumstances described below. Under the Deficit Reduction Act of 2005 (DRA), a principal residence that is not inhabited by a spouse or dependent relative is exempt only to the extent that the applicant's equity is less than $500,000, with the states having the option of raising this limit to $750,000. Although a home is not counted as an asset, it may be subject to recovery (discussed later) if it passes through the estate of the Medicaid recipient.
- Prepaid funeral plans and a small amount of life insurance.
- Assets that are considered "inaccessible," such as certain trusts described later.

Tip

Where does your state stand on consideration of income and home equity limits? See *http://www.statehealthfacts.org/comparemaptable.jsp?ind=817&cat=4.*

If the client has too many resources to be eligible, the process ends until those resources are depleted. If the client's resources allow him to qualify, income determines how much he pays toward his own care each month. For a single client (unmarried, no dependents), the resource determination is generally fairly simple. As you can see from Exhibit 7.1 on the next page, in North Carolina, such a client may have no more than $2,000 in resources.

Protecting the Community Spouse

But what if one spouse needs nursing home care and the other does not? Does the spouse who is still living at home in the community (the "community spouse") have to lose everything before Medicaid "kicks in" to cover the cost of nursing home care? Much of the practice of elder law involves planning to avoid impoverishment of the community spouse and any dependent children of the spouse in the nursing home. In some circumstances, it may be possible to preserve some assets for other family members with careful planning.

Federal spousal impoverishment provisions enacted in 1988 (42 U.S.C. §1396r-5) apply when one spouse enters a nursing facility or other medical institution and is expected to remain there for at least 30 days. When a Medicaid application is filed, a caseworker does an analysis of the applicant's resources. The resources of both spouses, regardless of ownership, are combined. The couple's home, household goods, a vehicle, and burial funds are not included in the couple's combined resources. The result is used to determine the spousal share, which is one-half of the couple's combined countable resources.

If the individual's countable resources are above the state resource standard, the applicant may be able to divest herself of assets to become eligible. Advance planning sometimes consists of a "spend down" to get to the eligibility level, which can mean:

- Paying for home care prior to entry into a facility, by entering into a detailed care contract under which the patient pays a friend or relative for care. In order to not be considered a transfer subject to penalty (described later), the contract must be in place at the time the care is given and the caretaker should keep careful records.
- Purchasing a newer car for the community spouse.
- Paying off the mortgage or other debts.
- Making upgrades to the house and furnishings (even buying a new house) if the house is exempt as the applicant's homestead or as the home of a spouse or relative as described later.
- Purchasing medical equipment, such as a wheelchair, lift van, or hearing aid.
- Purchasing a prepaid funeral package for the applicant and the spouse.
- Purchasing an **immediate annuity** to provide a regular income for the community spouse or the nursing home spouse. This is discussed in the next section.

Immediate Annuity
Purchase of a series of payments, to begin immediately after purchase

EXHIBIT 7.1
State Medicaid Guidelines

Because Medicaid differs from state to state, you must determine the information
for your own state. First, find and bookmark the Web site for your state agency,
using either *http://www.nasmd.org/links/state_medicaid_links.asp* or*http://www.
ncsl.org/default.aspx?tabid=20044*. Next, find the eligibility requirements for
aged beneficiaries.

For example, the North Carolina Web site (*http://www.dhhs.state.nc.us/dma/
medicaid/basicmedelig.pdf*) provides the following guidelines for full Medicaid
coverage:

Basic Eligibility Requirement:	Age 65 or older
Whose Resources Count:	Spouse's income and resources if live together
Income Limit:	100% of Poverty 1 person in household: $ 903/mo 2 people in household: $1,215 /mo
Resource Limit:	SSI Limits 1 person in household: $2,000 2 people in household: $3,000

Furthermore, note these provisions:

*Individuals in nursing facilities generally do not have to meet a de-
ductible to be eligible for Medicaid. However, they must pay all of their
monthly income, less a $30 personal needs allowance and the cost of
medical expenses not covered by Medicaid or other insurance to the
nursing facility. Medicaid pays the remainder ... . When an individual is in a nursing facility and has a spouse living at home, a
portion of the income of the spouse in the facility may be protected to bring
the income of the spouse at home up to a level specified by federal law ...
$1,822 [to] $2,739 depending upon ... cost for housing. The amount
protected for the at-home spouse is not counted in determining the eligibility of the spouse in the nursing facility ... . Additionally, the
countable resources of the couple are combined and a portion is protected
for the spouse at home. That portion is 1/2 the total value of the countable
resources, but currently not less than $21,912 or more than $109,560.
The amount protected for the at-home spouse is not countable in determining the eligibility of the spouse in the facility ... . When a person
gives away resources and does not receive compensation ... he may be
penalized. Medicaid will not pay for care in a nursing facility or care
provided under the Community Alternative Placement program or other
in-home health services and supplies for a period of time that depends on
the value of the transferred resource.*

From the combined countable resources, a protected resource amount (**PRA**) is subtracted. The PRA is the greatest of the following:

(**PRA**) **Protected Resource Amount**
Exempt from inclusion in Medicaid eligibility calculation

- The state spousal resource standard, which a state can set at any amount between $21,912 and $109,560 (as of 2010).
- An amount transferred to the community spouse for support as directed by a court order.
- An amount designated by a state hearing officer to raise the community spouse's protected resources up to the minimum monthly maintenance needs standard.

After the PRA is subtracted from the combined countable resources, the remainder is considered available to the spouse residing in the medical institution. If the amount (called "countable resources") is below the state's resource standard, the individual is eligible for Medicaid. Once resource eligibility is determined, any resources belonging to the community spouse are no longer considered available to the spouse in the medical facility.

In some states, most notably New York, the PRA may be inadequate to support the community spouse. In 1998 New York passed a law that authorized a community spouse to refuse to have his assets used in the computation of the institutionalized spouse's Medicaid eligibility. This is called **spousal refusal.**

Spousal Refusal
Spouse refuses to support Medicaid patient

Transfers, Trusts, "Look-Backs," and Estate Recovery

What if the client is not married but does not want to spend her own money on care? In most states a person with more than $2,000 in assets cannot qualify for Medicaid. As previously mentioned, the client's equity in her home, up to $750,000, is not counted as an asset if the client meets state guidelines for determining "intent to return." Many clients believe that they can give gifts of a certain amount each year ($13,000 per recipient in 2009) "with no consequences," but they are confusing estate and gift tax consequences (see Chapter 8) with Medicaid eligibility. While Medicaid looks to care for the institutionalized individual without impoverishing the community spouse or dependents, it is not intended to protect the "inheritance" of others. The common theme of the DRA provisions, as you will see, is that you cannot have your cake and eat it too! Some strategies may help a family in a particular situation, but they are not intended to allow a person to be cared for by Medicaid while leaving substantial assets to non-disabled heirs.

The transfer provisions examine gifts—not transfers for market value—or valid spend-downs such as the purchase of a new car or a new furnace before entering a nursing facility. Since enactment of the DRA, most states "look back" to find transfers of assets by the institutionalized person (or on behalf of that person) for 60 months prior to the later of the date the individual was institutionalized or the date of application for Medicaid. Before the DRA, a 36-month look-back was standard, and many people may still believe that is the law.

If a transfer of assets for less than fair market value occurred during the look-back period, the state must withhold payment for long-term care services for a period of time referred to as the penalty period. The length of the penalty period is determined by dividing the value of the transferred asset by the average monthly private-pay rate for nursing facility care in the state. There is no limit to the length of the penalty period. If there is a transfer during the look-back period, the penalty period is calculated, not from the date of the transfer, but from a date when the transferor has moved to a nursing home, has spent down to the asset limit for Medicaid eligibility, has applied for Medicaid coverage, and has been approved for coverage but for the transfer. This is a relatively new law, and implementation may differ from state to state—under prior law the penalty period began with the date of the gift.

Example

Pat Patient had assets of $100,000 and gave each of her three children $10,000 per year during each of three years, assuming that she would never need a nursing home. Pat was not motivated to "cheat the system"—she was helping her children through times when they had to pay medical bills and college tuition for their own children and experienced periods of unemployment. About 18 months after giving the last gift, Pat is disabled by a stroke and her condition is such that her children cannot provide the care she needs. Pat enters a nursing home with a cost of $5,000 per month. Because of her monthly income and $10,000 in remaining cash, Pat is able to pay for three months of care before her savings run out. The total transferred amount, $90,000, is divided by a $3,000 average monthly private-pay rate for Pat's state, resulting in a 30-month penalty period. Her income is insufficient to cover the cost. Unfortunately for Pat, under the DRA the 30-month penalty period starts now—how will she pay for care?

The DRA calculation of the penalty period from the date of eligibility, rather than the date of transfer, has largely limited a strategy previously used, called "half a loaf." Under "half a loaf" planning, Pat could have given away $50,000, creating a 17-month penalty, but at the same time kept $50,000 to pay for care during the penalty period. Under the DRA the penalty period does not start until Pat is down to $2,000, leaving her with no assets to pay for care during the penalty period.

The principal exceptions to which the penalty is not applied are as follows:

- Transfers to a spouse, or to a third party for the sole benefit of the spouse.
- Transfers by a spouse to a third party for the sole benefit of the spouse.
- Transfers to certain disabled individuals (a blind or disabled child or any permanently disabled individual younger than 65 years of age), or to trusts established for those individuals.
- Transfer of a home to a child who is under age 21 or who has lived with and provided care for the parent for at least two years prior to the parent's move to a nursing home.
- Transfer of a home to a sibling who has an equity interest and who lived in the home for at least a year before the move to a nursing home.
- Transfers for a purpose other than to qualify for Medicaid; and "transfers where imposing a penalty would cause undue hardship." (See Exhibit 7.2 for an example of hardship waiver guidelines.)

EXHIBIT 7.2
Hardship Waivers[2]

States generally have procedures for waiving requirements that would result in undue hardship. However, in most states it is still unclear how these waivers will be applied under the new DRA. Here is an example from the North Carolina statute:

§108A-58.2. Waiver of transfer of assets penalty due to undue hardship.

(a) Prior to imposition of a period of ineligibility for long-term care services because of an asset transfer, also known as a penalty period, the county department of social services shall notify the individual of the individual's right to request a waiver of the penalty period because it will cause an undue hardship to the individual. The director of the county department of social services, or the director's designee shall grant a waiver of the penalty period due to undue hardship if the individual meets the conditions set forth in subsection (e) of this section. As used in this section, "long term care services" are those services described in 42 U.S.C. §1396p(c)(1)(C)(i) and (ii).

(b) When a Medicaid applicant who is requesting Medicaid to pay for institutional care requests a waiver of a penalty period due to undue hardship, the determination of whether to waive the penalty period shall be processed as part of the Medicaid application and is subject to the application processing standards set forth in 10A NCAC 21B.0203.

(c) When an ongoing Medicaid recipient applies for institutional care or is receiving Medicaid payment for institutional care receives the notice described in subsection (a) of this section, the recipient has 12 calendar days from the date of the notice to request a waiver of the penalty due to undue hardship . . . .

The method by which assets are transferred generally makes no difference. So, if Pat Patient transferred $90,000 to an annuity for herself or a trust for her children during the look-back period, nothing changes. Suppose that Pat Patient had thought ahead and, six years before she went into the nursing home, established the "Patient Family Trust" into which she deposited $90,000. Would the money be "protected"? Probably not.

In determining whether a trust is available as a resource, the most important factor is how the trust fits into the exceptions previously discussed. Regardless of whether there are any trusts involved, the first step in determining Medicaid eligibility is calculation of combined countable resources, as described above. Trusts that will be included in that calculation:

---

[2]*http://www.ncga.state.nc.us/EnactedLegislation/Statutes/pdf/BySection/Chapter_108A/GS_108A-58.2.pdf*

Self-settled Trusts
Trust created by an individual, with her own assets, for her own benefit

Self-settled trusts: Principal of a trust created with the potential Medicaid recipient's ("patient") own assets if the patient can potentially benefit, either because the trust is revocable or because the patient could receive principal — regardless of whether the patient actually receives that benefit. Even if principal is not available to the patient for purposes of determining eligibility, income of such a trust that is available must be applied to pay for care. Like the non-trust assets of the patient's spouse, a trust created by a living spouse is counted to the extent that the patient or spouse could potentially benefit.

There are exceptions — the so-called "payback" trusts or "pooled" trusts. Funds remaining in a "payback" trust after the patient's death are used to pay Medicaid for the cost of the patient's care. The purpose of these "d(4)" (a reference to 42 U.S.C. §1396p(d)(4)) exceptions is to provide the patient with a better quality of life. Payback trusts can serve to pass wealth to family members after the patient's death only in the unlikely situation that the funds remaining upon the patient's death exceed what Medicaid paid for care:

Supplemental Needs Trusts
Created to fund needs of a disabled individual that are not covered by public funds

- Irrevocable **supplemental needs trusts** (also called "special needs trusts") established by a parent, grandparent, guardian, or court for the benefit of a disabled patient under the age of 65, using the patient's own funds.
- Irrevocable supplemental needs "pooled" trusts established by or for a disabled patient, using the patient's own funds. The trust must be part of a pool managed by a nonprofit organization for the benefit of each individual included in the trust. Funds remaining upon the patient's death are used to reimburse Medicaid or remain with the nonprofit organization.
- Some states permit a disabled patient age 65 or older to use his own money to create a pooled payback trust to pay for special needs not covered by Medicaid, such as mobility devices, hair care, dental care, and many other therapies.
- In states that impose an income limit on Medicaid eligibility, so-called "Miller" or "Utah Gap" trusts may be funded with pension, Social Security, and other non-investment income of the patient whose income would otherwise be too high to qualify for Medicaid, but insufficient to pay for care.

Vested Interest
A right protected by law

Discretionary
Including the ability to act or decide according to one's own judgment

A trust created by a third party for the benefit of the patient is counted as an asset of the patient only if the patient has a **vested interest** in the assets. Such trusts are generally structured to cover special needs, not the general support of the patient, and distribution to the patient is **discretionary.**

The next step is determining whether there were transfers within the look-back period. In general, any trust created by the patient or spouse during the look-back period that was not part of the countable resources described above will result in a penalty. The exceptions mirror the exceptions that exist for gifts without a trust:

- Transfer to a trust for the benefit of a spouse, but remember, the spouse's assets will be countable assets.
- Transfer to a trust for a blind or disabled child.
- Transfer to a trust for the sole benefit of a disabled person under age 65.

After a patient qualifies for Medicaid, the community spouse may want to create a **testamentary trust** to pay for the special needs of the institutionalized spouse, leaving any assets remaining after the death of institutionalized spouse to other family members. In such cases, the state may seek recovery of those assets, as described later in this chapter, as reimbursement for the Medicaid expenditures.

What else should a family consider in preparing for future Medicaid application?

- If a family member provides care for the patient prior to admission to a nursing home, a care contract may be structured so that the payment for care is not a transfer subject to penalty. Because these contracts may be challenged, careful documentation and record keeping are essential.
- The patient may make a loan to family members, provided that the loan is not "forgiven" upon the patient's death and that payments are structured in compliance with very strict regulations. During the patient's life, payments are income that can be used to pay for nursing home care, if needed. After the patient's death, the payments become part of the patient's estate and subject to recovery by Medicaid. Depending on the amount of care needed by the patient, there may be something left over for family.
- The patient may purchase a life estate in a family member's home. The payment for the life estate is a transfer for value, not a gift. A life estate is the right to live in the home. The patient must actually live in the home for a year. State agencies have tables for calculating the value of a life estate, based on life expectancy. For example, assume that a woman, age 75, does not have a house, but has $130,000 in the bank. She can buy a life estate in her son's home. If her state life expectancy table gives her a life estate value of 0.52149 and her son's house is worth $300,000, she could pay her son her entire savings for the right to live in the house for the rest of her life, then live there for one year. She received fair market value for what she transferred.

These strategies and the trusts described earlier—requiring that funds remaining at the patient's death be used to reimburse Medicaid—may have an advantage despite the Medicaid reimbursement. Qualifying the patient for Medicaid may mean that the patient's nursing care costs less than the private-pay rate.

A federal law called **OBRA**, enacted in 1993, requires states to seek recovery of amounts correctly paid by the state for certain people with Medicaid. Estate recovery procedures are initiated after the beneficiary's death and can seek assets held in the name of the patient as well as assets that pass from the patient to another without probate. States are required to establish procedures for waiving estate recovery when recovery would cause undue hardship.

Testamentary Trust
Trust that is implemented after creator's death

OBRA
Omnibus Budget Reconciliation Act of 1993, sets estate recovery guidelines

---

Example

When Frank Farmer entered a nursing home, the family home and farm were exempt from consideration because Frank's wife continued to live there and work the farm with their children. Frank's wife died last year and Frank died a month later. The state may seek recovery against the value of the farm, but if recovery would deprive the children of the ability to continue farming, they may be able to obtain a waiver.

In addition to the right to recover from the estate of the Medicaid beneficiary, state Medicaid agencies must place a lien on real estate owned by a Medicaid beneficiary during her life unless certain dependent relatives are living on the property. If the property is sold while the Medicaid beneficiary is living, not only will she cease to be eligible for Medicaid because of the cash she would net from the sale, but she would have to satisfy the lien by paying back the state for its coverage of her care to date. The exceptions to this rule are cases in which a spouse, a disabled or blind child, a child under age 21, or a sibling with an equity interest in the house is living there. Other property, such as payments in negligence lawsuits, can also be subject to a lien.

Example

A child, deprived of oxygen at birth and severely disabled, has lived in a nursing facility all of his life, with the cost paid by Medicaid. Under what circumstances might the state be able to seek reimbursement for the child's care? Is it possible that this child will ever have any assets?

In 1998 the North Carolina Division of Aging and Adults conducted a survey comparing efforts of states at recovery, *http://www.dhhs.state.nc.us/aging/estate.htm*, but the survey has not been updated. Enter the name of your state and "Medicaid estate recovery" in a search engine and determine whether your state seeks recovery against non-probate assets. To see what other measures your state may be taking for cost containment, see *http://www.statehealthfacts.org/comparetable.jsp?ind=187&cat=4*.

Treatment of Income

Once an individual is determined to be eligible for Medicaid (based on the countable resources analysis described above), a determination is made of how much that person must contribute toward the cost of his own nursing facility care. The community spouse's income is not considered available to the spouse who is in the medical facility. The two are not considered a couple for income eligibility purposes.

The process starts by determining the total income of the spouse in the medical facility — for example, Social Security and pension payments — and deducting the following:

- Personal needs allowance of at least $30 per month.
- Community spouse monthly income allowance (between $1,750 and $2,739 for 2010), from the institutionalized spouse's income as long as the income is actually made available to the community spouse.

- A family monthly income allowance, if there are other family members living in the household.
- An amount for medical expenses incurred by the spouse who is in the medical facility.

If the community spouse has income of her own, the amount of that income is deducted from the community spouse's monthly income allowance. Similarly, any income of family members, such as dependent children, is deducted from the family monthly income allowance. Once the above items are deducted, any remaining income is contributed toward the cost of care in the institution.

Step-by-Step Medicaid Preparation

1. Keep in mind that not all families want or need Medicaid. In those cases, the transfer rules do not apply. The elder patient may want to transfer all of her assets (taking the gift tax exclusion described in Chapter 8) so that her child can at least get an income tax deduction for the payment of her care bills.

2. When preparing to apply, investigate whether any assets can be protected.

   a. Transfers before the look-back period are risky. Even if recipients (assume these are children) are well-meaning, these assets are subject to claims in the event of the recipient's divorce, accident, or bankruptcy, and the assets should be regarded as gone. A possible exception is putting house in trust so that the parents have the right to inhabit it during their life and the children get the remainder, or putting income-producing assets into a trust so that the parents are entitled only to income and the children get the remainder of the principal. Keep in mind that determining when the need for care will arise is impossible, so the look-back date cannot be predicted.

   b. Transfers (including into a trust) during the look-back period are allowed without penalty if they are to or for a spouse, a blind or disabled child, or any permanently disabled individual younger than 65 years of age, or if they consist of transfer of a home to a child who is under 21 or who has lived with and provided care for parent for at least two years prior to the parent's move to a nursing home, or transfer of a home to a sibling who has an equity interest and who lived in the home for at least a year before the move to a nursing home.

   c. If the individual is married, the spend-down on a house and furnishings, car, burial plan, and perhaps an immediate annuity can be protected.

3. Deduct assets protected for a community spouse and determine eligibility based on the remaining assets—including assets in trust that are available to an individual in need of care.

4. Now look at income, including amounts available from trust, to determine how much the patient must pay for care each month. From the total income amount, deduct spouse/family allowance, medical care, and personal care allowances.

EXHIBIT 7.3
Kathy Says

PACE-certified paralegal Kathy Motley is Executive Vice President of Operations at Law ElderLaw, LLP. Kathy worked in the legal field even before earning her ABA-approved paralegal degree more than ten years ago. She did not have any knowledge of (or interest in) elder law until she answered an ad posted on her professor's bulletin board ... and the rest is history.

A frequent speaker at seminars, Kathy now coordinates a team that guides the firm's clients through medical and financial problems. She is known as a fierce advocate for the firm's vulnerable clients, but also as a cool head in a crisis—one with a love for seniors.

One of Kathy's "missions" is to educate the legal community about the practice of elder law, which is *not* general practice. She understands the unique needs of people who have suddenly been faced with the loss of the person who did the driving and paid the bills or those who have received a devastating diagnosis. She listens to their stories and tailors the firm's work to the client's needs.

Assignments

---

1. Find the Medicaid income and resource limits for your state.
2. Find your state's provisions for Medicaid Hardship Waivers. Under what circumstances might a waiver be granted? For example, might the state waive estate recovery if it would impoverish an heir?
3. Critical Thinking: Read the summary of the *Bergman* case at the end of the chapter. The opinion of the lower court, which is reversed in this decision, is in italics to avoid confusion.
   • As is typical, the facts are not given in chronological order. Construct a timeline of events.

- Why do you think Lucille withdrew $10,000 for her own funeral?
- Why did Lucille's estate make claims against her own sons?
- How does a person retain an interest in a house after transferring title (homestead rights)? Do you think it should make a difference whether the person retains a legal interest after transferring property?
- Does timing make any difference? Why did the Department not try to reclaim money from Lucille while she was alive, before or after she made the gifts?
- Do you think lawsuits like this are likely to become more common? Why?
- Do you think the outcome is fair? Why?

4. Examine 42 CFR 433.36, the regulations concerning liens for incorrect payments:

http://frwebgate1.access.gpo.gov/cgi-bin/TEXTgate.cgi?WAISdocID=KKzAbw/ 1/1/0&WAISaction=retrieve"""

- Under what circumstances may a state impose such a lien?
- Under what circumstances may a state impose a lien on the home of a patient correctly receiving Medicaid? Under what circumstances would the lien dissolve?

Review Questions

1. What are the protections against spousal impoverishment?
2. Explain why a client might say, "I am giving each of my kids and grandkids $10,000 so that if I ever need a nursing home, Medicaid will pay."
3. Suppose the client also says, "I will have given away everything by the end of this year. I am in good health and I don't think there is any chance I will need a nursing home for at least a couple of years." What might the client not understand?
4. What is meant by the look-back? What kinds of transfers can be made during the look-back without triggering a penalty period?
5. Explain what is meant by a self-settled trust, a supplemental needs trust, a testamentary trust, a vested right to income, and a trustee's discretionary power.

Bergman v. Bergman

688 N.W.2d 187 (N.D., 2004)

The North Dakota Department of Human Services appealed from a judgment dismissing its claim against the Estate of Lucille Bergman for Medicaid benefits provided to Bergman's deceased husband, Carl, and dismissing the Estate's action to void transfers made by Lucille to two of her sons, Robert and Doug, shortly before her death. We reverse the judgment and remand.

Carl Bergman resided in a nursing home from June 1, 1996, until his death on April 12, 1998, and he received $31,425.64 in Medicaid benefits from the Department during that time. In 1993, Carl Bergman purchased a $50,000 single payment annuity from Lutheran Brotherhood. The annuity was wholly owned by Carl. In 1995, he transferred about $5,000 from the annuity to a Lutheran Brotherhood joint money market account for himself and Lucille. In 1996, Carl applied for Medicaid benefits, and in order to qualify under the impoverished spouse rules, he transferred the proceeds from the annuity and the joint money market account to his community spouse, Lucille, who used the funds to open a Lutheran Brotherhood money market account in her name. In 1998, Lucille transferred $40,000 from her money market account to a Lutheran Brotherhood investment account, and retained $13,790.24 in the money market account. In July 2001, Lucille arranged to withdraw $250 a month from her money market account for deposit into her checking account.

Lucille was diagnosed with cancer in 2002, and was informed by counsel that her estate may be responsible for reimbursement of Medicaid benefits provided to Carl. November 6, 2002, Lucille withdrew $10,000 from her money market account for her funeral expenses. On November 11, 2002, Lucille redeemed the shares in her Lutheran Brotherhood investment account and transferred the funds into her money market account. On December 6, 2002, Lucille withdrew $34,000 from her money market account, and deposited that money in her personal checking account. On December 6, 2002, Lucille signed a power of attorney granting Robert authority to withdraw funds from her checking account. On December 6, 2002, Bergman withdrew $500 from Lucille's checking account. On December 9, 2002, Lucille issued a $30,000 check to Robert for gifts to her four children and a $2,800 check to Doug for gifts to her children and her grandchildren. Lucille died December 28, 2002.

> The Estate of Lucille sought to void the transfers to Robert and Doug, and the Department filed a claim against the Estate for the cost of Medicaid benefits, plus interest, provided to Carl. The trial court granted the Department's motion to intervene in the Estate's action against Robert and Doug. The court dismissed the Estate's action against Robert and Doug and the Department's claim against the Estate, reasoning: Using the North Dakota definition of the estate subject to probate, there was no property in the recipient's estate, as determined at the time of his death. Carl transferred ownership of the annuity on December 20, 1996, long before his death, and he had no interest in the annuity at the time of his death. No part of the value of the annuity was included in his estate. There is no claim that the transfer by Carl was fraudulent in any way. It was a legal transfer permitted by federal law and the funds were not considered available for payment of medical costs in the Medicaid qualification process. The Court finds that the claim of the State must fail against the estate of Lucille since there were no assets in the probate estate of Carl that are

traceable to Lucille and which were not the separate property of Lucille. [E]ven assuming that the expanded definition of the probate estate was somehow adopted in North Dakota, the expanded definition requires that Carl must have had some interest of title in the asset at the time of his death. He had no such interest. He had transferred all of his right, title and interest in the annuity to his wife in 1996. This is not a case where the decedent recipient had a statutory homestead interest at the time of his death in the family home previously transferred to his wife. In the case of joint or survivor interests, life estates and other arrangements, the list of retained interests clearly evidences a clear intent, expressed in the optional federal definition of probate estate, to include those non-probate transfers where the transferor retains an interest in the property up until the time of death, (or more properly, the moment before death) when it passes without probate proceedings to the survivor or beneficiary. No such interest is involved in this case. The assets sought to be applied in this case to reimbursement of the Medicaid claim are not available and the state's claim must be denied to that extent. Lucille gifted some of the annuity funds to her children. She had the right to do that. She could have spent all of the disputed funds on her living expenses and other needs, and the state would not have even had a colorable claim to the funds. She should not be penalized for preserving some of those funds that were not fraudulently transferred by her husband to her in 1996, and were not fraudulently transferred by her before her death. The funds were her separate property, to do with as she pleased.

The Department argues the trial court erred in determining there were no assets in the Estate of Lucille which were traceable to Carl [and that] Lucille's gifts of assets traceable to Carl avoid reimbursing the Medicaid program were a fraud on creditors, including the Department.

In *Thompson*, 586 N.W.2d 847, this Court construed applicable Medicaid law in N.D.C.C. §50-24.1-07 and 42 U.S.C. §1396p(b) to allow states to trace the assets of recipients of medical assistance and to recover the benefits paid when the recipient's surviving spouse dies. We said "because the expansive federal definition of 'estate' in 42 U.S.C. §1396p(b)(4) extends only to assets in which the medical assistance benefits recipient 'had any legal title or interest in at the time of death,' it is a matter of little moment whether the Department seeks to recover the benefits paid by filing a claim in the estate of the recipient after the death of the recipient's surviving spouse or by filing a claim in the surviving spouse's estate."

In *Wirtz*, 607 N.W.2d 882, we again considered the meaning of those statutes. We relied on 42 U.S.C. §1396p(b) to provide meaning to N.D.C.C. §50-24.1-07, stating the federal statute limits the situations in which states can recover Medicaid benefits from the surviving spouse's estate. [W]e construed those statutes to allow states to trace a recipient's assets and to recover money from the estate of a recipient's surviving spouse . . . any assets conveyed by [institutionalized spouse] to [community spouse] before [the institutionalized spouse's] death and traceable to [community spouse's] estate are subject to the department's recovery claim. However, recoverable assets do not include all property ever held by either party during the marriage. 42 U.S.C. §1396p(b) contemplates only that assets in which the deceased recipient once held an interest will be traced. It does not provide that separately-owned assets in the survivor's estate, or assets in which the deceased recipient never held an interest, are subject to the department's claim for recovery. Thus, recovery from a surviving spouse's separately-owned assets because of a past obligation to pay a now deceased Medicaid recipient's medical expenses as necessaries, or recovery from the surviving spouse's entire estate, including assets not traceable from the recipient, is not allowed.

Our decisions authorize the Department to trace assets formerly held by a Medicaid recipient and to recover from the estate of the recipient's surviving spouse assets in which the deceased recipient once had an interest. The trial court's reasoning that there was no property in Carl's probate estate at the time of his death that was traceable to Lucille and that he had no interest in the annuity at the time of his death is inconsistent with our decision that "any assets conveyed by [institutionalized spouse] to [community spouse] before [institutionalized spouse's death] and traceable to [community spouse's] estate are subject to the department's recovery claim."

Here, before his death and to qualify for Medicaid benefits, the institutionalized spouse, Carl, conveyed assets to the community spouse, Lucille. Before her death, Lucille transferred assets in which Carl once had an interest, and the issue is whether those assets are subject to a claim by the Department. Doug and Robert argue those assets were outside Lucille's estate at the time of her death, and there is no authority allowing the Department to recover funds that are outside of a community spouse's estate at the time of her death.

Although those assets may not have been in Lucille's estate when she died, she purported to gift those assets to her children in contemplation of death and after being informed of a possible claim by the Department. Under N.D.C.C. §30.1-18-10, a personal representative may recover property transferred by the decedent to avoid the decedent's creditors. Under N.D.C.C. §50-24.1-07, the obligation to repay Medicaid benefits arises upon receipt of the benefits and the Department has a claim against assets traceable to the institutionalized spouse in the surviving community spouse's estate. Under N.D.C.C. §13-02.1-05(1) of the Uniform Fraudulent Conveyance Act, a debtor's transfer of property is constructive fraud as to a creditor if the debtor made the transfer without receiving a reasonably equivalent value in exchange for the transfer and the debtor was insolvent at the time of, or became insolvent as a result of, the transfer.

We conclude N.D.C.C. §30.1-18-10 and N.D.C.C. ch. 13-02.1 authorize the Department, as intervenor in the action against Robert and Doug, to void Lucille's gifts because the Department was a creditor and Lucille made those transfers without receiving a reasonably equivalent value in exchange, which rendered her estate insolvent to pay the Department's claim. See N.D.C.C. §§13-02.1-01; 13-02.1-02; 13-02.1-03; 13-02.1-05; and 13-02.1-07. We reject the trial court's conclusion that any assets that Carl transferred to Lucille were her separate property to do with as she pleased . . . assets traceable to Carl are subject to a claim against Lucille's estate for benefits provided to Carl.

Doug and Robert argue that allowing the Department to pursue funds outside of a community spouse's estate at the time of the community spouse's death would set a dangerous precedent because community spouses would not know whether they could spend their money. However, there is a difference between spending money for something which has a reasonably equivalent value and gifting property that is subject to a creditor's claim. Accepting the argument would circumvent the purposes of Medicaid law by permitting an institutionalized spouse to receive Medicaid benefits after transferring assets to a community spouse and precluding the Department from recouping any remaining part of those assets after the community spouse died.

www.CrosswordWeaver.com

ACROSS

2. Exemption of home may be subject to limit on _____
3. PRA, _____ resource amount
6. _____ administer Medicaid with partial federal funding
7. Principal _____, not considered in determining eligibility
13. _____ needs allowance, $30/month
15. _____-back, 60 months
16. Prepaid _____ plans, not considered in determining eligibility
17. _____ period for non-exempt transfers
18. Purchased to provide regular income

20. Trust created at death
22. Waiver and demonstration projects give states this

DOWN

1. Self-_____ trust, for one's own benefit
4. Cannot reach special needs trusts
5. Can be placed on real property to secure repayment
8. _____ care, a current trend
9. _____ needs trust
10. Initials, federal law requires states to seek recovery
11. _____ eligibles, both Medicare and Medicaid
12. In the future, Medicaid will be based on person's income in relation to the _____ level
14. Spouse not in nursing home
17. Trust created with individual's own funds
19. Medicaid can reach assets if individual has a _____ interest
21. Initials, Medicaid for children

8

◆ ◆ ◆

Estate Planning

◆ ◆ ◆

Overview
Intestacy
Documenting the Plan
Wills and Codicils
     Formalities
     Probate
     Challenges
Trusts

Objectives

When you complete this chapter you will:

- Understand your state's law concerning intestate succession.
- Know what can be accomplished by will and the formalities required for a will.
- Describe the advantages of living and testamentary trusts.
- Prepare a codicil.
- Know the features of your state's probate code.

Overview

Any paralegal who plans to work in the field of elder law will want to take an entire course in estate planning and probate. If you have not yet had the class, this chapter will serve as an overview of the field; if you have had the class, this will be an opportunity to review your knowledge.

As discussed in the preceding chapters, it is all about planning. Even a simple estate plan can save survivors money, stress, and time, but, as indicated in Exhibit 8.1, many people fail to plan. The lack of a plan can be disastrous.

EXHIBIT 8.1
AARP SURVEY: It Seems Like a "No Brainer," But... [1]

Among age 50+ Americans, 60 percent have a will, 45 percent have a durable power of attorney, and 23 percent have a living trust; but 36 percent have none of these legal documents and only 17 percent have all three. The proportion of persons having each kind of document increases with age, particularly for wills and durable powers of attorney. While 44 percent—or fewer than half—of persons age 50 to 54 have a will, 85 percent of those age 80 or older have one. Both income and education affect the likelihood of having a will. For example, while just 51 percent of those with a high school education or less have a will, 80 percent of those with a college degree have one.

Intestacy

Intestate
To die without a will

Estate
Entirety of person's assets and liabilities

Probate
Process of determining will is valid, appointing administrator

Decedent
Person who has died

Per Capita
Per person

Per Stirpes
Per family line

To die **intestate** is to die without advance planning in the form of a will or trust. The result is that many assets of the **estate** are distributed, after a process known as **probate,** according to a plan described in state law. That state law plan may not reflect the wishes of the deceased individual (the **decedent**).

Examine Exhibit 8.2 and consider the plan for distribution. **Per Capita** distribution means that an individual descendant takes a share that is equal in size to the shares of each of the other descendants. **Per Stirpes** distribution is a method under which a group represents its deceased ancestor to take the proportional share to which the deceased ancestor would have been entitled if still living. For example, say a man died intestate, and his wife predeceased him. He had four children, three of whom are still living at the time of his death. The deceased child (Jordan) had three children, all still living. If Jordan's three children share, as a group, in one-fourth of their grandfather's estate, the share the deceased parent would have taken if still alive, their shares have been

---

[1] *http://www.aarp.org/research/surveys/money.html*

determined using the per stirpes method. The three living children will also each receive one-fourth of the estate.

EXHIBIT 8.2
Find Your State Law

Start your search at *http://topics.law.cornell.edu/wex/table_probate*.

Example: Connecticut Law

If survived by . . .	
Spouse and children* of both decedent and spouse	Spouse takes first $100,000, + 1/2 of remainder. Children* take the other 1/2.
Spouse and children* of decedent, one or more of whom is not the child of the spouse	Spouse takes 1/2. All the children* share other 1/2 equally.
Spouse and parent or parents (no children**)	Spouse takes first $100,000 + 3/4 of remainder. Parent(s) takes the other 1/4.
Spouse only (no children**, no parents)	Spouse takes all.
Children* only (no spouse)	All goes to children*.
Parent(s) (no spouse, no children**)	All goes to parent(s).
Brothers* and sisters* (no spouse, no parents, no children**)	All goes to brothers* and sisters*.
Next of kin (no spouse, no children**, no parents, no brothers** or sisters**)	All goes to the next of kin. If there is no next of kin, but there is a step-child*, he or she will be next in line to take. If there is no step-child**, all goes to the State of Connecticut[2].

---

*If this person(s) has died before the decedent, his or her descendants may take instead.
**or descendants : *http://www.jud.ct.gov/probate/ProbCourtYou.pdf*

---

[2]In escheat, the state claims assets of deceased in the absence of a will or statutory kin.

Documenting the Plan

Fortunately, a client can easily override the state intestacy scheme by properly documenting her wishes. She may wish to go further and plan for management of her assets after her death and even while she is alive. This chapter will discuss the documentation — namely, wills and trusts.

Tip

Clients should be reminded of the importance of reviewing, and possibly updating, this documentation with every life change, including significant illness. As discussed in the Medicaid chapter, the family may need to divert assets away from a person with illness that may require institutional care.

Wills and Codicils

Administrator
Person appointed to manage estate

Executor
Person appointed to manage an estate

Testator
One who writes a will

Bond
A security, to guarantee performance

Testamentary Trust
Trust created in a will

Inter Vivos Trust
Trust created during settlor's lifetime, also called living trust

Pour-over Will
Transfers assets to a trust

A will is the fundamental estate-planning document. Any adult with mental capacity may execute a will. Its basic functions include identifying the person who will manage the estate, the **administrator** or **executor**, and describing the wishes of the **testator** with respect to distribution of property. As described later in this chapter, whether those wishes can be implemented depends on the claims of creditors and the forced heirship laws of some states that prevent disinheriting a spouse and, in some cases, children. See Exhibit 8.3.

In addition, a will can identify individuals to act as guardians and trustees, list the powers of the executor/administrator and any guardians or trustees, and eliminate the need for court supervision or a **bond**. If a will provides for the outright distribution of assets, it is sometimes called a simple will. If it establishes one or more trusts, it is called a **testamentary trust** will. A will may leave probate assets to a preexisting **inter vivos trust**, in which case it is called a **pour-over will**. Trust arrangements (as opposed to outright distribution) ensure continued property management and can have benefits ranging from protection against debts to tax reduction, described later in this chapter.

There are other limits, beyond the requirement of paying claims and forced heirship, to what can be achieved in a will. A testator's wishes concerning the care of a child are always subject to a court's determination about the child's best interests. A will cannot govern assets that pass outside the probate estate (such as property owned in joint tenancy with right of survivorship, pay-on-death accounts, life insurance, retirement plans, and employee death benefits as described in Chapter 11) unless they are payable to the estate or have named the estate of the deceased individual as beneficiary.

EXHIBIT 8.3
Forced Heirship

Forced heirship is also called the force share or spousal "**elective share.**"

Utah Code 75-2-202. Elective share—Supplemental elective share amount—Effect of election on statutory benefits—Nondomicilary.

(1) The surviving spouse of a decedent who dies domiciled in Utah has a right of election, under the limitations and conditions stated in this part, to take an elective-share amount equal to the value of 1/3 of the augmented estate.

(2) If the sum of the amounts described in Subsection **75-2-209**(1), and that part of the elective-share amount payable from the decedent's probate estate and nonprobate transfers to others under Subsections **75-2-209**(2) and (3) is less than $25,000, the surviving spouse is entitled to a supplemental elective-share amount equal to $25,000, minus the sum of the amounts described in those sections. The supplemental elective-share amount is payable from the decedent's probate estate and from recipients of the decedent's nonprobate transfers to others in the order of priority set forth in Subsections **75-2-209**(2) and (3).

(3) If the right of election is exercised by or on behalf of the surviving spouse, the surviving spouse's homestead allowance, exempt property, and family allowance, if any, are charged against, and are not in addition to, the elective-share and supplemental elective-share amounts.

Elective Share
Also called forced inheritance, legal requirement that spouse inherit percentage

Formalities

Any person who has reached the age of majority and has capacity (is of "sound mind") may execute a will. The testator must:

- Generally know the nature and extent of her property.
- Generally be able to identify the natural objects of her bounty—this means that the testator is aware of her relatives who would take the estate if she were intestate.
- Understand that she is making a will and intend to make a will.
- Be free of any delusions that would influence the disposition of her property.

Every state has its own laws concerning formalities of preparation, **attestation** (witnessing), and execution. A will need not be prepared by a lawyer to be valid, if it meets the statutory requirements. Wills may be categorized as follows:

Attestation
Witnessing the signing of a will and signing as verification

Holographic
Intestator's own handwriting

Nuncupative
Oral, spoken to another person — generally valid only for testators in the armed services.

Self-proving
Witnesses have signed sworn statement, testimony in court may be excused

Affidavit
Sworn statement

Mystic
Sealed until testator's death

Reciprocal
Wills with mirror terms as an agreement between testators

Interested Witnesses
Person who stands to benefit by some provision in will

Codicil
Amendment or addition to will

Incorporation by Reference
Making an outside document part of the current document by description

- **Holographic:** In the testator's own handwriting, which may make a difference with respect to witness requirements.
- **Nuncupative (non-culpatory):** Oral, spoken to another person — generally valid only for testators in the armed services.
- **Self-proving:** Witnesses sign a sworn statement (**affidavit**) and their testimony may be excused in probate proceedings.
- **Mystic:** Sealed until death.
- **Reciprocal:** Made by two or more parties (typically spouses) to make similar or identical provisions in favor of each other.

States have their own requirements, as shown in Exhibit 8.4, but in general, wills are signed by the testator in the presence of witnesses, and certain formalities must be observed. In some states, two witnesses must sign in the presence of the testator and of each other. Some states even require that the signatures and date be at the end of the will and disqualify **interested witnesses**. Some lawyers use more witnesses than required by law to avoid any disqualification problems. Other states no longer require witnesses. A later amendment to a will is called a **codicil** and must be signed under the same conditions.

Some states require that the testator "publish" the will by clearly identifying herself and stating that the document is a will. Failure to state, in the will, that the testator is revoking prior wills and codicils may result in all the documents being read together. In some states a will may refer to a memorandum disposing of tangible personal property, such as furniture, jewelry, automobiles, etc., which may be changed from time to time without the formalities of a will. Other states do not allow such **incorporation by reference**. States also have their own requirements on revocation of a will

Clients often ask where they should keep their wills. The will must be safe, in case of fire, flood, or other disaster, and readily accessible when the testator dies, so a safe-deposit box may not be the best place. Some clients have their lawyers keep their wills. The client should tell his family and close friends where his will is kept to make sure that statutory deadlines and probate requirements can be met.

Probate

Ancillary Administration
Additional probate process because decedent owned property in another state

Probate is the process by which a will is determined to be valid and which confirms the appointment of an administrator or executor. Paralegals commonly perform much of the work in probating an estate, as described in Exhibit 8.7 at the end of this chapter. The process is generally initiated in the county of the decedent's last domicile, but if the decedent owned real estate in another state, **ancillary administration** may be necessary in that state. State law dictates who may initiate probate, the documentation required, and whether notice must be given particular individuals. After the appointment is made, the administrator identifies, gathers, and values assets; identifies debts and claims against the estate; pays those debts and claims as well as taxes and expenses of administration according to priorities set by state law (sometimes called an abatement law), then distributes remaining assets to those designated as beneficiaries in the will.

EXHIBIT 8.4
Maine Statutes

§2-502. Execution

Except as provided for holographic wills, writings within section 2-513, and wills within section 2-506, every will shall be in writing signed by the testator or in the testator's name by some other person in the testator's presence and by his direction, and shall be signed by at least 2 persons each of whom witnessed either the signing or the testator's acknowledgment of the signature or of the will.

§2-503. Holographic will

A will which does not comply with section 2-502 is valid as a holographic will, whether or not witnessed, if the signature and the material provisions are in the handwriting of the testator.

§2-504. Self-proved will

(a). Any will may be simultaneously executed, attested, and made self-proved, by acknowledgment thereof by the testator and affidavits of the witnesses, each made before an officer authorized to administer oaths under the laws of the state where execution occurs and evidenced by the officer's certificate in substantially the following form: . . .

§2-505. Who may witness

(a). Any person generally competent to be a witness may act as a witness to a will.

(b). A will is not invalid because the will is signed by an interested witness.

§2-507. Revocation by writing or by act

A will or any part thereof is revoked

(1). By a subsequent will which revokes the prior will or part expressly or by inconsistency; or

(2). By being burned, torn, canceled, obliterated, or destroyed, with the intent and for the purpose of revoking it by the testator or by another person in his presence and by his direction . . . . . .

Valuing the assets became a particular problem in 2010. Historically, property has been inherited on a **step-up basis.** For example, if Aunt Olga bought her house in 1979 for $150,000 and it was worth $3,000,000 at the time of her death, Nephew Neal would inherit the house with a basis of $3,000,000.

Step-up Basis
Readjustment of "beginning" value of property upon inheritance

Capital Gains Tax
Tax on difference between sales price and acquisition price

Carry-over Basis
Beneficiary inherits property subject to gain during testator's lifetime

When he sold the house, he would have to pay **capital gains tax** only on the amount of the sale price over $3,000,000. Without the step-up, Neil would inherit the property with a **carry-over basis** and would have to pay capital gains tax on the amount of the sales price over $3,000,000 ($2,850,000 gain during Olga's lifetime).

In 2010, step-up basis is limited to $1,300,000 for property passing to someone other than a decedent's spouse and to $3,000,000 for property passing to a decedent's spouse. In addition to the obvious problem of increased capital gains tax, carry-over basis presents problems, such as determining the basis in property that may have been owned for many years and changed forms (for example, reinvested stock dividends or improvements to a house) and allocating the basis for each of several beneficiaries.

Another common probate issue is inheritance by children, who legally cannot hold title to property. Most states have a version of either the Uniform Gifts to Minors Act or Uniform Transfers to Minors Act that allows creation of a trust or appointment of a custodian to manage the minor's assets. Access to the gift must be given to the minor when he or she reaches the age of majority, either 18 or 21 (sometimes even 25), depending on state law.

For information about the Uniform Transfers to Minors Act and the earlier Uniform Gifts to Minors Act and whether your state has adopted either law, visit the Web site for the Uniform Law Commission at *http://www.nccusl.org/nccusl/ DesktopDefault.aspx?tabindex=2&tabid=60.*

The probate process may be supervised by the probate court, or it may be unsupervised or informal. Contrary to what many people believe, probate need not be long or expensive. In many states, a small estate (for example, consisting of an old car and a bank account with $3,000) may be handled by affidavit, a sworn statement, like the California form shown in Exhibit 8.5.

Example

Like the laws of many other states, and the Uniform Probate Code, Illinois law provides for shorter, simpler forms of probate, including Independent Administration:

755 ILCS 5/28-1) (from Ch. 110 1/2, par. 28-1)

Sec. 28-1. Purpose and scope of Article. This Article permits an executor or administrator to administer the estate without court order or filings, except to the extent that court order or filing is required by this Article or is requested by any interested person pursuant to this Article . . . . . .

And disposition of small estates by affidavit:

755 ILCS 5/25-1) (from Ch. 110 1/2, par. 25-1) Sec. 25-1. Payment or delivery of small estate of decedent upon affidavit.

(a) When any person or corporation (1) indebted to or holding personal estate of a decedent, (2) controlling the right of access to decedent's safe deposit box or (3) acting as registrar or transfer agent of any evidence of interest, indebtedness, property or right is furnished with a small estate affidavit in substantially the form hereinafter set forth, that person or corporation shall pay the indebtedness, grant access to the safe deposit box, deliver the personal estate or transfer or issue the evidence of interest, indebtedness, property or right to persons and in the manner specified in paragraph 11 of the affidavit or to an agent appointed as hereinafter set forth.

Sometimes a will is challenged by an individual who questions the testator's intent, whether the testator was subject to undue influence, whether there was fraud, or whether the testator was competent to make the will. A will may include an **in terrorem clause,** providing that any beneficiary challenging the will loses her own inheritance under the will. The enforcement of these clauses varies by state, but the law generally requires strong evidence of improper execution, the testator's incapacity, or suggestion that the will (or trust) was based on **undue influence**, **fraud**, or **duress**.

Challenges

There is no "bright-line test" for determining whether a will was the product of undue influence or duress. Courts will balance the interests of the parties and consider evidence relating to domination and manipulation of the testator and whether the testator was exercising her own free will or acting under threat or domination, including:

- Old age, illness, or other factors making the testator susceptible to undue influence.
- Whether the testator lived under the control and supervision of the beneficiary being challenged.
- The nature of the relationship between the testator and the challenged beneficiary.
- Whether there was a prior will that was significantly different.
- Whether the challenged beneficiary is a non-relative.
- Whether family members were disinherited.
- Whether the beneficiary hired a lawyer to draft the will or otherwise arranged for its creation.

A will, a trust, or a provision of a will or trust, may be declared invalid if based on fraud—a false representation by someone who knew it was false, intended to deceive the testator, and did deceive the testator. The false statement has to be material—important enough that it was the basis of the testator's action. Fraud differs from undue influence in that it involves the testator acting voluntarily, but relying on false information, whereas with undue influence the will of another person is being substituted for the testator's. Common instances of fraud involve a testator who did not know that she was executing a will, or was misled as to the contents of the will.

Fraud in the execution is a false statement about the nature or contents of the document: "We know you are too tired to read this Uncle Bob—don't worry, it says everything you want it to say." "Uncle Bob, sign this—it authorizes the nursing home to send your laundry out for washing." Fraud in the inducement relates to reasons for signing: "You need to leave everything to me, Uncle Bob, so that I can take care of Billie." Testator does not know that Billie died weeks ago.

In Terrorem Clause
Provision threatening that anyone challenging legality of will or any part of it will be cut off or given a dollar, instead of the gift provided in the will

Undue Influence
Domination such that victim cannot exercise free will

Fraud
False statement of material fact, made with intent to deceive, on which the victim reasonably relied

Duress
Compulsion by threat

EXHIBIT 8.5
Affidavit for Collection of Personal Property

California Probate Code Section 13100

The undersigned state(s) as follows:

1. _____ died on _____, 20____, in the County of _____, State of California.
2. At least 40 days have elapsed since the death of the decedent, as shown by the attached certified copy of the decedent's death certificate.
3. • No proceeding is now being or has been conducted in California for administration of the decedent's estate. OR
   • The decedent's personal representative has consented in writing to the payment, transfer, or delivery to the declarant of the property described below, and a copy of the consent and of the personal representative's letter is attached to this affidavit.
4. The current fair market value of the real and personal property owned by the decedent, less property described in Section 13050 of the California Probate Code, does not exceed $100,000.
5. • An inventory and appraisal of the real property included in the decedent's estate is attached.
   • There is no real property in the estate.
6. The following property to be transferred, delivered, or paid to the affiant under the provisions of California Probate Code section 13100:
7. The successor(s) of the decedent, as defined in Probate Code Section 13006 is/are:
8. The undersigned
   • is/are successor(s) of the decedent to the decedent's interest in the described property.
   • is/are authorized under California Probate Code Section 13051 to act on behalf of the successor(s) of the decedent with respect to the decedent's interest in the described property.
9. No other person has a right to the interest of the decedent in the described property.
10. The undersigned request(s) that the described property be paid, delivered or transferred to the undersigned.
    I/we declare under penalty of perjury under the laws of the State of California that the foregoing is true and correct.

Dated: _____

Signed: _____

EXHIBIT 8.5
(continued)

State of California   )

)   ss.

County of   )

On____, 20____, before me, _____, personally appeared _____, who proved to me on the basis of satisfactory evidence to be the person(s) whose name(s) is/are subscribed to the within instrument and acknowledged to me that he/she/they executed the same in his/her/their authorized capacity(ies), and that by his/her/their signature(s) on the instrument the person(s), or the entity upon behalf of which the person(s) acted, executed the instrument. I certify under PENALTY OF PERJURY under the laws of the State of California that the foregoing paragraph is true and correct.

Witness my hand and official seal

_____

Trusts

The term **trust** describes the holding of property by a **trustee** (which may be one or more persons or a corporate trust company or bank) in accordance with the provisions of a written trust instrument executed by a **grantor** or **settlor** who transfers assets into the trust for the benefit of one or more persons called **beneficiaries**. This splits the legal title to the property from the equitable right to the property: The trustee holds title, but the right to benefit from the property belongs to the beneficiary. One person may be the settlor, a trustee, and a beneficiary of the same trust, but cannot be both the sole trustee and the sole beneficiary. A trust can be entirely independent of a will, or, as mentioned earlier, a will can create a trust at death or can "pour over" assets into an existing trust.

    Some people think that trusts are only for the wealthy and are intended to avoid probate and reduce taxes. While a trust can serve those goals, as described later in this chapter, the most significant feature of a trust is that it can provide for management of property. This can be a benefit to people at any income level. A

Trust
Property is held in name of trustee for benefit of beneficiaries

Trustee
One who holds property for benefit of another

Grantor
Person who creates trust

Settlor
Person who creates trust

Beneficiaries
Persons who receive the benefit of trust assets

Totten Trust, the simplest and most common form of trust, is simply a way of owning a bank account and is discussed in Chapter 11.

Example

Pedro, age 49, is a divorced, middle-income father of two. His daughter, Lourdes, is 27 and is an accountant; his son, Guillermo, is 14. Pedro's own health is not good. He is worried about how his financial matters would be handled if he became disabled. He is also concerned about providing for Guillermo without allowing his ex-wife control of any assets. Finally, he wants to make sure that his children ultimately share his assets.

Pedro establishes a **revocable trust** by naming himself as initial trustee and beneficiary and transferring his property (house, bank and investment accounts) to the name of the trust—the assets are sometimes called the "corpus" or body of the trust, which will produce income. Because Pedro can continue to control and use his own asset, he has a **life estate**. As described in Chapter 7, he might create an irrevocable trust and limit his use of the assets to **interest** and not **principal**, if he were trying to establish Medicaid eligibility. Pedro names Lourdes as **successor trustee**, to manage the assets if he becomes incompetent or dies. Pedro names the trust department of his bank to act if Lourdes cannot or does not serve as trustee. When Pedro dies, the trustee is to use the assets to provide for the support and education of Guillermo until Guillermo reaches age 25 or dies without having reached that age; at that time, the trustee is to distribute the remaining assets equally to Lourdes and Guillermo, or, if one has died, all to the other. The children are the **remaindermen**.

Pedro's trust can serve all of his important goals at little cost. His only cost is likely the lawyer's fee for preparing the documents. Pedro's goals have nothing to do with avoiding estate taxes (described later in this chapter), which are generally not an issue to middle-income individuals. When Pedro dies, probate may or may not be necessary, depending on the state in which he was living and whether he had any assets outside the trust. Pedro will probably also execute a pour-over will to ensure that any assets outside the trust become part of the trust upon his death.

One of the most important tasks for a law office is explaining the trust to the client. If a client does not understand how the trust works, she may not understand the importance of putting newly acquired assets in the name of the trust or may even unintentionally move assets out of the trust, thereby defeating the purpose of the trust.

The trustee is in a **fiduciary** position and may also need counseling about appropriate investments and distributions and how to sign when acting on behalf of the trust. As a fiduciary, a trustee (or an executor under a will) can be liable for mishandled funds. For that reason, and because administration of a large trust or estate is a lot of work, the laws of many states provide that fiduciaries are entitled to reasonable compensation for their work, even if the document (will or trust) makes no reference to compensation. Many trustees and executors employ professional trust departments to handle investments and disbursements, produce required account statements, and prepare required tax forms. A trust or an estate is a taxpayer in its own right and must obtain its own tax identification number.

Revocable Trust
Trust in which settlor can terminate trust and regain control of assets

Life Estate
Ownership that terminates with death

Interest
Revenue generated by principal assets

Principal
Capital or asset as distinguished from the interest or revenue from it

Successor Trustee
Person who serves if initial trustee does not

Remaindermen
Persons who receive what remains in trust after initial beneficiaries

Fiduciary
Acts on behalf of another, in a relationship of trust, with special obligations

---

Tip

The common form for a trust title and trustee signature is "Vipak Patel, as Trustee for the Vipak and Shirley Patel Trust, Dated May 15, 2010."

There are several different types of trusts, to serve the various goals of settlers. A **spendthrift trust** can be used to care for an individual who would otherwise lose his assets to wasteful spending, gambling, or outsiders. The trustee is instructed to use assets directly on the beneficiary's behalf (for example, pay the rent) or to make limited disbursements to the beneficiary. Such a trust is not available to creditors. A **discretionary trust** allows the trustee to make decisions about how to distribute assets, perhaps according to the needs of various beneficiaries, and is sometimes called a "sprinkling" or "spray" trust. A **special needs support trust**, also discussed in Chapter 7, is generally set up for a minor or a person with disabilities, to provide for the beneficiary's needs without giving that beneficiary access to the trust that might disqualify her from public benefits or result in wasteful spending.

Trusts are sometimes used to receive and manage the proceeds of a life insurance policy payable at the death of the grantor. These irrevocable life insurance trusts keep the policy out of the decedent's estate (a tax benefit, described below) while preventing the money from going directly to individuals who might not manage it well. A trust can be established to give the grantor income for life, while leaving the remainder to charity (charitable remainder trust), with the benefits of avoiding capital gains and estate taxes (discussed below). Many states now allow for creation of a trust to care for pets.

For people with more assets, trusts may be structured to minimize estate tax — although the same results may be accomplished by wills. The federal estate tax is a tax on a person's right to transfer property at death. Because people with a lot of assets might try to avoid estate tax by giving property away during their lives, it is tied into the federal gift tax, which is also paid by the giver. Although the estate tax and gift tax are referred to as a "unified system" and do have the same tax rates, the exclusion amounts are different.

Let's start at the beginning. A wealthy individual may want to make gifts during her lifetime. Generally, the following are not taxable gifts:

1. Gifts not more than the annual exclusion for the calendar year.
2. Tuition or medical expenses paid for someone (the educational and medical exclusions).
3. Gifts to a spouse.
4. Gifts to a political organization for its use.

If a gift is taxable, for many people it may fall within the exclusion. The annual exclusion for gifts after January 1, 2009, was $13,000 to each donee. In other words, a parent could give each of his children, sons- and daughters-in-law, and grandchildren $13,000 per year, up to the lifetime cap. The lifetime cap

Spendthrift Trust
Trust in which distributions prevent beneficiary from wasting assets

Discretionary Trust
Trust in which trustee has flexibility in making distributions

Special Needs Support Trust
Trust structured for the needs of disabled person or minor, to prevent loss of public benefits or wasteful spending

(total amount of excludable taxable gifts) is $1,000,000 as of this writing. The donor's spouse could give the same amount in gifts. If a decedent has not reached that lifetime cap or exclusion, any unused amount exempts property that passes at her death.

Tip

Remember, as discussed in Chapter 7, clients may confuse the annual gift tax exclusion with the ability to transfer assets and be eligible for Medicaid. The two are not related.

As of this writing, the status of the federal estate tax is unclear. The Economic Growth and Tax Relief Reconciliation Act of 2001 had gradually increased the annual exclusion and decreased the tax rate. The estate tax was repealed for 2010, but then the Act "sunsets" in 2011, and the estate tax reappears with an applicable exclusion amount of only $1,000,000, as shown in Exhibit 8.6 (unless Congress acts before then). It is very likely that Congress will act to freeze the numbers at or near the 2009 level, rather than let the estate tax remain expired for 2010 and then return at the 2001 level for 2011 and future years.

In order to take advantage of that exclusion and of the unlimited exclusion for gifts to a spouse, while keeping money in the family, many wealthy people have historically used an "AB Trust" in their wills or in the creation of living trusts. The "A Trust" is also commonly referred to as the "Marital Trust," "QTIP Trust," or "Marital Deduction Trust." The "B Trust" is also commonly referred to as the "Bypass Trust," "Credit Shelter Trust," or "Family Trust." For example, assume that the estate tax is in effect, with the 2009 lifetime exclusion of $3,500,000. Here is how it works:

1. *The couple divides assets so that each spouse has about the same value of assets in his or her individual name or in his or her revocable living trust.* This is important because many couples leave assets in joint accounts, which will pass outright to the surviving spouse instead of through the deceased spouse's will or trust. If that happens, the benefits of the plan are lost.

2. *Each will or trust provides that when the first spouse dies, assets amounting to the total exclusion will go into the B Trust.* This uses the first spouse's $3,500,000 federal exemption from estate taxes. The B Trust can be flexible because the lifetime exclusion does not depend on who receives the money. It can be used for the benefit of the surviving spouse (while alive) and later be distributed to descendants or other beneficiaries, or it can go directly to descendants or others if the A Trust, described below, contains adequate assets to provide for the surviving spouse.

EXHIBIT 8.6
Tax Status 2010 TRANSFERS

Transfer	2010	2011+
Applicable Exclusion Amount	Repealed	$1.1 Million
Lowest Estate Tax Rate	Repealed	41%
Highest Estate Tax Rate	Repealed	55%
Lifetime Gifts Market Value Exemption	$1 Million	$1.1 Million
Lowest Gift Tax Rate	35%	41%
Highest Gift Tax Rate	35%	50%
GST* Exemption Amount Allowable	Repealed	$1.1 Million
GST Transfer Tax Rate	Repealed	55%

GST
Generation-skipping
transfer rate

*The GST (generation-skipping transfer) tax applies to gifts and transfers in trust to or for persons two or more generations younger than the donor, like a grandchild or a non-relative more than 37 1/2 years younger.

3. *If the deceased spouse's assets exceed the exclusion amount ($3,500,000), the excess goes into the A Trust for the surviving spouse.* This takes advantage of the exclusion for gifts to spouses to defer payment of estate taxes on the assets above the deceased spouse's $3,500,000 exemption until after the surviving spouse's death. To take advantage of the exclusion, the A Trust can be used only for the benefit of the surviving spouse; the surviving spouse is required to receive all of the income from the A Trust.

4. *When the surviving spouse later dies, he or she will take advantage of his or her own estate tax exemption when the A Trust passes to the beneficiaries, typically the children.* If the exemption is $3,500,000 when the surviving spouse dies, then the first $3,500,000 of the surviving spouse's separate assets will pass estate tax free to the final beneficiaries. Anything over $3,500,000 will be taxed.

Effective use of the AB Trust system can allow married couples to pass on $7,000,000 to their final beneficiaries, free from any federal estate taxes. This example assumes that the federal estate tax is in effect with an exemption of $3,500,000 per spouse. Are you wondering whether the grantor could continue the trust, down through the generations, to make sure that the money never leaves the family? The answer is no. The **rule against perpetuities** limits the duration of trust ownership.

Rule Against Perpetuities
Limit on duration of
ownership in trust

Many states have their own inheritance taxes, sometimes called "death taxes," which often must be paid by the person who receives inherited property (as opposed to estate taxes, which are paid from the decedent's estate). Inheritance tax exemptions and rates may vary depending on who received the property—for example, the decedent's spouse may be taxed at a lower rate than would be a friend of the decedent. A number of states are phasing out their inheritance tax systems, and some are in limbo as of this writing because of the estate tax issues discussed above. You can find out whether your state has an inheritance tax at *http://estate.findlaw.com/estate-planning/estate-planning-law/estate-planning-law-state-taxes.html*.

Constructive Trust
Implied to prevent inequity

A **constructive trust** is a trust that was not formally created by a grantor, but is implied by law to prevent injustice. For example, Uncle Lou, losing his sight and not able to write checks anymore, transfers his bank account to his niece, who takes care of his finances. He also has two nephews and they are of great help, taking care of his yard, driving him to appointments, and spending time with him. When Lou dies, if his niece attempts to claim that the entire account was a gift to her, the nephews may claim constructive trust.

EXHIBIT 8.7
Tina Says

I have been working as a Paralegal in the area of Elder Law for approximately ten years. I was drawn to Elder Law due to an interest in the rights of the elderly and disabled. I pursued and obtained my Associates Degree in Applied Science—Paralegal Studies, and have found so many rewards in this career path. I cannot see myself doing anything else!

My work is devoted to the areas of guardianship, probate, trust administration, Medicaid planning, veterans' benefits, and so many other pieces of the Elder Law puzzle. I am able to work directly with the disabled or their families in client interviews, preparing a legal plan, implementing the plan, and seeing clients through this process. Components of the Elder Law plan can include working with the courts on disabled estates, working with state agencies to obtain public assistance such as Medicaid benefits, assisting veterans with benefit applications, and the list goes on. These benefit programs and procedures are complex and the stakes are usually high. The client and their families often need the advice and assistance of a qualified Elder Law attorney and their paralegal staff to help them navigate through the process.

It can truly be crisis management, but our clients are so grateful and relieved when they get to the end of the process and know that their loved one is protected and well cared for. This helps make this type of work so extremely rewarding.

I work for the Law Offices of Wilson & Wilson, The Center for Estate Planning and Elder Law, located in LaGrange, Illinois, near Chicago. Our principal attorney, William S. Wilson, is a charter member of the Academy of Special Needs Planners, a member of the National Academy of Elder Law Attorneys, and of the Chicago Bar Association Committees on Trust Law, Asset Protection, and Elder Law. We also provide assistance to clients in the areas of nursing home litigation, real estate, and advising small businesses and not-for-profit organizations.

Assignments

1. Find and write a short summary of your state's law concerning gifts to minors.
2. Find and summarize your state's laws providing for informal, unsupervised, or other "shortened" forms of probate.
3. Find your state's law concerning spousal "forced share."
4. Use the IRS Web site to determine the current status of federal estate tax rates and exclusion.
5. Critical Thinking: Read the case at the end of the chapter.
   - Discuss the court's apparent distinction between the influence the testator's sister had over the testator and "undue influence."
   - Do you think the result would be different if the sister had told the testator, "My sons have farmed your land for many years and if they don't have some guarantee about the future, they want to move on and get their own land."
6. Using the IRS Web site, examine the gift tax form (709).
   - What other type of tax uses the same form?
   - Why does it ask about consent by spouse?
   - When is the tax due?
7. Do you think that a person acting as a guardian or under a power of attorney could amend or revoke a will or a trust signed by the ward/principal? *See Bernard v. Foley,* 139 P.3d 1196 (Cal. 2006); *Matter of Chiaro,* 903 N.Y.S.2d 673 (2010); *Zagorski v. Kaleta,* 2010 Ill. App. LEXIS 869 (Ill. App.) 2010. Can you find a case from your jurisdiction that addresses the issue?
8. Find the statutory requirements for execution of a will or a codicil in your state.
   - How many witnesses are required? May they be interested witnesses?
   - Use a search engine, such as Google, and search for "free legal form codicil." Examine the form you find and determine whether using it without modification would comply with the law of your state.
   - Does your state allow incorporation by reference of an outside document?

Review Questions

1. What is intestacy?
2. What is meant by forced heirship?
3. What is the difference between an inter vivos trust and a testamentary trust, and how does a pour-over will relate to those?
4. What is a holographic will? a self-proving will? a reciprocal will?
5. What is the purpose of an AB Trust?
6. What are the duties of a trustee and of an executor?
7. Why might a person with modest assets want to establish a trust?
8. What types of property pass to the new owner, upon the death of an owner, outside the probate process?
9. Identify the grounds for a challenge to a will.

Pope v. McWilliams

632 S.E.2d 640 (Ga. 2006)

In the presence of two witnesses and a notary public, Gordon Grigsby executed a Last Will and Testament on April 14, 2004. His sister, Ruth McWilliams, named as executrix, accompanied him to the lawyer's office where the will was executed. Grigsby died on October 14, 2004. On November 9, 2004, James Pope, Grigsby's nephew by a deceased sister, filed a pro se document with the probate court, titled "Objection to Gordon K. Grigsby's Last Will." Pope's objections included: the will was secretly made and altered a prior will; the new will was made because of undue influence, fraudulent practices, and duress; Grigsby's mental capacity was inadequate at the time of the new will; and parts of the will were "overly broad and overly vague which may conflict with some laws."

The will devised real estate to McWilliams, and in the event that McWilliams predeceased Grigsby, to her lineal descendants; McWilliams's two sons had farmed Grigsby's land for about 15 years. Also, the will bequeathed the remainder of Grigsby's estate to his brother, a niece who is Pope's sister, and to Pope; there were investments included in the estate valued at approximately $300,000 to $400,000. Apparently, in a prior will, Pope's mother was to get a share of the estate, including the real property.

The probate court granted summary judgment to McWilliams, Pope appealed to the superior court, which denied the appeal and granted summary judgment to McWilliams. As evidence of this alleged undue influence, Pope cites numerous circumstances and a statement made by Pope's sister that before the creation of the new will, McWilliams told Grigsby that "We have got to go make that will." Pope also emphasizes that the change to the will was not made known to him at the time. He urges that this coupled, with Grigsby's susceptibility because of his age, infirmity, and mental deterioration, the confidential relationship enjoyed by McWilliams, the unreasonableness of the will, and actions by McWilliams including her taking Grigsby to her attorney's office without the knowledge of the others named in the will and her paying the attorney with a check drawn on an account held jointly with Grigsby demonstrate McWilliams's undue influence on Grigsby. But that is hardly the case.

[T]he cited statement does not aid Pope. It does not demonstrate that McWilliams forced Grigsby to make the will. In fact, McWilliams testified that Grigsby changed his will in order to be more specific about what he wanted done with his estate so as not to leave the disposition of the estate "all on [McWilliams's] shoulders." Second, there . . . is no requirement that a testator notify anyone expecting to inherit from the testator that a will is being executed. In fact, when asked in deposition if creating a will should be a matter of public record, Pope acknowledged that it is a private matter.

It is true that "[a] presumption of undue influence arises when it is shown that the will was made at the request of a person who receives a substantial benefit, who is not a natural object of the maker's estate, and who held a confidential relationship with the testator. However, a person standing in confidential relation to another is not prohibited from exercising any influence whatever to obtain a benefit to himself. The influence must be what the law regards as undue influence. Such influence that . . . "would give dominion over the will to such an extent as to destroy free agency, or constrain one to do against his will what he is unable to refuse." First, it is plain that McWilliams was a natural object of Grigsby's estate. But, [even if] she was not, such influence as would destroy Grigsby's free agency or constrain him to act against his will has not been shown to be the case here. McWilliams stated that the relationship was one of mutual trust. In contrast, "[a] confidential relationship is one where one party is so situated as to exercise a controlling influence over the will, conduct, and interest of another. Evidence showing only that the deceased placed a general trust and confidence in the primary beneficiary is not sufficient to trigger the rebuttable presumption that undue influence was exercised . . . . In order to give rise to the rebuttable presumption . . . , the evidence must show a confidential relationship wherein the primary beneficiary was capable of exerting the power of leadership over the submissive testator."

Pope's argument that the will was unreasonable and indicative of undue influence is unavailing. The disposition of the real estate is readily understandable inasmuch as McWilliams's sons had been farming the property for more than a decade prior to Grigsby's death. Indeed, another family member averred that he had expected Grigsby to give his land to McWilliams because her sons had farmed the land and thus, she would be able to pass the land to them so they could continue to farm it.

In summary, [u]ndue influence which operates to invalidate a will is such influence as amounts either to deception or to force and coercion, destroying free agency. The improper influence must operate on the testator's mind at the time the will is executed. Evidence that shows no more than an opportunity to influence and a substantial benefit falls short of showing exercise of undue influence.

Pope next contends that summary judgment was not warranted because there are genuine issues of material fact concerning Grigsby's mental incapacity. But here again, Pope's showing falls far short. A testator possesses the mental capacity to make a will if he understands that his will has the effect of disposing of his property at the time of his death, is capable of remembering generally what property is subject to disposition by the will and remembering those persons related to him, and is capable of expressing an intelligent scheme of disposition.

A stringent standard must be met in order to set aside a will because to do so is to deprive a person of the valuable right to dispose of his property as he wishes. Id. Beyond his own opinion about Grigsby's forgetfulness and state of mind, the only arguably significant evidence that Pope presents on the subject of lack of capacity is a hospital discharge paper stating that the doctors "[c]ould not exclude some early dementia." But, the mere presence of that notation does not demonstrate incapacity. Id. Moreover, this was six months after Grigsby's execution of the will in question. What is more, in affidavit, Pope acknowledges that he is not contending that Grigsby was "completely or severely mentally incompetent," but rather that he was merely "in the early state of mental deterioration."

The witnesses to the will were unequivocal in their opinions that Grigsby was fully aware of what he was doing. The notary public on the will averred that there was no question in her mind that Grigsby acted competently and freely and voluntarily in executing his will. In fact, she averred that Grigsby stated that "he was leaving his real property to his sister, Ruth McWilliams, because her sons, Mark and David had worked his farm since he wasn't able to do as much, and knew that his sister would keep his land in the family." The notary further related that she remembered Grigsby "laughing and stating that he knew if his nephew, Jim Pope, had his way, he would want everything."

www.CrosswordWeaver.com

ACROSS

1. Have equitable interest in trust
6. Step-up _____, when inheriting property
9. Witness who will inherit
15. Trust, trustee can make choices
16. Income on trust assets
17. Self-_____, witnesses need not testify
18. Sworn statement
21. Pour _____ will, into a trust
26. Secures performance of executor
27. Rule against _____ limits trust duration
28. Inter _____, living trust
29. Process: validate will, appoint administrator
30. Body of assets that funds a trust

DOWN

2. Next in line trustee
3. Per _____, per person
4. Trust implied by law
5. Trust that would be good for a gambler
7. Per _____, family line
8. Makes a will
10. Person who has died
11. Dying without a will
12. Administration in another state
13. Wills are mirror image
14. Acts on behalf of another in special relationship
19. Trust created by will
20. Hand-written will
22. _____ share, also called forced inheritance
23. Person's assets and liabilities
24. Amends a will
25. Holds legal title

9

◆ ◆ ◆

Housing

◆ ◆ ◆

Objectives

When you complete this chapter, you will:

- Be aware of the financial and support resources available to help clients stay in their own homes.

- Know the types of congregate housing available to seniors, the regulation of those housing types, and how to evaluate whether a facility is an appropriate choice.
- Understand housing needs and considerations

Housing can present a number of challenges for older people: finding the services and financial support necessary to stay in their current homes, finding new homes that are affordable and accessible, finding community living facilities that meet service and care needs. A paralegal working with older clients must be able to recognize the issues a client may be facing and direct the client to the appropriate resources.

Aging in Place

The image of senior citizens "retiring to Florida" or moving into an assisted-living community is not necessarily accurate. According to the National Council on Aging,[1] a nonprofit service and advocacy organization, 90 percent of seniors would prefer to stay in their own homes. In some cases, clients require assistance, including remodeling to accommodate mobility problems, in-home care, and housekeeping and shopping help. In-home care can range from a regular phone call to check on the individual's well-being to live-in skilled nursing care. While these services are generally available, older clients may not be able to do the research necessary to locate and evaluate services or to afford the services they need using their savings and income.

Resources for Staying in the Home

OAA
Older Americans Act

AoA
Administration on Aging, a federal agency

In order to address some of these concerns, the Older Americans Act (**OAA**), 42 U.S.C. §3001 *et seq*, established the federal Administration on Aging (**AoA**) and funds the delivery of services through state and area agencies. These agencies can refer clients to a variety of services, such as housekeeping and meal delivery, and may provide those services to clients meeting certain criteria, generally related to ability to pay. The AoA Web site (*http://www.aoa.gov*) provides a description of the types of programs available, links to state and local agencies, and even a link to a "benefit finder" to help seniors determine whether they might qualify for programs such as food stamps. Another federal government Web site that is useful for locating services for aging in place is the Department of Health and Human Services Elder Care Locators at *http://www.eldercare.gov/Eldercare.NET/Public/Index.aspx*.

Other resources can be used to find checklists of what to look for in housing and information about financial assistance for low-income homeowners. Among the best starting points for help with housing issues are the United States

---

[1] *http://www.ncoa.org*

Department of Housing and Urban Development (**HUD**) (*http://portal.hud.gov/portal/page/portal/HUD/topics/information_for_senior_citizens*) and AARP (*http://www.aarp.org/home-garden/housing/*). Senior citizen homeowners should also take advantage of any property tax reductions available.

As the aging population becomes an important force in the housing market, we are likely to see innovations in dealing with the unique needs—and wants—of older people. For example, on August 29, 2010, the *Chicago Tribune* reported on the formation of "intentional communities" to help seniors remain in their homes. Seniors pay an annual fee to join a neighborhood or "village" group that organizes social activities and provides assistance with chores. To find out whether such a program exists in your area, visit *http://vtvnetwork.clubexpress.com*.

Medicare Coverage of Home Services

A common saying among elder law paralegals is that "Medicare only cares if you can get better." In other words, like a traditional health insurance plan, Medicare does not cover housing needs, only medical needs. Medicare covers home health care services only if the client meets all of the following conditions:

- Doctor decides that medical care at home is necessary, and makes a plan for care at home.
- Patient needs intermittent skilled nursing care, physical therapy, speech-language therapy, or continued occupational therapy.
- The home health agency is approved by the Medicare program (Medicare-certified).
- Patient is homebound or normally unable to leave home without help. To be homebound means that leaving home takes considerable and taxing effort. A person can be homebound and still leave home for medical treatment or short, infrequent absences for nonmedical reasons, such as trips to a barber or church, or even adult day care.

If those conditions are met, Medicare will cover the following types of home health care:

- Skilled nursing care on a part-time or intermittent basis. Skilled nursing care includes services and care that can be performed safely and correctly only by a licensed nurse (either a registered nurse or a licensed practical nurse).
- Home health aide services on a part-time or intermittent basis. A home health aide doesn't have a nursing license but supports the nurse by providing services such as help with bathing, using the bathroom, dressing, or other personal care. These types of services don't require the skills of a licensed nurse. Medicare doesn't cover home health aide services unless the patient is also getting skilled care such as nursing care or other therapy. The home health aide services must be part of the home care for the patient's illness or injury.

- Physical therapy for as long as the doctor deems necessary. Physical therapy includes exercise to regain movement and strength in a body area, and training on how to use special equipment or do daily activities, such as how to get in and out of a wheelchair or bathtub.
- Speech-language therapy for as long as the doctor deems necessary. Speech-language therapy (pathology services) includes exercise to regain and strengthen speech skills.
- Occupational therapy for as long as the doctor deems necessary. Occupational therapy includes exercise to help the patient perform usual daily activities, such as new ways to eat, put on clothes, or comb hair. Occupational therapy can continue beyond skilled care, if ordered by a doctor.
- Medical social services to help with social and emotional concerns related to illness. This might include counseling or help in finding resources in the community.
- Certain medical supplies, such as wound dressings (but not prescription drugs or biologicals).
- Durable medical equipment, such as a wheelchair or walker.
- Food and Drug Administration (FDA)–approved injectable osteoporosis drugs in certain circumstances.

Currently, Medicare does not cover any of the following:

- 24-hour-a-day care at home
- Meals delivered to the home
- Homemaker services such as shopping, cleaning, and laundry
- Personal care given by home health aides (such as bathing, dressing, and using the bathroom) when this is the only care needed

Equity
Difference between value and amount owed

Home Equity Loan
A traditional mortgage, with monthly payments due

Reverse Mortgage
A loan against equity, not paid back until owner vacates

FHA
Federal Housing Administration

HECM
Federal Home Equity Conversion Mortgage

Reverse Mortgages

To cover other costs, a senior citizen might look to the value of his or her home. If the owner does not want to sell or lease her home, she may consider borrowing against her **equity**. If cash flow is a problem, a **home equity loan**, requiring monthly payments, is not a good option. The client might instead consider a **reverse mortgage**, a home loan that lets a homeowner convert the equity in her home into cash to cover unexpected medical expenses, make home improvements, travel, or just make ends meet. The homeowner can receive a lump sum or monthly payments, with no payments due until the borrower leaves the home (as described below) or defaults on the agreement. Unfortunately, reverse mortgages have often been used to defraud seniors and clients must be counseled) to be careful in entering this type of arrangement. See Exhibit 9.1.

The Federal Housing Administration (**FHA**) has a program, the Home Equity Conversion Mortgage (**HECM**), that allows senior property owners to

EXHIBIT 9.1
FBI Reverse Mortgage Alerts[2]

The FBI and the U.S. Department of Housing and Urban Development Office of Inspector General (HUD-OIG) urge consumers, especially senior citizens, to be vigilant when seeking reverse mortgage products. Reverse mortgages, also known as home equity conversion mortgages (HECM), have increased more than 1,300 percent between 1999 and 2008, creating significant opportunities for fraud perpetrators.

Reverse mortgage scams are engineered by unscrupulous professionals in a multitude of real estate, financial services, and related entities to steal the equity from the property of unsuspecting senior citizens aged 62 or older or to use these seniors to unwittingly aid the fraudsters in stealing equity from a flipped property.

In many of the reported scams, victim seniors are offered free homes, investment opportunities, and foreclosure or refinance assistance; they are also used as straw buyers in property flipping scams. Seniors are frequently targeted for this fraud through local churches, investment seminars, and television, radio, billboard, and mailer advertisements.

A legitimate HECM loan product is insured by the Federal Housing Authority (FHA). It enables eligible homeowners to access the equity in their homes by providing funds without incurring a monthly payment. Eligible borrowers must be 62 years or older, occupy their property as their primary residence, and own their property or have a small mortgage balance. See the FBI/HUD Intelligence Bulletin (*http://www.fbi.gov/scams-safety/fraud/seniors/intelbulletin_reversemortages*) for specific details on HECMs as well as other foreclosure rescue and investment schemes.

Seniors should consider the following:

- Do not respond to unsolicited advertisements.
- Be suspicious of anyone claiming that you can own a home with no down payment.
- Do not sign anything that you do not fully understand.
- Do not accept payment from individuals for a home you did not purchase.
- Seek out your own reverse mortgage counselor.

Victims of this type of fraud can file a complaint at the FBI's Tips and Public Leads Web site (*http://tips.fbi.gov*) or at a local FBI office (*http://www.fbi.gov/contact-us/field/field-offices*).

---

[2] *http://www.FBI.gov*

work with approved lenders to obtain a reverse mortgage and to choose to withdraw funds in a fixed monthly amount, as a line of credit, or a combination of the two. The amount available to a borrower under a reverse mortgage depends on the borrower's age, the value of the property, and whether the borrower opts for a fixed or variable interest rate, but the payments to the borrower are not taxed as income. Eligibility does not depend on income or credit rating; the property must meet certain requirements, and the borrower must:

- Be 62 years of age or older
- Own the property outright or have a small mortgage balance
- Occupy the property as a principal residence
- Not be delinquent on any federal debt
- Participate in a consumer information session given by an approved HECM counselor

Under FHA-approved reverse mortgages, the borrower will never owe more than the property is worth. Payment becomes due when the owner dies, sells the house, moves out permanently or fails to occupy the house for 12 months, or violates the agreement by failing to pay taxes or insurance or to perform maintenance. If sales proceeds are insufficient to pay the amount owed, FHA pays the lender the amount of the shortfall. FHA collects an insurance premium from all borrowers to provide this coverage. HECM borrowers can choose an adjustable or fixed interest rate.

Potential pitfalls in a reverse mortgage include the possibility that the cash flow generated by the payments might make the borrower ineligible for some means-based benefits. Most federal and state programs do not view such payments as "income," but if the payments are not spent and accumulate as savings, they might become a "resource." While a home itself is often an "exempt resource" in determining eligibility for programs such as Medicaid, the money from a reverse mortgage on that home lowers the value of the exempt resource and may not have the same protected status if it is in a bank account. Another problem could arise if it becomes necessary for the client to sell the mortgaged home, for example to move into a care facility. If the client has a taxable **capital gain** on the house and the tax liability exceeds what the client nets after paying the reverse mortgage, the client will have to look to other assets to pay the tax. This situation is uncommon given the exemption (currently $250,000 for a single taxpayer, $500,000 if married), but the client should be advised to talk to her tax professional.

Capital Gain
Amount by which selling price exceeds purchase price, may be taxed

Because of abuse and scams involving reverse mortgages, the 2010 Dodd-Franks Wall Street Reform and Consumer Protection Act (Public Law No: 111-203) targets mortgage lending, credit cards, and "payday" lending practices and creates a new independent Consumer Financial Protection Bureau (CFPB) within the Federal Reserve. CFPB is to conduct a study on reverse mortgages, to examine deceptive and abusive practices and determine the need for standards to protect consumers from being sold reverse mortgages to fund inappropriate annuities, investments and other financial products. CFPB also has authority to issue regulations, orders, or guidance that apply to reverse mortgages prior to the completion of the study. In the meantime, the Department of the Treasury issued "Reverse Mortgage Products: Guidance for Managing Compliance and

Reputation Risks" (known simply as "Guidance").[3] The Guidance document focuses on consumer counseling and conflicts of interest

Cohabitation

Some older people control living costs by sharing housing. A homeowner might take in a tenant, or two or more older people might rent together; either situation implicates the same landlord-tenant or house-sharing concerns that younger people would face:

- Does local zoning permit rental of an accessory apartment or individual room in the client's home?
- What impact does the rental agreement have on the client's homeowners' insurance?
- If the occupants do not have separate space, is the client's personal property safe? Are there any concerns for the client's own safety? Might a background or credit check be necessary?

If the situation involves a relationship beyond a landlord-tenant or co-tenancy, there can be additional concerns. According to Forbes.com,[4] 1.8 million Americans aged 50 and older lived in heterosexual "unmarried-partner households" in 2006. Most of these people have been married and believe in marriage. They may face disapproval by family and friends, but as discussed in Chapter 13, their reasons for not marrying include:

- Inheritance concerns—they are concerned (and they believe their children are concerned) that their assets will be inherited by a new spouse and that person's family.
- Alimony from a former spouse ending.
- Widows and widowers receiving a pension, health benefits, military survivors' benefits, or a public-service worker's annuity losing those benefits or having those benefits reduced upon remarriage.
- Concern about responsibility for other partner's existing or future debts and expenses, especially health care expenses.
- Loss of social security survivor's benefits if remarried before age 60.
- Possible loss of financial aid eligibility for children in college.
- Income tax "marriage penalty."

But cohabitation without marriage can carry its own risks. Some states recognize **"palimony"** or common-law marriage.[5] (These concepts are discussed further in Chapter 13.) Couples residing in those states must be very careful to not to represent themselves as being married, use the same surname, or take other actions that might be interpreted as forming a common-law marriage, and

Palimony
Payment of support (alimony) to a non-spouse companion

[3] http://www.ots.treas.gov/_files/25362.pdf and http://www.ffiec.gov/press/pr081610.htm
[4] http://members.forbes.com/forbes/2007/1112/DONOTTOUCH086.html
[5] http://www.ncsl.org/default.aspx?tabid=4265

should clarify, in writing, their expectations regarding support in the event that the relationship ends. Such couples should consider a cohabitation agreement, making sure it is consistent with the terms of advance directives, estate plans, and any ownership agreements. In addition, all cohabiting individuals, regardless of where they live and the nature of the relationship, should:

- Execute advance directives and estate planning documents, as described in earlier chapters.
- Consider long-term care insurance.
- Not combine assets or hold investments in joint name; even personal property should be clearly identified as belonging to one of the parties.

Leaving the Traditional Home

Some seniors do not want to age in place, perhaps because of financial concerns, wanting to move to a different climate or closer to family, or not wanting to do the maintenance required by a traditional home. Seniors who are relocating need to consider their wants and needs with respect to cost, whether to live in age-restricted housing, and whether they need services or care on-site. There are many options, ranging from so-called "granny flats," or cottages on property shared with a family member, to full nursing care facilities.

If cost is the client's most pressing concern, he may want to investigate public options. The United States Department of Housing and Urban Development has a variety of programs for older people with limited assets, including rental subsidies and housing choice vouchers (often called Section 8 vouchers), loans, and grants.

Age-Restricted Housing

Seniors who plan to move often choose age-restricted housing because such communities may provide security, services, and an atmosphere targeted to their preferences and needs. While the Fair Housing Act, 42 U.S.C. §3601 *et seq*, generally prohibits discrimination based on, among other things, family status (i.e., having children), housing that meets the definition of "housing for older persons" is exempt from the law's familial status requirements, provided that:

- HUD has determined that the dwelling is specifically designed for and occupied by elderly persons under a federal, state, or local government program *or*
- It is occupied solely by persons who are 62 or older *or*
- It houses at least one person who is 55 or older in at least 80 percent of the occupied units, and adheres to a policy that demonstrates intent to house persons who are 55 or older.

Age-restricted living facilities vary considerably in the amenities offered, cost, and restrictions imposed. Residents may be owners or renters or both—for example, in a mobile home community, the occupants may own their individual units, but rent the lots on which they are located. Services may range from none or minimal to round-the-clock skilled nursing care. Clients considering buying or renting in an age-restricted community should carefully compare the monthly cost to the cost of comparable services in a non-restricted setting, investigate the solvency and history of any entity providing **common elements** or rented facilities, and examine **restrictive covenants** carefully, especially any covenants relating to resale.

Common Elements
Parts of common ownership development shared by all owners

Restrictive Covenants
Legal obligation imposed by deed or contract, may limit use or sale of property

Rentals and Disabilities

The Fair Housing Act also requires that owners of housing facilities (such as apartment buildings) make reasonable exceptions in policies and operations to afford people with disabilities equal housing opportunities. For example, a landlord with a "no pets" policy may be required to grant an exception to this rule and allow an individual who is blind to keep a guide dog in the residence. The Act also requires that landlords allow tenants with disabilities to make reasonable access-related modifications to their private living space, as well as to common use spaces, although the landlord is not required to pay for the changes. The Act requires that new multifamily housing with four or more units be designed and built to allow access for persons with disabilities. This includes accessible common use areas, doors that are wide enough for wheelchairs, kitchens and bathrooms that allow a person using a wheelchair to maneuver, and other adaptable features within the units. The Act is enforced by the U.S. Department of Housing and Urban Development (*http://portal.hud.gov/portal/page/portal/HUD/program_offices/fair_housing_equal_opp*).

Assisted Living and Care Facilities

As people age, they often need additional assistance with daily activities, such as preparing meals and bathing. Those needs sometimes increase to a point where the person requires on-site skilled health care professionals 24 hours a day. Facilities providing assistance and care vary greatly in size, services, cost, and quality. Services can be provided in a "foster care" setting, with one or more individuals living in a family-type arrangement; in a group home; in a large community of apartments, condominiums, or single-family housing; or in a traditional "nursing home" setting. Large continuing care retirement communities (**CCRC**) or "progressive care" facilities offer different levels of service and care to meet clients' evolving needs.

CCRC
Continuing Care Retirement Community

There is no universal definition of the terms used to describe the levels of care and service. "Independent living" is a marketing term often used to describe an apartment, condominium, or single-family housing association that may have features particularly attractive to seniors, such as accessibility, social and recreational options, and, sometimes, housekeeping, transportation, and meals. "Assisted living" generally refers to assistance with medications, bathing and grooming, and other, more personal, services. Some facilities advertised as providing assisted living are not regulated in any way greater than traditional housing. The federal government does not regulate independent or assisted living (or, as you will learn, pay for those facilities) and each state is different in defining the level of services and supervision that requires licensing.

Example

California: Oversight of Continuing Care Retirement Communities[6]

Today's seniors are faced with many attractive options for retirement living. One of these options is a continuing care retirement community, or CCRC. CCRCs offer a long-term continuing care contract that provides for housing, residential services, and nursing care, usually in one location, and usually for a resident's lifetime.

All providers offering continuing care contracts must first obtain a certificate of authority and a residential care facility for the elderly (RCFE) license. In addition, CCRCs that offer skilled nursing services must hold a Skilled Nursing Facility License issued by the Department of Health Services.

The California Department of Social Services (Department), is responsible for the oversight of continuing care providers. The Department's Community Care Licensing Division has two branches that participate in the regulation. The Senior Care Program monitors continuing care providers for compliance with the Community Care licensing laws and regulations regarding buildings and grounds, accommodations, care and supervision of residents, and quality of service. The Continuing Care Contracts Branch is responsible for reviewing and approving applications to operate a CCRC and monitors the ongoing financial condition of all CCRC providers and their ability to fulfill the long-term contractual obligations to residents.

The National Center for Assisted Living published a state regulatory review in 2009. Find out where your state stands at *http://www.ahcancal.org/ncal/resources/Pages/StateRegulatoryReview.aspx*. Starting at *http://www.ltcombudsman.org/ombudsman*, find the agency that regulates nursing homes in your state and the contact information for your state ombudsman. Bookmark the link for an assignment at the end of this chapter.

Regulation of Nursing Facilities

The licensing of nursing and skilled nursing facilities is a state function, but federal regulations play an important role because a facility must be certified to receive Medicare or Medicaid payments. Among other things, the federal regulations, 42 CFR §483.1 *et seq*, establish a patient bill of rights, admission and transfer requirements, standards for facility practices and for assessment of

---

[6]*http://www.calccrc.ca.gov*

residents, standards requiring that the facility provide care and services to help residents attain or maintain the highest practicable level of well-being, and even requirements concerning food and nutrition. Many states have nursing home patients' bills of rights and may provide even greater protection than the federal rules.

The Centers for Medicare and Medicaid Services (*http://www.cms.hhs.gov*) contracts with state governments to do health inspections and fire safety inspections of certified nursing homes and to investigate complaints about nursing home care. Inspections take place, on average, about once a year, but may be done more often if the nursing home is performing poorly.

Care facilities may also obtain **accreditation** from a private-sector organization (such as the Joint Commission on the Accreditation of Healthcare Organizations or the Long-Term Care Evaluation Program) if they meet standards established by that organization. Accreditation is voluntary and does not affect the home's eligibility to act as a Medicare or Medicaid care provider.

Accreditation
Verification of compliance with standards by a private group

Assessing Quality

While quality facilities are available in most areas, people often wait until the situation reaches a crisis point and they are rushed into making a decision. Paralegals should be aware of resources available to help clients make good decisions, even in emergency situations. In addition to government agencies previously mentioned, be aware of nonprofit advocacy groups, such as the National Consumer Voice for Quality Long-Term Care (*http://www.nccnhr.org*) and the National Senior Citizens' Law Center (*http://www.nsclc.org*).

To begin the search for the right facility, the client or caregiver can obtain a list of facilities from the local AoA agency, the state licensing agency, or associations such as the American Association of Homes and Services for the Aging (not-for-profit facilities) and the Assisted Living Federation of America (mostly for-profit). These agencies may help narrow the search to facilities that meet the needs of the resident. Some facilities focus on rehabilitation, generally with the goal of eventual discharge. Others focus on special care for particular physical and mental conditions, such as Alzheimer's disease. Still others provide hospice care to meet the physical and emotional needs of terminal patients.

According to the Centers for Medicare and Medicaid Services:

Hospice provides comfort and support services to people who are terminally ill. It helps them live out the time they have remaining to the fullest extent possible. Hospice care is provided by a specially trained team that cares for the "whole person," including his or her physical, emotional, social, and spiritual needs. Hospice provides support to family members caring for a terminally ill person. Hospice is generally given in the home. Hospice services may include drugs, physical care, counseling, equipment, and supplies for the terminal illness and related conditions. Hospice doesn't shorten or prolong life. Hospice focuses on comfort, not on curing an illness.[7]

---

[7] *http://www.medicare.gov/Publications/Pubs/pdf/02154.pdf*

Medicare can cover hospice benefits under the following conditions:

- The patient is eligible for Medicare Part A (Hospital Insurance).
- The patient's doctor and the hospice medical director certify that the patient is terminally ill and has six months or less to live if the illness runs its normal course.
- The patient signs a statement choosing hospice care instead of other Medicare-covered benefits to treat a terminal illness.
- The patient gets care from a Medicare-approved hospice program.

No facility should be given serious consideration until its status (Medicare/Medicaid certification, license, and complaints) is verified. The client or caregiver should conduct at least one unannounced visit in addition to the scheduled guided tour, and talk to residents and staff. The visitor should obtain written copies of all rules and contracts for careful review. In order to remember what she has seen and heard, the client can print a checklist of questions and considerations from *http://www.medicare.gov/Publications/Pubs/pdf/02174.pdf*.

EXHIBIT 9.2
Compare Definitions

Remember, federal definitions determine whether a nursing facility is eligible for Medicare and Medicaid payments and, therefore, whether it must be certified in compliance with federal regulations. State licensing is a separate function.

Federal Law

Sec. 1819. [42 U.S.C. 1395i--3]

(a) Skilled Nursing Facility Defined. — In this title, the term "skilled nursing facility" means an institution (or a distinct part of an institution) which —
(1) is primarily engaged in providing to residents —
(A) skilled nursing care and related services for residents who require medical or nursing care, or
(B) rehabilitation services for the rehabilitation of injured, disabled, or sick persons, and is not primarily for the care and treatment of mental diseases;
(2) has in effect a transfer agreement (meeting the requirements of section 1861(l)) with one or more hospitals having agreements in effect under section 1866; and
(3) meets the requirements for a skilled nursing facility described in subsections (b), (c), and (d) of this section.

EXHIBIT 9.2
(continued)

Wisconsin Statutes

Section 50.01(3)

NURSING HOME: A place where 5 or more persons who are not related to the operator or administrator reside, receive care or treatment and, because of their mental or physical condition, require access to 24-hour nursing services, including limited nursing care, intermediate level nursing care and skilled nursing services.

Minnesota Statutes

Subd. 5. Nursing home.

"Nursing home" means a facility or that part of a facility which provides nursing care to five or more persons. "Nursing home" does not include a facility or that part of a facility which is a hospital, a hospital with approved swing beds as defined in section 144.562, clinic, doctor's office, diagnostic or treatment center, or a residential program licensed pursuant to sections 245A.01 to 245A.16 or 252.28.

Subd. 6. Nursing care.

"Nursing care" means health evaluation and treatment of patients and residents who are not in need of an acute care facility but who require nursing supervision on an inpatient basis. The commissioner of health may by rule establish levels of nursing care.

Iowa Code

135C.1

"Nursing facility" means an institution or a distinct part of an institution housing three or more individuals not related to the administrator or owner within the third degree of consanguinity, which is primarily engaged in providing health-related care and services, including rehabilitative services, but which is not engaged primarily in providing treatment or care for mental illness or mental retardation, for a period exceeding twenty-four consecutive hours for individuals who, because of a mental or physical condition, require nursing care and other services in addition to room and board.

Cost and Contracts

Of course, cost is also a huge factor. According to the *New York Times*, in 2010 the average cost of nursing home care, not including special care services, was $200 per day.[8] Some facilities charge a substantial entry fee in addition to monthly fees. Some facilities are all-inclusive; others charge for services separately. Most residents of assisted living facilities pay the costs out of their own pockets. Most facilities have one thing in common: Residents can expect costs to increase with time. Arrangements under which residents would pay a substantial fee up front (sometimes all of their assets) in return for a guarantee of shelter, services, and care for life (sometimes called life care) have largely disappeared; to the extent that such arrangements are available, clients should carefully consider the provider's financial ability to fulfill its obligations.

Medicare does not cover assisted living; in some states Medicaid or other programs may pay for assisted living if the individual qualifies financially. Keep in mind that Medicare is like health insurance, whereas Medicaid is assistance for low-income individuals and varies by state.

Example[9]

Illinois developed the Supportive Living Program as an alternative to nursing home care for low-income older persons and persons with disabilities under Medicaid.

By combining apartment-style housing with personal care and other services, residents can live independently and take part in decision-making. Personal choice, dignity, privacy, and individuality are emphasized.

The Department of Healthcare and Family Services has obtained a "waiver" to allow payment for services that are not routinely covered by Medicaid. These include personal care, homemaking, laundry, medication supervision, social activities, recreation, and 24-hour staff to meet residents' scheduled and unscheduled needs. The resident is responsible for paying the cost of room and board at the facility.

Custodial
Protective care, generally on-site with caretaker

Under certain limited conditions, discussed in Chapter 6, Medicare will pay some nursing home costs for beneficiaries who require skilled nursing or rehabilitation services and receive those services at a Medicare-certified skilled nursing home after a qualifying hospital stay of at least three days immediately before entering the nursing home. The coverage is only for medically necessary services and care; **custodial** care and services, such as help with daily tasks and specialized care for conditions such as Alzheimer's, are not covered.

Lien
Claim against property to secure payment of a debt

About half of all nursing home residents pay costs out of their own savings; after their savings and assets are exhausted they can become eligible for Medicaid. As discussed in Chapter 7, Medicaid does not generally require a spouse to sell the marital home in order to pay for nursing home care, but may impose a **lien** on the property. Medicaid will pay most nursing home costs for people with limited income and assets, in certified facilities. Clients should consult their income tax advisors; some expenses may qualify as deductible medical expenses.

---

[8] *http://www.nytimes.com/2010/03/20/health/20patient.html*
[9] *http://www.slfillinois.com*

Some individuals have private insurance. Medigap insurance (a supplement to Medicare, discussed in Chapter 6) will generally pay a portion of the cost of skilled nursing care if the care is covered by Medicare. A managed care insurance plan will not help pay for care unless the nursing home has a contract with the plan. Long-term care insurance policies are also available, but they vary widely in terms of benefits. The National Association of Insurance Commissioners, which represents state health insurance regulators, provides a free publication called "A Shopper's Guide to Long-Term Care Insurance" as well as guides for Medigap and other insurance. See *http://www.naic.org/store_pub_consumer.htm*.

Contract Questions

While state and federal regulations do limit, to some extent, the rights that nursing facilities can give themselves and take from clients by means of a contract, not all contracts comply with those regulations. If the facility is not a state-licensed or Medicare/Medicaid nursing facility, it may be subject to few limits on what it can include in its contract. It is important to review any contract before the client signs it and carefully consider:

- If the client needs a higher level of care in the future, can the facility provide that care? Does it guarantee that it will make that care available? If that higher level of care might be paid by Medicare or Medicaid, is the facility certified?
- Does the contract mirror what the client was told during a visit or in brochures, in terms of services, options, staffing, visitation hours, rules, etc.?
- Is the client promised a particular room? Can the facility move the client or assign a new roommate without consent?
- How can the client terminate the contract and move?
- Under what circumstances might the facility terminate the contract and discharge the client?
- What will happen if the facility closes or changes ownership?
- To what extent are entry or other up-front fees refundable?
- Is there any limit on the frequency or amount of cost increases?
- What happens if costs exceed a resident's ability to pay?
- If the residents are a couple, what if marital status changes? What if one partner needs a different level of care?
- What if the resident leaves the facility for hospitalization or to spend time with family—will her bed still be available upon her return (often referred to as a **bed-hold**)?
- What is the grievance process? Does the contract call for arbitration or mediation in the event of a dispute?
- Does the contract contain any provisions purporting to allow the facility to control the client's accounts or property or to constitute advance consent to medical procedures?
- Does the contract attempt to require a deposit or a guarantor?

Bed-hold
Resident is not in facility, space is held pending return

Exculpatory Clause
Relieves a party of liability

Hold Harmless
Exculpatory clause

- Does the facility attempt to limit its liability (with respect to client's property as well as client's well-being), called an **exculpatory clause** or **hold harmless**?

Once a facility has been selected, it should be provided with copies of the client's advance directives, powers of attorney, and contact information for interested relatives and others.

EXHIBIT 9.3
Heather Says

Before taking her current corporate managerial position, Heather Finn worked at a suburban Elder Law boutique practice outside a major city. When asked about advice she might give a new paralegal, planning to work with seniors, Heather said:

> Many initial intake calls were from the client's adult child, asking what to do because Mom or Dad was sick and needed advance directives or an entire estate plan. Quite often the parent(s) have never been to an attorney, other than for purchasing a home. They were often apprehensive and anxious about the entire process. They need to feel confident that your firm is going to take care of them. That includes preparing the proper legal documents and providing peace of mind that their families will be taken care of.
>
> I recall a situation where an elderly client was very nervous about the process and simply did not like attorneys. To make him feel more comfortable, the firm asked me to buy his favorite cherry pie for the signing of his documents. When the client arrived in the conference room and the pie was waiting for him he immediately began to smile and we all felt a sense of ease throughout the room. It is amazing how a simple, inexpensive gesture made such a difference in the client's experience and, we hoped, changed his mind about the legal profession. Clients often just want to be heard and feel important. When you truly listen to their stories and needs, you are able to give the clients so much more than legal documents.
>
> Another important factor to keep in mind is who the client is. Very often you receive the initial call from an adult child, but when you are representing the parent(s), it is important to keep discussions confidential, unless you have permission from the client(s) to share. This can be tricky, because the adult child may be paying fees on behalf of the parent(s) and feel entitled to the privileged information. If your firm is representing the parent, you need to be careful not to breach attorney-client privilege. If the situation gets uncomfortable or you are uncertain how to handle things, it is always best to inform your supervising attorney and forward the child's questions directly to that attorney. The most important point to keep in mind is mental capacity. It is important to determine any client's mental capacity before executing legal documents, but it is even more important when dealing with clients who might be suffering from

---

**EXHIBIT 9.3
(continued)**

---

degenerative mental diseases, such as Alzheimer's and other forms of dementia. Often the supervising attorney will provide a simple competency test, such as asking the client the date, the name of the president, and the name(s) of their children. To avoid offending the client, explain that this is done before all signings, regardless of age. Documenting the questions and answers will protect your firm if the documents are later challenged.

Assignments

---

1. Use the reverse mortgage calculator (*http://rmc.ibisreverse.com//rmc_pages/rmc_aarp/aarp_index.aspx*) to determine the monthly payment that would be available for a client born August 10, 1947, who is the sole owner of a house worth $400,000 in your zip-code area.
2. Use the Administration on Aging Web site (*http://www.aoa.gov/AOARoot/AoA_Programs/OAA/Aging_Network/Index.aspx*) to find the agency nearest your location and the poverty guidelines for a household with two people.
3. Search the Internet or form books in a law library for non-marital cohabitation agreements. Many online form sites require you to pay to download or use a form but allow you to look at and preview the form without paying. Based on the forms you see, develop a checklist of issues that should be addressed in such an agreement.
4. Consider the summary of *Moffett* at the end of the chapter. Why do you think Ms. Moffett's children do not want to participate in arbitration? Why was the arbitration agreement on a separate page?
5. Use a search engine, such as Google, to search the name of your state and "senior citizens property tax exemption." Report your findings.
6. Visit a nursing home, assisted living facility, or seniors-only housing facility in your area and report to your classmates on the physical features that make the facility accessible to seniors, whether the facility provides social or recreational opportunities, and your observations about the condition of the facility and the attitude of any residents you encountered.

7. Critical Thinking/Ethical Issues: Read the two summaries of Washington cases at the end of this chapter. These cases have been drastically edited so that you are seeing nothing but the facts. Before you read the full opinions, consider:
   - What is it about living trusts and reverse mortgages and about the way they are sold that make them an attractive "scam" on senior citizens?
   - Defend the lawyer (Shepard). What might the salesman have said about this arrangement to make him think it was not a bad thing?
   - Go to your state's ethical rules (rules of professional conduct). Identify rules that the lawyer has likely violated.
   - Do you think that taking away the insurance agent's license is adequate?
   - What more could be done to protect the victims of these scams?
8. Determine whether your state has a nursing home patients' bill of rights. Use the Code of Federal Regulations (*http://www.gpoaccess.gov/cfr/index.html*) to answer the following from the regulation concerning patient rights:
   - Do the regulations provide any particular protections for patients who do not speak English?
   - What types of changes require consultation with the client's physician and notification of a representative or family member?
   - What are the requirements for a facility holding a client's personal funds? What types of items or services may be charged against those personal funds?
   - In your own words, what are the client's rights with respect to visitation and with respect to transfer or discharge?
   - Under what circumstances can the facility use restraints or seclusion?
   - What are the requirements for the presence of a registered nurse on the premises?
9. Why is zoning for "granny cottages" controversial? Visit *http://www.nytimes.com/2006/12/02/nyregion/02attics.html* and *http://articles.latimes.com/2004/apr/11/local/me-granny11*. Would your municipal zoning allow such an arrangement?

Review Questions

1. What are the differences between an independent living community, an assisted living community, and a nursing home?
2. When will Medicare contribute to the cost of home care? of nursing home care?
3. What happens if a patient is in a nursing home and his assets run out, so that she is no longer able to pay?
4. What are the advantages and disadvantages of a reverse mortgage?

5. A client calls and says she plans to move into a progressive care facility. What are your top "factual" concerns?

6. A client's son calls and says he is worried because, having recently moved, he cannot get to Mom's nursing home before late evening and the nursing home does not allow visitors after 8:00 P.M. He has not been able to visit on weekends because of his visitation schedule with his children. On the phone, Mom sounds unusually tired and confused, but the nurses say she is fine. Which laws are implicated? Who would you contact to help resolve this?

MOFFETT V. LIFE CARE CENTERS,

187 P.3d 114 (Colo. App., 2008) [summary]

In 2004 Dorothy Moffett, suffering from Alzheimer's disease, was admitted to Briarwood. As part of the admission process, Dorothy's son, James Moffett, signed documents provided by Briarwood, including an arbitration agreement. Ms. Moffett had executed powers of attorney appointing her son and daughter attorneys-in-fact. The arbitration agreement . . . states that the parties agree to arbitrate

> any claim, including, but not limited to, any claim that medical services were unnecessary or unauthorized or were improperly, negligently, or incompetently rendered or omitted . . . [and] all disputes . . . arising out of and in any way connected to the Resident's stay and care provided at the Facility, including but not limited to any disputes concerning alleged personal injury to the Resident caused by improper or inadequate care, including allegations of medical malpractice; any disputes concerning whether any statutory provisions relating to the Resident's rights under Colorado law were violated; and any other dispute under Colorado or federal law based on contact, tort, or statute. . . .
>
> THE UNDERSIGNED ACKNOWLEDGE THAT EACH OF THEM HAS READ THIS ARBITRATION AGREEMENT AND UNDERSTANDS THAT BY SIGNING THIS ARBITRATION AGREEMENT EACH HAS WAIVED HIS/ HER RIGHT TO A TRIAL, BEFORE A JUDGE OR JURY, AND THAT EACH OF THEM VOLUNTARILY CONSENTS TO ALL OF THE TERMS OF THE ARBITRATION AGREEMENT. . . . NOTE: BY SIGNING THIS AGREEMENT YOU ARE AGREEING TO HAVE ANY ISSUE OF MEDICAL MALPRACTICE DECIDED BY NEUTRAL BINDING ARBITRATION RATHER THAN BY A JURY OR COURT TRIAL. . . . YOU HAVE THE RIGHT TO SEEK LEGAL COUNSEL AND YOU HAVE THE RIGHT TO RESCIND THIS AGREE-MENT WITHIN NINETY DAYS FROM THE DATE OF SIGNATURE BY BOTH PARTIES. . . . NO HEALTH CARE PROVIDER SHALL WITHHOLD THE PROVISION OF EMERGENCY MEDICAL SERVICES TO ANY PERSON BECAUSE OF THAT PERSON'S FAILURE OR REFUSAL TO SIGN AN AGREEMENT CONTAINING A PROVISION FOR BINDING ARBITRA-TION OF ANY DISPUTE ARISING AS TO PROFESSIONAL NEGLIGENCE OF THE PROVIDER. . . . NO HEALTH CARE PROVIDER SHALL REFUSE TO PROVIDE MEDICAL SERVICES TO ANY PATIENT SOLELY BECAUSE SUCH PATIENT REFUSED TO SIGN SUCH AGREEMENT OR EXERCISED THE NINETY-DAY RIGHT OF RESCISSION.

Following this text are lines for "Signature of Resident/Date," which was left blank; "Signature of Legal Representative/Date," signed by James Moffett, but not dated; and "Signature of Facility Representative/Date," signed by a Briarwood employee and dated. Ms. Moffett [died after admission to a hospital]. Plaintiffs filed a complaint for wrongful death against Briarwood. . . . Briarwood filed a motion to compel arbitration. The trial court concluded that the arbitration agreement was invalid because it did not comply with §13-64-403, C.R.S. 2007, of the Colorado Health Care Availability Act (HCAA) . . . that (1) the arbitration agreement was "illegally tendered" because Briarwood knew "Ms. Moffett lacked rational capacity to sign" (2) a copy of the agreement was not given to Ms. Moffett as required; and (3) Mr. Moffett was impermissibly told that, if he did not sign the arbitration agreement, his mother would be refused and denied urgently needed care, in violation of §13-64-403(7), C.R.S. 2007.

[T]he trial court must first determine whether a valid agreement to arbitrate exists between the parties . . . The court may refuse to compel arbitration "only upon a showing that there is no agreement to arbitrate or if the issue sought to be arbitrated is clearly beyond the scope of the arbitration provision." . . . We conclude the statute allows an attorney-in-fact with sufficient authority to execute such an agreement. However, on the record before us, we cannot determine whether Mr. Moffett had authority to do so.

Section 13-64-403(11) provides, "No such [arbitration] agreement may be submitted to a patient for approval when the patient's condition prevents the patient from making a rational decision whether or not to execute such an agreement." The plain language of 13-64-403(11) neither expressly includes nor expressly excludes a person who holds a power of attorney from entering into an arbitration agreement on behalf of a patient who is unable to make a rational decision whether to enter into such an agreement. . . . [E]xecution of a power of attorney creates a principal-agent relationship . . . because an attorney-in-fact stands in the shoes of the . . . patient, it would be unnecessary . . . to have a separate provision in §13-64-403 explaining that a person who holds a power of attorney has the authority to sign an arbitration agreement on behalf of the principal-patient. . . . [T]o construe §13-64-403(1) as prohibiting a person who holds a power of attorney from executing an arbitration agreement on behalf of a patient would frustrate the very purpose of many powers of attorney. For example, in a statutory power of attorney, an agent may be given the power to "*[s]ubmit to arbitration,* settle, and propose or accept a compromise with respect to a claim or litigation." §15-1-1313 (1) (e), C.R.S. 2007 (emphasis added). However, plaintiffs' interpretation of 13-64-403(1) would effectively defeat an attorney-in-fact's power to "submit to arbitration."

In addition, the medical durable power of attorney statute, §15-14-506, C.R.S., expressly allows a person who holds a power of attorney to exercise all medical treatment decisions on behalf of the patient who lacks decisional capacity: An agent appointed in a medical durable power of attorney may provide informed consent to or refusal of medical treatment on behalf of a principal who lacks decisional capacity and *shall have the same power to make medical treatment decisions the principal would have if the principal did not lack such decisional capacity.* §15-14-506(3), C.R.S. 2007.

The provision . . . clearly indicates that, absent a limitation in the medical durable power of attorney, an attorney-in-fact can make exactly the same types of medical treatment decisions that the principal could make if he or she had the mental capacity to do so. "Medical treatment" is defined as "the provision, withholding, or withdrawal of any health care, medical procedure, including artificially provided nourishment and hydration, surgery, cardiopulmonary resuscitation, or service to maintain, diagnose, treat, or provide for a patient's physical or mental health or personal care. §15-14-505(7), C.R.S. 2007. [A] decision to admit the patient to a nursing home clearly constitutes a "medical treatment decision. . . . Courts in other jurisdictions have . . . [held] that a person who holds a medical durable power of attorney, in selecting a long-term health care facility, has the power to execute applicable admissions forms, including arbitration agreements, unless that power is restricted by the principal.

Although the existence of the powers of attorney is enough to find error in the trial court's conclusions, because they are not in the record we are unable to determine whether they contained any restrictions that would have prevented Mr. Moffett from executing the arbitration agreement. Therefore, on remand, the trial court should determine whether . . . Mr. Moffett . . . was validly exercising the authority vested in him by his mother's medical durable power of attorney or general power of attorney. . . . [I]t is undisputed that Mr. Moffett received a copy of the arbitration agreement. Therefore, if on remand the trial court concludes that Mr. Moffett had the authority to sign the arbitration agreement as his mother's attorney-in-fact, the trial court must find that §13-64-403(6) was also satisfied. There are disputed issues . . . regarding whether Mr. Moffett was impermissibly told that if he did not sign the arbitration agreement, his mother would be refused and denied urgently needed care. . . . [T]he trial court should revisit this issue on remand. §13-64-403(7) states: "No health care provider shall refuse to provide medical care services to any patient solely because such patient refused to sign such an [arbitration] agreement or exercised the ninety-day right of rescission." . . . Mr. Moffett was a competent individual signing a well-marked, highly visible agreement which indicated very clearly that dispute resolution would be accomplished by way of arbitration. In addition, having the arbitration agreement printed and executed as a separate agreement "cuts strongly against" plaintiffs' position because it suggests that Briarwood made clear that the arbitration agreement was not a condition of admission. . . . The judgment and order are reversed, and the case is remanded to the trial court for further proceedings consistent with this opinion.

In re SHEPARD

2010 Wash. LEXIS 723 (Wash. 2010) [summary]

Shepard was a solo practitioner in Tacoma who focused about a third of his practice on basic estate planning. In 2003, he was contacted by Cuccia, President of Coranda Living Trust Services, about entering into a business arrangement. Cuccia intended to sell living trusts to seniors in Washington and wanted Shepard to be available to provide legal advice to his customers . . . clients who purchased a Coranda Living Trust Package (CLTP) from Cuccia would be referred to Shepard for legal services relating to those trusts. Cuccia would independently market and sell the trusts and would have each purchaser sign a fee agreement with Shepard. The fee agreement required clients to pay Shepard $200 for his agreement to independently review and make recommendations regarding each client's estate planning needs. During the meeting, Cuccia informed Shepard that he was not a lawyer, but was a "certified estate planner." Cuccia did not mention that he had been previously convicted in California for selling fraudulent insurance products to seniors. Shepard agreed to the proposal.

After affiliating with Shepard, Cuccia began [visiting] the homes of prospective clients and gave a presentation about the benefits of using a living trust. Many of the elderly couples visited by Cuccia did not understand the differences between various estate planning options, and much of the information Cuccia provided them was either inaccurate or misleading. In particular, Cuccia exaggerated the costs and difficulty of probating an estate. Many clients were sold trusts that they did not need without being fully informed on how the living trusts worked. Most clients would have been better served by executing simple wills and advance medical directives rather than the living trusts. Shepard never accompanied Cuccia on sales visits. He did not discuss other estate planning options with prospective clients or review their financial situations before they agreed to purchase the CLTP.

As part of Cuccia's sales pitch, prospective clients were told that an attorney would review the estate planning documents and were presented with an attorney-client fee agreement whereby the clients retained Shepard and agreed to pay him $200 for his services. Among other things, the fee agreement provided: 1. SCOPE OF SERVICE. Client(s) retain Attorney to provide the following legal services: (a) Review and Consultations. Independent review of Client(s) estate planning needs to make recommendations regarding appropriate planning tools and supporting documents. Includes a personal telephone consultation to verify key information and provide answers to Client(s) legal questions. (b) Document and Asset Review. Review available financial and real estate documents for proper title designation. Order and supervise drafting of all plan documents, review final documents, and issue opinion letter with plan documents.

Shepard did not draft or produce trust packages. Both the CLTP and Shepard's fee agreement were generated by ATDS, a contract paralegal service that provides legal forms to attorneys. Shepard discussed the CLTP with ATDS and suggested changes. Upon agreement to purchase a CLTP, clients were asked to fill out a questionnaire that included assets and names, addresses, and ages of intended beneficiaries. The questionnaire was sent to ATDS which would generate trust documents and a short table summarizing the client's answers on the questionnaire. These were forwarded to Shepard, but he did not carefully review them. Shepard simply called to verify the information provided in the questionnaire was accurate. Once the information was verified, the trust packages were forwarded to Cuccia who delivered them, along with a form letter by Shepard explaining how to execute the trusts, to the clients. When the trusts were delivered, Shepard considered his job complete and never followed up to ensure that the documents were executed correctly.

Shepard did not provide the services promised in his fee agreement. He never discussed with his clients their estate planning needs and never discussed with them the advisability of entering into a living trust. He did not review their assets to determine an appropriate estate planning strategy. Though he did speak with his clients after they had already purchased the CLPT, conversations were very brief and were limited to verifying the information provided on the questionnaire. Shepard never discussed the financial condition of his clients, the size of their estates, or other simpler estate planning options. During the brief telephone calls he did make, Shepard never disclosed that he had an ongoing business relationship with Cuccia and Coranda and that this might give rise to a conflict of interest. Shepard represented over 70 people or couples and received $200 from Cuccia for each.

Although many purchasers of the CLTP were couples, Shepard often only spoke to one spouse over the phone. In some cases, Shepard made notes about concerns regarding competency of clients. In one instance, Bishop, specifically notified Shepard that his wife, Lavera, was incompetent to execute a trust. Although Shepard's fee agreement stated that "an in-office consultation . . . is required if undue influence or incapacity issues appear possible," Shepard made no effort to investigate, nor did he require the Bishops to come to his office. Mr. Bishop signed the trust documents for his wife using a previously executed power of attorney that specifically did not allow Mr. Bishop to revoke or change any estate planning or testamentary documents for Mrs. Bishop. Shepard did not discuss the prior power of attorney with the Bishops, and as a result the trusts they purchased were legally invalid.

[I]n 2003, Shepard was introduced to Steven Cuccia's brother, Anthony Cuccia, an insurance agent. Steven informed Shepard that Anthony would be working with him, offering insurance products to clients who purchased CLTPs. Steven and Anthony, along with Steven's wife Michelle and two other individuals, intended to use personal and financial information obtained through the sale of the CLTPs to sell annuities and reverse mortgages to clients through fraudulent means. Many clients who purchased the trust packages were pressured into purchasing these insurance products. Most of the insurance products purchased from the Cuccias were eventually canceled, and the premiums returned, but only after intervention by the office of the insurance commissioner (OIC).

Shepard became aware of possible problems by March 2004, when he was contacted by Prendergast, the daughter of two of his clients. Prendergast was upset and informed Shepard that she believed her parents were not competent to execute the trust documents because her mother had Alzheimer's disease and her father was bedridden. She was concerned that the documents they had signed were not executed properly, which turned out to be correct. She also informed Shepard that in addition to the CLTP, Cuccia had attempted to sell her parents both an annuity and a reverse mortgage. Shepard spoke with Cuccia about his conversation with Prendergast, but made no changes.

In December 2004, Shepard sent a letter to the Washington State Bar Association (Bar) requesting an informal opinion about possible RPC violations that an attorney might commit while performing "estate planning consultation services." In the letter, Shepard presented a "hypothetical" situation that essentially outlined the practices of Cuccia and Coranda. However, the hypothetical lawyer actually performed the services promised his clients. Shepard never received a response from the Bar.

In February 2005, Shepard was contacted by Overholt, an investigator with OIC. Overholt informed Shepard that OIC was investigating the Cuccias for their role in selling insurance products to seniors and told Shepard about Steven Cuccia's prior felony conviction in California. Despite this information, Shepard continued to accept clients referred to him through Coranda well into 2005. Overholt informed both the Bar and the attorney general's office about his concerns regarding the Cuccias, Coranda, and Shepard. The Bar began investigating Shepard's role in the scheme.

In response, Shepard initiated efforts to mitigate problems with his conduct. On April 20, 2006, he sent a letter to his clients urging them to make an appointment with him to review their trust documents. The letter informed clients of the three separate investigations by OIC, the attorney general, and the Bar. Shepard explained that he had no reason to believe that anything "improper" occurred during the preparation of trust documents, but that he was concerned that some of the trusts were not executed properly or were never received. On January 29, 2007, Shepard sent a follow-up letter to his clients again urging them to make an appointment to see him or another attorney of their choice to review the trust documents purchased from Coranda. The Bar filed a formal complaint against Shepard alleging [violation of] seven Rules of Professional Conduct. The State Bar Association Disciplinary Board recommended Shepard be suspended from the practice of law for two years. Shepard argues that a two-year suspension is too harsh.

CHANDLER V. OFFICE OF THE INSURANCE COMMISSIONER

173 P.3d 275 (Wash. App., 2007)

Chandler challenges the order revoking his Washington insurance agent's license. [T]he Office of the Insurance Commissioner (OIC) issued an order revoking Chandler's license on the ground that he was untrustworthy, a source of injury and loss to the public, and not qualified to be an insurance agent. The matter was referred to an administrative law judge (ALJ) [who] issued an initial decision which rejected the revocation order on the ground that there was insufficient evidence of untrustworthiness and that the "law of *caveat emptor* remains the general rule in the consumer marketplace." . . . [The review judge made the findings below,] rejected the ALJ's initial decision and issued a final order revoking Chandler's license. Superior Court affirmed the review judge's final order. Chandler appeals.

FINDINGS OF FACT

1. The Licensee is a 50 year old man who, until 2001, was a resident of California. He held a California insurance agent's license and worked as an insurance agent there until he surrendered that license in 2001. He is now a resident of Washington. The Licensee's primary clientele has always been senior citizens. Throughout his career, Licensee has made it a normal practice to meet with senior[s] in their homes. In addition to selling insurance products, the Licensee offers estate planning services to his clientele, including long term care insurance products, living trusts and reverse mortgages. . . .

2. As a means of making contact with potential clients, Licensee has used lead cards. Generally, lead cards are mailed to prospective clients, advertising access to some information or service. When the recipient mails back the card, the card is sold to an insurance agent (or the insurance agent has paid for the mailing of these cards initially) and the insurance agent then calls at the home of the prospective client. Often the insurance agent then takes that opportunity to attempt to sell the recipient/prospective client other insurance products (long term care insurance, etc.) or other noninsurance products (living trusts, reverse mortgages, etc.), or to provide other information, in addition to that which has been advertised in the lead cards to which the recipients have responded.

3. Licensee arranged with a Texas company to mass mail some 128,000 lead cards to seniors in King and Snohomish Counties, which advertised the availability of a possible property tax exemption or federally insured reverse mortgage programs. Interested seniors were to complete the card and mail it back to the Texas company which then refers them on to the Licensee. The Licensee then

arranged to come to the seniors' home to sell them insurance or other products. . . .

5. Licensee created, with another individual, several limited liability corporations, including The Life Insurance Store, Inc., Senior Loan Center, LLC, and The Centre, LLC (also known as the Centre for Living Trusts) . . . and another organization entitled Elder Planners of Washington. The Licensee represented himself as an "elder planner," who helps "seniors understand their options by intertwining the benefits available from . . . government entities along with the private sector, such as insurers . . . to better handle life's certainties and uncertainties." . . . Thus, the Licensee acknowledges that he offers to assist seniors in getting property tax exemptions as a "gimmick" to allow him access to seniors' homes and the opportunity to evaluate them for other potential sales. . . .

7. April 13, 2000, the Consumer Services Division of California's Department of Insurance wrote to the Licensee informing him that an elderly consumer had filed a request for assistance, claiming that the Licensee had refused to return various documents regarding a living trust. Cal Insurance instructed the Licensee to respond directly to the consumer's "complaint" and noted that he would not hear from Cal Insurance again unless the agency determined that the consumer's complaint was justified. . . .

8. Further, although the Licensee had never been involved in any "formal disciplinary action resulting in administrative penalties," in California, he had been the subject of eight investigations conducted by Cal Insurance, five of which were the result of citizen complaints. Four of these cases were closed with a "field warning given to the Licensee." . . .

10. Betty Husby is an approximately 77 year old woman who resides in Everett, Washington. Ms. Husby had responded to a lead card advertising information about living trusts. In response, on February 5, 2002, Mickey Larson, an associate of the Licensee, came to her home. The Licensee had conducted research into Ms. Husby's property, accessing public records to confirm property ownership and any existing liens. . . . Mr. Larson advised Ms. Husby that he was helping senior citizens pay fewer taxes, and she let him inside. Mr. Larson showed Ms. Husby a copy of her county property assessment record and said that he would return. On February 12, 2002, Mr. Larson and the Licensee returned to Ms. Husby's home. The Licensee talked with Ms. Husby for some two hours, and attempted to sell her a reverse mortgage so that, he advised, she could have more income and pay fewer taxes. Ms. Husby advised the Licensee that she was not interested in a reverse mortgage. At that point, the Licensee became agitated and when she refused to sign some papers he put in front of her, the Licensee stood over Ms. Husby and said "I'm not losing my commission. . . . You're going to sign this." Ms. Husby was alone with these two men, felt threatened and feared for her physically [sic] safety. Ms. Husby reluctantly signed the paper. The Licensee then put two more pages in front of her and told her to sign them as well, which she did out of fear. The Licensee then took papers Ms. Husby had signed, leaving no copies at all and advised her he would return the following week. . . . Ms. Husby then contacted a friend, who contacted Licensee and [t]old him not to return to her home, served papers upon Licensee rescinding any transaction which he might have entered into and who proceeded to investigate the Licensee, which eventually culminated in Ms. Husby filing a complaint with the OIC. . . .

Ms. Husby's complaint filed with the OIC, her subsequent deposition testimony and her testimony at hearing are all quite consistent.

11. Bill and Evelyn Kristjanson (Kristjansons) are a married couple who are each over 80 years old. Bill Kristjanson, at least, has a difficult time with memory loss and understanding financial documents. . . . While getting out of the car to attend and testify at the hearing herein, Mr. Kristjanson fell and injured himself and so neither he nor his daughter, Phyllis, were able to testify herein. However, Mr. Kristjanson did provide deposition testimony earlier and Phyllis' complaint to the OIC was included as evidence herein. In the summer of 2001, the Licensee sold the Kristjansons a will and living trust for approximately $8900. A few months later, the Licensee returned to sell long-term care coverage for Evelyn Kristjanson. The payment for the long-term care coverage was to come from a reverse mortgage on their home. When Phyliss [sic] Kristjanson discovered this, her husband (a former OIC examiner) called the Licensee [and said] that the reverse mortgage transaction was to be cancelled and requested that, because the elder Kristjansons experience memory loss and confusion, he did [sic] not directly contact the elder Kristjansons further, but instead work through Phyliss [sic] or himself. In January 2002, Phyliss [sic] Kristjanson discovered that the Licensee had returned to her parents' home with the intention of selling the long-term care coverage via a reverse mortgage. Phyliss [sic]Kri[s]tjanson advised the Licensee again not to contact her parents, but, a few hours later, she discovered that the Licensee had again contacted her parents against her wishes. The Licensee stated that he believed that the Kristjansons were competent to conduct an estate planning transaction with him and explained that he would not honor Phyliss [sic] Kristjanson's request to provide her with her parent's document because he honors his clients' right to privacy. . . .

14. In January 2002, Harold and Juanita Boeckel (Boeckels), elderly Washington residents, contacted the Licensee to update their living trust. . . . The Licensee convinced them that it would be easier to create a new one and charged them $965 to do so. . . . The Licensee drafted the new trust document, and when the Boeckels received it, they discovered many errors: Mr. Boeckel's first name was misspelled several times, two of their daughters were disinherited, monies previously given to their children were shown as loans instead of gifts, and the Licensee had inserted himself as an alternate Trustee, alternate Executor, and alternate Attorney-in-Fact and notarized the trust documents himself after bringing his own witnesses (two business associates, DeRenzo and Larson) to serve as witnesses even though Mr. Boeckel had already arranged for his neighbors to witness his documents. . . . Mr. Boeckel never indicated that he wanted the Licensee to be the alternate executor of his will nor [sic] give him power-of-attorney over his assets. . . . When the Boeckels were unable to have the Licensee correct the Trust, they sought the assistance of another attorney and for an additional $280 made the necessary changes. . . . Licensee also tried to sell them annuities, but when they told him they were not interested in buying the annuities, the Licensee persisted in attempting to sell them and eventually became angry and intimidating to the Boeckels. . . . The Licensee's activities in regard to the Boeckel transaction demonstrate that he is untrustworthy and a source of injury and loss to the public.

15. Prior to May 2002, the Licensee entered into an agreement with Alpha Telecom to sell, and subsequently did sell, public-use pay telephones and tele-

phone services to senior citizens on behalf of Alpha Telecom. . . . The "investor" was to receive 30% of the adjusted gross revenue generated by the telephones, or a monthly base amount of $46.67 per $4,000 [worth of] telephone[s] purchased or $58.34 per $5,000 [worth of] telephone[s] purchased, which equated to a 14% annual return. . . . The Licensee was not licensed as a securities agent to sell these securities.

16. As a result of his activities regarding Alpha Telecom, the Washington State Department of Financial Institutions (DFI), Securities Division, issued a Cease and Desist Order, SDO-9-02 against the Licensee and other individuals based upon its determination that the Licensee had engaged in offering and/or selling securities without a Washington securities license. On May 22, 2002, the Licensee agreed to a Consent Order, SDO-48-02 with DFI vacation Order No. SDO-9-02 and agreed to pay DFI $7,500 for its costs incurred in its investigation of the matter. The Licensee further agreed that, based on the Findings of Fact and Conclusions of Law, he would be subject to a fine in the amount of $50,000 with the entire amount suspended based on future compliance with DFI's Order. In the event of a violation of the Order, DFI will seek enforcement of the Order pursuant to RCW 21.20.395.

17. Eileen Johnston, a 75 year old widow, was visited by the Licensee in her home after she had mailed in a lead card requesting information on living trusts. As Ms. Johnston had limited financial resources, the Licensee set up a reverse mortgage and sold her $55,000 investment in Alpha Telecom paid out of the proceeds of the reverse mortgage. As a result, Ms. Johnston filed for bankruptcy and expected to lose her home of 50 years. . . .

19. As found in Findings of Facts 2 and 3 above, the Licensee uses a direct marketing service to mail postcards to senior citizens regarding the possibility of a senior citizen property tax exemption, and listed his identity as "Chandler and Assoc., Everett, WA,["] or "information provided by www.epwa.org," referring prospective clients to his "Elder Planners of Washington["] web site. . . . These mailers were confusing consumers and many consumers believed that these cards were being sent to the county assessors' offices. . . . Further, there is no indication a response to this card will result in a visit from an insurance agent who will likely to attempt to sell the senior insurance products and/or reverse mortgages, living trusts and the like. Additionally, the Office of the Attorney General, Consumer Protection Division performed an investigation into the Licensee's use of these lead cards . . . and found that these mailers were misleading. As a result, on May 7, 2003, the Attorney General issued a consumer alert to warn consumer[s] of the Licensee's direct mail solicitation. . . . These mailings were, indeed, misleading and deceptive. Further, the Licensee used these marketing cards as a "gimmick" [Testimony of the Licensee] to get his foot in the door of elderly consumers' homes to then sell them other products such as reverse mortgages, living trusts, long term care and other insurance policies. . . . Based upon this finding that these specific marketing cards are misleading and deceptive, the Licensee's use of these specific cards demonstrates that the Licensee is untrustworthy, which bears upon his qualifications to act as an insurance agent.

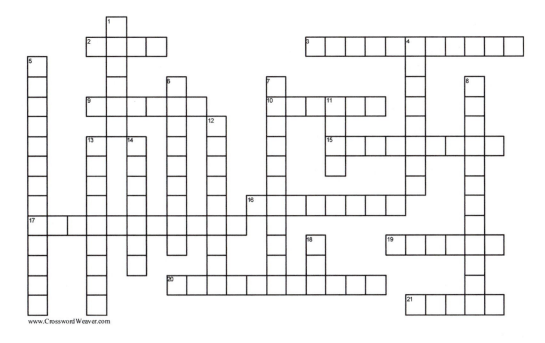

www.CrosswordWeaver.com

ACROSS

2. Bed _____, nursing home patient is absent and wants to return
3. Clause attempts to limit liability
9. _____ elements, such as swimming pool in condo development
10. Nursing home patients bill of _____
15. _____ care, patient stays with caregiver
16. _____ living, help with daily functions
17. Used for resolving disputes without litigation
19. Department of _____ and Human Services has elder care locator
20. _____ living, a marketing term, not generally regulated
21. Federal Administration on _____ (AoA)

DOWN

1. _____ law marriage, not formalized
4. Term for support of unmarried companion
5. Voluntary process, private organization verifies compliance with standards
6. Restrictive _____, restrict owner's use or sale of property
7. _____ care facility, also called CCRC
8. Living together
11. Initials, FHA reverse mortgage program
12. One of the requirements for Medicare coverage of home care
13. Nursing homes must be _____ to qualify for Medicare funds
14. Mortgage that borrows against equity
18. Initials, agency for housing issues

10

◆ ◆ ◆

Abuse, Neglect, and Financial Exploitation

◆ ◆ ◆

Objectives

When you complete this chapter, you will:

- Recognize the signs of neglect and abuse.
- Know the governmental agencies responsible for investigating and prosecuting abuse.
- Recognize the signs of an overly stressed caregiver and the resources available in such situations.
- Know the common schemes for financial exploitation and the remedies available.

Abuse and Neglect

Definitions

"Elder abuse" is a catchall term referring to any knowing, intentional, or negligent act by a caregiver or any other person that causes harm or a serious risk of harm to a vulnerable adult. The specificity of laws varies from state to state, but broadly defined, abuse may be:

- **Physical Abuse:** Inflicting, or threatening to inflict, physical pain or injury on an elder person, or depriving them of a basic need.
- **Emotional Abuse:** Inflicting mental pain, anguish, or distress on an elder person through verbal or nonverbal acts.
- **Sexual Abuse:** Nonconsensual sexual contact of any kind with an elder person.
- **Exploitation:** Illegal taking, misuse, or concealment of funds, property, or assets of an elder person.
- **Neglect:** Refusal or failure by those responsible to provide food, shelter, health care, or protection for an elder person.
- **Abandonment:** The desertion of an elder person by anyone who has assumed the responsibility for care or custody of that person.

Unfortunately, abuse, neglect, and financial exploitation of the elderly are major problems—and are on the rise. When discovered, these misdeeds can result in criminal, civil, or administrative actions. The type of action may depend on the "quantity" of the abusive or negligent behaviors. Some situations fall into a gray area. In general, *abuse* is physical or emotional mistreatment or harm, and *neglect* is the purposeful failure to provide needed care or services. But the appropriate action may depend on the level of the problem. A caregiver might go on vacation, leaving an elderly dementia patient alone for a week, or might dash out for 20 minutes to pick up an important prescription at the store. The result might be the same: The elderly person is badly injured or even dies. But should the penalty be the same?

According to AARP, statistics concerning instances of physical and financial abuse have spiked during from 2007 to 2009.[1] A paralegal working with senior clients must be particularly alert to the signs of abuse, because she may be among the few "outsiders" in communication with the victim.

It is difficult to say how many people are abused, neglected, or exploited, in large part because the problem remains greatly hidden. Findings from the often-cited National Elder Abuse Incidence Study suggest that more than 500,000 Americans age 60 and older were victims of domestic abuse in 1996. While the study is outdated, it is significant because it also found that only 16 percent of the abusive situations are referred for help—84 percent remain hidden. While a couple of studies estimate that between 3 percent and 5 percent of the elderly population have been abused, the Senate Special Committee on Aging estimates that there may be as many as 5 million victims every year.[2]

Causes

This chapter will focus on abuse and neglect of a vulnerable older person, the person most likely to be the client. As previously mentioned, economic factors underlie many instances of neglect, exploitation, and abuse, whether perpetrated by a family member or an outsider. The cause may also be psychological: a history of violence in the family or alcohol or substance abuse. Sometimes the cause is simply opportunity: An older person may be socially isolated, and the abuser senses vulnerability and a likelihood that the abuse will not be discovered. However, one reason that people often overlook signs of abuse or neglect is failure to understand the pressures on a common perpetrator of abuse: the caregiver. Knowing that the caregiver is a generous person, making sacrifices to care for a loved one, and has no history of violent or criminal character, makes it difficult to imagine that abuse or neglect are taking place.

Perpetrators

Abuse, neglect, and exploitation may be committed by a loved one, who may or may not be a caretaker; by an individual nonfamily caretaker or an institution; or by an outsider, without the caretaker or family's knowledge. All an abuser needs is access to the vulnerable older person, who may be unable or afraid to report. The abuse can be active and either physical or verbal or it can be passive and take the form of failing to meet the individual's needs. It is often hard to define the boundaries: Is a caregiver who loudly demands that the patient follow instructions exercising firm control over a difficult patient or being emotionally abusive? If a caregiver restrains a dementia patient so that the patient cannot get out of a chair, is the caregiver being physically abusive or simply ensuring the patient's safety? What about actions that amount to denials of rights—say a caregiver tells a patient that if she does not cooperate in taking her medications, she will not be allowed to visit with her family later in the week?

---

[1]AARP Bulletin print edition, July 1, 2009.
[2]*http://www.ncea.aoa.gov/ncearoot/main_site/FAQ/Questions.aspx*

Caretakers

According to the National Alliance for Caregiving (NAC) (*http://www.caregiv-ing.org/pubs/data.htm*), there are at least 43.5 million caregivers age 18 and over, equivalent to 19 percent of all adults, who provide unpaid care to an adult family member or friend age 50 years or older. Among the problems explored by the report:

- Financial burden
- Impact on caregiver's employment
- Physical strain and impact on caregiver's health
- Emotional stress

In addition, the elderly patient may be physically or verbally abusive toward the caregiver, particularly if the patient is suffering from mental deterioration.[3] Substance or alcohol abuse can also be a factor. The patient may have been abusive even as a young person. About one-third of caregivers are men, who are historically less likely to seek needed assistance.[4]

Regardless of the cause and regardless of whether the law office has any relationship with the caregiver, the situation is a matter of concern to a firm representing the elder patient. A caregiver who is under stress or is the victim of abuse is more likely to become abusive in response or to avoid and neglect the patient. Every caregiver should be made aware of the resources available, including:

- The NAC Web site (*http://www.caregiving.org/resources*)
- The National Family Caregivers Association Web site (*http://www.familycaregiving101.org*)
- The AARP Web site (*http://www.aarp.org/relationships/caregiving-resource-center/*)
- State respite care programs—start at *http://www.aoa.gov/AoARoot/Elders_Families/index.aspx*

Self-Neglect

Whether self-neglect constitutes a form of neglect or abuse can be controversial. If an individual is competent and able to care for herself, but chooses not to do so, should society intervene? Should it make a difference whether the choice involves poor grooming, such as failure to bathe, or refusal to seek medical treatment? Perhaps the answer depends on why the neglect is occurring: Is the individual making a choice or is she physically or mentally impaired or depressed? Is substance abuse or over-medication to blame? Might the cause be poverty or physical limitations making self-care difficult? If self-neglect is considered a form

---

[3]*http://www.ncbi.nlm.nih.gov/pmc/articles/PMC2745572*
[4]Gail Sheehy, *The Secret Caregivers,* AARP Magazine, May/June 2010, p. 43.

of abuse or neglect, it is a very large part of the problem. Some experts think it is the largest category within the umbrella of neglect and abuse.[5] At the very least, evidence of self-neglect must be evaluated to determine whether the individual is capable of self-care.

According to the AoA Web site, the signs of self-neglect include:

- **Hoarding**
- Failure to take essential medications or refusal to seek medical treatment for serious illness
- Leaving a burning stove unattended
- Poor **hygiene**
- Not wearing suitable clothing for the weather
- Confusion
- Inability to attend to housekeeping
- Dehydration[6]

Hoarding
Acquiring and failing to throw out a large number of items that appear to have little or no value

Hygiene
Conditions and practices, such as cleanliness, that promote or preserve health

Signs of Abuse and Reporting

Anyone in contact with a vulnerable older person must be able to notice changes in personality or behavior, and willing to ask hard questions. While one sign does not necessarily indicate abuse, some signs that there could be a problem are:

- Bruises, pressure marks, broken bones, abrasions, and burns may be an indication of physical abuse, neglect, or mistreatment.
- Unexplained withdrawal from normal activities, a sudden change in alertness, and unusual depression may be indicators of emotional abuse.
- Bruises around the breasts or genital area can occur from sexual abuse.
- Sudden changes in financial situations may be the result of exploitation.
- Bedsores, unattended medical needs, poor hygiene, and unusual weight loss are indicators of possible neglect.
- Behavior such as belittling, threats, and other uses of power and control by spouses are indicators of verbal or emotional abuse.
- Strained or tense relationships, or frequent arguments between the caregiver and elderly person are also signs.[7]

Victims are often reluctant to disclose abuse and neglect and even more reluctant to accept a remedy that will include leaving home or the eviction of or an order of protection against the perpetrator. Despite the abuse, the victim may love the perpetrator and feel that life would be worse without this person. It may, therefore, fall to others to report the situation. Visit *http://www.ncea.aoa.gov/ncearoot/main_site/Find_Help/State_Resources.aspx* to determine who should be called in your state to report possible abuse.

---

[5] *http://www.webster.edu/~woolflm/abuse.html*
[6] *http://www.ncea.aoa.gov/ncearoot/main_site/FAQ/Questions.aspx*
[7] *http://www.ncea.aoa.gov/ncearoot/main_site/FAQ/Questions.aspx*

Some states have laws mandating that certain professionals report abuse and protecting those who make reports, like the Illinois law shown in the Example below. Mandatory reporting laws generally apply to health care and social workers and have been criticized as ineffective. Prosecution for failure to report is rare, and some commentators believe that these laws should distinguish between competent individuals and those unable to help themselves to respect the autonomy of the victims.[8]

Example: Illinois Law[9]

Anyone can report a case of elder abuse in good faith.
The Elder Abuse and Neglect Act provides that people who in good faith report suspected abuse or cooperate with an investigation are immune from criminal or civil liability or professional disciplinary action. It further provides that the identity of the reporter shall not be disclosed except with the written permission of the reporter or by order of a court. Anonymous reports are accepted.

Certain professionals are required by law to report suspected elder abuse.
Illinois has a law which requires certain professionals to make reports of suspected abuse of older persons who are unable, due to dysfunction, to report for themselves. This law applies to persons delivering professional services to older persons in the following fields:

- social services
- adult care
- law enforcement
- education
- medicine
- state service to seniors
- social workers.

Mandatory reporting requirements only apply when the reporter believes that the older person is not capable of reporting the abuse themselves.

Few states specifically make lawyers mandatory reporters, although lawyers may fall within the broad coverage of a general law. For example, Texas Human Resources Code §48.051 provides, "(a) Except as prescribed by Subsection (b), *a person* having cause to believe that an elderly or disabled person is in the state of abuse, neglect, or exploitation, including a disabled person receiving services as described by Section 48.252, shall report the information required by Subsection (d) immediately to the department" (emphasis added).

Similarly, in Indiana, IC 35-46-1-13 provides:

(a) A person who:

(1) believes or has reason to believe that an endangered adult is the victim of battery, neglect, or exploitation as prohibited by this chapter, IC 35-42-2-1(a)(2)(C), or IC 35-42-2-1(a)(2)(E); and

---

[8]See, e.g., Jennifer Glick, *Protecting and Respecting Our Elders,* 12 Va. J. Soc Pol'y & Law 714 (Spring 2005).
[9]*http://www.state.il.us/aging/1abuselegal/abuse_reporting.htm*

(2) knowingly fails to report the facts supporting that belief to the division of disability and rehabilitative services, the division of aging, the adult protective services unit designated under IC 12-10-3, or a law enforcement agency having jurisdiction over battery, neglect, or exploitation of an endangered adult; commits a Class B misdemeanor.

Arizona Revised Statutes §46-454 creates a limited duty with respect to financial exploitation:

> An attorney, accountant, trustee, guardian, conservator or other person who has responsibility for preparing the tax records of a vulnerable adult or a person who has responsibility for any other action concerning the use or preservation of the vulnerable adult's property and who, in the course of fulfilling that responsibility, discovers a reasonable basis to believe that exploitation of the adult's property has occurred or that abuse or neglect of the adult has occurred shall immediately report or cause reports to be made of such reasonable basis to a peace officer, to a protective services worker or to the public fiduciary of the county in which the vulnerable adult resides.

How does reporting fit with the ethical obligation of confidentiality? The client might specifically request that the abuse not be revealed, or the client might be the perpetrator. Few states specifically address the question. For example, in South Carolina, 43-35-50 provides:

> Abrogation of privilege for certain communications. The privileged quality of communication between husband and wife or between a professional person and the person's patient or client, except that between attorney and client or priest and penitent, are abrogated and do not constitute grounds for failing to report or for the exclusion of evidence in any civil or criminal proceeding resulting from a report made pursuant to this chapter.

To analyze the issue, start by finding your state law on mandatory reporting: *http://www.abanet.org/aging/docs/MandatoryReportingProvisionsChart.pdf*. Next, examine your state ethics rules: *http://www.abanet.org/cpr/links.html#States*. What do the confidentiality provisions say about disclosure to prevent substantial bodily harm or reasonably certain harm to financial interests? Do the rules allow a lawyer to act on behalf of a client with diminished capacity to protect that client's interests?

Financial Exploitation

Senior citizens are not only the fastest growing segment of the population, they are also most likely to have a "nest egg" and be at home, answering the phone and the door. Those factors, coupled with social isolation, loneliness, and confusion, make senior citizens particularly vulnerable to financial crimes, such as fraud. Even a victim who is intelligent and not impaired may be vulnerable because of her beliefs about politeness, having a trusting nature, lack of understanding about technical matters or the law, and even embarrassment about being alone.

Some states, including California and Colorado, specifically criminalize financial abuse of the elderly, while others rely on general criminal statutes. Others use the age or vulnerability of the victim as a sentencing enhancement. State laws prohibiting financial exploitation are often classified as consumer protection acts and enforced by the state's attorney general. To find the responsible agency in your state, visit *http://www.consumeraction.gov/state.shtml*. At the federal level, the Federal Trade Commission (FTC) enforces a number of laws, including, among others, the laws summarized in Exhibit 10.1.

EXHIBIT 10.1
FTC Enforcement

Fair Packaging and Labeling Act (15 U.S.C. §§1451-1461) requires that consumer commodities other than food, drugs, therapeutic devices, and cosmetics be labeled to disclose net contents, identity of commodity, and name and location of manufacturer or distributor.

Truth in Lending Act (15 U.S.C. §§1601-1667f) requires creditors who deal with consumers to make written disclosures concerning finance charges and related matters and establishes three-day right of rescission in certain transactions.

Fair Credit Billing Act (15 U.S.C. 1666-1666j) requires prompt written acknowledgment of consumer billing complaints and investigation of billing errors; prohibits creditors from taking adverse actions until investigation is completed.

Fair Credit Reporting Act (15 U.S.C. §§1681-1681(u)) protects privacy of information collected by credit bureaus, medical information companies, and tenant screening services.

Gramm-Leach-Bliley Act (15 U.S.C. §§6801-6809 and §§6821-6827) requires that financial institutions protect financial privacy.

Fair Debt Collection Practices Act (15 U.S.C. §§1692-1692o) prohibits third-party debt collectors from employing deceptive or abusive conduct in the collection of consumer debts.

Electronic Fund Transfer Act (15 U.S.C. §§1693-1693r) establishes the rights, liabilities, and responsibilities of participants in electronic fund transfer systems.

Consumer Leasing Act (15 U.S.C. §§1667-1667f) regulates personal property leases that exceed four months in duration, made to consumers for personal, family, or household purposes.

Magnuson Moss Warranty-Federal Trade Commission Improvements Act (15 U.S.C. §§2301-2312) is the basis for FTC regulation of product warranties.

Hobby Protection Act (16 U.S.C. §§2101-2106) outlaws manufacturing or importing imitation numismatic and collectible political items unless they are marked in accordance with FTC regulations.

EXHIBIT 10.1
(continued)

Postal Reorganization Act of 1970 (39 U.S.C. §3009(a)) authorizes the FTC to prosecute unfair or deceptive practices involving use of the mail to send unordered merchandise.

Federal Deposit Insurance Corporation Improvement Act of 1991 (12 U.S.C. §1831t) requires non–federally insured depository institutions to disclose that the institution is not federally insured.

Energy Policy Act of 1992 (42 U.S.C. §§6201 *et seq.*) concerns energy efficiency labeling.

Telephone Disclosure and Dispute Resolution Act of 1992 (15 U.S.C. §§5701 *et seq.*) allows FTC regulation of pay-per-call or "900 number" telephone services.

Telemarketing and Consumer Fraud and Abuse Prevention Act (15 U.S.C. §§6101-6108) allows the FTC to prohibit deceptive telemarketing practices, to prohibit unsolicited telephone calls that a reasonable consumer would consider coercive or an invasion of privacy, to restrict hours when unsolicited calls may be made to consumers, and to require disclosure of the nature of the call at the start of an unsolicited call.

Home Equity Loan Consumer Protection Act/Home Ownership and Equity Protection Act (15 U.S.C. §§1637, 1639 and 1647) requires disclosures and imposes limits on open-end credit secured by consumer's home; prohibits equity stripping and other abusive practices with high-cost mortgages.

Credit Repair Organizations Act (15 U.S.C. §§1679-1679j) prohibits misrepresentations and requires certain affirmative disclosures in the offering or sale of "credit repair" services.

Identity Theft Assumption and Deterrence Act of 1998 (18 U.S.C. §1028) makes the FTC a central clearinghouse for identity theft complaints.

Do-Not-Call Registry Act of 2003 (15 U.S.C. §6102 note) prohibits commercial telemarketers from calling people on the registry, with some exceptions, to reduce the number of solicitation calls.

Fair and Accurate Credit Transactions Act of 2003 (15 U.S.C. §§1681-1681x) entitles consumers to one free credit report a year and enables consumers to place fraud alerts in their credit files.

Unlawful Internet Gambling Enforcement Act (31 U.S.C. 5361 *et seq.*) prohibits any person engaged in the business of betting from knowingly accepting credit, electronic fund transfers, checks, or any other payment involving a financial institution to settle unlawful Internet gambling debts.

Example

The Florida Attorney General Web site (*http://www.myfloridalegal.com/#*) is typical:

What Florida Law Provides
The Attorney General's Office is an enforcing authority of Florida's Deceptive and Unfair Trade Practices Act, which is meant to protect individual consumers and legitimate businesses from various types of illegal conduct in trade or commerce. Pursuant to the Act, the attorney general investigates and files civil actions against persons who engage in unfair methods of competition, unfair, unconscionable or deceptive trade practices, including, but not limited to, pyramid schemes, misleading franchise or business opportunities, travel scams, fraudulent telemarketing, and false or misleading advertising.

According to the federal Department of Justice Community Oriented Policing Services (COPS) Web site, financial exploitation is likely very underreported. In addition, an elder who has been victimized is particularly likely to be re-victimized. Some scams even target previous victims with promises to recover money lost to an earlier scam. The COPS guide, "Financial Crimes Against the Elderly,"[10] classifies financial crimes according to whether they are committed by strangers or by relatives or caregivers. When a relative or caregiver commits a financial crime, it typically consists of:

- Exploiting legal arrangements, such as joint accounts, powers of attorney, or trusts.
- Simply taking the elder's money, property, or valuables without permission (possibly without the elder's knowledge), often selling or giving away the property.
- Borrowing money (sometimes repeatedly) and not paying it back.
- Denying services or medical care to conserve funds for inheritance.
- Signing or cashing pension or social security checks without permission.
- Misusing ATM or credit cards, or using them without permission.
- Forcing the elder to part with resources by making empty promises (such as lifelong care) or threats (to put the elder in a nursing home).

Example

A new scam has been making its way through the elder community. The elder receives a call from a person who announces, "Grandma, it's me!" When the elder answers, "Jason, is it you?" the caller claims to be Jason. The elder often has poor hearing and may not have seen or spoken to the grandchild in a long time. The "grandchild" claims to be in trouble while on vacation or at college and afraid to contact his parent. The grandparent is asked to send money for legal fees or medical treatment immediately.

---

[10]*http://www.cops.usdoj.gov/ric/ResourceDetail.aspx?RID=91*

Common Schemes

Crimes committed by strangers often involve sweepstakes and contests, home and auto repairs, investment scams, charitable giving, health remedies, travel, loans, insurance, and funeral planning. The fraud may be committed by means of mail, telephone, face-to-face contact, or the Internet. A common element to fraud by strangers is building confidence or trust by use of a charismatic personality, use of a business or charity name that is similar to that of a well-known organization, and use of personal flattery — implying that the older person has been "specially selected." The implication that the victim was individually selected often assists in another goal: keeping the transaction secret.

The Federal Bureau of Investigation (FBI) maintains a Common Fraud Schemes Web site (*http://www.fbi.gov/majcases/fraud/seniorsfam.htm*) that details scams involving reverse mortgages (discussed in Chapter 9) and funeral planning scams (Chapter 12) among other featured scams.

Here are some warning signs of consumer fraud or exploitation:

- Stacks of unsolicited mail proclaiming the recipient to be a "guaranteed winner."
- Unusual number of packages containing cheap costume jewelry, plastic cameras, and watches.
- Excessive magazine subscriptions.
- Unsolicited calls from operators offering "fantastic opportunities" for prizes or investments.
- Difficulty covering expenses such as food, utilities, etc., if income should support these needs.
- Housing or possessions inconsistent with supposed finances (e.g., elder with a good pension unable to replace television).
- New relationships in which the "friend" does not meet family members or friends and is not a usual social companion (older, wealthy man or much younger woman with financial problems).
- Elder visits bank with a stranger who encourages a large withdrawal.
- Unusual interest in the elder's finances by a caregiver, a friend, or even a relative.
- Anyone preventing others from communicating with elder or access to financial documents.
- Checks and withdrawals for individuals, marketing companies, or other businesses, or transactions that the elder cannot explain.

Health Insurance Frauds

In the case of medical equipment fraud, equipment manufacturers offer "free" products. Insurers are charged for products that were not needed and may not have been delivered.

In "rolling lab" schemes, unnecessary and sometimes fake tests are given to individuals at health clubs, retirement homes, or shopping malls and billed to insurance companies or Medicare.

Medicare fraud can take the form of any of the frauds described above. Senior citizens are frequent targets, especially by equipment manufacturers who offer seniors free medical products in exchange for their Medicare numbers. Because a physician has to sign a form certifying that equipment or testing is needed before Medicare pays for it, con artists fake signatures or bribe corrupt doctors to sign.

These are some tips for avoiding health insurance fraud:

- Never sign blank insurance claim forms.
- Never give blanket authorization to a medical provider to bill for services rendered.
- Ask medical providers what they charge and what you will be expected to pay out-of-pocket.
- Carefully review your explanation of benefits statement. Call your insurer and provider if you have questions.
- Do not do business with door-to-door or telephone salespeople who tell you that services or medical equipment are free.
- Give your insurance/Medicare identification only to those who have provided you with services.
- Keep accurate records of all health care appointments.
- Know if your physician ordered equipment for you.

These are some tips for avoiding counterfeit prescription drugs:

- Closely examine packaging and lot numbers of prescription drugs and be alert of any changes from one prescription to the next.
- Consult your pharmacist or physician if your prescription drug looks suspicious.
- Alert your pharmacist and physician immediately if medication causes side effects or if your condition does not improve.
- Do not purchase medications from unlicensed online distributors or those who sell medications without a prescription. Reputable online pharmacies have a seal of approval called the Verified Internet Pharmacy Practice Site (VIPPS).
- Promotions or cost reductions and other "special deals" may involve counterfeit products.

These are some tips for avoiding fraudulent "anti-aging" products:

- If it sounds too good to be true, it probably is. Watch for "secret formulas" or "breakthroughs."
- Don't be afraid to ask questions about the product.
- Research a product thoroughly before buying it. Call the Better Business Bureau to find out if other people have complained about the product.
- Be wary of products that claim to cure a wide variety of illnesses that don't appear to be related.
- Testimonials and/or celebrity endorsements are often misleading.
- Be very careful of products that are marketed as having no side effects.
- Products that are advertised as making visits to a physician unnecessary should be questioned.
- Always consult your doctor before taking any dietary or nutritional supplement.

Telemarketing Fraud

If you're age 60 or older, you may be a special target for people who sell bogus products and services by phone. Telemarketing scams often involve offers of prizes, low-cost vitamins and health care products, and travel offers. There are warning signs to these scams, including promises of "free" or "low-cost" vacations and get-rich-quick schemes. If you hear these — or similar — "lines" from a telephone salesperson, just say, "No thank you," and hang up the phone:

- "You must act now or the offer won't be good."
- "You've won a free gift, vacation, or prize." You have to pay postage and handling or other charges.
- "You must send money, give a credit card or bank account number, or have a check picked up by courier." You may hear this before you have had a chance to consider the offer carefully.
- The callers say you do not need to speak to anyone including your family, lawyer, accountant, local Better Business Bureau, or consumer protection agency.
- "You don't need any written information about their company or their references."
- "You can't afford to miss this high-profit, no-risk offer."

Here are some tips for avoiding telemarketing fraud. It's difficult to get your money back if you've been cheated over the phone. Before you buy, remember:

- Don't buy from an unfamiliar company. Legitimate businesses understand that you want more information about their company and are happy to comply.
- Always wait until you receive written material about any offer or charity. If you get brochures about investments, ask someone whose financial advice you trust to review them. Keep in mind that not everything written down is true.
- Check out unfamiliar companies with your local consumer protection agency, Better Business Bureau, state attorney general, the National Fraud Information Center, or other watchdog groups. Unfortunately, not all bad businesses can be identified through these organizations.
- Some con artists give out false names, telephone numbers, addresses, and business license numbers. Verify the accuracy of these items.
- Before you give money to a charity or make an investment, find out what percentage of the money is paid in commissions and what percentage actually goes to the charity or investment.
- Before you send money, ask yourself, "What guarantee do I really have that this solicitor will use my money in the manner we agreed upon?" Pay only after delivery.
- Some con artists will send a messenger to your home to pick up money, claiming it is part of their service. In reality, they are taking money without leaving any trace of who they are.
- Always take your time making a decision. Legitimate companies won't pressure you.
- Don't pay for a "free prize." If a caller tells you payment is for taxes, he is violating federal law.

- It's never rude to wait and think about an offer. Be sure to talk over big investments offered by telephone salespeople with a trusted friend, family member, or financial advisor.
- Never respond to an offer you don't understand thoroughly.
- Never send money or give out credit card numbers and expiration dates, bank account numbers, dates of birth, or social security numbers to unfamiliar companies or unknown persons.
- Your personal information is often brokered to telemarketers through third parties.
- If you have been victimized, be wary of calls offering to help you recover your losses for a fee.
- Report fraud to state, local, or federal law enforcement agencies.

Identity Theft

The Federal Trade Commission (FTC) estimates that as many as nine million Americans are victims of identity theft each year and provides resources and information to victims. Identity theft occurs when a thief uses personal information, such as name, social security number, or credit card number, without permission. The thief may commit fraud in obtaining government benefits or other crimes, using the victim's name, by obtaining a driver's license or other identification with the victim's information but the thief's picture. The thief may order goods or services charged to an existing account, rent housing, obtain a new credit card or open a new bank account in the victim's name for use by the thief, obtain a loan, or establish new phone or utility accounts. Some victims resolve the problem quickly, but others spend large amounts of time and money repairing damage to reputation and credit record. Some may lose job opportunities, or be denied loans because of negative credit report information. In rare cases, they may even be arrested for crimes they did not commit.

Among the methods used to obtain personal information:

- **Dumpster Diving:** Rummaging through trash for bills or other paper with personal information.
- **Skimming:** Use of a device to steal credit and debit card numbers while processing a card.
- **Phishing:** Pretending to be a financial institution or company and sending spam or pop-up messages to get victims to reveal personal information.
- **Changing Address:** Diverting statements to another location using a change of address form.
- **Stealing:** Taking wallets and purses; mail, including bank and credit card statements; pre-approved credit offers; new checks; tax information; personnel records.
- **Pretexting:** Using false pretenses to obtain personal information from financial institutions, telephone companies, and other sources.

To catch identity theft quickly and limit the damage, people should monitor accounts and bank statements each month, and check their credit reports on a regular basis. Often, however, victims are not aware of identity theft until they are contacted about overdue bills they did not incur or they are denied a loan or a credit card. Once identity theft is spotted, the victim should:

1. File an FTC ID Theft Complaint at *https://www.ftccomplaintassistant. gov*, print out the complaint, and take it to the local police.
2. File an Identity Theft Report with the police, which entitles the victim to certain legal rights when it is provided to the three major credit reporting agencies or to companies where the thief misused the victim's information. An Identity Theft Report must contain specific detailed information. It can be used to block fraudulent information, such as accounts or addresses, from appearing on the victim's credit report and to ensure that fraudulent debts do not reappear on credit reports. Identity Theft Reports can prevent a company from continuing to collect debts that result from identity theft. An Identity Theft Report is also needed to place an extended fraud alert on the victim's credit report. A police report is needed to get copies of information from companies that dealt with the thief.
3. Contact companies to correct fraudulent information and regularly monitor credit reports for additional fraudulent information.

Advance Fee, Pyramid, and Ponzi Schemes

An advance fee scheme involves persuading a victim to pay money in anticipation of receiving something of greater value, such as an inheritance, prize, "found money," loan, contract, investment, or gift. The victim actually receives little or nothing in return. The advance fee may be characterized as a "finder's fee," a delivery fee, "earnest money," a legal fee, or some other kind of fee.

A Ponzi scheme is an investment fraud that promises high financial returns or dividends that are not available through traditional investments. Instead of investing victims' funds, the operator pays "dividends" to initial investors using the principle amounts "invested" by later investors. The scheme generally falls apart when the operator flees with all of the proceeds, or when a sufficient number of new investors cannot be found to allow the continued payment of "dividends."

Pyramid schemes, also referred to as franchise fraud or chain referral schemes, are marketing and investment frauds: An individual is solicited to buy a distributorship or franchise to market a particular product. The real profit is earned, not by sale of the product, but by sale of new distributorships. Emphasis on selling franchises rather than the product eventually leads to a point where the supply of potential investors is exhausted and the pyramid collapses. At the heart of each pyramid scheme there is typically a claim that new participants can recoup their original investments by inducing two or more prospects to make the same investment.

Some pyramid schemes do not even involve a product, but work more like a chain letter. Each new participant is asked to give money to participants "up the chain" and then recruit new participants who will give them money.

Home Repair Fraud

Because older people may be unable to perform their own home maintenance and repairs, they are particularly vulnerable to this type of fraud. Some states have enacted laws governing the contents of home repair contracts, requiring insurance, and imposing other safeguards. Seniors have to be particularly alert to unmarked trucks, "repairmen" who cruise neighborhoods looking for work, companies unwilling to provide references, stories involving "leftover materials from another job," companies that offer to pay for referrals to other customers or that promise loans without respect to credit ratings, and companies that demand payment in advance.

The Role of Government: Federal

As abuse and neglect of elders began to come to the public attention, there was a call for governmental action. In response, 1987 amendments to the Older Americans Act (42 U.S.C. §3001) required that each state create a plan for prevention of abuse. As a result, primary responsibility for protection of the elderly lies with the states, but the AoA provides grants to the states (see Exhibit 10.2). The state agency on aging coordinates efforts, and many states choose to use their AoA funds to support local service providers and area agencies on aging. Other than providing funding through grants, the federal role has historically been limited to dissemination of information. The "Prevention of Elder Abuse, Neglect, and Exploitation Program" of the federal AoA provides a number of resources through the National Center on Elder Abuse (NCEA) (*http://www.ncea.aoa.gov*).

The AoA has also developed the National Legal Resource Center (*http://www.nlrc.aoa.gov*), a collaborative effort that supports legal professionals working with the elderly. The center provides access to materials on a variety of legal issues, models of effective programs and practices, and even case consultations.

The latest federal enactment is the Elder Justice Act, Pub. Law 111-148. The Act was part of the Patient Protection and Affordable Care Act, which became law in 2010, and, among other provisions, authorizes an Elder Justice Coordinating Council to make recommendations within two years to the Secretary of Health and Human Services on coordination of activities of federal, state, local, and private agencies relating to elder abuse, neglect, and exploitation. The law also authorizes funding for Adult Protective Services; for state demonstration grants to test methods to detect and prevent elder abuse; for Elder Abuse, Neglect, and Exploitation Forensic Centers to develop forensic expertise and provide services relating to elder abuse, neglect, and exploitation; for the Long-Term Care Ombudsman Program; for training programs for national organizations and state long-term care ombudsman programs; and for enhancing long-term care staffing through training and recruitment and incentives for individuals seeking or maintaining employment in long-term care, in either a facility or a community-based long-term care entity.

EXHIBIT 10.2
Examples of State Programs Funded by AoA in 2007

- In Kentucky, the statewide network of Local Coordinating Councils on Elder Abuse has developed "visor cards" for law enforcement officers that contain contact and resource information to assist victims of elder abuse. The Councils also produced "fraud fighter" forms that are distributed to thousands of seniors to help in the prevention of exploitation and scam artists. Other public awareness activities include renting billboards with elder abuse awareness messages and the state reporting number, hosting community trainings on the various forms of elder abuse, and other events and resources to raise awareness in communities.
- In Rochester, New York, Lifespan used OAA funding to train nontraditional reporters, such as hairdressers, store clerks, and others who have frequent contact with the elderly, on how to identify and report suspected cases of elder abuse. Additionally, a series of television ads were developed and aired.
- The Wisconsin Bureau of Aging and Disability Resources, in collaboration with the National Clearinghouse on Later Life, developed a series of pamphlets to raise awareness for caregivers of the risks and signs of abuse in later life, or "domestic violence grown old."

The Role of Government: State

Many state and local agencies have some role in dealing with elder abuse and exploitation. If violence or criminal behavior occur in the community, the police or sheriff's office may be the first responder. If the abuse, neglect, or exploitation occurs in a care facility, the best resource may be the state long-term care ombudsman (described in Chapter 9). A previous section in this chapter led you to a list of other offices in your state, which may include an abuse hotline, the office of the state's attorney general, and links to area agencies on aging. Local Adult Protective Services (APS) offices are generally under the umbrella of one of these agencies. A local APS office is often the first responder to reports of abuse, exploitation, and neglect. APS interventions include, but are not limited to, receiving and investigating reports, case planning, monitoring, and evaluation. APS may also provide or arrange for the provision of medical, social, economic, legal, housing, law enforcement, or other protective, emergency, or supportive services. In some states, local APS functions may be contracted to a private organization.

Civil Actions

Regardless of whether governmental action has occurred in a case involving a senior citizen, the victim may seek a civil order of protection or "stay away" order against the perpetrator. In addition, civil remedies may be available to provide the victim with funds to aid in her recovery and care. If the abuse occurred in a care facility, a malpractice claim may be appropriate. Other abusers may be sued for assault, battery, false imprisonment, or intentional infliction of emotional distress.

Helping Older Victims

In some cases, the exploitation of a senior citizen does not rise to the level of a criminal matter that would cause a governmental agency to intervene. In other cases (as in the case summarized at the end of the chapter), the exploitation may not be discovered until after the victim's death — in fact, many perpetrators count on that. In such cases, the victim or her family may resort to a private lawsuit. An exploitation victim may sue for the return of property on the same grounds that may be used to challenge a will: incapacity, fraud, duress, or undue influence (Chapter 8).

Example

Maine has codified the concept in its Improvident Transfer Act, Title 33, Ch. 20 §1022. Undue influence
1. Presumption. In any transfer of real estate or major transfer of personal property or money for less than full consideration or execution of a guaranty by an elderly person who is dependent on others to a person with whom the elderly dependent person has a confidential or fiduciary relationship, it is presumed that the transfer or execution was the result of undue influence, unless the elderly dependent person was represented in the transfer or execution by independent counsel. When the elderly dependent person successfully raises the presumption of undue influence by a preponderance of the evidence and when the transferee or person who benefits from the execution of a guaranty fails to rebut the presumption, the elderly dependent person is entitled to avoid the transfer or execution and entitled to the relief set forth in section 1024

Regardless of whether there is criminal prosecution, action by a governmental agency, or a civil suit, remember that an older person may be a particularly fragile victim and witness. Always proceed with caution and act respectfully to all of the individuals involved, regardless of what you believe may have happened or the individual's competency. Interview everyone out of the presence of others. Consider interviewing older people at different times of day and videotaping interviews. Try to obtain all necessary facts from a variety of sources, to minimize reliance on an older witness.

EXHIBIT 10.3
LaShonda Says

A graduate of the University of Michigan, Bachelor of Applied Science Degree with an emphasis in Criminal Justice and Business, LaShonda Dillard obtained an Associate Degree in Applied Science — Paralegal Technology from Mott Community College in Flint, Michigan. LaShonda is currently a litigation paralegal specializing in special education law at the Weatherly Law Firm in Atlanta, Georgia. She is serving her fourth term on the Georgia Association of Paralegals Board of Directors. She represents the local paralegal association nationally. Ms. Dillard is also a member of the National Federation of Paralegals Association (NFPA) wherein she has been a delegate to the national convention for the past two years. Before taking her current position, LaShonda worked in elder law and says that being an elder law paralegal can be very rewarding.

However, one must be very personable, friendly, and trustworthy. I assisted clients with their long-term care and/or nursing home needs. I met with the client's children and/or other relatives to discuss the needs of aging individuals who were unable to live alone and/or care for themselves any longer due to the onset of dementia and/or Alzheimer's. Oftentimes, a paralegal in this field will have access to clients' retirement accounts, and bank and investment accounts. Because clients may feel vulnerable, it is very important to make them feel comfortable. While reviewing and maintaining decades of financial documents, it was very common to stumble across bank accounts the elderly client forgot existed. As such, a paralegal's attention to detail and investigative skills are very important.

Assignments

1. Visit the AoA Web site and prepare a short report (1–2 pages) on the latest available statistics about elder abuse and neglect.
2. Find the FTC three-day "cooling-off" rule and describe when it applies.
3. Ethical Thinking: Find and read the March 2006 Illinois Supreme Court case, *In re Winthrop*, 848 N.E.2d 961, at *http://www.state.il.us/court/Opinions/archive.asp*
   - Do you think a two-year suspension was appropriate?
   - Do you think lawyers should have a heightened duty to clients in this type of situation?

4. Search your state's laws concerning consumer fraud and regulated businesses. Does your state regulate dance studios, weight-loss businesses, or health clubs? Does it have a "lemon law" for purchasers of automobiles? Does it include special provisions relating to home repair fraud? Does it include any business regulations that surprise you?

5. Find your state's statutory law concerning undue influence. Start at *http://www.abanet.org/aging/about/pdfs/Undue_Influence_Context_Provisions_and_Citations_Chart.pdf.*

6. View and write a short report on one of the webinars identified by the National Legal Resource Center as a resource for elder law professionals: *http://www.nlrc.aoa.gov/nlrc/Resources/WebCasts.aspx.* (The available resources will change with time.) You may be able to link directly to the webinars through *http://www.nlrc.aoa.gov/Legal_Issues/Consumer_Protection/Consumer_Scams.aspx.*

7. Determine whether your state has a law mandating reports of elder abuse by certain professionals and protecting reporters.

8. Browse the Fraud Prevention page of the AARP Web site (*http://www.aarpelderwatch.org/public/fraud_prevention.html*) and then write a short memo describing how elder clients can protect themselves against travel scams, home repair scams, and chain letter scams.

9. Critical Thinking: Read the case at the end of the chapter.
   - Find your state law on annulment; what does it say about annulment after the death of a spouse?
   - Why did Nidia have the right to take an elective share of the estate, despite the annulment of the marriage?
   - How does the court avoid giving Nidia the money, despite her statutory right to an elective share?
   - Do you think criminal sanctions might be appropriate in a case like this? Can you identify criminal statutes in your state that might apply?

Review Questions

1. Describe four common financial "scams" and how they can be avoided.
2. What civil remedies are available for financial exploitation and for physical abuse?
3. What laws and resources does your state have concerning reporting of abuse?
4. Identify four common signs of abuse.
5. Identify signs of self-neglect; under what circumstances is it particularly important to address the situation?
6. What is the role of federal agencies with respect to abuse and exploitation?

CAMPBELL V. THOMAS

897 N.Y.S.2d 460 (N.Y. App 2010) [summary]

Elder abuse, including financial exploitation of elderly individuals who have become mentally incapacitated, is an "often well hidden problem" in part because the perpetrator in many cases is a member of the victim's family. New York does not yet have a statute specifically addressing a situation in which a person takes unfair advantage of an individual who clearly lacks the capacity to enter into a marriage by secretly marrying him for the purpose of obtaining a portion of his estate at the expense of intended heirs. When a marriage to which one of the parties is incapable of consenting due to mental incapacity is not annulled until after the death of the nonconsenting party, a strict reading of existing statutes requires that the other party be treated as a surviving spouse and afforded a right of election against the estate, without regard to whether the marital relationship came about through overreaching or undue influence. On this appeal, we have occasion to consider whether the surviving party may nonetheless be denied the right of election, based on the equitable principle that a court will not permit a party to profit from his or her own wrongdoing.

In early 2000 Howard Thomas was diagnosed with terminal cancer and severe dementia. In 2001 Nancy Thomas, Howard's daughter and primary caretaker, went away on a one-week vacation, and left Howard, 72 years old, in the care of defendant Nidia Colon Thomas, then 58 years old. Nancy and Howard's other children, Christopher and Keith later learned that, during Nancy's vacation, Nidia married Howard, and transferred his assets into her name. Nidia caused the ownership of an account at Citibank worth $150,000 to be changed from Howard individually to Nidia and Howard jointly, and caused herself to be named as sole beneficiary of Howard's account with the defendant New York City Teachers' Retirement System (TRS), valued at $147,000. Howard died in August 2001.

Nidia previously was one of five beneficiaries of the TRS account, with Christopher, Keith, Nancy, and Nancy's son, Peter.

In November 2001 Christopher, Nancy, and Keith commenced this action seeking a judgment declaring Nidia's marriage to Howard, as well as the changes to the bank account ownership and the TRS account beneficiaries, to be null and void. They contended that Howard lacked legal capacity to enter into marriage or execute changes to his accounts due to his severe dementia, effects of medications he was taking, and progression of his cancer. The plaintiffs amended their complaint to add causes of action alleging undue influence, conversion, and fraud.

In December 2002 Howard's will, dated 1976, providing that if his first wife predeceased him, his estate was to be divided among his children, was admitted to probate. In January 2003 Christopher was issued letters of administration. In May 2003 Nidia filed a right of election, which Christopher challenged. Since the Court and the parties agreed that the determination of the right-of-election issue would depend upon the outcome of the dispute in the Supreme Court as to the validity of Nidia's marriage to Howard, the Surrogate's Court stayed the proceedings.

According to Nancy, during the last three years of Howard's life, his dementia had caused him to become "paranoid, extremely forgetful, and prone to temper outbursts" he "experienc[ed] great confusion as to who various individuals were," and called almost all females "Nancy." Nancy asserted that he required constant monitoring . . . tended to "wander off or just remain standing in one spot with a fixed stare" . . . during two hospital stays, Howard could not feed himself, was "combative and aggressive," had to be sedated and restrained, and "would pull out his IV tubes and catheter." Nancy explained that, late in 2000, Howard's primary physician advised her that "there was nothing more that could be done and it was simply a matter of time until the [cancer] took its course." Nancy stated that she conveyed this information to Nidia . . . when Nancy found out about the marriage and confronted Howard, Howard . . . adamantly denied that it, stating: "What are you talking about? . . . I'm not married. . . . Are you crazy?" Nancy asserted that Howard kept his will in a safe at his home, and had shown her the will in the fall of 2000, but that when Howard died, Nidia claimed that she was unable to locate the will. The will, however, was later produced by Nidia's attorney.

Peter averred that, despite having a close bond with his grandfather throughout his childhood, he began to notice bizarre behavior in 1999. During his hospitalization, Howard became "belligerent" and "threatened to kill [Peter]," then failed to recall [the threat] when confronted later. Peter stated that, beginning in 2000, Howard "required constant supervision," and "would soil himself," requiring Nancy or Peter to clean him, "because he had lost the ability to understand that he needed to be clean." As Peter recalled, on one occasion in 2000, Howard walked out of Nancy's house, where he was living temporarily, and was found several blocks away in a confused state of mind. After Howard "ran away" on one or more additional occasions, Nancy decided that Howard should move back into his own home, where she would continue to care for him, with the assistance of others, including Nidia.

Christopher alleged that one month prior to Howard's death, Nidia sold land owned by Howard for $90,000, and deposited proceeds into the now-joint Citibank account. As of the date of Christopher's affidavit, the balance of the Citibank account was 54 cents. The plaintiffs also submitted medical records as well as affidavits, one from Howard's primary care physician, who treated him for the last 13 years of his life, and one from a neurologist. Both physicians, who examined Howard in 2000, confirmed that he suffered from "severe dementia" and that his condition made it inadvisable for him to be left unsupervised, "even for a minute." Both recommended that Howard be placed in a nursing home, and both would have supported appointment of a legal guardian. Howard was taking numerous medications, including psychotropic medication. As one physician described it, Howard "was confused and had lost the mental capacity to provide for himself or understand his legal and financial affairs," and his mental condition continued to deteriorate after October 2000.

Nidia made the statement: "I did not know that he had transferred the [TRS] account until three months after [his] death. He had taken the steps . . . without my knowledge or my help." Nidia averred that she and Howard met in 1975, after Howard's first wife died. Nidia explained that Howard was a school principal, while she was a school safety officer. . . . [S]he and Howard had a 25-year relationship, during which Howard asked her to marry him in 1979, in 1980, in 1981, and in 2001. Nidia claimed that she accepted the last proposal, even though she knew that Howard's children were against it. According to Nidia, "[W]hile [Howard] did have moments of forgetfulness, he did seem to have the requisite mental capacity to enter into the marriage vows." Nidia's relationship with Howard was not exclusive; she admitted that she was aware during Howard's lifetime that he was dating other women. According to Christopher, Howard jointly owned property with one such woman.

Nidia also submitted affidavits from the pastor who performed the ceremony and the two witnesses to the marriage, each of whom asserted that Howard "knew that he was marrying Nidia." The pastor, however, testified that, had he known about Howard's medical condition . . . he would not have performed the ceremony. The plaintiffs pointed out that Nidia had admitted that the handwriting on the change-of-beneficiary form was hers, exposing the representations made in her affidavits as untruthful.

[Following remand], the Supreme Court found that Nidia had admitted that she had use of, at minimum, $101,997.00 from [Howard's] Citibank account," and directed entry of judgment in favor of Howard's estate and against Nidia in the amount of $101,997. The order directed that Nidia shall have no legal rights and can claim no interest as a spouse of [Howard] . . . that Nidia provide accounting of all property obtained from Howard; that TRS make Keith, Peter, and Christopher sole beneficiaries of Howard's account; that Citibank provide complete accounting to Howard's estate and those accounts be placed in the sole name of Howard's estate; and that Howard's estate be given ownership of all property in the name of Howard N. Thomas as of October 1, 2000. . . . Nidia appeals.

This Court concluded that the marriage was . . . void on the ground that Howard was "incapable of consenting. . . ." The Domestic Relations Law deems such a marriage to be voidable, meaning that the marriage "is void from the time its nullity is declared by a court. . . ." . . . No consent, no marriage. . . . A void marriage is void for all purposes from its inception. . . . "[T]he legislature has chosen, without regard to whether the marriage is void or voidable, to attach to annulled marriages sufficient validity . . . to support an award of alimony, in other words, to serve, the same as any valid marriage would, as the foundation of a continuing duty to support the wife after the marriage is terminated"

The Domestic Relations Law provides that: "An action to annul a marriage on the ground that one of the parties thereto was a mentally ill person may be maintained at any time . . . after the death of the mentally ill person . . . and during the life of the other party . . . by any relative" . . . the . . . interest of a relative . . . is preventing the living spouse from sharing in the estate. Yet, the Estates, Powers and Trusts Law provides that a husband or wife is considered a "surviving spouse" with a right of election against the deceased spouse's estate unless, "(1) A final decree or judgment of divorce, of annulment or declaring the nullity of a marriage . . . was in effect when the deceased spouse died." This provision appears to render the right . . . to obtain a post-death annulment largely illusory. . . . [It] appears to be among those statutory provisions in which, the Legislature has "attached to annulled marriages, for certain purposes, the same significance that a valid marriage would have." In this case, the marriage was not declared a nullity until this Court issued its decision in January 2007, more than five years after Howard's death. Nidia technically had a legal right to an elective share as a surviving spouse.

"[N]o one shall be permitted to profit by his own fraud, or to take advantage of his own wrong, or to found any claim upon his own iniquity, or to acquire property by his own crime." . . . In determining whether Nidia engaged in wrongdoing from which she now seeks to profit, this Court determined that Howard lacked mental capacity to enter into marriage. Nidia was aware of this lack of capacity. As Nidia knew, Howard's dementia had advanced to the point that he had difficulty recognizing family members, had lost ability to understand his legal and financial affairs or even to attend to his own hygiene, and could not be left alone. Nidia had been informed that Howard was not expected to live much longer. With knowledge of these facts, Nidia waited until Nancy left for a vacation, and then married Howard, without informing Nancy or any other member of Howard's family until after the fact. Nidia quickly arranged to have her name added to Howard's bank account, secretly made herself sole beneficiary on Howard's retirement account . . . then attempted to cover up by falsely stating that Howard made her the beneficiary without her knowledge or assistance. . . . Nidia procured the marriage through overreaching and undue influence. Nidia should not be permitted to benefit from that conduct any more than should a person who engages in overreaching and undue influence by having herself named in the will of a person she knows to be mentally incapacitated. Nidia has forfeited any rights that would flow from the marital relationship, including the statutory right she would have to an elective share of Howard's estate. Moreover, the facts that Nidia had known Howard for 25 years, had a close relationship with him, and had been legitimately named as one of the beneficiaries of his account do not diminish Nidia's culpability . . . those facts-which Nidia has in common with a large percentage of perpetrators -indicate that Nidia was in a position of trust, which she abused, and that she could not plausibly deny awareness of Howard's incapacity. Nidia wrongfully altered Howard's testamentary plan, just as if she had exploited his incapacity to induce him to add her to his will. Under such circumstances, equity will intervene to prevent the unjust enrichment of the wrongdoer . . . [because of the] need to protect vulnerable incapacitated individuals and their rightful heirs from overreaching and undue influence, [and] to protect the integrity of the courts. A court, "even in the absence of express statutory warrant," must not allow itself to be made the instrument of wrong.

[T]he Legislature was focused on preventing an individual from disinheriting his or her spouse [and] did not intend to provide refuge for a person seeking to profit by a nonconsensual marriage. And our holding is limited to [when an] individual, knowing that a mentally incapacitated person is incapable of consenting, deliberately takes unfair advantage for the purpose of obtaining pecuniary benefits . . . available by virtue of being that person's spouse, at the expense of . . . intended beneficiaries.

www.CrosswordWeaver.com

ACROSS

3. Initials, developed by AoA for legal professionals serving elderly
4. Acquiring and keeping items of little value, resulting in cluttered living space
6. Scams involving phones
8. _____ diving, going through garbage
10. Use of the Internet for identity theft by pretending to be financial institution
12. APS, Adult _____ Services
13. Main role of federal AoA with respect to elder abuse

DOWN

1. _____ scheme, perpetrator uses investments by new people to pay dividends to first investors
2. Scheme, profits from bringing in new distributors rather than actual sales
5. Use of device to steal credit card numbers
7. Using false information to acquire personal information
9. Practices related to preservation of health
11. Federal agency, information about identity theft

11

◆ ◆ ◆

Financial Matters

◆ ◆ ◆

Retirement Plans
Annuities
Insurance
Bank Accounts
Tax Concerns of Elder Clients
     Income
     Family and Caretaker Issues

Objectives

When you complete this chapter, you will:

- Use terminology associated with retirement and investment plans appropriately.
- Understand the features of life insurance policies.
- Know the most common tax issues for senior citizens.
- Know the issues confronting and the legal protections for clients planning funerals.
- Define common tax terms.

Financial concerns are a major component of an elder law practice. Pension law and tax law are very complex, and it would be impossible to become truly knowledgeable in those subjects, even in a whole year of study. However, you can at least learn the terminology and become familiar with the particular issues that affect older clients. You should make a practice of staying up-to-date on the ever-evolving investment schemes used to defraud seniors.

Retirement Plans

Qualified Plan
Pension meeting requirements of IRC §401(a), eligible for tax-favored treatment

Employers are not required to provide a retirement plan for their employees; indeed, fewer than half of employees in the private sector are covered by retirement plans. An employer-sponsored plan is likely to be a **qualified plan** so that the employer can take a tax deduction for contributing to the plan, and employees typically do not pay taxes on plan assets until the assets are distributed. Earnings on qualified plans (such as interest earned on contributions) are tax-deferred. A qualified plan may be a defined-benefit plan or a defined-contribution plan (discussed below). Qualified plans must comply with requirements of the Internal Revenue Code, the Department of Labor, and ERISA (described below).

For those who are covered, a retirement plan may take one of several forms (see Exhibit 11.1). This chapter will describe only some of the major options. Those options can often be combined in ways that best meet the needs of the employer, who may not be in a financial position to commit to a particular level of contribution each year or who may want to motivate employees by giving them an interest in the company's profitability.

Defined Benefit Plan
Plan in which benefits do not depend on how plan investments have fared financially

Under a traditional pension or **defined benefit plan**, payments in retirement are based on the length of a worker's employment and the level at which the worker was paid. A worker with more years of service will have better retirement benefits than a worker with fewer years as an employee of the company. An employee does not have a separate account in such programs; the pension fund is generally a trust established by the employer. The employer bears the cost and the entire risk of a defined benefit plan — and many employers have discontinued such plans for that reason.

EXHIBIT 11.1
Talk the Talk

Client Says: "Our profit-sharing plan. . . . "
Paralegal Thinks: Used for sharing profits with employees, but discretionary so that an employer may make contributions regardless of whether the business had profits or may choose not to contribute to the plan every year. A stock-bonus plan is a type of profit sharing — a corporation uses its own stock to make contributions. These may be set up as 401k plans.

Client Says: "My 401k. . . . "
Paralegal Thinks: A qualified plan, established by an employer. Employees have contributions deducted from salary (the amount that may be contributed is capped — $16,500 in 2010 or $22,000 if age 50); the employer may also contribute. Employee contribution may be taken before or after tax calculation. Earnings (interest on contributions) are not subject to taxes until withdrawn

EXHIBIT 11.1
(continued)

(**tax-deferred**). Investments may be managed by the employee, who may choose from a group of options, including annuities and mutual funds, or by a professional investment manager. Penalties may apply for early withdrawal (generally before age 59 1/2), but the penalty does not apply if the employee, age 55 or older, takes the funds upon leaving employment. A **403b** plan, which is for employees of public schools or other tax-exempt organizations, is very similar.

Client Says: "My IRA. . . . "
Paralegal Thinks: A savings plan to which an individual may contribute on a flexible basis. Contributions may be tax-deductible, depending on the individual's income and other retirement plans, but income is always tax-deferred. Funds can be invested in stocks, bonds, certificates of deposit, or even annuities. A "simple" IRA can be established by the employer (or a self-employed individual) to allow contributions of pre-tax earnings, with tax on earnings deferred until distribution. A **rollover IRA** receives contributions from distributions from a qualified retirement plan. A **Roth IRA** is funded with after-tax contributions (all money is taxed at the current rate before any is put into Roth account) and earnings are tax-deferred until distribution. Distributions of contributions that were already taxed are not taxed again. Whether an individual benefits from pre-tax contributions and tax-exempt earning versus post-tax contributions and taxable earnings depends on her tax rates at the time of contributions (usually while working) and at the time of distribution (retirement). An early withdrawal penalty can apply to IRA withdrawals before age 59 1/2.

Client Says: "My 457 plan. . . . "
Paralegal Thinks: A nonqualified, deferred compensation plan established by governmental and tax-exempt employers. Eligible employees are allowed to make salary deferral contributions to the 457 plan, as in a 401k or 403b plan. Earnings grow on a tax-deferred basis, and contributions are not taxed until the assets are distributed from the plan. In addition to providing an additional source of retirement funds for senior workers, these plans have a benefit for newer workers: They can withdraw funds without penalty upon separation from employment.

Client Says: "My money purchase plan. . . . "
Paralegal Thinks: A plan in which the employer is required to make an annual contribution to each employee's account regardless of profitability—contributions and earnings accumulate tax-free until withdrawn by the participant.

Client Says: "I have a **Keogh**. . . . "
Paralegal Thinks: A plan set up by a self-employed person, partnership, or owner of an unincorporated business as either a defined benefit or defined contribution plan—as a profit-sharing, a money purchase, or a combined profit-sharing/money purchase plan.

Tax-deferred
Tax paid at a later date, possibly in a lower tax bracket

403b
Similar to 401, for educators

Rollover IRA
Account into which employee may deposit distribution of another retirement account to avoid tax penalty

Roth IRA
Plan in which contributions are not tax-deferred, but funds may grow tax-free

Keogh
A tax-deferred qualified retirement plan for self-employed individuals and unincorporated businesses

Defined Contribution Plan
Plan in which retirement benefits depend on how plan investments have fared

ESOP
Employee Stock Ownership Plan

401k
Plan that allows employee to put part of earnings into tax-deferred investment account

Annuity
Contract, usually sold by an insurance company, to provide regular payments

Actuarial Calculations
Use of statistics to determine probability (e.g., of life span)

IRA
Individual Retirement Account

ERISA
Employee Retirement Income Security Act

PBGC
Pension Benefit Guaranty Corporation

In a **defined contribution plan**, regular deposits are made to an account established for the individual employee. The retirement benefit depends on the amount in the account at retirement, and the employee may have options in managing the investments in the account, so there is greater risk for the employee. A defined contribution plan can be an Employee Stock Ownership Plan (**ESOP**) or profit-sharing plan; a savings or thrift plan, such as a **401k**; or a money purchase plan. These plans can be entirely employee-funded or can involve matching contributions by the employer.

An employee under either type of plan may face a choice upon retirement. The employee may:

- Transfer the funds to another retirement account (a "rollover," described below).
- Take a lump sum payment of some or all of the benefits.
- Request regular, systematic payments in an amount of the employee's choosing.
- Choose an **annuity**, providing the employee with income for life — the regular payment amount will depend on **actuarial calculations** concerning life expectancy.

The employee must consider that any amount he receives is taxable income — a large lump sum distribution can result in substantial tax liability. The custodian of the plan will generate a Form 1099 for the employee and for the IRS. An employee who receives a lump sum payment of retirement benefits upon leaving a plan before retirement will usually invest the funds into an Individual Retirement Accounts (**IRA**) or a new retirement plan, to avoid immediate tax liability for the distribution. Remember that any funds not taxed when going into the plan are going to be taxed when they come out!

An IRA is a plan that an employee may establish if her employer does not have a plan or to supplement an employer's plan. It is generally not done through an employer, but an employee may be able to take a tax deduction for IRA contributions — depending on income and existence of an employer plan — and the income will grow tax-free until distribution. It is important that the client understand that an IRA is not just another form of savings — with the recent downturn in the economy, people have withdrawn money from IRAs to pay living expenses, only to find that they are subject to a tax penalty as described below.

A plan may create a "joint and survivor annuity" so that the worker gets a regular payment for the rest of her life and her spouse receives a reduced amount in regular payments for the rest of his life. In most cases, ERISA (described below) requires a joint and survivorship annuity for married employees. An employee who receives a lump sum may use it to purchase an annuity.

The Employee Retirement Income Security Act (**ERISA**), 29 U.S.C. §1001, *et seq*, governs defined benefit plans from private-sector employers who engage in interstate commerce. ERISA established the Pension Benefit Guaranty Corporation (**PBGC**) to insure defined benefits plans (except plans for government and certain other workers) up to a certain level. Employers must pay premiums for PBGC coverage. ERISA also extensively regulates termination of plans. ERISA does not apply to defined contribution plans except 401k plans. ERISA requires that:

- Employers provide both the Department of Labor and its own employees with detailed descriptions of the benefits they are to receive.
- Certain employees must receive a pension if a pension is offered — the plan need not cover all workers, but it cannot cover only higher-paid employees.
- A percentage of the retirement benefits contributed by the employer must be **vested** for the employees after the employee has worked for a given number of years and/or reached a given age. (Employee contributions are always vested.)
- Pension plans provide benefits to an employee's survivors upon the employee's death.
- Employers adequately fund the program.
- Employers adhere to **fiduciary** responsibilities.

Vested
Legal right to current or future possession

When a worker who has a retirement plan is divorced, the spouse may be entitled to a share of the benefits. The court awards those benefits by entering a **QDRO**, or qualified domestic relations order. This may not be done automatically as part of divorce proceedings, so it is important to determine whether the client had a QDRO entered if a divorce occurred before your firm's representation of the client. Retirement plans require designation of a beneficiary to receive benefits upon the worker's death; the assets generally transfer outside the probate process (described in Chapter 8).

Fiduciary
Acting on behalf of another in a relationship with special obligations

QDRO
Qualified Domestic Relations Order

Tip

Clients often forget to change the beneficiary designation when they experience a life-changing event, such as divorce, illness or disability, or death of a spouse. It is important to remind clients to make sure their designations comply with their current situations and wishes.

If a working client is in need of immediate funds, he may be allowed to borrow from a 401k plan for a relatively short term — one to five years, or up to ten years for purchase of a primary residence. The advantages are that such a loan does not require a credit check or (usually) application fee, and the interest is paid into the employee's own account. On the other hand, the employee loses all potential investment gains from the borrowed funds and the loan is repaid in after-tax dollars (and, when withdrawn in retirement, taxed again). If the employee stops working for any reason, the entire loan is usually due within a short period. If it is not paid, the outstanding balance may be considered an early distribution, subject to tax and penalties described later in this chapter.

Annuities

The previous section discussed retirement annuities, but not all annuities are alike. Some are purchased by periodic contributions, invested on behalf of the contributor, and are designed to build value for retirement in the future. These have a contribution/accumulation phase and a payout phase; the beneficiary is not taxed on investment income until she takes a payout. An **immediate annuity**, on the other hand, is designed to provide income immediately; it is a contract between the purchaser and an insurance company, purchased with a large lump sum (generally a single payment) in exchange for payments over the rest of the beneficiary's life. The amount of the cost/payments depends on life expectancy. It's like a wager: The insurance company is "betting" that the beneficiary won't live beyond life expectancy, which will increase its profit, while the purchaser is "betting" on a longer life. Some annuities have a lump sum refund option or death benefit (with a correspondingly higher cost or lower periodic payments) so that, upon the death of the beneficiary, the heirs will get a lump sum.

An annuity can be **fixed** so that the beneficiary has the security of a guaranteed income stream, but it is not a good protection against inflation. On the other hand, it might be indexed or tied to investments, providing a potentially greater return, but less security.

Some annuities are a means of investing to build value, but what are the advantages to an immediate annuity? Why not just keep the money and use it as needed? One reason may be favorable tax treatment of the income from the annuity. Another is to remove the money from a person's estate so that the person can qualify for Medicaid as described in Chapter 7, while providing a stream of income for a spouse or dependent. Some people also use annuities as protection from creditors if they anticipate future financial problems, perhaps because of disability or illness—this depends on state law.

Discussing all the possible features of annuities is beyond the scope of this book. Understanding the options is also beyond the understanding of many elder clients, so annuities are a common means of committing fraud on seniors. (To learn about common schemes, see *http://www.sec.gov/spotlight/seniors/elder-fraud.pdf.*) What is most important? Investors must avoid high-pressure sales techniques, cold callers, and products that sound too good to be true. They should deal only with reputable financial professionals who will ask the right questions and guide them to products that meet their individual needs.

Insurance

Life insurance is another benefit, often provided by an employer, that generally passes to a designated beneficiary outside the probate process. It is important to remind clients to make sure their beneficiary designation is current. Failure to change beneficiaries can "undo" Medicaid and tax planning described in previous chapters. It is also important to determine how the policy was paid for; if the employer deducted money from salary (pre-tax dollars), tax will be due upon payment of the policy.

When clients experience financial distress, they sometimes look to life insurance as an asset. Whether the policy has that potential depends on the type of

Immediate Annuity
Contract purchased for income immediately, not in the future

Fixed
Payments do not adjust with inflation or performance of investments

policy. Term or temporary insurance has no investment component—there is no **equity** in the policy. It is coverage that lasts for a set period of time, provided the monthly premium is paid. Once the term ends, the policy has no value and, during the term, the policy has no loan value. Annual renewable term insurance is purchased year by year, although requalification, by showing evidence of good health each year, is not required.

A **whole life** policy is permanent insurance, combining life coverage with an investment fund—it pays a stated, fixed amount at death, and part of the premium builds cash value from investments. Cash value builds tax-deferred each year, and the owner can borrow against the cash accumulation. A **universal life** policy is also a type of permanent insurance policy that combines **term insurance** with a money market–type investment that pays a market rate of return. To get a higher return, these policies generally do not guarantee a certain rate. Universal life policies are more flexible and often less expensive than whole life policies. The return on the investment component many even be applied to pay for the premiums on the term insurance component. **Variable life** and variable universal life are permanent policies with an investment fund tied to a stock or bond mutual-fund investment. Returns are not guaranteed.

If a client has adequate equity in a life insurance policy, she may be able to use it as **collateral** for a loan—usually from the insurance company and usually at a good interest rate because it is solid collateral—or cash it in outright. The first thing to consider is the cost of money. Policies differ, but many have a loan clause that allows the owner to borrow, from the insurance company, 90 percent of the policy's cash value.

A client who is terminally ill may also consider a **viatical settlement**. These arrangements to accelerate financial benefits from life insurance policies, sometimes called "living benefits," have complicated legal, financial, and tax consequences. In a viatical settlement, the insured party assigns a life insurance policy to a viatical settlement company in exchange for a lump sum payment equal to a percentage of the policy's face value. The viatical settlement company becomes the beneficiary on the policy, pays the premiums, and collects the face value of the policy after the insured party dies.

The Federal Trade Commission has issued a brochure (*http://www.ftc.gov/opa/1995/12/via.shtm*) to help people evaluate the viatical settlement arrangement and explore alternatives. The FTC brochure cautions that certain choices may have state or federal tax implications and that collecting benefits in advance may affect eligibility for public assistance programs. The brochure specifically advises consumers contemplating viatical or other accelerated benefit programs to:

- Contact several viatical companies to be sure they're getting the best value.
- Check state regulators to determine whether the company meets licensing requirements.
- Resist high-pressure sales tactics.
- Verify that the company has money on hand and is not shopping to sell the policy to a third party.
- Ask about the company's policy for protecting the consumer's privacy.
- Check the tax consequences and implications for public assistance benefits.
- Consult a lawyer about probate and estate considerations.

Equity
Difference between market value of property and claims against it

Whole Life
Insurance with fixed amount benefits and definite premiums

Universal Life
Hybrid insurance combining protection of conventional term insurance policy with cash values and investment yields

Term Insurance
Low-cost insurance valid only for stated period; no surrender or loan value

Variable Life
Insurance in which death benefit and cash value policy fluctuate according to investment performance of a separate account fund

Collateral
Promised or given to a creditor (e.g., bank) to guarantee payment of debt

Viatical Settlement
Purchase of a terminally ill person's life insurance

Long-term Care Insurance Insurance providing coverage for necessary medical or personal care services outside hospital setting (e.g., in nursing home or insured's home)

Many individuals now purchase **long-term care insurance** to pay for institutional care, which is not covered by Medicare (discussed in Chapter 6). It is important to remember that the features of such policies and, therefore, their value, differ depending on the contract terms. Some states now provide resources to assist seniors in evaluating policies, as shown in Exhibit 11.2. The sale of long-term care policies is particularly susceptible to fraud, and many senior clients may not think to ask whether the policy limits will adjust with inflation, whether the policy covers in-home care, whether there is a waiting period before which coverage is not available, whether the policy can be cancelled by the company or is guaranteed renewable as long as premiums are paid, whether there can be any refund if the purchaser pays premiums for many years but never needs long-term care, or who makes the determination of when long-term care is necessary and what appeals are available. On the "plus" side, states may disregard long-term care policies in determining Medicaid eligibility—a rule intended to encourage the purchase of such policies.

Bank Accounts

Senior citizens often add the name of a child or other relative to a bank account for a variety of reason. The older person may worry about disability or hospitalization and want to make sure someone can pay the bills or may want to avoid probate. There are often better ways to address those concerns.

EXHIBIT 11.2
Assessing Long-Term Care Policies

Most states offer many resources for consumers. Here is an example from the Texas Department of Insurance Web site (*http://www.tdi.state.tx.us/pubs/consumer/cb032.html*):

Tax-Qualified Long-Term Care Policies

You may be able to deduct part of the premium for a tax-qualified long-term care policy from your taxes as a medical expense. In addition, you are generally not required to claim your qualified long-term care policy benefits as taxable income. However, in the case of an indemnity policy, there is an annual dollar cap.

All policies sold before January 1, 1997, are automatically tax-qualified. Policies sold on or after January 1, 1997, may be either tax-qualified or non-tax-qualified. To determine whether your policy is tax-qualified, look for a statement on your policy similar to this: "This policy is intended to be a qualified long-term care insurance contract as defined by the Internal Revenue Code of 1986, Section 7702B(b)."

If the client adds the name of her child to an account, so that the child becomes a joint owner of the account, that child has the legal right to the entire account. "Spending" the money in the account may be beyond the child's control. For example, the child may be involved in a car accident and unable to pay the bills, or the child's spouse may try to claim the assets in a divorce. While the parent might be able to recover the money, at the very least there would be delay, legal expenses, and possibly harm to the relationship. In addition, holding title to a parent's assets may affect the child's ability to obtain need-based benefits ranging from Medicaid to scholarships. These same concerns are relevant to putting another person's name on the title to any property.

If the client's objective is avoidance of probate, in most states the client can make the account payable on death (**POD**). In some states these are called **Totten trusts**. The theory is this: The creator controls the account during her life, but it is held in trust for a designated survivor. Upon the owner's death the account will automatically become the property of the designated beneficiary, without making that person an owner immediately. Consider whether having the assets bypass the rest of the client's estate plan will have a negative impact on that plan. For example, if Punit wants his three sons to share his estate equally and his will says so, creating a POD account in the name of one of the sons could frustrate his wishes.

> **POD**
> Pay-on-death bank account
>
> **Totten Trust**
> Bank account controlled by creator during life, but in trust for beneficiary on creator's death

If the primary concern is convenience in the event of disability or absence, the client would likely be better served by a power of attorney (discussed in Chapter 2). A power of attorney can give as much or as little power as desired: A limited power might allow the agent "to sell my car and deposit the sale proceeds to my bank account" or "to write checks on my bank account to pay my utility bills." A power of attorney can become effective when it is signed or at some future date or event, such as "only in the event of my disability." A power of attorney can be revoked at any time as long as the principal remains mentally competent. A client concerned about convenience and probate can have both a POD account and a power of attorney.

Tax Concerns of Elder Clients

According to Ben Franklin, in this world, nothing is certain except death and taxes. He was correct: Every competent adult in the United States has to think about both. Estate and gift tax consequences are discussed in Chapter 8; property taxes on real estate are discussed in Chapter 9. This chapter will deal with income tax, but will cover only those issues most likely to be of concern to elder clients.

Income

- The **tax threshold** is higher for senior citizens because there is an additional **standard deduction** for people age 65 or older or blind.
- **Pension and annuity** payments, which were not taxed to the employee when deposited into an account for the employee, are like a substitute paycheck and are taxed as received. If the employee paid part of the cost of a plan with taxed (post-tax) dollars, part of each payment can be

> **Tax Threshold**
> Level above which income is taxed
>
> **Standard Deduction**
> IRS-specified amount by which taxpayer is entitled to reduce income, alternative to itemizing deductions

excluded from income as a recovery of cost (investment in the contract). This tax-free part of the payment is figured when the annuity starts and remains the same each year, even if the amount of the payment changes. The rest of each payment is taxable. The payer of a pension, profit-sharing, stock bonus, annuity, or deferred compensation plan generally will withhold income tax on the taxable part.

Workers Compensation
State program to pay workers suffering from work-related injury or illness

- Amounts received as **workers compensation** for an occupational sickness or injury are exempt from tax if they are paid under a statute in the nature of a workers' compensation act. The exemption also applies to survivors. The exemption, however, does not apply to retirement plan benefits based on age, length of service, or prior contributions to the plan, even if the recipient retired because of an occupational sickness or injury.

- **Life insurance proceeds** paid because of the death of the insured person are not taxable unless the policy was turned over to the beneficiary for a price — but if the death benefit is paid in installments, interest included in installments may be taxable.

- In the case of **surrender of policy for cash**, any proceeds that are more than the cost of the life insurance policy are taxable as income.

- Certain amounts paid as **accelerated death benefits** under a life insurance contract or **viatical settlement** before the insured's death are generally excluded from income if the insured is terminally or chronically ill. For a chronically ill individual, accelerated death benefits paid on the basis of costs incurred for qualified long-term care services are fully excludable. Accelerated death benefits paid on a per diem or other periodic basis without regard to the costs are excludable up to a limit. In addition, if any portion of a death benefit under a life insurance contract on the life of a terminally or chronically ill individual is sold or assigned to a viatical settlement provider, the amount received is also excluded from income.

- **Social security benefits** (monthly retirement, survivor, and disability benefits, but not supplemental security income [SSI] payments, which are not taxable) and equivalent railroad retirement benefits may be taxable depending on the recipient's total income and marital status.

- **Military retirement** pay based on age or length of service is taxable and must be included in income as a pension, but certain military and government disability pensions that are based on a percentage of disability from active service are not taxable.

- **Disability payments** received under a plan that is paid for by an employer are taxable.

- **Long-term care insurance contracts** are treated as accident and health insurance contracts. Amounts received from them (other than policy-holder dividends or premium refunds) are generally excludable from income.

- **Gifts and inheritances** are usually not included in income of the recipient, but income produced by that property later is income.

- **Medicare** benefits are not included in income.

- **Reverse mortgages** are loan advances, not income, and money received by the homeowner is not taxable. Any interest (including original issue discount) accrued on a reverse mortgage is not deductible until it is actually paid.

- Support services or reimbursement for out-of-pocket expenses for **volunteer work** are not taxable income.
- Distributions from a **traditional IRA** (but not a Roth or simple IRA) are generally taxable in the year when received.
- **Early distributions**, amounts distributed from a traditional IRA account or annuity before age 59 1/2, or amounts received by cashing in retirement bonds before age 59 1/2, must be included in gross income and are also subject to an additional 10 percent tax unless the distribution qualifies for an exception. The owner of a traditional IRA must receive the entire balance or start receiving periodic distributions by April 1 of the year following the year in which she reaches age 70 1/2 to avoid a penalty. There are exceptions, and a client considering early distribution should consult a tax professional.
- A **Roth IRA** can be either an account or an annuity and features tax-free distributions.
- **Capital gains** from the **sale of a main home** is generally excludable up to $250,000 ($500,000 on a joint return in most cases), but special rules govern how long the owner must have had the home, people who must leave home because of disability, and other unusual situations.

Capital Gain
Amount by which selling price of asset exceeds purchase price

Family and Caretaker Issues

- When acting as **personal representative** of a person who died during the year, a client may have to file a final return for that decedent and notify the IRS that he is acting as personal representative, using Form 56, Notice Concerning Fiduciary Relationship. If no personal representative has been appointed by the filing date, a surviving spouse may file a joint return (if not remarried) and, in the signature area, write, "Filing as surviving spouse."
- An adult child serving as caretaker may claim a parent as a **dependent** in some circumstances; a caretaker may also claim a tax credit for dependent care for services such as adult day care.
- Other credits are available to **low-income tax filers**.
- A deduction is available for **medical expenses** paid for the taxpayer or a spouse or dependents if the expenses exceed a specific percentage of income.

Assignments

1. Use the PBGC Web site (*http://www.pbgc.gov*) to search for missing participants with your surname. How many did you find? Find the list of what may not be required of PBGC under the terms of a QDRO.

2. Using the same Web site, find and describe the right of appeal when a plan participant receives a formal determination with respect to a terminated plan. Describe the procedure by which a participant can request an estimate of her pension payment.

3. Determine whether POD or Totten trust accounts are recognized in your state.

4. Using the Web site for the agency that regulates insurance companies in your state, determine how you would find out whether a viatical settlement company is licensed. Start with the National Association of Insurance Commissioners (*http://www.naic.org/state_web_map.htm*).

5. Starting at the same Web site, determine how your state regulates long-term care insurance and write a short summary. What resources are available to consumers?

6. The IRS Volunteer Income Tax Assistance Program (VITA) and the Tax Counseling for the Elderly (TCE) programs offer free tax help for taxpayers who qualify. How would you locate a site for a client? What information is a client asked to bring in order to obtain assistance?

7. Determine whether/how your state regulates prepaid funeral plans and whether your state has a personal preference law.

8. Victor and Lourdes, ages 55 and 56, have worked in construction and home maintenance their entire adult lives. Neither is a high school graduate, so they have been in jobs with no benefits and no retirement plans, but they are frugal people. They bought a small house four years ago and have about $25,000 in individual IRAs. Last year, things fell apart. Both lost their jobs and they have been unable to find work. Many houses in their neighborhood are in foreclosure and they are unable to sell their house for enough to pay off the mortgage. Now they have run out of savings and are unable to make monthly mortgage, car, and health insurance payments. Not understanding the consequences, they withdrew money from their IRAs. Use the IRS Web site, particularly Publication 590 and the instructions for Form 5329, to answer the following questions:

   • Will the withdrawal be subject to a penalty? Might there be a way to use the money and avoid the penalty? Would the answer be different if these were Roth IRAs? Why?
   • Assume that they took $8,000 out and used $4,000 to pay health insurance premiums and the rest to pay mortgage and car payments. What is the tax penalty?
   • Is the penalty calculated above the only payment that will have to be made to the IRS on account of this distribution?

9. Critical Thinking: Read the *Miller* case summary at the end of this chapter.

   • One of Muzzy's alternatives would have been to buy an annuity with a death benefit. Can you think of a downside to doing so?
   • Might Muzzy have made a reasoned decision to buy the annuity naming only himself as a beneficiary? Is there any fact in the case that might give you a clue? Note the executor of the estate.

- Knowing the options available for annuities, do you think an average older person would understand the options and risks?
- Did Muzzy essentially decide to leave his money to an insurance company rather than to Medicaid reimbursement? Why might he have made this decision? Would there be any benefit to him? Is there a particular risk he might have been worried about?

10. Visit *http://www.sec.gov/investor/seniors.shtml*. Suppose that a client told you that she was considering purchasing a variable annuity with a "bonus credit feature." Find out what that is and what the client should consider.

11. Using the Web site of the Securities and Exchange Commission (*http://www.sec.gov/investor.shtml*) and other credible Web sites, write a report on investment scams targeting seniors, including an explanation of "churning."

12. Using the AARP Web site (*http://www.aarp.org/money/*) and other credible Web sites, write short answers:
- What are the benefits and detriments to paying off a mortgage early?
- What is a mutual fund?

Review Questions

1. Describe the differences between a traditional defined-benefit pension and a 401k plan. What is an IRA? A Keogh?
2. Your supervisor has asked you to contact a client and get information about a problem "involving life insurance." What questions would you ask about the policy and the problem to get a thorough picture?
3. Why is it not a good idea for a parent to add a child to a bank account? What are the alternatives?
4. What is the problem with early withdrawals from a retirement plan? What might be done to avoid the problem if the client urgently needs money?
5. Are pension payments taxable income?
6. Identify the major issues in making a decision about long-term care insurance.

MILLER V. HARTFORD LIFE INSURANCE CO.

64 FED. APPX. 795 (2nd CIR. 2003)

Plaintiff Miller appeals from the Memorandum Decision and Order, dated May 17, 2002, of the U.S. District Court for the Northern District of New York granting defendant Hartford Life Insurance Company's motion for summary judgment and denying her motion for summary judgment.

Miller brings this diversity action as the executrix of the estate of Orman Muzzy. Miller is Muzzy's grandniece. Muzzy was born in 1915, as was his wife, Helen, whom he married in 1944.

In late 1994, when he was 79 years old, Muzzy contacted his attorney, Mills, concerning the purchase of an annuity . . . [and] told Mills that he want[ed] to purchase a "single premium immediate life annuity" as a means of shielding his assets from any attempt by the Government to seek reimbursement for Medicaid benefits. Muzzy expected that he would be vulnerable to an attempt at reimbursement because Helen, who had been diagnosed with Alzheimer's disease, would soon need to enter a nursing home, the cost of which would largely be borne by Medicaid.

Muzzy told Mills that he wished to purchase an annuity which would name him as sole beneficiary. This wish was based upon Muzzy's belief that naming a beneficiary other than himself would not protect the annuity from Medicaid reimbursement. It is not contested that this belief was false, and that Muzzy received no [Medicaid] benefit by not naming someone else as a beneficiary. Mills testified that he had no experience in legal matters involving Medicaid, and no experience in "elder law" generally. Mills also testified that he did not opine on the wisdom of the purchase beyond asking Muzzy if he understood the risk in a single premium immediate life annuity, i.e., that he would receive payment under the annuity only so long as he lived and that, should he die before his expected life span, the seller of the annuity would retain the balance of the purchase price. It was Mills' impression that Muzzy was fully aware of this risk. Indeed, Mills was convinced that Muzzy "had his mind made up" regarding the annuity purchase. He also testified that Muzzy was to all indications of sound mind.

According to Mills, all Muzzy asked him to do with respect to the purchase was to inquire among various insurance agents as to which of them offered the best deal. Mills eventually recommended that Muzzy contact the Rowledge Agency, which was an authorized dealer of Hartford insurance products. The agency had provided ordinary insurance services to Muzzy in the past. Muzzy went to speak to Rowledge in January 1995. Rowledge testified that Muzzy told him that he was intent upon purchasing an annuity naming himself as sole beneficiary and wanted no recommendation from Rowledge as to whether this was a good idea. Like Mills, Rowledge also testified that he inquired as to whether Muzzy understood the risks of an annuity and was convinced that he did.

As with Mills, Rowledge testified that he discussed Medicaid with Muzzy and that Muzzy asserted that he had "checked it out" and was under the impression that naming a beneficiary on the annuity other than himself would subject the annuity funds to Medicaid reimbursement. Rowledge asserted that he had no prior knowledge as to whether or not Muzzy was correct, but that he telephoned a Hartford sales representative, who agreed with Muzzy's position. Rowledge testified that he saw no indication that Muzzy was not of sound mind. Further, after speaking with Muzzy, Rowledge called the vice-president of Muzzy's bank, who confirmed that Muzzy was in full possession of his faculties.

Muzzy purchased the annuity on January 18, 1995 for $180,000. On the application form, he elected the form of annuity that promised payments only for the remainder of his life, rather than one of the available options for somewhat reduced payments for life with a guarantee of a minimum number of years of benefits to designated beneficiaries. Five days later, his wife Helen entered a nursing home. It is uncontested that Muzzy made no effort to rescind the annuity during the 10-day grace period provided for this purpose. Under the terms of the annuity, Muzzy received monthly payments of $2,192.40. He died of "end stage congestive heart failure" on September 23, 1996. Thus, Muzzy received $43,848 on the annuity, leaving Hartford $136,152 on his death.

In considering whether to establish a constructive trust, the elements a court may consider include the existence of "1) a confidential or fiduciary relation, 2) a promise, 3) a transfer in reliance thereon and 4) unjust enrichment." "Although these factors provide important guideposts, the constructive trust doctrine is equitable in nature and should not be rigidly limited." Still, "under New York law, one who seeks to impose a constructive trust must establish the facts giving rise to that remedy by clear and convincing evidence." A constructive trust should not be established here. The central allegation in Miller's complaint is that Muzzy "was easily confused, given his advanced age, deteriorating health and the effects in which the diagnosed malady of kidney failure impaired his ability to comprehend." But Miller also asserts that "it is not herein contended that [Muzzy] was mentally incapacitated[,] but, instead, if matters had been better explained . . . some other prudent choice could have been made."

Muzzy's purchase of the annuity was not impulsive; he asked Mills to find him the best deal and the purchase itself did not take place until weeks later. Mills and Rowledge believed Muzzy to be of sound mind. The most Miller testified to was that Muzzy was sometimes depressed and confused in his last years. And Miller's expert witness merely opines that the purchase of the annuity was "totally inappropriate," not that Muzzy did not understand what he was buying into. At most, the evidence in the record establishes that Muzzy made an unwise decision, not that he was incapable of making an informed choice. What is more, "under New York law the relationship between an insurance company and a policyholder is a contractual relationship, not a fiduciary one." Miller's assertion that "it goes without saying" that such a relationship must exist here because of the size of the investment is wholly unsupported. There is no contention here that Rowledge was—or that he held himself out to be—an investment advisor, someone who does have a fiduciary relationship with clients. A corollary of this lack of a fiduciary relationship is that "there [is] no duty cast upon the defendant to investigate the health of those seeking annuities." Thus, even if Muzzy was occasionally confused due to poor health, there was no obligation on the part of Rowledge or Hartford to ascertain this. Further, the only promise that Rowledge and Hartford made to Muzzy is that he would be paid $2192.40 a month until he died. It is undisputed that this promise was carried out. It is thus incorrect for Miller to assert that Muzzy "received nothing" or "truly received no benefit whatsoever" pursuant to the annuity.

Again, it is not disputed that both Muzzy and Hartford were incorrect in their assessment about the effect of the annuity upon Medicaid reimbursement. But an essential element of a claim of negligent misrepresentation is the existence of a duty on the part of the defendant, arising from a fiduciary relationship, to impart correct information. No such relationship exists in this case.

"Annuity agreements, like other contracts, may be rescinded, set aside, or voided upon proper grounds. Thus, where an annuity agreement apparently was entered into through fraud, duress, misrepresentation, or undue influence, or where it appears that the underlying transaction was unconscionable under the circumstances, the agreement may be set aside or recovery back of the consideration may be permitted." None of these grounds is present here. Indeed, as the District Court found, Muzzy effectively ratified the annuity contract by not availing himself of the ten-day grace period in which he could have rescinded the contract, and by accepting payments under the contract for nineteen months. Accordingly . . . the judgment of the District Court is hereby AFFIRMED.

www.CrosswordWeaver.com

ACROSS

1. IRA is _____ Retirement Account
3. Difference between value and debt
4. Gain on selling asset above purchase price
8. Tax _____, above this, income is taxed
10. Initials, bank account bypasses probate
11. Type of life insurance tied to value of investment account
14. Pension Benefit _____ Corporation
15. Legal entitlement
17. _____ settlement, terminally ill person sells insurance policy
20. _____ Life insurance, fixed benefit and premium
21. Federal law regulating pensions
24. Defined _____; retirement income depends on performance of investments in account
26. Acts on behalf of another with special obligations
27. Retirement plan for self-employed
28. Initials — covers pension in divorce

DOWN

2. Standard _____, taxpayer does not itemize
4. Secures payment of debt
5. Usually taxable as a replacement for paycheck
6. Initials, gives employees ownership in employer company
7. Workers' _____, for work-related injuries
9. Tax-_____, pay tax later
12. Early distribution from IRA may result in this
13. Provides regular payments
16. Retirement plan with tax benefits for employer
18. _____ IRA can receive pension distributions without penalty
19. Defined _____ retirement income does NOT depend on performance of investments in account
22. Initials, implements Funeral Rule
23. _____ IRA, contributions not tax-deferred
25. Insurance for a specified period

12

♦ ♦ ♦

End-of-Life Issues

♦ ♦ ♦

Right to Die
    Surrogate Decisions Versus Patient's Expressed Wishes
    Hastening Death
Funerals
Dealing with Grief

Objectives

When you complete this chapter, you will:

- Know how the courts assess cases in which a patient has not expressed clear wishes concerning life-sustaining treatment.
- Understand how the law views "assisted suicide."
- Be aware of the laws governing providers of funeral services.

Right to Die

In Chapter 2 you were introduced to end-of-life issues in the context of learning the importance of advance directives. This chapter will revisit those issues from an ethical perspective and take it a step further: Does a patient have the right to end her life and what is the liability of a person who assists her in doing so?

Surrogate Decisions Versus Patient's Expressed Wishes

The term "right to die" normally refers to the patient's wish that caregivers allow death by not providing medical intervention under conditions when recovery is highly unlikely or impossible. The very controversial *Cruzan, Schiavo,* and *Quinlan* cases involved situations in which the patient had not expressed her wishes in an advance directive. In each case, the court set the bar very high for those who wanted to discontinue life support.

Nancy Cruzan moved from a coma to a full vegetative state after a single-car accident. Years later her parents sought to remove life support. Nancy had no written advance directive but had stated that "if sick or injured she would not wish to continue her life unless she could live at least halfway normally." The state court[1] held that, absent clear and convincing evidence of her wishes, she should remain on life support. The Supreme Court affirmed. You can listen to the oral arguments on the Supreme Court Web site (*http://www.oyez.org/cases/1989*).

Terri Schiavo collapsed in her home in 1990 and, several weeks later, was declared to be in a vegetative state. In 1998, her husband sought removal of her feeding tube, arguing that she had no hope of recovery and would not have wanted to be kept alive by artificial means. Terri's parents opposed removal of life support, expressing belief that Terri had a level of consciousness and that removal of the feeding tube was akin to euthanasia and contrary to her religious beliefs. The case involved multiple state court hearings, initial removal and reinsertion of the feeding tube, intervention by the governor, and enactment (and subsequent invalidation) of a special law. The final state court ruling allowed removal of the feeding tube, based on "clear and convincing evidence."[2] After Terri's parents and pro-life activists sought federal intervention, there were several rulings by federal courts refusing to require restoration of the feeding tube before Terri Schiavo died in 2005.

Years earlier, 21-year-old Karen Quinlan had lapsed into a persistent vegetative state after consuming drugs and alcohol at a party. The New Jersey Supreme Court had permitted removal of a respirator, basing its decision on the patient's right to privacy, her guardian's right to assert that interest, and medical evidence that the patient would never recover.[3]

If the legal pattern to these cases seems clear, consider some particularly disturbing factual aspects and the old adage "hard cases make bad law." All of these cases involved previously healthy young women. All had close family ties. All of those families were subjected to unimaginable pain and humiliation in the hospital, in court, and in the media in attempting to do what they thought was right. None of the families made their decisions quickly; all initially hoped that their loved ones would recover. Two of these patients could be seen opening their eyes, groaning, appearing to smile, and exhibiting other reflexive responses. These facts alone made the cases difficult, and the issues were further complicated by evidence concerning religious beliefs of the patients and by confusing medical

---

[1] *Cruzan v. Director, Missouri Dept. of Health,* 497 U.S. 261 (1990)
[2] 780 So. 2d 176 (Fla. App. 2001)
[3] *In re Quinlan,* 355 A.2d 647 (N.J. 1976)

evidence. Future cases may be further complicated by the fact that states have different definitions of death.

William Colby, who represented the Cruzan family, gave this compelling example in *From Quinlan to Cruzan to Schiavo: What Have We Learned?*:

> A well-known local rabbi is driving down the New Jersey turnpike and has a horrible car accident. EMTs arrive, resuscitate the rabbi, and then rush him to the hospital. But it's not just any hospital. This hospital is a new joint venture between the states of Pennsylvania and New Jersey, and it was built straddling the state line between the two states. As fate would have it, the bed that they took the rabbi to that night in the ER is in fact straddling the state line between the two states. The medical team does everything they can to bring about recovery for the rabbi, without success. The attending physician does the various clinical tests, like testing the corneal reflex, to see if there's any brain activity. There's not. Two separate EEGs, or electroencephalograms, are performed, and the result is a flat line — no electrical activity in his brain whatsoever. But, the rabbi's heart and his lungs continue to function with all of the support that we can bring to bear in the modern day emergency room. Dejected, the doctor walks out of the ER, just as the rabbi's brother rushes into the waiting room, sees the doctor, and says, "Oh my God, doctor, my brother, is he dead?" . . . He meets the Pennsylvania definition of brain death. In New Jersey, he may or may not be dead, depending on what the attending physician knows about the tenets of the rabbi's faith, and depending on what's written in his medical chart. . . . [4]

Colby particularly notes that Florida law clearly favored allowing Cruzan's husband to make the decision and concludes that what these cases have taught us is the importance of both documenting your wishes and discussing your beliefs with your family.

Powers of attorney, living wills, and DNR orders (discussed in Chapter 2) are legal instruments that make a patient's treatment decisions known ahead of time; allowing a patient to die based on such decisions is not considered to be euthanasia or homicide. The patient's wishes generally indicate that the patient wants only **palliative care**.

Palliative Care
Care that slows or reduces symptoms of disease, but does not cure

Hospitals that have or are seeking accreditation from the Joint Commission of Accreditation of Health Care Organizations are required to have DNR policies. If a patient with a DNR consents to surgery, the patient and doctor should discuss whether to suspend the DNR during surgery. An individual patient's DNR may be very specific. If it is not, the state may have a statute clarifying the meaning of DNR orders.

For example, under Ohio law, the DNR Comfort Care protocol (OAC rule 3701-62-04) permits various means of identification to communicate the patient's status:

- A state-approved DNR Comfort Care form, signed by a physician or advanced practice nurse
- A DNR necklace or bracelet
- A DNR wallet card

---

[4]*http://luc.edu/law/activities/publications/lljdocs/vol37_no2/colby.pdf*, visited September 4, 2010

- A living will specifying that a DNR order should be written when the living will becomes effective

The protocol requires that professionals:

- Will suction the airway, administer oxygen, position for comfort, splint or immobilize, control bleeding, provide pain medication, provide emotional support, and contact other appropriate providers.
- Will not administer chest compressions, insert an artificial airway, administer resuscitative drugs, defibrillate or cardiovert, provide respiratory assistance (other than suctioning the airway and administering oxygen), or initiate cardiac monitoring.

A DNR can be revoked at any time, by the patient, the patient's surrogate decision maker, or the physician. Keep in mind that calling for an ambulance may create confusion if there is a DNR in place; emergency personnel will generally not comply with oral instructions.

Hastening Death

Euthanasia
To intentionally painlessly kill

"Passive Euthanasia"
Withdrawal of medical treatment intended to cause death

"Double Effect"
High dose of medication, intended to relieve pain, causes death

Terminal Sedation
Deep sedation continued until patient dies

As these cases indicate, an individual clearly has a right to refuse treatment. What if the individual is in extreme pain and not only wants to refuse life-sustaining treatment but wants help in hastening death? In discussing the "right to die," some people automatically think of **euthanasia** and the trial of Dr. Jack Kevorkian.[5] In reality, however, euthanasia or "mercy killing," which involves active participation by a person other than the patient, is not legal in the United States, even with the patient's fully informed consent. Even physician-assisted suicide, in which a doctor provides, but does not administer, lethal medications (discussed below) is lawful only under limited circumstances in some states.

"Passive euthanasia" may result from the **"double effect,"** defined as "the administration of opioids or sedative drugs with the expressed purpose of relieving pain and suffering in a dying patient." The unintended consequence may be respiratory depression. In other words, the medication required to relieve suffering cannot be given without the probable result of hastening death. Similarly, if a patient is very ill and does not respond to pain medications, a last-resort therapy that can be used is **terminal sedation**, in which a patient is given medications that induce sleep or unconsciousness until death occurs as a result of the underlying illness. In either case, if the intention is only to relieve suffering and not to cause death, this is a lawful and accepted medical practice; death is attributed to the disease or complications of the disease, combined, in some circumstances, with withdrawal of life-sustaining treatments, such as intravenous liquids, nutrition, and artificial respiration.

At least two states have taken it a step farther. The 1994 Oregon Death with Dignity Act, ORS 127.800 (*http://www.oregon.gov/DHS/ph/pas/docs/statute.*

---

[5] *People v. Kevorkian*, 639 N.E.2d 291 (Mich. App. 2001)

pdf), and the 2008 Washington Death with Dignity Act (below) are sometimes called physician-assisted suicide laws. At least one state, Montana,[6] has held that, even without a specific statutory authorization, a physician is not liable for acting in accordance with a patient's end-of-life wishes, even if the physician must actively pull the plug on a patient's ventilator or withhold treatment that will keep him alive.

Under the Oregon law, both an attending and a consulting physician must first determine that a patient, who is mentally capable and a resident of Oregon, is suffering from a terminal disease. A prescription for a lethal dose of drugs is written only after both patient and doctor have followed a strict protocol. The patient makes two oral requests and one written request for medication over the course of 15 days; the prescription can be filled on the fifteenth day, which is also when the second oral request is presented. Doctors cannot administer the medication; Oregon law requires that patients be able to take the lethal dose themselves. If a doctor suspects that a patient is depressed or otherwise mentally incapable of making an informed decision, she can refuse the prescription requests and refer the patient to a mental health professional. The Washington Department of Health has collected and compiled data on the use of its law and released its first report on March 4, 2010, indicating that 36 terminally ill patients used the law to hasten their death, 63 people received prescriptions, and 53 physicians participated in 2009.

The Washington Death with Dignity Act (*http://apps.leg.wa.gov/RCW/default.aspx?cite=70.245*) provides similarly:

(1) An adult who is competent, is a resident of Washington state, and has been determined by the attending physician and consulting physician to be suffering from a terminal disease, and who has voluntarily expressed his or her wish to die, may make a written request for medication that the patient may self-administer to end his or her life in a humane and dignified manner in accordance with this chapter.

(2) A person does not qualify under this chapter solely because of age or disability.

State law is not consistent. Read the summary at the end of this chapter, *Vacco v. Quill,* and compare your state's law, as described in an assignment.

Funerals

Death visits every client eventually, so an elder law practice is likely to get a call at some time with the news that a client has died or a client's loved one has died. The caller may have no idea what to do. The first step depends on the circumstances of the death. When someone dies in a hospital or similar care facility, the staff will usually take care of some arrangements, such as contacting the funeral home (if a choice has been made) and, if necessary, arranging an autopsy. The staff will also institute procedures if the deceased has made an anatomical gift (organ donation or donation of body to science) as discussed in Chapter 2. In such cases, the survivor's first task may be to call relatives, friends, and clergy to start to spread the word.

---

[6]*Baxter v. State,* 224 P.3d 1211 (Mont., 2009)

If the death occurs at home or at work, the first call should generally be to 911 or the police because most deaths occurring without a physician or medical personnel in attendance require an investigation. If the deceased individual was in hospice care at home, a call to the hospice organization should be the first call—hospice personnel will help with the rest. After the coroner's examination, the body will either be transported to the morgue for autopsy or to the funeral home chosen by the survivor, depending on the circumstances of death. If the deceased was under medical care, the doctor should be notified.

Once the survivor has chosen a licensed funeral director, the staff will:

- Transport the body
- Obtain a death certificate
- Help select a casket, urn, and/or grave marker
- Arrange the funeral and memorial and/or burial service
- Prepare the obituary
- Help with necessary notifications
- Offer grief support or direct to other resources

FTC
Federal Trade Commission

If the deceased individual or survivor preplanned the funeral, the arrangements should require few decisions. Without preplanning, the survivor will have to make many decisions under stressful circumstances and may spend more money than necessary or desirable. Preneed planning has had a bad reputation in the past, but the federal Funeral Rule, 16 CFR Part 453 (enforced by the Federal Trade Commission **FTC**), has made preplanning safer and easier. Planning can be done through an individual funeral home or through a not-for-profit organization, such as those found at the Web site for the Funeral Consumers Alliance (*http://www.funerals.org/affiliates-directory*).

Your state may also have resources for those planning funerals. Check out New York's very helpful Web site (*http://www.health.state.ny.us/professionals/ patients/patient_rights/funeral.htm*). The U.S. General Accounting Office posted the results of a survey on state regulation of the death care industry (*http:// www.gao.gov/special.pubs/gao-03-831sp/toc.html*). It's a bit tricky to navigate, but is partially reproduced below:

Q25. What consumer protections, if any, does your state have in place concerning funeral homes that address issues beyond the Federal Trade Commission's requirement that funeral homes provide clients with a General Price List? See chart on page 271.

State	Requires death care businesses to provide general price lists	Provides one or more state sponsored complaint hot lines	Provides information through state sponsored Web page	Conducts educational outreach programs	Provides information on licensed facilities in good standing	Holds public hearings	Conducts investigations of legitimate consumer complaints
AK			X		X		X
AL					X	X	X
AR	X	X	X	X	X	X	X
AZ	X		X		X		X
CA	X	X	X		X	X	X
CO	X		X		X		X
CT	X	X	X		X		X
DE		X	X		X		X
FL	X	X	X	X	X		X
GA	X		X		X	X	X
HI	X	X	X		X		X
IA	X	X		X	X		X
ID	X	X	X				X
IL	X	X	X	X	X	X	X
IN	n/r	n/r	n/r	n/r	n/r	n/r	n/r
KS	X	X	X	X	X		X
KY		X	X	X	X		X

n/r = State did not respond to survey
For information on other states, visit *http://www.gao.gov/new.items/d03757.pdf*

Keep in mind that preplanning does not have to mean prepayment, but prepaid burial plans are an exempt asset in assessing Medicaid eligibility (see Chapter 7). The payment need not be to an individual funeral home — an individual may be able to obtain burial insurance, which is, essentially, life insurance without the complicated procedures. Whether prepayment to a funeral home is wise may depend on the state. Some states require the funeral home or cemetery to place a percentage of the prepayment in a state-regulated trust or to purchase a life insurance policy with the death benefits assigned to the funeral home or cemetery; other states have little meaningful regulation. The purchaser should also know whether the plan can be cancelled or changed for a refund, and what happens if the funeral home goes out of business or the purchaser moves out of the area. The purchaser should get a detailed list of the products and services to be provided and make sure copies will be available to survivors, to avoid any chance that they will pay for the same things again.

The client may have a preconceived notion of a traditional funeral and may not be aware that many "traditional" products are not required. Embalming is not always required; a casket is not required for cremation. Even the most expensive casket does not provide perfect protection of the remains, and a vault or liner may not be necessary. Under the Funeral Rule, a funeral director may not require a client to purchase a "package" that includes items or services that are not legally required and that the client does not want, may not refuse to use a casket or urn purchased elsewhere, and must identify items and services that are required by law. See Exhibit 12.1 for a checklist of planning considerations.

EXHIBIT 12.1
Planning for a Funeral[7]

---

1. **Shop around in advance.** Compare prices from at least two funeral homes. Remember that you can supply your own casket or urn.
2. **Ask for a price list.** The law requires funeral homes to give you written price lists for products and services.
3. **Resist pressure** to buy goods and services you don't really want or need.
4. **Avoid emotional overspending.** It's not necessary to have the fanciest casket or the most elaborate funeral to properly honor a loved one.
5. **Recognize your rights.** Laws regarding funerals and burials vary from state to state. It's a smart move to know which goods or services the law requires you to purchase and which are optional.
6. **Apply the same smart shopping techniques** you use for other major purchases. You can cut costs by limiting the viewing to one day or one hour before the funeral, and by dressing your loved one in a favorite outfit instead of costly burial clothing.
7. **Plan ahead.** It allows you to comparison shop without time constraints, creates an opportunity for family discussion, and lifts some of the burden from your family.

---

[7] http://www.ftc.gov

Might the stated wishes of the deceased individual be disregarded by a survivor who wants different arrangements? In some states, the answer is yes, even if the stated wishes of the deceased are reasonable and not unduly burdensome. Of course, circumstances may change, and even preplanning should include some flexibility. If Samira planned her funeral while she was a popular college professor and her family was financially well off, would she want the same arrangements if she died at age 97, having spent 22 years in a nursing home and depleted her assets? State "personal preference" laws may give an individual the right to appoint an agent to make funeral arrangements or may require that survivors comply with the wishes of the deceased. For an overview of these laws, visit the Funeral Consumers Alliance Web site (*http://www.funerals.org/your-legal-rights/funeral-decision-rights*).

Remember, all veterans, their spouses, and dependents, are entitled to a free burial site in a veterans' cemetery, as discussed in Chapter 15. Veterans are also entitled to a grave marker, and there is no charge for opening and closing the grave. For more information, visit *http://www.cem.va.gov/cems_nmc.asp*. Many private cemeteries offer "veterans' specials" but make their profit in selling adjoining space for family members or in fees for opening and closing the graves.

In dealing with a client who has just survived the death of a spouse or other close loved one, a paralegal will have to call on the skills described in Chapter 1. In addition to understanding the client's state of mind and using your best communications skills, you may have to use detective skills. The survivor may be totally unprepared to provide important information and documents and may rely on the law office for assistance, as described in Chapter 1.

The following are the "first month" tasks for the survivor (all requests should be in writing):

- If the deceased was employed, contact the employer about benefits (life insurance, accrued vacation time) and pay owed the deceased, and the availability of continued benefits.
- If the deceased had life insurance, the beneficiary must submit a claim with a death certificate and may have to choose a payment option.
- Notify the Social Security Administration of the death.
- Call any unions or professional or service organizations your loved one belonged to — life insurance and other benefits are sometimes available through these organizations.
- Start gathering essential documents — will or trust, deeds, business agreements, tax returns, bank accounts, earnings statements, birth and marriage certificates, military discharge papers, Social Security number, vehicle registration, loan payment books, bills, etc., for the probate process described in Chapter 8.
- Notify creditors (credit card companies, etc.).
- Contact banks and other financial institutions to have deceased individual's name removed from accounts — in most states survivor will continue to have access to funds (it used to be common for banks to freeze accounts upon notice of death). Make sure that survivor understands that any property held in trust needs no action. A survivor may not understand that transferring funds out of the "William and Lorraine Warner Trust" into her own name can seriously jeopardize a good financial plan.

Dealing with Grief

Be aware that your client's religious or cultural beliefs may dictate how some of these matters should be handled. For example, Judaism[8] and Islam accept autopsy only if a need is demonstrated. Buddhism, which may include a denial of appearances, is finding ways to accommodate the need of medical practices in the western world. Judaism and some other beliefs require that the funeral occur as soon as possible; some religions disfavor cremation.

Religions and cultures also differ with respect to beliefs about an afterlife and expressions of grief. Be sensitive to the fact that your client may have traditions and beliefs different than your own and, in communicating with the client, do not make assumptions based on your own culture. While you cannot ignore the client's loss and act as if it is "business as usual," a simple "I am so sorry for your loss," followed by a sincere offer of help is generally best. If you knew the deceased, you can say something like, "I will always remember his contagious laugh." Keep it short and, if possible, upbeat. Avoid statements like, "I knew he was in terrible pain, but he was so brave." Older clients may feel a strong need to keep their emotions under control, particularly in a place of business and particularly in front of younger people. Do not make it more difficult for them.

- Your most important task is to listen. Do not interject your own experiences or feelings or say, "I know how you feel."
- Follow the client's lead. She may not want to talk about her feelings. She may not want to talk about the manner of her spouse's death. She may not want to talk about the future. She may just want to get through the day by accomplishing a particular task.
- Do not make "comforting" statements, based on your own beliefs, such as "It is for the best," "At least he is not suffering," or "He is in a better place."
- Do not expect grief to have a timetable or for the client to find "closure" and move on. Continue to be sensitive to the fact that the client may be suffering, even long after the loss.

EXHIBIT 12.2
Amity Says

The Reverend Amity Carrubba grew up as an "Air Force brat," living around the United States and Germany, and pursued a career in the pharmaceutical industry prior to discovering her passion for ministry. She was ordained an Episcopal priest in 2006 and currently serves at Church of the Redeemer in Elgin, Illinois, a

---

[8]For a list of cases involving wrongful autopsy, see *http://www.jlaw.com/Summary/autopsy.html* (visited September 4, 2010).

EXHIBIT 12.2
(continued)

diverse congregation that worships in two languages. When asked about dealing with grief, she said:

> I have noticed some differences in the grieving process between older and younger people. Often older individuals, particularly if they are widowed, are more isolated physically and emotionally, which leads to even greater isolation during a time of loss. This common reality makes it all the more important for these older individuals to have people to take the initiative and reach out to them. Also, members of the older generation tend to hold more traditional views on suffering and grief that are not always helpful — for example, thinking that their loss is a form of God's punishment. Conversely, older individuals also have more life experience, which can help the person gain perspective on the situation, difficult though it may be.
>
> Younger adults tend to have a more extended support system and other aspects of life (work, social, children) that can serve at least as distractions and at best as mechanisms of healing in themselves. Younger adults tend to be more open and accepting of seeking counseling services and tend to have more contemporary understandings of suffering and loss. On the other hand, I think of one young family from my last parish whose five-year-old daughter died. While it is always tragic and painful for a parent to lose a child, to suffer a loss at such a young age (both young parents and young child), the grief is even more acute.
>
> My only observations in cultural differences are very superficial. For example, at funeral receptions in the Anglo culture, people are eating, drinking, talking, perhaps laughing and telling stories of the departed. The idea is often to celebrate the life of the person and so in our grief we include celebration. In Latino culture the events tend to be much more somber and serious, with prayers continuing after the funeral is over. In the Jewish tradition, there are very particular rituals, forms, and community roles/expectations for grief. As a non-Jew, I find these helpful since so often in Christian culture we don't know what to say or do, so we end up doing nothing and isolating the person/individuals in their grief. At least in the Jewish culture everyone knows what is expected, so you have a pre-set roadmap and don't have the extra burden of trying to find your way during a difficult time.
>
> In dealing with grief in a professional role, be honest and direct. Be sensitive, but it is appropriate to ask for what you need as a professional to serve the person. Some push-back or "nudging" may be needed. As a priest I try to avoid euphemisms for death (passed away, lost, etc.) and articulate the truth: "When your mother died. . . . " Sometimes out of pity or an attempt at sensitivity we tiptoe too much and try to avoid the truth, which is not always helpful. And sometimes people get bogged down in their grief and need a helpful nudge in order to overcome emotional inertia and do the real life chores that need to be done.

Assignments

1. Report on hospice services available in your area.
2. Critical Thinking/Ethical Dilemma: Read the summary of the *Vacco* case at the end of this chapter.
   a. Does your state have a law similar to the one at issue? Use these starting points for your research: *http://www.nightingalealliance. org/pdf/state_grid.pdf* and *http://www.deathwithdignity.org.*
   b. The court distinguishes the Cruzan situation, but might the situation of a patient wanting to end her life be more compelling? In the *Cruzan* case the patient was not functioning, but there was no indication that she was in intolerable pain. Do people have a "right" to be free of pain that cannot be relieved?
   c. Do you think that the removal of life support equipment, with knowledge that death will follow, is essentially assisted suicide?
   d. Can you think of other reasons to prohibit assisted suicide? Can you imagine situations in which a patient would be subject to pressure?
   e. Suppose that a client confided in you her intention to commit suicide because of the pain she is enduring. Discuss your ethical obligations. Would it make a difference if the patient, unable to leave home, has a friend who has agreed to bring the pills and sit with her while she takes them?
3. Use the Internet to find the regulatory agency that licenses funeral directors in your state. Is it possible to determine whether a funeral director has been disciplined? Report on the consumer protections in place in your state with respect to the death care industry.
4. Critical Thinking/Ethical Dilemma:

Linda, a 68-year-old married woman, suffers a seizure while at a movie with friends and is rushed to the hospital in an unresponsive state. While Linda appears to be healthy, she recently learned that a cancer for which she was treated several years ago has returned and is likely terminal. A scan reveals that her cancer has spread to her brain and she has a hemorrhage from one of the cancerous spots that led to her seizure and coma. The doctors say that if they do not evacuate the hemorrhage immediately she will die in the next 24 to 48 hours. If they evacuate it, there is no way to predict whether she will wake up and how much functioning she will have. Because the hemorrhage is in the motor portion of her brain, it is likely Linda will be at least partially paralyzed and will always be dependent on others for care.

Linda has told her friends that she would prefer to die quickly rather that suffer the deterioration of cancer and that she might consider taking her own life as the disease progresses. Linda has been married to Phil for 15 years and Phil agrees with Linda that natural death is preferable to life-prolonging measures. Unfortunately, Linda's children from her first marriage do not like Phil and have always thought he married their mother for financial reasons. The children firmly believe in preserving life at all costs and believe that their mothers' cancer might be cured by a medical miracle. Linda's only sibling, Marie, agrees with the children. At the time of Linda's emergency, Phil is in an airplane over the Atlantic Ocean, returning from a visit to his elderly mother, who lives in England. He cannot be reached. Linda's children and sister, called by her friends, will arrive at the hospital in about an hour. Linda's friends are with her at the hospital and have told the doctors of Linda's stated preferences.

Linda has not yet executed any advance directives. She planned to do so next week. At the emergency room, the doctors are aware of her cancer because her oncologist is on staff. The doctors remember, from the limited legal training they have received, that treating a person without consent can constitute **medical battery**, but that there is an exception to the **informed consent doctrine** for medical emergencies. They wonder whether the exception applies in situations where the doctors are aware that the patient would likely not consent if conscious.

Analyze the situation based on your own state's surrogate decision-making statute, or under the common law and the Illinois statute (see below).

Medical Battery
Treatment without informed consent

Informed Consent Doctrine
Requirement that patient understand procedure or treatment before giving consent

There are four essential elements required to establish that the common-law emergency exception applies: (1) there was a medical emergency, (2) treatment was required in order to protect the patient's health, (3) it was impossible or impractical to obtain consent from either the patient or someone authorized to consent for the patient, and (4) there was no reason to believe that the patient would decline the treatment, given the opportunity to consent.[9]

The text of the relevant Illinois statute follows:

(755 ILCS 40/25) (from Ch. 110 1/2, par. 851-25)

Sec. 25. Surrogate decision making.

(a) When a patient lacks decisional capacity, the health care provider must make a reasonable inquiry as to the availability and authority of a health care agent under the Powers of Attorney for Health Care Law. When no health care agent is authorized and available, the health care provider must make a reasonable inquiry as to the availability of possible surrogates listed in items (1) through (4) of this subsection. For purposes of this Section, a reasonable inquiry includes, but is not limited to, identifying a member of the patient's family or other health care agent by examining the patient's personal effects or medical records. If a family member or other health care agent is identified, an attempt to contact that person by telephone must be made within 24 hours after a determination by the provider that the patient lacks decisional capacity. No person shall be liable for civil damages or subject to professional discipline based on a claim of violating a patient's right to confidentiality as a result of making a reasonable inquiry as to the availability of a patient's family member or health care agent, except for willful or wanton misconduct.

---

[9] *See, e.g., Restatement (Second) of Torts,* §892A (1979); *Planned Parenthood Minn. v. Rounds,* 650 F. Supp. 2d 972 (D.S.D. 2009); *Moriarity v. Rockford Health Sys.,* 848 N.E.2d 202 (Ill. App., 2006)

The surrogate decision makers, as identified by the attending physician, are then authorized to make decisions as follows: (i) for patients who lack decisional capacity and do not have a qualifying condition, medical treatment decisions may be made in accordance with subsection (b-5) of Section 20; and (ii) for patients who lack decisional capacity and have a qualifying condition, medical treatment decisions including whether to forgo life-sustaining treatment on behalf of the patient may be made without court order or judicial involvement in the following order of priority:

(1) the patient's guardian of the person;
(2) the patient's spouse;
(3) any adult son or daughter of the patient;
(4) either parent of the patient;
(5) any adult brother or sister of the patient;
(6) any adult grandchild of the patient;
(7) a close friend of the patient;
(8) the patient's guardian of the estate.

The health care provider shall have the right to rely on any of the above surrogates if the provider believes after reasonable inquiry that neither a health care agent under the Powers of Attorney for Health Care Law nor a surrogate of higher priority is available.

Where there are multiple surrogate decision makers at the same priority level in the hierarchy, it shall be the responsibility of those surrogates to make reasonable efforts to reach a consensus as to their decision on behalf of the patient regarding the forgoing of life-sustaining treatment. If 2 or more surrogates who are in the same category and have equal priority indicate to the attending physician that they disagree about the health care matter at issue, a majority of the available persons in that category (or the parent with custodial rights) shall control, unless the minority (or the parent without custodial rights) initiates guardianship proceedings in accordance with the Probate Act of 1975. No health care provider or other person is required to seek appointment of a guardian.

Review Questions

1. Discuss the differences between a client refusing treatment and assisted suicide.
2. Identify the tasks that should be performed soon after death.
3. What is the Funeral Rule and which agency enforces it?

VACCO V. QUILL

521 U.S. 793 (1997) [footnotes, internal citations, quotations, and concurring opinions omitted]

In New York, as in most States, it is a crime to aid another to commit or attempt suicide, but patients may refuse even lifesaving medical treatment. The question presented by this case is whether New York's prohibition on assisting suicide therefore violates the Equal Protection Clause of the Fourteenth Amendment. We hold that it does not.

Petitioners are various New York public officials. Respondents Timothy E. Quill, Samuel C. Klagsbrun, and Howard A. Grossman are physicians who practice in New York. They assert that although it would be "consistent with the standards of [their] medical practices" to prescribe lethal medication for "mentally competent, terminally ill patients" who are suffering great pain and desire a doctor's help in taking their own lives, they are deterred from doing so by New York's ban on assisting suicide. Respondents, and three gravely ill patients who have since died, sued the State's Attorney General in the United States District Court. They urged that because New York permits a competent person to refuse life-sustaining medical treatment, and because the refusal of such treatment is "essentially the same thing" as physician-assisted suicide, New York's assisted-suicide ban violates the Equal Protection Clause

The District Court disagreed: "It is hardly unreasonable or irrational for the State to recognize a difference between allowing nature to take its course, even in the most severe situations, and intentionally using an artificial death-producing device." The court noted New York's "obvious legitimate interests in preserving life, and in protecting vulnerable persons," and concluded that "under the United States Constitution and the federal system it establishes, the resolution of this issue is left to the normal democratic processes within the State."

The Court of Appeals for the Second Circuit reversed. The court determined that, despite the assisted-suicide ban's apparent general applicability, "New York law does not treat equally all competent persons who are in the final stages of fatal illness and wish to hasten their deaths," because "those in the final stages of terminal illness who are on life-support systems are allowed to hasten their deaths by directing the removal of such systems; but those who are similarly situated, except for the previous attachment of life-sustaining equipment, are not allowed to hasten death by self-administering prescribed drugs." In the court's view, "the ending of life by [the withdrawal of life-support systems] is nothing more nor less than assisted suicide." The Court of Appeals then examined whether this supposed unequal treatment was rationally related to any legitimate state interests, and concluded that "to the extent that [New York's statutes] prohibit a physician from prescribing medications to be self-administered by a mentally competent, terminally-ill person in the final stages of his terminal illness, they are not rationally related to any legitimate state interest." We granted certiorari, and now reverse.

The Equal Protection Clause commands that no State shall "deny to any person within its jurisdiction the equal protection of the laws." This provision creates no substantive rights. Instead, it embodies a general rule that States must treat like cases alike but may treat unlike cases accordingly. If a legislative classification or distinction "neither burdens a fundamental right nor targets a suspect class, we will uphold [it] so long as it bears a rational relation to some legitimate end."

New York's statutes outlawing assisting suicide affect and address matters of profound significance to all New Yorkers alike. They neither infringe fundamental rights nor involve suspect classifications. These laws are therefore entitled to a "strong presumption of validity."

On their faces, neither New York's ban on assisting suicide nor its statutes permitting patients to refuse medical treatment treat anyone differently than anyone else or draw any distinctions between persons. Everyone, regardless of physical condition, is entitled, if competent, to refuse unwanted lifesaving medical treatment; no one is permitted to assist a suicide. Generally speaking, laws that apply evenhandedly to all "unquestionably comply" with the Equal Protection Clause.

The Court of Appeals, however, concluded that some terminally ill people — those who are on life-support systems — are treated differently than those who are not, in that the former may "hasten death" by ending treatment, but the latter may not "hasten death" through physician-assisted suicide. . . . This conclusion depends on the submission that ending or refusing lifesaving medical treatment "is nothing more nor less than assisted suicide." Unlike the Court of Appeals, we think the distinction between assisting suicide and withdrawing life-sustaining treatment, a distinction widely recognized and endorsed in the medical profession and in our legal traditions, is both important and logical; it is certainly rational.

The distinction comports with fundamental legal principles of causation and intent. First, when a patient refuses life-sustaining medical treatment, he dies from an underlying fatal disease or pathology; but if a patient ingests lethal medication prescribed by a physician, he is killed by that medication. . . . Furthermore, a physician who withdraws, or honors a patient's refusal to begin, life-sustaining medical treatment purposefully intends, or may so intend, only to respect his patient's wishes and "to cease doing useless and futile or degrading things to the patient when [the patient] no longer stands to benefit from them." The same is true when a doctor provides aggressive palliative care; in some cases, painkilling drugs may hasten a patient's death, but the physician's purpose and intent is, or may be, only to ease his patient's pain. A doctor who assists a suicide, however, "must, necessarily and indubitably, intend primarily that the patient be made dead." Similarly, a patient who commits suicide with a doctor's aid necessarily has the specific intent to end his or her own life, while a patient who refuses or discontinues treatment might not.

The law has long used actors' intent or purpose to distinguish between two acts that may have the same result. Put differently, the law distinguishes actions taken "because of" a given end from actions taken "in spite of" their unintended but foreseen consequences. . . . Given these general principles, it is not surprising that many courts, including New York courts, have carefully distinguished refusing life-sustaining treatment from suicide. In fact, the first state-court decision explicitly to authorize withdrawing lifesaving treatment noted the "real distinction between the self-infliction of deadly harm and a self-determination against artificial life support." And recently, the Michigan Supreme Court also rejected the argument that the distinction "between acts that artificially sustain life and acts that artificially curtail life" is merely a "distinction without constitutional significance — a meaningless exercise in semantic gymnastics," insisting that "the Cruzan majority disagreed and so do we."

Similarly, the overwhelming majority of state legislatures have drawn a clear line between assisting suicide and withdrawing or permitting the refusal of unwanted lifesaving medical treatment by prohibiting the former and permitting the latter. And "nearly all states expressly disapprove of suicide and assisted suicide either in statutes dealing with durable powers of attorney in health-care situations, or in 'living will' statutes." Thus, even as the States move to protect and promote patients' dignity at the end of life, they remain opposed to physician-assisted suicide.

New York is a case in point. The State enacted its current assisted-suicide statutes in 1965. Since then, New York has acted several times to protect patients' common-law right to refuse treatment. In so doing, however, the State has neither endorsed a general right to "hasten death" nor approved physician-assisted suicide. Quite the opposite: The State has reaffirmed the line between "killing" and "letting die." More recently, the New York State Task Force on Life and the Law studied assisted suicide and euthanasia and, in 1994, unanimously recommended against legalization. In the Task Force's view, "allowing decisions to forego life-sustaining treatment and allowing assisted suicide or euthanasia have radically different consequences and meanings for public policy."

This Court has also recognized, at least implicitly, the distinction between letting a patient die and making that patient die. In *Cruzan v. Director*, Mo. Dept. of Health, 497 U.S. 261, 278 (1990), we concluded that "the principle that a competent person has a constitutionally protected liberty interest in refusing unwanted medical treatment may be inferred from our prior decisions," and we assumed the existence of such a right for purposes of that case. But our assumption of a right to refuse treatment was grounded not, as the Court of Appeals supposed, on the proposition that patients have a general and abstract "right to hasten death," but on well established, traditional rights to bodily integrity and freedom from unwanted touching. In fact, we observed that "the majority of States in this country have laws imposing criminal penalties on one who assists another to commit suicide." Cruzan therefore provides no support for the notion that refusing life-sustaining medical treatment is "nothing more nor less than suicide."

For all these reasons, we disagree with respondents' claim that the distinction between refusing lifesaving medical treatment and assisted suicide is "arbitrary" and "irrational." Granted, in some cases, the line between the two may not be clear, but certainty is not required, even were it possible. Logic and contemporary practice support New York's judgment that the two acts are different, and New York may therefore, consistent with the Constitution, treat them differently. By permitting everyone to refuse unwanted medical treatment while prohibiting anyone from assisting a suicide, New York law follows a longstanding and rational distinction.

New York's reasons for recognizing and acting on this distinction — including prohibiting intentional killing and preserving life; preventing suicide; maintaining physicians' role as their patients' healers; protecting vulnerable people from indifference, prejudice, and psychological and financial pressure to end their lives; and avoiding a possible slide towards euthanasia — are discussed in greater detail in our opinion in Glucksberg, ante. These valid and important public interests easily satisfy the constitutional requirement that a legislative classification bear a rational relation to some legitimate end. The judgment of the Court of Appeals is reversed.

13

◆ ◆ ◆

Family Matters

◆ ◆ ◆

Objectives

When you complete this chapter, you will:

- Understand the legal requirements of marriage, annulment, separation, and divorce.
- Know the rights of unmarried couples in committed relationships.
- Describe the requirements of a valid prenuptial agreement.
- Know whether your state has a process for ordering grandparent visitation.
- Describe the alternatives available to grandparents raising grandchildren.

A thorough exploration of family law requires an entire course and is far beyond the scope of this book. After a short overview, to introduce some essential terminology, this chapter will focus on particular issues of concern to older clients.

Family issues, by necessity, involve more people than the individual client, so the law firm must pay particular attention to ethical concerns, especially confidentiality. If representation will involve a couple, planning to be married or planning not to be married, that planning may involve areas in which their interests potentially are adverse. If the representation involves custody or visitation of grandchildren, it is very likely that interests will clash. Be alert for conflicts of interests! Family members, who either disapprove of the relationship or have their own interests at heart, may challenge the client's plans or directives. Be cautious to protect the client interests when preparing documents.

Check your state rules of ethics at *http://www.abanet.org/cpr/links.html*. Do they allow an attorney to represent conflicting interests with full disclosure and waiver?

Overview of Marriage and Divorce

Marriage is a legal union, by consent, of parties with the legal ability to marry each other. That ability is defined by state law. State laws set the minimum age for marriage, identify familial relationships between the parties that preclude marriage (for example, many states prohibit marriage between first cousins), require mental capacity, and require that neither party be married to anyone else. Most states require that marriage be between a man and a woman, but some states recognize "domestic partnership" unions for same-sex couples, described later in this chapter. States also regulate how marriage can occur: Some recognize common-law marriages, with almost no formalities (discussed later in this chapter); others require that the parties obtain a license, have blood tests, and go through a ceremony with an authorized individual presiding. With elder clients, competency to consent can be an issue, as demonstrated by the case at the end of Chapter 10.

Marriage gives spouses certain legal and property rights; of course, the end of a marriage changes or ends those rights. Clients who are getting married or going through a separation or divorce have many things on their minds, and legal documents are often last on the list. Good legal counsel includes reminders. If a client gets married, separated, or divorced, estate planning documents and advance directives should be reviewed.

In general, a marriage that is valid in the state in which it was entered is considered valid in other states. For example, if first cousins married in California (which permits such marriages) their marriage would be considered valid if they moved to Iowa (which does not). The apparent exception to states giving marriages "full faith and credit" stems from the 1996 Defense of Marriage Act, which defines marriage as "only a legal union between one man and one woman as husband and wife" and provides that "No State, territory, or possession of the United States, or Indian tribe, shall be required to give effect to any public act, record, or judicial proceeding of any other State, territory, possession, or tribe respecting a relationship between persons of the same sex that is treated as a marriage under the laws of such other State, territory, possession, or tribe, or a right or claim arising from such relationship" (28 U.S.C. §1738C).

Annulment, separation, and divorce are also governed by state law. **Annulment** is a decree that no valid marriage occurred, perhaps because a party lacked mental capacity or consented based on fraud. While annulment does not depend on the length of the relationship, courts are very reluctant to annul a marriage after children have been born. The parties do not necessarily have the same rights they would have in the event of a divorce, but a court may still award support and determine property rights.

A **separation**, sometimes called a limited divorce, does not dissolve the marriage, but defines the rights of spouses who are not living together (cohabitating). In some states a legal separation can "convert" to a divorce after a specified period.

A **divorce** formally dissolves a legal marriage and in some states is called dissolution of marriage. Some states require a "cooling-off period," a time period after legal separation that must pass before divorce proceedings can begin. Some states require a showing of misconduct or wrongdoing, such as adultery or abandonment, by a spouse. The requirement of proving fault sometimes led to couples indulging in "legal fictions" to obtain a divorce. In recent years almost all states have adopted "no fault" divorce provisions. In those states a court typically must find only (1) that the relationship is no longer viable, (2) that irreconcilable differences have caused an irremediable breakdown of the marriage, (3) that discord or conflict of personalities have destroyed the legitimate ends of the marital relationship and prevent any reasonable possibility of reconciliation, or (4) that the marriage is irretrievably broken. The "fault" requirement for granting a divorce is generally not related to the court's decisions concerning children and property.

Property and Children in Divorce

Property Division and Support of Spouse

There are two basic models of property distribution in divorce: the so-called equitable or common-law model and the community property model. In states following the common-law or equitable distribution method, the court identifies assets as either marital property or separate property. **Marital property** is property that the spouses own jointly or that either acquired individually during the marriage (in most states, excluding gifts to or inheritance by one spouse). **Separate property** is property that one spouse possessed prior to the marriage and that did not substantially change in value during the marriage because of the efforts of one or both spouses. If a spouse trades separate property for other property or sells the property, the newly acquired property or funds remain separate property. In some states a court can transfer separate property from one spouse to the other; in other states the court can only declare ownership of marital property.

An equitable division of the marital property does not necessarily mean an equal division, but rather a division that is fair and just, considering the circumstances. The court generally attempts to enable both parties to start their divorced lives with some degree of financial self-sufficiency. While states differ, most courts

Annulment
Declaration that no valid marriage existed

Separation
Sometimes called limited divorce, married people no longer cohabitate

Divorce
Dissolves a lawful marriage

Marital Property
Acquired after marriage, not by gift or inheritance to one spouse

Separate Property
Owned by a spouse before marriage or inheritance or gift after marriage

at least recognize contribution to the accumulation of marital property, the respective parties' liabilities, whether one spouse received income-producing property while the other did not, duration of the marriage, age and health of the parties, earning capacity and employability of the parties, value of each party's separate property, pension and retirement rights of each party, whether one party will receive custody and/or child support, **dissipation of assets** by either spouse, respective contributions of the spouses to the home and parenting, outside obligations, and tax consequences of the allocations. Some courts consider whether one spouse's marital misconduct caused the divorce; others do not.

Dissipation of Assets
Wrongful use of marital assets by a spouse

Tip

Despite the presumptions that apply to marital property in divorce situations, title does matter in other situations. As discussed in Chapter 8, if property is held in "joint tenancy with right of survivorship" or "tenancy by the entirety," the property automatically belongs to the surviving spouse when the other dies—no matter what the decedent's will says. But if the property is held in "tenancy in common" (unusual with married couples), the decedent's interest is inherited by her heirs as described in a will or by the state's law of **intestacy**.

Intestacy
Dying without a will—state law governs distribution of property

---

Community Property
Laws in some states, governing property acquired during marriage

Some states[1] have **community property** laws. Typically, money earned by either spouse during the marriage, and any property purchased with that money, belongs to both of them. Debts incurred during the marriage also belong to both. Money that one spouse had before the marriage or got by inheritance or gift during the marriage belongs to that spouse as separate property. Increased equity in separate property may become community property in certain circumstances, and separate property that is commingled with community property can become community property. If a spouse dies, the surviving spouse is presumed to inherit the decedent's share of community property unless there is a will stating otherwise. The courts in community property states usually divide the **net value** (value of assets minus debt) of community property equally between the parties and give each spouse his or her separate property. There can be exceptions—for example, if a spouse is unable to work. In recent years, the differences between common law and community property have blurred because courts are more focused on fairness to the parties.

Net Value
Assets minus debts

The future retirement benefits of a spouse may be the most valuable marital asset, and the other spouse may obtain an award of part of that property. A qualified domestic relations order (**QDRO**) is a court order by which ownership of part of that asset can be transferred to a former spouse.

QDRO
Qualified Domestic Relations Order, regarding ownership of retirement benefits

---

[1] Arizona, California, Idaho, Louisiana, Nevada, New Mexico, Texas, Washington, and Wisconsin. In Alaska, spouses can sign an agreement making specific assets community property.

Alimony, sometimes called spousal support or maintenance, is the payment of a regular amount by one former spouse to the other. Permanent alimony requires the paying spouse to continue paying until one of them dies or the spouse receiving payments remarries. Temporary alimony requires payments while the case is pending. Similar to temporary alimony, rehabilitative alimony requires payments for a specific period after the property division proceedings have concluded. Rehabilitative alimony is intended to help a spouse with lesser employability or earning capacity become financially independent. The court can award more than one type of alimony and generally attempts to allow the recipient to maintain the standard of living to which the recipient has become accustomed. Factors include the length of the marriage; length of separation before divorce; the parties' ages, respective incomes, and future financial prospects; the health of the parties; and (in some states) the parties' respective faults in causing the marriage to end.

Alimony
Support of former spouse

Many of the benefits previously discussed in this book have specific rules relating to divorce and support. For example, Chapters 4 and 6 discussed the ability of a divorced spouse to claim social security and Medicare benefits based on an ex-spouse's earnings record. The rules applicable to those claims — particularly the "10 years of marriage" rule — can make the timing of divorce critical. On the other hand, divorce generally terminates a spouse's eligibility for veterans' benefits and reduces the veteran's number of dependents, as discussed in Chapter 15.

In addition, divorce and support may have an impact on Medicaid eligibility or payments, as discussed in Chapter 7. Remember, the process first looks at assets to determine eligibility and then looks at income to determine what the patient can pay. In general, court-ordered transfers of property in divorce are not subject to penalties that would attach to other transfers in determining a person's eligibility for Medicaid.

Example

Howard and Wendy divorced in 2010 and, as part of the court-ordered settlement, Howard transferred $100,000 to Wendy. If, in 2011, Howard applies for Medicaid, he will not be penalized for having transferred property. On the other hand, if Wendy applies for Medicaid, she will no longer have a "community spouse" and the money will be part of her assets, unless some other exception applies, and will have to be depleted before she qualifies. For this reason, the likelihood of need for skilled care may be an important factor in settling property matters in divorce.

Support payments (alimony or maintenance) constitute income for the recipient and are considered in determining what Medicaid will pay each month. It is, therefore, common for the spouse paying support to attempt to have payments reduced once the recipient is institutionalized and receiving Medicaid. Because a reduction in support will increase the public's burden, a court may not be receptive to such a plan. If the spouse receiving the support consents to a reduction, it is possible that Medicaid will consider the agreement a "gift" and impose a penalty. The case at the end of this chapter demonstrates some of these issues.

Custody and Support of Children

Jurisdiction
Court's power to decide a case, based on type of case and/or geographical concerns

The court with **jurisdiction** over divorce proceedings also determines child custody and support. Custody refers not only to where the children will live, but also to the right to make decisions about their education, health care, and other matters.

As a starting point, parents generally have joint guardianship over children of the marriage, and parental rights are equal. Parents are presumed fit to have custody, and each parent has an equal right to the custody of the children when they separate. The court will typically award temporary custody to one parent during the proceedings, while it decides whether to award exclusive custody to one parent, joint custody to both, or custody to a third party. The court will consider the best interests of the children and the ability of the spouses to properly perform their duties as parents. Relevant factors include the wishes of the parents; the wishes of the children (depending on age); avoiding splitting siblings; each child's relationship with each parent, siblings, and other persons who may substantially impact the child's best interests; the child's comfort in her home, school, and community; and the mental and physical health of the involved individuals. Courts will sometimes appoint a guardian ad litem, an attorney for the children, a psychologist, or a court-appointed special advocate (**CASA**) to assist in the determination. For more information about CASA volunteers, visit *http://www.casaforchildren.org.*

CASA
Court-appointed special advocate for a child

When a court awards exclusive custody to one parent, the noncustodial parent retains the right to see and visit the child, except in extraordinary circumstances. There is a strong presumption in favor of visitation rights and in favor of attempting to heal parent-child relationships. Courts may impose restrictions on visitation and will often do so rather than deny visitation rights.

Support is a separate issue. Most states calculate child support using a formula that takes into account the income of the parent paying support and the number of children. Because failure to support children often results in a burden on taxpayers, states get involved in enforcing support orders, and the federal government has enacted laws to aid in the enforcement of those orders across state lines.

More information about family law in your state can be found at *http://topics. law.cornell.edu/wex/table_family.* Structuring support of a disabled child can be an important part of Medicaid planning. A full discussion is beyond the scope of this book.

Unmarried Couples

The terms "domestic partners" or "unmarried couple" can apply to same-sex couples who do not have the ability to marry in their home state or to opposite-sex couples who have chosen not to marry. A paralegal working in the field of elder law is likely to encounter many clients who do not marry for financial, legal, family, or philosophical reasons, but nonetheless have an exclusive and vital tie to another person. Good legal advice is essential to these clients because, despite their intentions, they may be "legal strangers" without the default protections of marriage, ranging from tax advantages to the right to visit in the hospital or plan a funeral. The Defense of Marriage Act, 28 U.S.C. §1738C, negates recognition of nontraditional relationships for federal purposes. The impact of the Act is discussed in more detail in chapters concerning federal benefits, such as social security. At the other end of the spectrum, these couples may wish to avoid financial obligations but not be aware that their actions could create those obligations.

At this writing, the future of same-sex marriage is very uncertain and, while some states and municipalities provide for registration of domestic partnerships, registration does not necessarily confer legal rights the partners might want. For example, the Washington statute (see Exhibit 13.1) states an intent to grant all of

---

EXHIBIT 13.1
Washington Statute on Domestic Partnership

RCW 26.60.015

Intent.

It is the intent of the legislature that for all purposes under state law, state registered domestic partners shall be treated the same as married spouses. Any privilege, immunity, right, benefit, or responsibility granted or imposed by statute, administrative or court rule, policy, common law or any other law to an individual because the individual is or was a spouse, or because the individual is or was an in-law in a specified way to another individual, is granted on equivalent terms, substantive and procedural, to an individual because the individual is or was in a state registered domestic partnership or because the individual is or was, based on a state registered domestic partnership, related in a specified way to another individual. The provisions of chapter 521, Laws of 2009 shall be liberally construed to achieve equal treatment, to the extent not in conflict with federal law, of state registered domestic partners and married spouses.

RCW 26.60.030

Requirements.

To enter into a state registered domestic partnership the two persons involved must meet the following requirements:

(1) Both persons share a common residence; . . .

(3) Neither person is married to someone other than the party to the domestic partnership and neither person is in a state registered domestic partnership with another person; . . .

(6) Either (a) both persons are members of the same sex; or (b) at least one of the persons is sixty-two years of age or older.

the rights of marriage, while the Boulder, Colorado ordinance (*http://www.bouldercolorado.gov/index.php?option=com_content&task=view&id=5269&Itemid=139*) confers no rights or responsibilities. Notice that the Washington law requires that opposite-sex domestic partners be age 62 or older. Why do you think the legislature added that limitation? Clients are likely to get the best result by tailoring a partnership agreement to their own wants and needs.

Documents discussed in other chapters are essential to spelling out exactly which rights each party wants to give the other with respect to decision making and distribution of property after death: advance directives for health care and property and a will or trust. But, keep in mind that those documents are executed by one party. If Pat writes a will that leaves nothing to Chris, with whom Pat has lived for 18 years, might Chris have enforceable expectations contrary to the will? In addition, unlike married couples, unmarried couples need to spell out their rights and responsibilities with respect to support and responsibilities while alive and healthy. Do they intend to form an "economic unit," with possible support obligations if the relationship ends, or do they wish to remain financially independent? A written agreement is crucial if the parties have intertwined their lives by living together, co-ownership of property, even presenting themselves as married in dealing with others.

To Wed or Not to Wed? That Is the Question

Married	*Not Married*
Legal assumptions regarding inheritance, support, decision making.	These issues can be handled by careful advance planning.
Increased access to institutionalized partner's assets when seeking Medicaid for long-term care.	No legal responsibility for partner's expenses and care.
Social "approval."	Possible disapproval or anger on the part of children of previous marriage.
Entitlement to certain social security, pension, insurance benefits of spouse.	Possible loss of those rights from prior spouse.

Common-law Marriage
Lacks formalities of license and ceremony

Palimony
Slang term, describes paying support to a non-spouse companion

A few states recognize **common-law marriage** and others do not; some states have recognized informal or implied agreements to support an unmarried partner—sometimes called **palimony**. Regardless of whether the couple wants to confer or avoid the obligations that come with marriage, they should not gamble on getting the result they want. Cohabitation agreements are generally enforceable under ordinary contract law principles and can address:

- Ownership, management, and control of assets
- Allocation or sharing of income and expenses
- Support if the relationship ends or a party becomes incapacitated or dies
- Taxation and other liabilities that may result from property transfers

Because some courts have found cohabitation agreements unlawful agreements to pay for sexual conduct, these agreements should carefully describe other **consideration**. Has either party foregone other opportunities (sold property, passed up a job promotion)? Are the parties performing other compensable services for each other (cooking, shopping, cleaning, yard work, home or vehicle maintenance)? While there may be no precedent indicating that a cohabitation agreement must be supported by full disclosure (prenuptial agreements, also discussed in this chapter, do require disclosure), any agreement based on false information is less likely to be upheld in court.

Consideration
Mutual give-and-take, separates a contract from a gift

Prenuptial Agreements

Some older people do marry. While younger people are often willing to rely on default law (known as divorce law) to resolve issues that arise if their marriage breaks up, older people typically have more property, more personal obligations, and more concern about estate planning. They can enter into a prenuptial agreement, also called a "prenup" or an **ante-nuptial agreement** to resolve rights and responsibilities in advance (see Exhibit 13.2). An agreement executed after marriage is not the equivalent of a prenup and is likely to be considered unenforceable.

Ante-nuptial Agreement
Contract in anticipation of marriage

Because these agreements have the potential to be unfair, states have fairly strict laws governing enforceability. State laws differ, but it is best to err on the side of caution. Many states have enacted the Uniform Premarital Agreement Act (*http://www.law.cornell.edu/uniform/vol9.html*), which focuses on full disclosure by each party. To avoid having a court declare the agreement unenforceable:

- Each party should be represented by his or her own lawyer and must have time to review the agreement without pressure.
- There must be no evidence of **duress**—many agreements include a statement that the parties were fully informed and signed under no pressure.
- The agreement must be in writing.
- Each party must fully and truthfully disclose his or her financial status before the agreement is signed—if a party has assets that are difficult to value, at least identify the assets and acknowledge the difficulty in assessing value.
- The agreement cannot leave a spouse **indigent**—unable to support himself, but not entitled to support from the spouse.

Duress
Threat or pressure

Indigent
Impoverished

Generally, a prenuptial agreement can address the following issues:

- Division of property on divorce
- Whether particular items are considered marital property, community property, or separate property

EXHIBIT 13.2
Anatomy of a Prenup

Pat Smith, ("Prospective Husband"), and Chris Jones ("Prospective Wife"), hereby agree on this 2nd day of August, 20XX, as follows:

1. Prospective Husband and Prospective Wife contemplate marriage in the near future and wish to establish their respective rights and responsibilities regarding each other's income, property, and obligations, and income, property, and obligations that may be acquired, either separately or together, during the marriage.
2. Prospective Husband and Prospective Wife have made a full and complete disclosure to each other of all of their financial assets and liabilities, as more fully set forth in the accompanying Financial Statements, attached hereto as Exhibits A and B.
3. Both Prospective Husband and Prospective Wife are currently self-supporting; each has separate assets and can provide for his or her own needs.
4. Prospective Husband has been previously married and has continuing support obligations to a child of that marriage, Jordan Smith ("Jordan"). Jordan is disabled and will require continuing parental support after reaching the age of majority.
5. Except as otherwise provided, Prospective Husband and Prospective Wife waive rights:
   - To share in each other's estates upon their death.
   - To spousal maintenance, both temporary and permanent.
   - To share in any increase in value of separate property of the parties.
   - To share in the pension, profit sharing, or other retirement accounts of the other.
   - To the division of the separate property of the parties, whether currently held or hereafter acquired.
   - To any claims based on the period of cohabitation of the parties.
6. Prospective Husband currently pays the sum of $XXX per month for the support of Jordan, has executed a Trust, attached hereto as Exhibit C, under which Jordan is the sole primary beneficiary of Husband's assets in the event of Prospective Husband's death, and has named Jordan as sole beneficiary of a life insurance policy listed in Exhibit A.
7. Prospective Husband and Prospective Wife agree that each is solely responsible for any debts incurred in his or her name alone, whether before or after marriage.
8. Prospective Husband and Prospective Wife have shared and will continue to share a home, identified in Exhibit B, owned by Prospective Wife; that home, and any substitute home held in the name of Prospective Wife, shall remain the sole property of Prospective Wife, free of any claims by Prospective Husband.

EXHIBIT 13.2
(continued)

9. Prospective Husband and Prospective Wife are each represented by separate and independent legal counsel of their own choosing; each has had adequate opportunity to examine this agreement and consider its contents.
10. This agreement constitutes the entire agreement of the parties and may be modified only in a writing executed by both Prospective Husband and Prospective Wife.
11. In the event it is determined that a provision of this agreement is invalid because it is contrary to applicable law, that provision is deemed separable from the rest of the agreement, such that the remainder of the agreement remains valid and enforceable.
12. This agreement is made in accordance with the laws of the state of ___, and any dispute regarding its enforcement will be resolved by reference to the laws of that state.
13. This agreement will take effect immediately upon the solemnization of the parties' marriage.

I HAVE READ THE ABOVE AGREEMENT, I HAVE TAKEN TIME TO CONSIDER ITS IMPLICATIONS, I FULLY UNDERSTAND ITS CONTENTS, I AGREE TO ITS TERMS, AND I VOLUNTARILY SUBMIT TO ITS EXECUTION. (signatures)

- Ownership of the marital residence
- Responsibility for premarital debts
- Distribution of property on death (make sure estate planning documents are consistent)
- Alimony obligations (in some states)[2]
- Financial responsibilities during the marriage
- Under which state's law the prenup is to be interpreted (default is generally state of divorce, not state of marriage)

---

[2]Keep in mind that, even if inclusion of support limits is not prohibited, a court can always strike the provision if it is unfair or if circumstances have changed. For example, if husband and wife agreed that there would be no support in the event of a divorce because they had similar assets and income at the time of the marriage, but husband is now disabled and cannot work, a court will not enforce the provision. In general, the longer the marriage lasts, the more likely a court is to invalidate a provision in a prenup.

- How disputes about the prenup are to be resolved (mediation or arbitration)
- Sunset clause — many couples state that the agreement will not be valid if they are married for a certain number of years
- Provisions concerning married life, such as division of chores — but many people believe these are unenforceable and belong in a separate agreement

In addition, the parties cannot contract away the rights of others, so a provision purporting to eliminate child support would be meaningless. Courts always look to the best interests of the children in making custody and care decisions, and contractual provisions are irrelevant. Of course, anything illegal is not allowed as is anything that might encourage a divorce.

Grandparents

For most older people, grandchildren are a source of great joy without responsibility. Unfortunately, it is increasingly common for grandparents to have to take responsibility for grandchildren or to be denied contract with grandchildren.

Visitation

Every state has or has had some type of "grandparent visitation" statute through which grandparents and sometimes others (foster parents and stepparents, for example) can ask a court to grant them visitation with children of whom they do not have custody. Some states restrict visitation to grandparents of children whose parents are divorcing or whose parent has died. In some states visitation rights end when the child is adopted by a stepparent or another grandparent. More permissive states allow courts to consider a visitation request even without the death of a parent or the dissolution of a marriage, if visitation would serve the best interests of the child.

These laws have been challenged with mixed results. In 2000, the Supreme Court said of a Washington statute that it characterized as "breathtakingly broad":

> There is a presumption that fit parents act in their children's best interests; . . . there is normally no reason for the State to inject itself into the private realm of the family to further question fit parents' ability to make the best decisions regarding their children. . . . The problem here is not that the Superior Court intervened, but that when it did so, it gave no special weight to Granville's determination of her daughters' best interests. More importantly, that court appears to have applied the opposite presumption, favoring grandparent visitation. In effect, it placed on Granville the burden of *disproving* that visitation would be in her daughters' best interest and thus failed to provide any protection for her fundamental right. *Troxel v. Granville*, 530 U.S. 57 (2000)

Contrary to what some people believe, the decision did not invalidate all grandparent visitation laws, but only ruled on the application of one particular law. Since the decision, some courts have relied on the *Troxel* court statement that a decision on visitation "must accord at least some special weight to the parent's own determination," and upheld laws that do properly weigh the decision of a fit parent.[3] Exhibit 13.3 shows how Illinois amended its law after determining that a previous version did not pass constitutional muster.

What is the law in your state? See *http://family.findlaw.com/child-custody/custody-more/state-grandparent-custody.html*.

Grandparents Raising Grandchildren

The United States Census of 2000 indicated that about 4.4 million children lived in households headed by a grandparent.[4] This often starts out as an informal arrangement, with grandparents agreeing to provide temporarily while a parent gets through a divorce, addiction, even incarceration. If the arrangement continues, the grandparents may find themselves in need of help with physical challenges, financial problems, and legal issues. They may have trouble getting the children enrolled in school or obtaining medical care. They may worry that an unfit parent will return and disrupt the stable home life they have created for the children.

In recognition of these issues, the Older Americans Act (OAA) was amended to establish the National Family Caregiver Support Program (**NFCSP**), *http://www.aoa.gov/AoARoot/AoA_Programs/HCLTC/Caregiver/index.aspx*, administered through the Administration on Aging (AoA). The program provides funds to states for five types of services to relative caregivers age 55 and older, even in informal arrangements:

NFCSP
National Family Caregiver Support Program

- Information to caregivers about available services
- Assistance to caregivers in gaining access to the services
- Individual counseling, organization of support groups, and caregiver training
- Respite care
- Supplemental services, on a limited basis

Priority is given to those with financial need and those caring for disabled grandchildren. See Exhibit 13.4 for an example of an NFCSP program enacted in Illinois.

A client who wants to formalize her role in her grandchild's life may have a number of options, depending on the state and on whether the child's parents are willing to consent. If the parents do not consent and have not been determined to be unfit, obtaining any formal arrangement can be very difficult. If, however, the grandparent has taken care of the child under an informal arrangement for long enough to become the child's "psychological parent," a court may act without consent or a determination that the parents are unfit.

---

[3] *See, e.g., Oldham v. Morgan*, 372 Ark. 159 (2008)
[4] The 2010 Census results were not available as of this writing; for further breakdown visit *http://www.census.gov/main/www/cen2000.html*.

EXHIBIT 13.3
Illinois Statute

750 ILCS 5/607(a-3)

Grandparents, great-grandparents, and siblings of a minor child, who is one year old or older, have standing to bring an action in circuit court by petition, requesting visitation in accordance with this Section. . . . Grandparents, great-grandparents, and siblings also have standing to file a petition for visitation and any electronic communication rights in a pending dissolution proceeding or any other proceeding that involves custody or visitation issues, requesting visitation in accordance with this Section. . . . Nothing in this subsection (a-3) and subsection (a-5) of this Section shall apply to a child in whose interests a petition is pending under Section 2-13 of the Juvenile Court Act of 1987 or a petition to adopt an unrelated child is pending under the Adoption Act.

    (a-5)(1) Except as otherwise provided in this subsection (a-5), any grandparent, great-grandparent, or sibling may file a petition for visitation rights to a minor child if there is an unreasonable denial of visitation by a parent and at least one of the following conditions exists: . . .

    (A-5) the child's other parent is deceased or has been missing for at least 3 months . . . (A-10) a parent of the child is incompetent as a matter of law; (A-15) a parent has been incarcerated . . . during the 3 month period preceding;

    (B) the child's mother and father are divorced or have been legally separated from each other or there is pending a dissolution proceeding involving a parent of the child or another court proceeding involving custody or visitation of the child (other than any adoption proceeding of an unrelated child) and at least one parent does not object to the grandparent, great-grandparent, or sibling having visitation with the child. The visitation of the grandparent, great-grandparent, or sibling must not diminish the visitation of the parent who is not related to the grandparent, great-grandparent, or sibling seeking visitation; . . .

    (D) the child is born out of wedlock, the parents are not living together, and the petitioner is a maternal grandparent, great-grandparent, or sibling of the child born out of wedlock; or (E) the child is born out of wedlock, the parents are not living together, the petitioner is a paternal grandparent, great-grandparent, or sibling, and the paternity has been established by a court of competent jurisdiction.

    (2) Any visitation rights granted pursuant to this Section before the filing of a petition for adoption of a child shall automatically terminate by operation of law upon the entry of an order terminating parental rights or granting the adoption of the child, whichever is earlier. If the person or persons who adopted the child are related to the child, as defined by Section 1 of the Adoption Act, any person who was related to the child as grandparent, great-grandparent, or sibling prior to the adoption shall have standing to bring an action pursuant to this Section requesting visitation with the child.

    (3) In making a determination under this subsection (a-5), there is a rebuttable presumption that a fit parent's actions and decisions regarding grandparent, great-grandparent, or sibling visitation are not harmful to the child's

EXHIBIT 13.3
(continued)

mental, physical, or emotional health. The burden is on the party filing a petition under this Section to prove that the parent's actions and decisions regarding visitation times are harmful to the child's mental, physical, or emotional health.

(4) In determining whether to grant visitation, the court shall consider the following:

(A) the preference of the child if the child is determined to be of sufficient maturity to express a preference;

(B) the mental and physical health of the child;

(C) the mental and physical health of the grandparent, great-grandparent, or sibling;

(D) the length and quality of the prior relationship between the child and the grandparent, great-grandparent, or sibling;

(E) the good faith of the party in filing the petition;

(F) the good faith of the person denying visitation;

(G) the quantity of the visitation time requested and the potential adverse impact that visitation would have on the child's customary activities;

(H) whether the child resided with the petitioner for at least 6 consecutive months with or without the current custodian present;

(I) whether the petitioner had frequent or regular contact or visitation with the child for at least 12 consecutive months;

(J) any other fact that establishes that the loss of the relationship between the petitioner and the child is likely to harm the child's mental, physical, or emotional health; and

(K) whether the grandparent, great-grandparent, or sibling was a primary caretaker of the child for a period of not less than 6 consecutive months.

Some states have caregiver authorization forms that enable a grandparent (or other relative) to enroll a child in school or obtain medical care without going to court. These forms are sworn statements that can be used even if the parents cannot be found. They do not terminate the rights of the biological parents.

Example

Typical Language from a Caregiver Authorization
Check one or both (for example, if one parent was advised and the other cannot be located):
[ ] I have advised the parent(s) or other person(s) having legal custody of the minor of my intent to authorize medical care, and have received no objection.
[ ] I am unable to contact the parent(s) or other person(s) having legal custody of the minor at this time, to notify them of my intended authorization.

EXHIBIT 13.4
Illinois Program Implementing National Family Caregiver Support Program[5]

In Illinois, over 200,000 children under the age of 18 are living in a grandparent-headed home. More than 100,000 grandparents are caring for their grandchildren. The Illinois Department on Aging, in cooperation with the Illinois Task Force on Grandparents Raising Grandchildren, works to locate, assist, and promote awareness of older caregivers who are currently raising their family's children.

The Grandparents Raising Grandchildren Program began in 1996 with a grant from the Brookdale Foundation. Additional legislative support has allowed the Department to expand the program, by:

- Establishing support groups and providing them with financial and technical assistance.
- Providing grandparents with information and referral assistance.
- Training professionals and facilitators to meet grandparents' needs.

Find the program in your area: *http://www.aoa.gov/AoARoot/AoA_Programs/OAA/How_To_Find/Agencies/find_agencies.aspx*

Guardianship
Gives guardian right to act on behalf of another

A legal **guardianship** is a simple procedure, with parental consent, that gives the grandparent authority to consent to medical care and enroll the child in school. Because children do not have the same rights that adults are assumed to have, the due process protections necessary in obtaining guardianship over an adult are not required. With a guardianship, the biological parents continue to have rights and may petition to end the guardianship. Some states have "permanent" guardianships or conservatorships that are more difficult to end, and some states have financial aid for guardians, particularly for guardians of children who have been in state custody. Some states recognize a status called "legal custody," which is similar to guardianship.

Foster Parent
Cares for child in custody of state

Adoption
Terminates rights of biological parents, names new parent(s)

A grandparent might become a **foster parent** to her grandchild. Foster parents receive financial assistance from the state, but the child is in state custody. State custody means that the state can overrule the grandparent on decisions and could even remove the child. **Adoption** means that the rights of the biological parents are terminated and the grandparent(s) become the parent(s). A court examines the grandparents' age, health, and ability to care for the child. A grandparent may lose some financial benefits by adopting a grandchild, although subsidies are available for

---

[5]*http://www.state.il.us/aging/1intergen/grg.htm*

adoption of special-needs children who have been in foster care and, once a grandchild becomes a child of the grandparent, the grandparent's social security benefits can extend to the child (as described in Chapter 4).

Financing Care of Grandchildren

While child support–related issues are not generally considered part of elder law practice, it may be useful to have some basic information, to help direct clients to needed resources. A grandparent's social security benefits do not extend to a grandchild who has not been adopted by a grandparent. If, however, a parent has died or has a disability, the child may be eligible for social security benefits through that parent. A grandparent can apply on behalf of a grandchild.

Temporary Assistance for Needy Families (**TANF**) is a federally funded, state-run (generally through a department of human services) program of cash assistance for families in financial need. A grandparent can apply for a "child-only" grant based only on the child's income. The adult's income is not investigated and the adult is not required to look for a job or attend job training. The amount of money available with a child-only grant is much lower than available through a family grant, but getting a family grant depends on the adult's income and requires the adult to look for a job. Some states try to get child support from the parents of children receiving TANF grants. Learn about your state's TANF program at *http://www.acf.hhs.gov/programs/ofa/data-reports/annualreport6/chapter12/chap12.htm*.

TANF
Temporary Assistance for Needy Families

A child, age five years or under, receiving TANF funds may also be eligible for the Special Supplemental Food Program for Women, Infants, and Children (**WIC**). The WIC program requires a medical examination at a WIC clinic to determine whether the child is at risk of poor nutrition. In addition, low-income families may qualify for food stamps (*http://www.fns.usda.gov/snap*).

WIC
Special Supplemental Food Program for Women, Infants, and Children

There are also income tax benefits. A low-income employed grandparent, with a child in the household, may be eligible for an earned income tax credit. Any adult caretaker may be eligible for a dependent child tax credit.

Assignments

---

1. Critical and Ethical Thinking: Read the case summary at the end of the chapter, keeping in mind that states operate their Medicaid programs differently
   - Do you think this decision is fair? Are H.K. and L.K. trying to "have their cake and eat it too"?
     The court mentions that H.K. and his wife did not get a complete divorce because then they would have lost the advantage of the community spouse provisions and because, in that situation, support for L.K. would not be deducted from H.K.'s income in determin-

ing how much of his income would be available. Can you think of reasons why this makes sense? Visit *http://humanservices.vermont .gov/boards-committees/hsb/decisions/fh-2009-01-to/fh-09-227/view* and *http://edocket.access.gpo.gov/cfr_2009/octqtr/42cfr435.725.htm.*

- If spouse A is relying on spouse B for support in retirement because B has a very good pension plan and A is concerned that B will need nursing care, how might A be protected?

2. Examine the summary at *http://family.findlaw.com/child-custody/custody-more/state-grandparent-custody.html,* and then visit *http://topics.law. cornell.edu/wex/table_family* to find the actual statute to verify that the summary is correct. Prepare a short summary of your state's law with respect to grandparents' rights, including correct citations.

3. Conduct an Internet search to determine whether your state or municipality provides for registration of domestic partnerships.

4. Determine whether your state has enacted the Uniform Premarital Agreement Act.

5. Use an Internet search engine to determine whether your state has a caregiver authorization form or affidavit.

Review Questions

1. Identify the options available to a grandparent, caring for a grandchild, who wants to have authority to put the child in school and consent to medical care.

2. Why might a court invalidate a prenuptial agreement?

3. What is marital property?

4. What option is available to a married couple if they want to live apart and formalize their obligations to each other, but do not want to divorce?

5. Why might a grandparent visitation statute be found to be unconstitutional?

6. What is a domestic partnership? Is this recognized in your state?

7. Why is a cohabitation agreement a good idea for couples who cannot or do not wish to marry? What are the characteristics of an agreement likely to be upheld?

H.K. V. DIVISION OF MEDICAL ASSISTANCE AND HEALTH SERVICES

878 A.2d 16 (N.J. App., 2005)

This case concerns the continuing tension between the State's effort to conserve Medicaid resources for the truly needy and the legal ability of institutionalized Medicaid recipients to shelter income for the benefit of their non-institutionalized spouses. In this case, we hold that the applicant and his wife transgressed the permissible limits of Medicaid planning by entering into a divorce from bed and board* and agreeing, in a consent order entered without judicial fact finding, that the institutionalized husband's pension benefits would be paid to the wife as alimony.

The husband, H.K., suffered a debilitating stroke and was admitted to a nursing home in May 2002. H.K. initially applied for Medicaid ... but could not qualify until he and his wife, R.K., had "spent down" their available resources. ... They reached that limit in August of 2002. H.K. was able to qualify for medically needy nursing home Medicaid even though he had Social Security and pension income of approximately $4,500 per month and his wife worked full-time and earned over $2,000 per month. However, H.K. was required to use his pension and Social Security benefits to pay part of the cost of his nursing home care. Medicaid would pay for the balance of the nursing home costs.

The Federal statute, 42 *U.S.C.A.* §1396r-5(d), and our regulations, *N.J.A. C.* 10:71-5.7(c), recognize that some portion of an institutionalized spouse's income may be used to support the community spouse to avoid the latter from becoming impoverished. ... But those same provisions place strict limits on the amount of a Medicaid recipient's income that can be used for the community spouse allowance. At the time H.K. qualified for Medicaid, the spousal allowance was normally limited to $1,493. ... A community spouse may obtain a larger allowance by demonstrating, at [a] hearing, that he or she suffers "exceptional circumstances resulting in financial duress." ... A separate provision, *N.J.A.C.* 10:71-5.7(f), permits an alternative means of obtaining support for the community spouse:

If a court has entered an order against an institutionalized spouse for ... support of a community spouse and the amount of the order is greater than the amount of the community spouse deduction, the amount so ordered shall be used in place of the community spouse deduction. This implements an analogous provision in the federal statute, 42 *U.S.C.A.* §1396r-5(d)(5). The federal statute provides that "If a court has entered an order against an institutionalized spouse for monthly income for the support of the community spouse, the community spouse monthly income allowance for the spouse shall be not less than the amount of the monthly income so ordered." 42 *U.S.C.A.* §1396r-5(d)(5).

R.K.'s monthly income was too high to entitle her to a community spousal allowance. ... Therefore, unless R.K. qualified for an exception to the cap set by section 5.7(c), H.K.'s entire income would be used to pay for his nursing home

---

Also known as a "limited divorce," a divorce from bed and board does not dissolve the marriage; it formalizes the couple's arrangement to live separately and requires one spouse to pay for the other spouse's separate living expenses. N.J.S.A. 2A:34-3; As a result of the divorce from bed and board, H.K.'s wife remained a "community spouse" for Medicaid purposes. See N.J.A.C. 10:71-5.7(c).

care. H.K. and R.K. attempted to invoke the "court order" exception . . . by obtaining a divorce from "bed and board" with a property settlement agreement providing for support to be paid from H.K.'s pension. The divorce action was . . . finalized by consent on December 24, 2002. The Final Judgment . . . specifically recited that the settlement agreement, incorporated in the judgment, was entered without the court having taken testimony "as to the merits thereof, and therefore [the court] makes no judgment with respect to the fairness thereof." Based on this final judgment, H.K. sought recalculation of H.K.'s Medicaid benefit, claiming that the court order for her support superseded the cap on the spousal allowance. But on March 20, 2003, the Board declined to recognize H.K.'s support obligation to R.K. as a deduction for Medicaid purposes.

The parties agreed that the purpose of the "bed and board" divorce (as opposed to a divorce from the bonds of matrimony) . . . was to avoid having the payments. . . . treated as "alimony" for Medicaid purposes. At the hearing . . . the parties agreed that ordinary alimony, resulting from a divorce from the bonds of matrimony, cannot be deducted from the calculation of a Medicaid applicant's income in determining what amount of his income must be paid to the nursing home before Medicaid will pay the balance. We do not address that issue, because it is not properly before us, and it affects the rights of H.K.'s first wife, who is not a party to this case. We note that H.K.'s first wife, who is 81 years old and appears to be genuinely impoverished, sent the Board of Social Services a letter protesting the disallowance of H.K.'s monthly alimony payment to her, an obligation set by court order in 1976.

H.K. appealed that determination before the Office of Administrative Law (OAL), claiming that *N.J.A.C.* 10:71-5.7(f) required the Board to recognize and include his court-ordered spousal support obligation in calculating his income. . . . Administrative Law Judge Miller rejected H.K.'s contention in an initial decision on February 10, 2004. He reasoned that a literal reading of the regulation would lead to an absurd result, allowing Medicaid applicants to transfer additional income to their spouses without a showing of exceptional circumstances and financial duress, which the Medicaid statute and regulations would otherwise require. . . . He concluded that "the evidence in this case did not involve financial duress or exceptional circumstances. Rather, it came about through crafty planning by combining an old divorce statute with a regulation intended to offer relief to those in financial need. . . . [A] substitute maintenance deduction is not presently necessary to alleviate financial duress."

The State Division of Medical Assistance and Health Services (DMAHS) adopted the Initial Decision in a final determination . . . reasoned that giving effect to the divorce judgment "would be contrary to the . . . Medicare Catastrophic Coverage Act" which was intended to avoid pauperization of the community spouse by assuring that she would be allowed "sufficient" but "not excessive" income. The agency also noted that "the support payment was not evaluated on the merits by the Judge" and "[t]hus, at no time did the court make a finding that the property settlement was equitable." The agency concluded: Moreover, New Jersey courts have opined that a property "agreement which would leave a spouse a public charge or close to it" . . . would probably not be enforced by any court.

Courts in other states . . . have held that relieving one spouse from all responsibility for spousal maintenance in order to force the other spouse into poverty and shift the responsibility to Medicaid violates public policy and the underlying policy of the Medicaid Act. We are satisfied that . . . the agency's decision is consistent with the language and purpose of the Medicaid statute. Accepting H.K.'s contentions would allow Medicaid recipients and their spouses to enter into collusive support agreements for the sole purpose of diverting the Medicaid recipient's income to the community spouse. . . .

H.K. contends [that] *N.J.A.C.* 10:71-5.7(f), permits a community spouse to obtain an unlimited increase in the spousal allowance by obtaining a court order. But accepting H.K.'s position would nullify the . . . limitations on the community spouse allowance. We will not construe a statute or a regulation in a manner that produces an absurd result or that renders a part of it meaningless. . . .

The 1988 amendments to the Federal Medicaid statute, which created the community spousal allowance, were intended to prevent community spouses from becoming impoverished. Congress recognized that, particularly for women who had been homemakers, and who relied on their husbands' pensions for support in their old age, the requirement that the husbands' entire income be used to pay nursing home bills represented an economic catastrophe. . . . Congress recognized that under the existing Medicaid law, some community spouses were forced, in desperation, to sue their institutionalized spouses for support. . . . The amendments were designed to avoid that need, by allowing some portion of the institutionalized spouse's pension or other income to be used to support the community spouse. Congress also recognized that under "special circumstances," a court order for support might supersede the normal community spouse allowance: Court ordered support. — The Committee recognizes that there will be some instances in which the rules set forth in the bill do not take adequate account of the *special circumstances* affecting a particular community spouse. The bill therefore provides that, if a court has entered an order against an institutionalized spouse for monthly income for the support of the community spouse, the community spouse monthly income allowance must be at least as great as the amount of the income ordered to be paid.

Nothing . . . suggests that Congress . . . intended the "court order" exception to apply to H.K. and R.K.'s agreement. This is not a situation where a court has held an evidentiary proceeding and determined independently that the community spouse is in need of support or has "special circumstances." Nor was the court . . . even notified that H.K. was receiving Medicaid benefits. This is also not a case where there was an existing support obligation that pre-dated the Medicaid application and was entered at a time when such an application was not anticipated. Rather, the property settlement agreement in this case was an undisguised attempt to circumvent the Medicaid regulations. . . .

We do not address whether a section (f) allowance is only permitted on a showing of exceptional circumstances, which is the standard under subsection (e). . . . H.K. and R.K. made no effort to prove exceptional circumstances, and we deem it injudicious to address such an important issue without a proper factual record. The applicants relied on an asserted absolute entitlement to the deduction under . . . *N.J.A.C.* 10:71-5.7(f), a position the agency correctly rejected. [A]lthough the purpose of the limited divorce was to affect H.K.'s benefit, the Medicaid program was not served . . . or otherwise given notice. [T]he proceeding was not genuinely adversarial . . . and the court that entered the order did not determine whether the award was justified in light of the countervailing interests of the State in having H.K. use his income to pay for his nursing home care.

Finally, we note that the issue was, to some extent, foreshadowed in the Supreme Court's decision in *L.M. v. Div. of Med. Assistance & Health Servs.*, 659 A.2d 450 (1995). The *L.M.* case was decided before the State amended its Medicaid statute to cover "medically needy" applicants such as H.K. In *L.M.*, an elderly couple, married for fifty-three years, obtained a divorce from bed and board and agreed to equitable distribution to the wife of the husband's entire pension through a QDRO . . . the Court held that since *L.M.*'s entire pension had been transferred to the wife, it was no longer the husband's asset and the income from the pension was no longer attributable to the husband. Therefore, under the then existing income-based test, he qualified for Medicaid. We do not find *L.M.* controlling here because *L.M.* preceded our State's adoption of the medically needy nursing home program, and unlike this case, the record in *L.M.* apparently established that the wife was elderly, impoverished, and clearly in need of support. But we find *L.M.* relevant. In ruling for the wife, the Court recognized that its decision potentially opened the door to abusive practices, and strongly suggested that the State adopt regulations to prevent collusive transfers of assets. . . . It is now ten years since *L.M.* was decided. The State has adopted the "medically needy" nursing home program. But the State has not adopted regulations giving content to the very general language of 42 *U.S.C.A.* §1396r-5(d)(5) and *N.J.A.C.* 10:71-5.7(f). Given the importance of clear guidelines to assist families in Medicaid planning, we add . . . our own suggestion that regulations be adopted to address the appropriate balance between legitimate provisions for division of property and income in cases of divorce, and protection of the intended purpose of the medically needy nursing home program. Affirmed.

www.CrosswordWeaver.com

ACROSS

1. Governs distribution if person dies without will: _____ law
2. Initials, aid for families
10. Slang term for support of unmarried partner
11. Allows grandparent to put child in school, get medical care
13. Initials, court may appoint for child
15. Value of assets minus debt
16. _____-law marriage
21. Mutual give-and-take that supports a contract
23. Terminates rights of birth parent
24. Without assets

DOWN

1. Best _____, relevant to custody
3. Property acquired before marriage
4. No-_____ divorce
5. Court's power to hear a case, based on geography or type of case
6. _____ parent, cares for child in state custody
7. Spousal support
8. Living together
9. _____ of assets,
12. No valid marriage existed
13. Few states have _____ property laws
14. Sometimes called limited divorce
17. Initials, established by OAA to help grandparents
18. Threats or pressure
19. Property acquired after marriage
20. Initials, nutrition program
22. Prenup, also called an _____-nuptial agreement

14

◆ ◆ ◆

Discrimination

◆ ◆ ◆

ADEA
    ADEA Waivers
    Proving Discrimination
    Enforcement
ADA
    Employment
    Governmental Services and Transportation
    Public Accommodations
    Telecommunications Relay Services
Other Laws

Objectives

When you complete this chapter, you will:

- Know the laws that protect senior citizens from discrimination in a variety of settings.
- Understand how those laws are enforced.
- Identify state and local resources that may assist a client in the event of discrimination.

Legal protection from discrimination based on age or disability is relatively new. Discrimination in the workplace was an acceptable business practice in the past: Older workers often cost more in salary and benefits, training an employee who may not stay with the company for long is inefficient, and many employers prefer to "grow" their workforces from within. In addition, the traditional doctrine of **employment at will** gave employers the right to terminate employees (and employees the corresponding right to quit) for a good reason or for no reason. While accommodating physical and emotional disabilities is not necessarily more expensive, many businesses simply never considered it until the law forced the issue. (Note that this chapter does not address the protections that might be available through a union, or specific state or local laws that may provide a client with additional options.)

Employment at Will
Doctrine allowing employer or employee to terminate employment relationship for no reason

ADEA

The Age Discrimination in Employment Act of 1967 (ADEA) and its amendments, 29 U.S.C. §621 *et seq*, protect individuals who are 40 years of age or older (there is no upper age limit) from employment discrimination based on age. ADEA protections apply to both employees and job applicants. The term *employee* does not include **independent contractors**, high-level decision makers who have nonforfeitable retirement benefits, and certain partners.

Independent Contractors
Those who perform work but are self-employed and not employees

The ADEA applies to employers with 20 or more employees; generally only full-time employees count in determining whether an employer is subject to the law, but if the employer is subject to the law, part-time workers are protected. The ADEA applies to state and local governments, to employment agencies and labor organizations, and to the federal government (although complaints against the federal government follow a process slightly different than the one described in this chapter).

Under the ADEA, it is unlawful to discriminate against a person because of age with respect to any term, condition, or privilege of employment, including hiring, firing, promotion, layoff, compensation, benefits, job assignments, and training. It is also unlawful to retaliate against an individual for opposing employment practices that discriminate based on age or for filing an age discrimination charge, testifying, or participating in any way in an investigation, proceeding, or litigation under the ADEA.

The ADEA *does* permit employers to favor older workers based on age even when doing so adversely affects a younger worker who is 40 or older. ADEA protections apply to:

- *Apprenticeship programs.*
- *Job notices and advertisements.* The ADEA generally makes it unlawful to include age preferences, limitations, or specifications in job notices or advertisements. A job notice or advertisement may specify an age limit only in the rare circumstances where age is a "bona fide occupational qualification" (**BFOQ**) reasonably necessary to the normal operation of the business.

BFOQ
Bona fide occupational qualification

- *Pre-employment inquiries.* The ADEA does not specifically prohibit an employer from asking an applicant's age or date of birth. However, because such inquiries may deter older workers from applying for employment or may otherwise indicate intent to discriminate based on age, requests for age information are closely scrutinized.
- *Mandatory retirement.* With limited exceptions for law enforcement and firefighters, mandatory retirement and maximum-hire ages are prohibited.
- *Benefits.* A 1990 amendment specifically prohibits employers from denying benefits to older employees. Congress recognized that the cost of providing certain benefits to older workers is greater than the cost of providing those same benefits to younger workers, and that those greater costs would create a disincentive to hire older workers. Therefore, in limited circumstances, an employer may be permitted to reduce benefits based on age, as long as the cost of providing the reduced benefits to older workers is the same as the cost of providing benefits to younger workers. Employers may not refuse to hire because of the higher cost of benefits for older workers, but may coordinate retiree health benefit plans with eligibility for Medicare or a comparable state-sponsored health benefit.

ADEA Waivers

An employer may ask an employee to waive rights or claims under the ADEA either in the settlement of an ADEA administrative or court claim or in connection with an exit incentive program or other employment termination program. However, the ADEA sets out specific minimum standards that must be met in order for a waiver to be considered knowing and voluntary and, therefore, valid. Among other requirements, a valid ADEA waiver must:

- Be in writing and be understandable.
- Specifically refer to ADEA rights or claims.
- Not waive rights or claims that may arise in the future.
- Be in exchange for valuable consideration.
- Advise the individual in writing to consult an attorney before signing the waiver.
- Provide the individual at least 21 days to consider the agreement and at least 7 days to revoke the agreement after signing it.

Proving Discrimination

Circumstantial Evidence
Evidence that requires inference or assumption

Employers know better than to put discriminatory intent into words. Although discrimination may be proven by statistical or **circumstantial evidence** in

Prima Facie Case
Case in which evidence is sufficient to prove case unless refuted

Direct Evidence
Evidence that does not require inference or assumption, often direct sensory evidence

Disparate Treatment
Treatment of a group different from treatment of other groups

some cases, employers are given fairly wide latitude in running their businesses. The difficulty of proving a discrimination case can be seen by reviewing the statistics in the chart reproduced in Exhibit 14.1. Discrimination in hiring is particularly difficult to prove; the mere fact that a younger person was hired does not establish discrimination. In addition, many jobs now require technical skills that younger workers are more likely to possess. As in most civil cases, the plaintiff has the burden of proving the elements of a **prima facia case** by a preponderance of the evidence. **Direct evidence** of discriminatory intent or **disparate treatment** is rarely available.

In Age Discrimination in Employment Act cases the plaintiff must produce evidence that is sufficient to convince a reasonable factfinder to find all of the elements of a prima facie case. When the plaintiff alleges unlawful discharge based on age, the prima facie case requires proof that (i) the plaintiff was a member of the protected class, i.e., was 40 years of age or older, 29 U.S.C.S. §631 (a), (ii) that the plaintiff was discharged, (iii) that the plaintiff was qualified for the job, and (iv) that the plaintiff was replaced by a sufficiently younger person to create an inference of age discrimination. *Showalter v. University of Pittsburgh Medical Center*, 190 F.3d 231 (3rd Cir., 1999)

The fourth element can also be established by showing that there was another available position for which the discharged employee was qualified and need not be proven if the plaintiff was not replaced.

EXHIBIT 14.1
Age Discrimination in Employment Act, FY1997-FY2009[1]

The following chart represents the total number of charge receipts filed and resolved under the ADEA. Receipts include all charges filed under the ADEA as well as those filed concurrently under Title VII, ADA, and/or EPA. Therefore, the sum of receipts for all statutes will exceed total charges received. The data are compiled by the Office of Research, Information, and Planning from data reported via the quarterly reconciled Data Summary Reports and compiled from EEOC's Charge Data System and, from FY 2004 forward, EEOC's Integrated Mission System.

---

[1] *http://www.eeoc.gov/eeoc/statistics/enforcement/adea.cfm*

EXHIBIT 14.1
(continued)

	FY 1997	FY 1998	FY 1999	FY 2000	FY 2001	FY 2002	FY 2003	FY 2004	FY 2005	FY 2006	FY 2007	FY 2008	FY 2009
Receipts	15,785	15,191	14,141	16,008	17,405	19,921	19,124	17,837	16,585	16,548	19,103	24,582	22,778
Resolutions	18,279	15,995	15,448	14,672	15,155	18,673	17,352	15,792	14,076	14,146	16,134	21,415	20,529
Settlements	642 / 3.5%	755 / 4.7%	816 / 5.3%	1,156 / 7.9%	1,006 / 6.6%	1,222 / 6.5%	1,285 / 7.4%	1,377 / 8.7%	1,326 / 9.4%	1,417 / 10.0%	1,795 / 11.1%	1,974 / 9.2%	1,935 / 9.4%
Withdrawals w/Benefits	762 / 4.2%	580 / 3.6%	578 / 3.7%	560 / 3.8%	551 / 3.6%	671 / 3.6%	710 / 4.1%	787 / 5.0%	764 / 5.4%	767 / 5.4%	958 / 5.9%	1,252 / 5.8%	1,161 / 5.7%
Administrative Closures	4,986 / 27.3%	4,175 / 26.1%	3,601 / 23.3%	3,232 / 22.0%	3,963 / 26.1%	6,254 / 33.5%	2,824 / 16.3%	3,550 / 22.5%	2,537 / 18.0%	2,639 / 18.7%	2,754 / 17.1%	6,387 / 29.8%	4,031 / 19.6%
No Reasonable Cause	11,163 / 61.1%	9,863 / 61.7%	9,172 / 59.4%	8,517 / 58.0%	8,388 / 55.3%	9,725 / 52.1%	11,976 / 69.0%	9,563 / 60.6%	8,866 / 63.0%	8,746 / 61.8%	10,002 / 62.0%	11,124 / 51.9%	12,788 / 62.3%
Reasonable Cause	726 / 4.0%	622 / 3.9%	1,281 / 8.3%	1,207 / 8.2%	1,247 / 8.2%	801 / 4.3%	557 / 3.2%	515 / 3.3%	583 / 4.1%	612 / 4.3%	625 / 3.9%	678 / 3.2%	614 / 3.0%
Successful Conciliations	74 / 0.4%	119 / 0.7%	184 / 1.2%	241 / 1.6%	409 / 2.7%	208 / 1.1%	166 / 1.0%	139 / 0.9%	169 / 1.2%	177 / 1.3%	186 / 1.2%	220 / 1.0%	202 / 1.0%
Unsuccessful Conciliations	652 / 3.6%	503 / 3.1%	1,097 / 7.1%	966 / 6.6%	838 / 5.5%	593 / 3.2%	391 / 2.3%	376 / 2.4%	414 / 2.9%	435 / 3.1%	439 / 2.7%	458 / 2.1%	412 / 2.0%
Merit Resolutions	2,130 / 11.7%	1,957 / 12.2%	2,675 / 17.3%	2,923 / 19.9%	2,804 / 18.5%	2,694 / 14.4%	2,552 / 14.7%	2,679 / 17.0%	2,673 / 19.0%	2,796 / 19.8%	3,378 / 20.9%	3,904 / 18.2%	3,710 / 18.1%
Monetary Benefits (Millions)*	$44.3	$34.7	$38.6	$45.2	$53.7	$55.7	$48.9	$69.0	$77.7	$51.5	$66.8	$82.8	$72.1

If the plaintiff establishes a prima facie case, the employer has the burden to produce a legitimate, nondiscriminatory reason for the action taken. Personality conflicts, insubordination, and reduction in forces can all be legitimate reasons for termination. A legitimate basis for firing, such as a worker lacking dexterity to perform necessary job functions, is not made illegal simply because it disproportionately adversely affects older workers. A plaintiff alleging a **disparate impact** must "isolat[e] and identif[y] the *specific* employment practices that are allegedly responsible for any observed statistical disparities . . . [which is] not a trivial burden"[2] There are certain reasons that are regarded as suspicious, such as claiming that the worker is "overqualified" for all available jobs or that the worker's job performance suddenly deteriorated after years of good performance, and the employer may be required to explain or document that the stated reason is not a **subterfuge**.

In addition, an employer may be able to establish a BFOQ, particularly for jobs involving strenuous work and public safety. In general, employers should test employees individually for ability to handle the physical requirements of a job, but individual testing is not always practicable. The court discussed the BFOQ defense in the case summarized at the end of this chapter.

Disparate Impact
Policy that appears neutral but has a disproportionate effect on a group

Subterfuge
Deceptive strategy

Enforcement

The ADEA is enforced by the federal Equal Employment Opportunity Commission (EEOC), which has 53 field offices. Many states and even some local governments have their own laws and agencies. If a complaint is filed with a state or local office, it is considered dual-filed and need not be separately filed with the EEOC.

Example

Chicago has its own law, in addition to state and federal law:

Discrimination Complaints Investigations[3]
The Commission on Human Relations receives, investigates, and rules on discrimination complaints filed under the Chicago Human Rights Ordinance and Chicago Fair Housing Ordinance. For more information about the kinds of discrimination these ordinances prohibit and what remedies the Commission can order if a respondent if found in violation, please see Discrimination Cases as well as the applicable Ordinances and Regulations.

Find your closest EEOC field office at *http://www.eeoc.gov/field/index.cfm* and your state agency at *http://www.eeocoffice.com*.

Exhaustion of Administrative Remedies
Requirement that complainant pursue all rights through agency before going to court

The process starts with filing a charge of discrimination with the agency. An employee/job applicant may not file a discrimination lawsuit without having first gone through the agency process, a requirement called **exhaustion of administrative remedies**. The charge must be filed within 180 days of the claimed

---

[2]*Meacham v. Knolls Atomic Power Laboratory,* 128 S. Ct. 2395 (2008)
[3]*http://www.cityofchicago.org/city/en/depts/cchr/supp_info/investigations.html*

discriminatory act. If a state agency is involved, the time may be extended to within 300 days of the discriminatory act, or 30 days after notice that the state agency has terminated its processing of the charge, whichever is earlier.

As of this writing, the EEOC does not accept filing of charges online, but does have an online tool that can be used to evaluate a claim: *http://www.eeoc.gov/employees/howtofile.cfm*. Filing is accomplished in person or by a signed letter containing information described on the Web site.

In some cases, a charge that lacks merit is dismissed without an investigation; this is called a "no cause finding." The agency may also propose **mediation**, an informal and confidential way to resolve disputes with the help of a neutral mediator. Mediation sessions typically last a few hours and cost the participants nothing. Either party may reject mediation. If the case is not sent to mediation, or if mediation doesn't resolve the problem, the charge will be given to an investigator.

Mediation
Neutral party who assists parties in reaching agreement without litigation

If an investigation finds no violation of the law, the complainant is given a Notice of Right to Sue, which is evidence of exhaustion of administrative remedies. If a violation is found, the agency attempts to reach a voluntary settlement with the employer. If settlement does not occur, the case is referred to the agency's legal staff (or the Department of Justice in certain cases) for a decision on whether the agency should file a lawsuit. If the agency does not file a lawsuit, it gives the complainant a Notice of Right to Sue.

Relief depends upon the discriminatory action and the effect it had on the victim. For example, if someone is not selected for a job or a promotion because of discrimination, the remedy may include placement in the job and/or back pay and benefits the person would have received. The employer will also be required to stop any discriminatory practices and take steps to prevent discrimination in the future. A victim of discrimination may also be able to recover attorney's fees, expert witness fees, and court costs.

In cases involving intentional age discrimination, victims cannot recover either compensatory or punitive damages but may be entitled to **liquidated damages**. The amount of liquidated damages that may be awarded is equal to the amount of back pay awarded the victim.

Liquidated Damages
Damages to compensate for actual loss

Can an ADEA case proceed if the victim dies? See the case at the end of the chapter for a discussion of that issue and of damages.

ADA

Many older people suffer from impairments that may qualify as disabilities, such as loss of hearing or vision or limited mobility. The Americans with Disabilities Act (ADA), 42 U.S.C. 12101, prohibits discrimination on the basis of disability in employment, state and local government, public accommodations, commercial facilities, transportation, and telecommunications. To be protected by the ADA, one must have a disability or have a relationship or association with an individual with a disability. An individual with a disability is defined by the ADA as a person who has a physical or mental impairment that substantially limits one or more major life activities, a person who has a history or record of such an impairment, or a person who is perceived by others as having such an impairment. The ADA does not specifically name all of the impairments that are covered.

Employment

Title I of the ADA is enforced by the EEOC and requires that employers with 15 or more employees provide qualified individuals with disabilities an equal opportunity to benefit from the full range of employment-related opportunities available to others. It prohibits discrimination in recruitment, hiring, promotions, training, pay, social activities, and other privileges of employment. It restricts questions that can be asked about an applicant's disability before a job offer is made, and requires that employers make reasonable accommodation to the known physical or mental limitations of otherwise qualified individuals with disabilities, unless it results in undue hardship. Reasonable accommodations typically include:

- Changing job schedules
- Providing assistive devices (such as telephone amplifiers)
- Making physical changes to the work environment

Governmental Services and Transportation

Sections of Title II, enforced by the Department of Justice, cover programs, policies, practices, services, and activities of state and local governments. Those governmental bodies are required to follow specific architectural standards in new construction and alteration of buildings, relocate programs or otherwise provide access in inaccessible older buildings, and communicate effectively with people who have hearing, vision, or speech disabilities. Public entities are not required to take actions that would result in undue financial and administrative burdens, but are required to make reasonable modifications to policies, practices, and procedures where necessary to avoid discrimination, unless they can demonstrate that doing so would fundamentally alter the nature of the service, program, or activity being provided.

The transportation provisions of Title II cover public transportation services, such as city buses and public rail transit (subways, commuter rails, Amtrak). Public transportation authorities may not discriminate against people with disabilities in the provision of their services. They must comply with requirements for accessibility in newly purchased vehicles, make good-faith efforts to purchase or lease accessible used buses, remanufacture buses in an accessible manner, and, unless it would result in an undue burden, provide **paratransit** where they operate fixed-route bus or rail systems. Paratransit is a service for individuals who are unable to use the regular transit system independently because of a physical or mental impairment; they are instead picked up and taken to their destinations. The transportation provisions are enforced by the Office of Civil Rights in the Federal Transit Administration.

Paratransit
Alternative public transportation for riders with special needs

Public Accommodations

Title III, enforced by the Civil Rights Division of the Department of Justice covers businesses and nonprofit service providers that are public accommodations, privately operated entities offering certain types of courses and examinations, privately operated transportation, and commercial facilities. Public accommodations are private entities that own, lease, lease to, or operate facilities such as restaurants, retail stores, hotels, movie theaters, private schools, convention centers, doctors' offices, homeless shelters, transportation depots, zoos, funeral homes, day care centers, and recreation facilities including sports stadiums and fitness clubs. The provisions do not apply to private clubs or religious entities, except in sponsoring public events, and do not apply to the provision of insurance. Housing is subject to the Fair Housing Act, discussed in Chapter 9, except for public areas such as an apartment rental office or party room.

Public accommodations must comply with basic nondiscrimination requirements that prohibit exclusion, segregation, and unequal treatment. They also must comply with specific requirements related to architectural standards for new and altered buildings; make reasonable modifications to policies, practices, and procedures; and have effective communication with people with hearing, vision, or speech disabilities. They must remove barriers in existing buildings where it is easy to do so without much difficulty or expense, given the public accommodation's resources.

Telecommunications Relay Services

Title IV, enforced by the Federal Communications Commission (FCC), addresses telephone and television access for people with hearing and speech disabilities. It requires common carriers (telephone companies) to establish interstate and intrastate telecommunications relay services (**TRS**) 24 hours a day, 7 days a week. TRS enables callers with hearing and speech disabilities who use telecommunications devices for the deaf (**TDD**s)—also known as teletypewriters (**TTY**s)—and callers who use voice telephones to communicate with each other through a third-party communications assistant. Title IV also requires closed captioning of federally funded public service announcements on television.

TRS
Telecommunications relay service

TDD
Telecommunications device for the deaf

TTY
Teletypewriter

Other Laws

Other laws that may apply to disabilities suffered by older clients:

- Air Carrier Access Act, 49 U.S.C. §41705, administered by the U.S. Department of Transportation
- Civil Rights of Institutionalized Persons Act, 42 U.S.C. §§1997 *et seq.*
- Fair Housing Act, 42 U.S.C. §§3601 *et seq.* (discussed in Chapter 9)
- Rehabilitation Act, 29 U.S.C. §791, prohibiting discrimination in federally funded activities

- Telecommunications Act of 1996, 47 U.S.C. §§255, 251(a)(2), also under the jurisdiction of the FCC
- Voting Accessibility for the Elderly and Handicapped Act of 1984, 42 U.S.C. §§1973ee *et seq.*, administered by the Department of Justice

---

**EXHIBIT 14.2
Eric Says**

Eric Matusewitch, a specialist in EEO law, holds a bachelor's degree in history and a master's degree in political science from the City College of New York, and a master's degree in library science from Columbia University. Eric also obtained a Certificate in Paralegal Studies from the ABA-approved program at George Washington University and is certified as a Professional in Human Resources (PHR) by the Human Resources Certification Institute and an Affirmative Action Professional (CAAP) by the American Association for Affirmative Action.

Eric recently retired as deputy director of the New York City Equal Employment Practices Commission. Prior to that position, he was assistant director of EEO for the New York City Health and Hospitals Corporation (the country's largest municipal hospital system), and an EEO specialist for the New York City Commission on Human Rights. Eric now lectures on EEO law for schools and organizations along the East Coast and teaches a full-semester course on that topic for the New York University School of Continuing and Professional Studies. He has also written the *Manager's Handbook on Employment Discrimination Law* (Andrews Publications, 2000) and more than 145 articles on that topic for legal, paralegal, and human resources publications. Mr. Matusewitch is a member of the Society for Human Resource Management, American Association for Affirmative Action, Law Library Association of Greater New York, and New York City Paralegal Association. In addition, he is a member of the Berkeley College Paralegal Studies Program Advisory Board.

> During my 27-year EEO career, I investigated and resolved hundreds of discrimination complaints—including many involving age bias. Sadly, I have found that older workers are often disproportionately terminated during company reorganizations or downsizing. Management teams may perceive these employees as "dead wood" and a hindrance to greater productivity. I have also found that many employers believe that those over age 50 are incapable of learning or adapting to new technologies. These attitudes are not supported by social science research, and deprive employers of experienced, competent, and loyal employees. Finally, during these difficult economic times, older workers face another barrier to employment: they may apply for entry-level positions and be rejected due to "overqualification." I was fortunate to have settled a number of cases involving older individuals who were discriminatorily denied employment or terminated from their private and public sector jobs. These workers were either hired or reinstated with back pay and other benefits, or given a lump sum in lieu of hiring or reinstatement.

Assignments

1. Critical Thinking: Read the summary of the *Fariss* case at the end of the chapter:
   - Why is it particularly important that a discrimination case be able to continue after the death of the victim?
   - Do we know whether Lynchburg Foundry acted in a discriminatory manner? Is it likely that that will ever be determined in court? Why?
   - Is it fair that Fariss cannot recover what the life insurance would have paid if Fariss had died while employed? Why?
   - What is the purpose of "liquidated damages" as described in this case, and why does the court think Fariss should not qualify for liquidated damages?
2. List the information that must be included in a charge filed with the EEOC. May someone file a charge on behalf of another? What can be done to protect the identity of the person alleging discrimination?
3. Use the online code of federal regulations: What specific language is suggested to be discriminatory if included in a help-wanted ad? What does an employer have to prove to establish a BFOQ? Is adoption of a seniority system that gives workers less protection for having worked longer always discriminatory?
4. Using *http://www.ada.gov*, determine whether a taxicab service may refuse service to a person with a guide dog.
5. Starting at the HUD Web site (*http://portal.hud.gov/portal/page/portal/HUD/topics/rental_assistance*), find your state rental laws and resources. Is there a state agency or any private group designated as helping renters in the event of discrimination?
6. Determine whether your community has any paratransit resources.

Review Questions

1. Read the summary of the *Western Airlines* case at the end of the chapter. Are you surprised that the Court upheld the decision in favor of the pilots? What is your opinion of requiring individual assessment in a job with major public safety implications?
2. Can you describe situations in which age might be a BFOQ? For instance, must a 45-year-old actress be considered to play a teenager?
3. Why are claims of age discrimination in employment difficult to prove?
4. What types of businesses are not subject to the various discrimination laws?

WESTERN AIR LINES, INC. V. CRISWELL
472 U.S. 400 (1985)

SYLLABUS OF THE COURT: The Age Discrimination in Employment Act of 1967 generally prohibits mandatory retirement . . . , but §4(f)(1) of the Act provides an exception "where age is a bona fide occupational qualification reasonably necessary to the normal operation of the particular business." Petitioner airline company requires that its flight engineers, who are members of the cockpit crews of petitioners' aircraft but do not operate flight controls unless both the pilot and the copilot become incapacitated, retire at age 60. A Federal Aviation Administration regulation prohibits any person from serving as a pilot or copilot after reaching his 60th birthday. Certain of the respondents, who include flight engineers forced to retire at age 60 and pilots who, upon reaching 60, were denied reassignment as flight engineers, brought suit in Federal District Court against petitioner, contending that the age-60 retirement requirement for flight engineers violated the ADEA. Petitioner defended, in part, on the theory that the requirement is a BFOQ "reasonably necessary" to the safe operation of the airline. The physiological and psychological capabilities of persons over age 60, and the ability to detect disease or a precipitous decline in such capabilities on the basis of individual medical examinations, were the subject of conflicting expert testimony presented by the parties. The jury instructions included statements that the "BFOQ defense is available only if it is reasonably necessary to the normal operation or essence of [petitioner's] business"; "the essence of [petitioner's] business is the safe transportation of passengers"; and petitioner could establish a BFOQ by proving both that "it was highly impractical for [petitioner] to deal with each [flight engineer] over age 60 on an individualized basis to determine his particular ability to perform his job safely" and that some flight engineers "over age 60 possess traits of a physiological, psychological or other nature which preclude safe and efficient job performance that cannot be ascertained by means other than knowing their age." The District Court entered judgment based on the jury's verdict for the plaintiffs, and the Court of Appeals affirmed, rejecting petitioner's contention that the BFOQ instruction was insufficiently deferential to petitioner's legitimate concern for the safety of its passengers.
Held:

1. The ADEA's restrictive language, its legislative history, and the consistent interpretation of the administrative agencies charged with enforcing the statute establish that the BFOQ exception was meant to be an extremely narrow exception to the general prohibition of age discrimination contained in the ADEA.

2. The relevant considerations for resolving a BFOQ defense to an age-based qualification purportedly justified by safety interests are whether the job qualification is "reasonably necessary" to the overriding interest in public safety, and whether the employer is compelled to rely on age as a proxy for the safety-related job qualification validated in the first inquiry. The latter showing may be made by the employer's establishing either (a) that it had reasonable cause to believe that all or substantially all persons over the age qualification would be unable to perform safely the duties of the job, or (b) that it is highly impractical to deal with the older employees on an individualized basis.

3. The jury here was properly instructed on the elements of the BFOQ defense under the above standard, and the instructions were sufficiently protective of public safety.

(a) Petitioner's contention that the jury should have been instructed to defer to petitioner's selection of job qualifications for flight engineers "that are reasonable in light of the safety risks" is at odds with Congress' decision, in adopting the ADEA, to subject such decisions to a test of objective justification in a court of law. The BFOQ standard adopted in the statute is one of "reasonable necessity," not reasonableness. The public interest in safety is adequately reflected in instructions that track the statute's language.

(b) The instructions were not defective for failing to inform the jury that an airline must conduct its operations "with the highest possible degree of safety." Viewing the record as a whole, the jury was adequately focused on the importance of safety to the operation of petitioner's business.

(c) There is no merit to petitioner's contention that the jury should have been instructed under the standard that the ADEA only requires that the employer establish "a rational basis in fact" for believing that identification of those persons lacking suitable qualifications cannot be made on an individualized basis. Such standard conveys a meaning that is significantly different from that conveyed by the statutory phrase "reasonably necessary," and is inconsistent with the preference for individual evaluation expressed in the language and legislative history of the ADEA. Nor can such standard be justified on the ground that an employer must be allowed to resolve the controversy in a conservative manner when qualified experts disagree as to whether persons over a certain age can be dealt with on an individual basis. Such argument incorrectly assumes that all expert opinion is entitled to equal weight, and virtually ignores the function of the trier of fact in evaluating conflicting testimony.

FARISS V. LYNCHBURG FOUNDRY

769 F.2d 958 (4th Cir., 1085)

Ewell W. Fariss, plaintiff under the Age Discrimination in Employment Act (ADEA), 29 U.S.C. Sec. 621 (1982) et seq., brought suit against Lynchburg Foundry, alleging he had been terminated from employment because of his age. He sought reinstatement, back pay and punitive damages. Mr. Fariss died and his widow, Marguerite . . . moved to substitute herself as plaintiff, which the district court permitted over defendant's objection. . . . The district court granted summary judgment for defendant. It held that plaintiff lacked a claim for monetary relief because pension benefits Mr. Fariss received after his termination exceeded defendant's liability for back wages and life insurance premiums. Plaintiff appeals, while defendant cross-appeals from the substitution of Mrs. Fariss as plaintiff.

We affirm. Mrs. Fariss was properly substituted as plaintiff. Plaintiff, however, would be entitled to no monetary relief even if she were to prevail on the
merits. The proceeds of an employer-provided life insurance policy may not be
claimed as damages from a wrongful termination, but only the premiums that
would have been paid had the plaintiff remained employed. These premiums,
together with back pay, are more than offset by the pension benefits Fariss received as a result of his termination, which must be deducted from any possible
damages award. . . . The principal question before us is whether plaintiff could
recover anything if she were to prove age discrimination. Thus, the substantive
issue of discrimination, which the district court did not resolve, is not relevant to
this appeal. . . .

Fariss worked for Lynchburg Foundry from 1941 until his termination on
April 30, 1981 at the age of 61. He continued to receive full salary and benefits
from his employer until September 1, 1981, enabling him to retire at age 62 with
no reduction in pension benefits. Had Fariss remained employed . . . until his
death on September 13, 1983, he would have earned, . . . approximately $42,000
in salary including projected increases. This amount may be claimed as back pay.
Upon his retirement, however, Fariss received a lump sum pension payment of
$64,742.85. Because Fariss declined a survivor benefit option in favor of the
lump sum, no pension benefits would have been paid had he remained employed
until his death. If the lump sum payment is offset from back wages, plaintiff falls
$22,742.85 short of having a claim. . . . she must thus identify potential damages
from other sources exceeding that sum.

Plaintiff attempts to identify such damages by reference to employer-
provided life insurance coverage. Fariss was entitled to fringe benefits of em-
ployer-paid group medical and life insurance. Full medical coverage continued
after retirement. Life insurance would have paid twice Fariss's annual salary, or
$42,000 . . . had he died while employed, but declined to only $2,000 after
retirement. Plaintiff seeks to recover the difference. Defendant expended
$5,085.28 in premiums to continue full medical and reduced life insurance
coverage until Fariss's death. Had Fariss remained employed, defendant would
have paid $6,422.98 in premiums, an additional $1,337.70, to insure him for the
same period. . . . Lynchburg Foundry employees could elect to convert their
group life insurance to an individual policy, thereby preserving full coverage after
retirement by paying the additional premium costs. No evidence has been presented that Fariss ever sought to purchase substitute life insurance.

[P]laintiff must offer some evidence that, were she to establish discrimination, monetary relief would be due. Three damages issues are presented: 1)
whether plaintiff may recover the proceeds of the life insurance policy that Fariss
would have received had he died while employed, or only the premiums the
employer would have paid for full coverage up to Fariss's death; 2) whether
pension benefits received as a result of the termination should be offset from
plaintiff's losses; and 3) whether plaintiff could recover liquidated damages under
the ADEA. We hold that only the premiums may be claimed as damages and that
no liquidated damages are available, while the pension benefits must be offset
from back pay and other fringe benefits due. Thus, no claim for monetary relief
exists.

Congress clearly intended that fringe benefits be available as monetary
damages under the ADEA, along with back pay. . . . It follows that a claim for lost

fringe benefits survives the death of an employee and is proper here. Overwhelming judicial authority recognizes that employers guilty of discrimination are liable for fringe benefits they would have provided to employees as well as back wages under the ADEA. . . . Thus, the value of health or life insurance provided by the employer . . . is recoverable where age discrimination has occurred. The question concerns the proper measure of value. We reject plaintiff's contention that the proceeds of the insurance are the appropriate measure of value here. Typically, as in this case, insurance proceeds are paid not by the employer but by a third party insurer with whom the employer contracts. By electing this method . . . the employer manifests an intent to limit its own expenditures to regular premiums, which ordinarily provide the basis for a damages calculation. . . .

We do not think Congress intended . . . to transform employers into insurers merely because an insurance policy is part of the compensation for employment. Although the insurance policy is the benefit an employee contracts to receive, the employer does not undertake to cover personally risks of loss of life or illness by purchasing a policy for employees. A large disparity exists between what the employer would have paid as premiums had Fariss remained on the job, $1,337.70, and liability for the face value of the policy . . . an additional $40,000. In many instances, an obligation to pay the full proceeds of a policy could be staggering, amounting to many hundreds of thousands of dollars. The disincentives to providing employees insurance as a fringe benefit are evident; faced with such enormous potential liability, employers could be expected to consider compensating employees entirely in cash.

We decline to follow those decisions [cited by plaintiff] . . . ADEA demands "'the most complete relief possible' toward putting the victim of age discrimination back into the position he would have been in but for the unlawful discrimination." . . . Had Fariss not been terminated, he would have been covered by a life insurance policy. . . . This insurance coverage, not the proceeds, is the benefit for which the employer must be held liable. Here the employer would in no event have been liable to the employee for the $42,000, but only for the continuing payment of premiums. The value of being insured for a given period is precisely the amount of the premiums paid. . . . in most instances, the employee can easily avoid the risk of being uninsured by purchasing an individual policy of comparable value. Where the employee elects to obtain substitute insurance, the "make whole" concept underlying ADEA damages . . . would permit full recovery of any additional premiums. . . . An ADEA plaintiff has a general duty to mitigate his damages "by seeking other available employment with reasonable diligence. . . . Because there is no evidence here that Fariss attempted to obtain any substitute coverage, plaintiff can recover only the premiums the employer would have paid. We need not consider the measure of damages had he . . . found insurance unavailable for a person of his age and health.

We agree . . . that the $64,742.85 lump sum [received] by Fariss following his termination should be offset from the damages. An ADEA damages award "should only make the wrongly discharged employee monetarily whole under his employment contract; it should not provide a windfall." . . . Had Fariss continued working until he died, the pension would not have been paid at all, since he had declined the survivorship option offered by the employer. . . . Employer-provided pensions received as a result of termination have been generally offset from back pay claims under the ADEA. . . . When pension benefits are wrongfully withheld due to termination, they may be claimed as damages in an ADEA action. If such benefits would not have been granted but for the termination, it is equally appropriate to offset them from an award for back pay and benefits. Otherwise, plaintiff would enjoy the rewards from the employer both of working and not working. . . . In this case, Fariss had a substantial financial gain from his termination. Whether or not he suffered discrimination, he was more than $20,000 ahead at the time of his death. We cannot ignore the reality of his position in resolving plaintiff's claim.

Liquidated damages are available under the ADEA in an amount equal to other damages where the employer is guilty of "willful violations." 29 U.S.C. Sec. 626(b). As interpreted by the Supreme Court, this standard requires at least a "reckless disregard" by the employer. . . . Here plaintiff alleged a "willful" violation . . . and has grounds for claiming liquidated damages if the . . . test is satisfied. The district court did not address this issue. We are concerned, however . . . with a question of calculation. Liquidated damages under the ADEA for nonpecuniary losses are to be "calculated as an amount equal to the pecuniary loss." . . . The question is whether the liquidated damages should be assessed only with relation to damages claimed before any offset, or in an amount equal to the net loss after offset. Under the former view, plaintiff's claim for $43,337.70 in back wages and insurance premiums would be doubled before deducting the $64,742.85 lump sum pension, creating a monetary claim for relief; under the latter, nothing would exist to be doubled. We hold that liquidated damages should be assessed only upon the net loss after offsets. Losses arising from a termination ought not to be artificially segregated from gains. Where there has been no overall pecuniary loss, we do not believe that Congress intended plaintiffs to receive a windfall liquidated damages award . . . it is just to withhold liquidated damages for presumed nonpecuniary losses where a plaintiff has fortuitously had a financial gain from termination. Liquidated damages are not punitive in nature but compensatory. . . . Unlike punitive damages [which are not available under ADEA], they are not designed to serve the independent purpose of deterring employer misconduct, and we see no reason to provide a compensatory award where there is no injury to compensate. We therefore determine that plaintiff could recover no liquidated damages here. AFFIRMED.

www.CrosswordWeaver.com

ACROSS

1. _____ accommodation, required by ADA
8. ADEA _____ voluntary settlement of claim
9. Initials, enforces discrimination law
11. Deceptive reason
12. Initials, investigates discrimination by landlords
13. _____ facie case, employer must rebut
16. Initials, law prohibiting discrimination, based on age, in workforce
19. Evidence, requires no inference or assumption
21. Initials, telephone companies must have for callers with hearing and speech difficulties
22. Initials, law for people with disabilities
23. Evidence, requires assumption to reach conclusion
24. Spell out number of employees to be covered by ADEA

DOWN

2. In some circumstances, employer can reduce _____ for older workers
3. Damages generally available for employment discrimination
4. Mandatory _____ generally prohibited
5. Bona fide _____ qualification
6. _____ accommodations, subject to ADA
7. _____ treatment of older workers is rarely direct
10. No _____ finding, case dismissed
14. Job requirements may have a disparate _____ on older workers
15. _____ of administrative remedies
17. Attempt to help parties settle without litigation
18. Right to _____ letter issues when agency is finished
20. Employment at will allows termination for no _____

15

◆ ◆ ◆

Veterans

◆ ◆ ◆

Objectives

When you complete this chapter, you will:

- Distinguish between "pension" and "compensation" type benefits and the eligibility for each.
- Describe what is required to apply for VA benefits and who can assist in the application.
- Understand how an elder veteran may qualify for VA health care.
- Know the benefits available to all veterans.
- Identify resources for detailed information/guidance.
- Understand how various legal professionals assist with VA benefit problems.

Overview

The United States Veterans Administration (VA) offers a broad range of services for both male and female veterans and their dependents. Some of those services are underused because older veterans and their families do not realize that these services exist or that they may qualify. Many senior veterans used VA education benefits or had a VA home loan when they were younger and recently out of the service. Those veterans may think that benefits are available later in life only if they had service-related injuries. Because the requirements have changed with time, some of the benefits now available might not have been available when these older people left service. As you will learn in this chapter, and as demonstrated in Exhibit 15.1, paralegals play important roles in helping veterans secure the benefits to which they are entitled.

EXHIBIT 15.1
The Federal Government Is a Major Employer of Paralegals[1]

Job Title: PARALEGAL SPECIALIST

Department: Department Of Veterans Affairs

Agency: Veterans Health Administration

Job Announcement Number: VG-10-MBE-320689

Salary Range: $42,406–$67,427/year

Open Period: Friday, February 12, 2010, to Friday, February 19, 2010
Series and Grade: GS-0950-07

Position Information: Full-Time Career/Career Conditional

Promotion Potential: 09

Duty Locations: 1 vacancy: Hanscom AFB, Bedford, MA

Who May Be Considered: United States citizens

Job Summary: Be a member of a team providing compassionate healthcare to veterans. The Department of Veterans Affairs is an employer of choice as a center of excellence in patient care, education and research. We value trust, respect, commitment, compassion, and excellence; we value you. For more information on the Department of Veterans Affairs, go to *http://www.va.gov*.

---

[1] *http://www.usajobs.gov*

According to the VA's 2009 analysis (*http://www1.va.gov/VETDATA/Specialreports/Special_Reports.asp*):

- 23,440,000 (estimate) living veterans as of 9/30/08
- 8,493,700 (36% of total living veterans according to Vetpop) received VA benefits and/or services in FY08
  - 87 percent (7.38 million) were male
  - 81 percent (6.89 million) were 45 years old or older
- 5,756,800 of veterans using VA used only one program
  - 84 percent (4.85 million) were male
  - 81 percent (4.68 million) were 45 years old or older
- 2,736,900 of veterans using VA used multiple programs
  - 93 percent (2.53 million) were male
  - 81 percent (2.21 million) were 45 years old or older

The federal statutes relevant to veterans' rights can be found at 38 USC 101 *et.seq.*; the regulations are in CFR Title 38. Some of the benefits particularly helpful to seniors include:

- Medical care for eligible veterans who were discharged with other than dishonorable discharge.
- Disability compensation for veterans with service-related injuries.
- Non–service connected pension for low-income disabled veterans who served during war times.
- Aid and attendance for eligible veterans and surviving spouses in need of the regular aid and attendance of another person.
- Respite care to relieve family caregivers of veterans.
- Burial benefits for eligible veterans.
- Death pension for low-income surviving spouse and dependents of veterans who served during war times.

In general, the term *compensation* is used to refer to benefits paid because of service-related death or disability; compensation does not depend on the recipient's need. The term *pension* refers to benefits paid because of need. Some benefits, such as pensions, have financial eligibility guidelines (**means test**) and may require a co-pay. Do not confuse a VA pension, which is based on need, with a **military retirement pension**, which is a non-VA earned benefit paid by the Department of Defense to those who have made military service a career.

Means Test
Considers income and assets to determine eligibility

Military Retirement Pension
Not a VA benefit, not need-based, paid by Department of Defense based on service

Process

Because some benefits are calculated from the time of filing, it is important that a claim be filed as soon as it is determined that a client may be eligible. Processing the claim can take months or even a year, but the award is retroactive. Filing can be done online through VONAPP (*http://vabenefits.vba.va.gov/vonapp/who_uses.asp*) or at any of the VA Regional Offices, called VAROs, which can be located by using the map at *http://www.vba.va.gov/vba/benefits/offices.asp*. Most filings require:

- Military discharge or separation papers (DD214 or equivalent)
- Dependency records (marriage and children's birth certificates)
- Medical evidence of disability (doctor and hospital reports)

The Veterans Claims Assistance Act of 2000, 38 U.S.C. §5100, requires the VA to assist claimants in obtaining evidence necessary to substantiate a claim for benefits unless there is no reasonable possibility that such help would do any good. This means the VA has to make reasonable efforts to locate relevant records that the VA as well as other public and private entities may have in their possession. If the claim is for disability compensation, the VA may have to provide for a medical exam or opinion. The requirement of assistance is discussed in both cases at the end of this chapter.

Here is a bare-bones overview of the process: Most claims begin at a VA regional office or medical center, and denial can be appealed within one year from the date of the notification by notifying the VA office that processed the claim. In some cases, a simplified procedure of review by a DRO (decision review officer) is available.

If the appeal is to proceed to the Board of Veterans' Appeals, the local office sends the applicant a summary of reasons behind its ruling in a Statement of the Case and a VA Form 9, to be completed and returned by the applicant. The VA office will then forward all claim materials to the Board and notify the applicant that it has done so. The applicant may submit additional evidence, appoint or change legal representation, or ask for a hearing within 90 days after the notification is mailed. The Board will conduct hearings, if requested, review the matter, and issue a decision. It may be more than a year before the Board issues a decision. If the appeal is denied, the applicant may pursue various motions with the Board, such as a motion for reconsideration, or may file another appeal to the U.S. Court of Appeals for Veterans Claims. A 120-day deadline is the same for either option.

The process can include variations, depending on the availability of teleconferencing, the applicant's willingness to travel, and the applicant's desire to give personal testimony. You can print a copy of Form 9 at *http://www4.va.gov/vaforms/va/pdf/VA9.pdf*. Note that it is written in language understandable to most laypeople. Note also the statement about "getting assistance."

Representation

A person seeking benefits can be represented by a licensed attorney, an official of a state department of veterans' affairs, an "agent," or a veterans' service organization such as Amvets, the VFW, or the American Legion. More than 80 percent of applicants use such an organization in pursuing an appeal. Representation by these organizations is critical because of the restrictions on paid representation described below. Service organizations may not charge fees.

To learn about the free services provided by service organizations, visit: *http://www.vfw.org/index.cfm?fa=vets.levelc&cid=3731*, *http://www.amvetsnsf.org*, and *http://www.legion.org/departmentofficers*. The National Resource Directory (*http://www.nationalresourcedirectory.gov*) provides information about veterans' service organizations and many other topics of interest to veterans.

When a law firm assists with veterans' benefits, it is often in the context of assisting with other matters, such as advance directives or Medicaid planning. This is because the attorney must do a certain amount of the work in filing for VA benefits without compensation. Read Exhibit 15.2 (emphasis added to particular provisions) for a detailed explanation of limitations on fees and note the reference to attorneys "admitted to practice before the VA." The standards for admission to practice are found at 38 CFR §14.629. Although financial product salespeople often offer to help veterans apply for benefits, their goal is usually the sale of a product, such as an annuity, and they may or may not have the knowledge necessary to actually help.

General Eligibility for VA Benefits

Eligibility for most VA benefits requires discharge from active military service under other than dishonorable conditions. Honorable and general discharges qualify a veteran for most VA benefits. Dishonorable and bad conduct discharges generally bar VA benefits. In addition, if benefits are based on an injury or disability, the harm cannot have been caused by the veteran's own willful misconduct.

For various programs, the VA distinguishes active service from time, for example, in reserve service. Active service means full-time service as a member of the Army, Navy, Air Force, Marines, or Coast Guard, or as a commissioned officer of the Public Health Service, the Environmental Services Administration, or the National Oceanic and Atmospheric Administration. Certain VA benefits require wartime service. The VA recognizes the following war periods:

- World War 1: April 6, 1917, through November 11, 1918; for veterans who served in Russia April 6, 1917, through April 1, 1920: extended through July 1, 1921, for veterans who had at least one day of service between April 6, 1917, and November 11, 1918
- World War II: December 7, 1941, through December 31, 1946
- Korean War: June 27, 1950, through January 31, 1955
- Vietnam War: August 5, 1964 (February 28, 1961, for those who served "in country" before August 5, 1964) through May 7, 1975
- Gulf War: August 2, 1990, through a date to be set by law or Presidential Proclamation

Some benefits require a minimum length of service, which is generally 24 months for those who enlisted on or after September 24, 1980. There are special rules for early discharge due to service-related disability.

EXHIBIT 15.2
VA Limits on Attorney Fees

---

38 CFR 636 (c) Circumstances under which fees may be charged. Except as noted in paragraph (c)(2) and in paragraph (d) of this section, **agents and attorneys** may charge claimants or appellants for representation provided: **after an agency of original jurisdiction has issued a decision** on a claim or claims, including any claim to reopen under 38 CFR 3.156 or for an increase in rate of a benefit; a Notice of Disagreement has been filed with respect to that decision on or after June 20, 2007; and the agent or attorney has complied with the power of attorney requirements in §14.631 and the fee agreement requirements in paragraph (g) of this section.

. . . See the full text of the regulation for exceptions and other details. . . .

(e) *Fees permitted.* Fees permitted for services of an agent or attorney admitted to practice before VA must be reasonable. They may be based on a fixed fee, hourly rate, a percentage of benefits recovered, or a combination of such bases. Factors considered in determining whether fees are reasonable include:

(1) The extent and type of services the representative performed;

(2) The complexity of the case;

(3) The level of skill and competence required of the representative in giving the services;

(4) The amount of time the representative spent on the case;

(5) The results the representative achieved, including the amount of any benefits recovered;

(6) The level of review to which the claim was taken and the level of the review at which the representative was retained;

(7) Rates charged by other representatives for similar services; and

(8) Whether, and to what extent, the payment of fees is contingent upon the results achieved.

(f) *Presumptions.* **Fees which do not exceed 20 percent of any past-due benefits awarded as defined in paragraph (h)(3) of this section shall be presumed to be reasonable. Fees which exceed 331/3percent of any past-due benefits awarded shall be presumed to be unreasonable.** These presumptions may be rebutted through an examination of the factors in paragraph (e) of this section establishing that there is clear and convincing evidence that a fee which does not exceed 20 percent of any past-due benefits awarded is not reasonable or that a fee which exceeds 331/3percent is reasonable in a specific circumstance.

(g) *Fee agreements.* All agreements for the payment of fees for services of agents and attorneys (including agreements involving fees or salary paid by an organization, governmental entity or other disinterested third party) must be in writing and signed by both the claimant or appellant and the agent or attorney.

(1) To be valid, a fee agreement must include the following:

(i) The name of the veteran,

(ii) The name of the claimant or appellant if other than the veteran,

EXHIBIT 15.2
(continued)

(iii) The name of any disinterested third-party payer (see paragraph (d)(2) of this section) and the relationship between the third-party payer and the veteran, claimant, or appellant,

(iv) The applicable VA file number, and

(v) The specific terms under which the amount to be paid for the services of the attorney or agent will be determined.

(2) Fee agreements must also clearly specify if VA is to pay the agent or attorney directly out of past due benefits. A direct-pay fee agreement is a fee agreement between the claimant or appellant and an agent or attorney providing for payment of fees out of past-due benefits awarded directly to an agent or attorney. A fee agreement that does not clearly specify that VA is to pay the agent or attorney out of past-due benefits or that specifies a fee greater than 20 percent of past-due benefits awarded by VA shall be considered to be an agreement in which the agent or attorney is responsible for collecting any fees for representation from the claimant without assistance from VA.

(3) A **copy of the agreement must be filed** with the Office of the General Counsel within 30 days of its execution. . . .

(h) *Payment of fees by Department of Veterans Affairs directly to an agent or attorney from past-due benefits.* (1) Subject to the requirements of the other paragraphs of this section, including paragraphs (c) and (e), the claimant or appellant and an agent or attorney may enter into a fee agreement providing that payment for the services of the agent or attorney will be made directly to the agent or attorney by VA out of any past-due benefits awarded in any proceeding before VA or the United States Court of Appeals for Veterans Claims. VA will charge and collect an assessment out of the fees paid directly to agents or attorneys from past-due benefits awarded. The amount of such assessment shall be equal to five percent of the amount of the fee required to be paid to the agent or attorney, but in no event shall the assessment exceed $100. Such an agreement will be honored by VA only if the following conditions are met:

(i) The total fee payable (excluding expenses) does not exceed 20 percent of the total amount of the past-due benefits awarded,

(ii) The amount of the fee is contingent on whether or not the claim is resolved in a manner favorable to the claimant or appellant, and

(iii) The award of past-due benefits results in a cash payment to a claimant or an appellant from which the fee may be deducted. An award of past-due benefits will not always result in a cash payment to a claimant or an appellant. For example, no cash payment will be made to military retirees unless there is a corresponding waiver of retirement pay. (*See* 38 U.S.C. 5304(a) and 38 CFR 3.750).

Benefit Categories

Health Care

The VA medical benefits system provides enrolled veterans (and eligible dependents of retired military veterans) with preventive outpatient and inpatient services at VA hospitals and clinics across the country and assistance with prescription medications. Some veterans even qualify for reimbursement of travel costs. Once a veteran is enrolled, she remains enrolled. Veterans can apply for enrollment online. Find a VA hospital or clinic in your area at *http://www2.va. gov/directory/guide/home.asp?isflash=1.*

Even career-long military retirees must enroll through the Defense Enrollment Eligibility Reporting System (DEERS). Care at a military hospital and eligibility for Tricare insurance (discussed below) is totally dependent upon proper registration in DEERS. (*http://tricare.mil/mybenefit/*). Paralegals and family members can get more information at any military base or at: *http://www. military.com/benefits/tricare/defense-enrollment-eligibility-reporting-system.*

The number of veterans enrolled each year depends on congressional funding, so enrollment is based on a system of priorities. Factors used to determine a veteran's priority include length of service, whether the veteran wants care for VA-adjudicated disabilities (commonly referred to as service-connected disabilities) and the level of disability, time since discharge and nature of service (for example, former prisoners of war and Purple Heart recipients), coverage under other health insurance plans, and (in certain priority groups) income level and assets. If income and assets are above the "means test" threshold, the veteran may be required to agree to make copayments; if the veteran is eligible for Medicare and is above the threshold, he may be responsible for the Medicare deductible for part of each year.

If a client is a veteran in need of health care, check the VA Web site (*http:// www4.va.gov/healtheligibility/application*) to determine eligibility and documentation needed to apply. The priority system is complicated and the VA periodically amends factors. For example, the VA recently announced that it has established a service connection to three diseases linked to herbicide Agent Orange use during the Vietnam War: B-cell leukemias, Parkinson's disease, and ischemic heart disease. The income level for priority group 8 was relaxed in 2009, so veterans previously denied enrollment may now be eligible.

Military retirees are also eligible for low-cost health insurance through the Tricare Insurance Programs (*http://www.tricare.mil*). Most military retirees use private health insurance through their civilian employer as their primary coverage, with Tricare as a secondary payer, so that they are not limited to use of military facilities. Spouses of retired veterans lose their military health care benefit when they become eligible for Medicare, but may still participate in the Tricare insurance program.

Disability Compensation

Veterans who are disabled by injury or disease incurred or aggravated during active military service are eligible for monthly compensation payments. The injury itself does not have to be service-related. For example, a service member who suffers disability as the result of a bad tackle during an impromptu football game is eligible, just as a service member who is hurt by enemy fire. The injury may, in fact, be the result of negligent treatment in VA-provided health care.

The amount of compensation varies with the degree of disability, number of dependents, and payment of military retirement or severance. Benefits are not subject to federal and state income tax. Former prisoners of war with specific conditions are presumed to be eligible.

In addition to monthly benefits, a service-related disabled veteran may qualify for:

- An automobile/transportation allowance.
- Guide dog(s) and equipment for the blind
- Prosthetic devices and rehabilitative aids
- A clothing allowance
- Drugs and medicine allowance
- Vocational rehabilitation under the "Chapter 31" program

Even veterans with disabilities that are not service-related may be eligible for support, called a pension and described below, if they have low income, are permanently and totally disabled for reasons other than the veteran's own willful misconduct, and have 90 days or more of active military service, at least one day of which was during a period of war.

Veterans with disabilities or enrolled for health care and in need of residential care may qualify for care in a VA Community Living Center (*http://www1.va.gov/geriatrics*) or in a state veterans' home (*http://www.longtermcarelink.net/ref_state_veterans_va_nursing_homes.htm#List*), or care in a nursing home with a VA contract.

Death compensation payments are made to surviving spouses, children, and dependent parents of those who died in service, and to the surviving dependents of veterans whose death before January 1, 1957, was service-connected. Surviving dependents of veterans who died from service-connected injuries or illnesses after January 1, 1957, are eligible for monthly benefits under a new program known as **Dependency and Indemnity Compensation** (DIC). Surviving dependents of veterans who died of service-connected causes prior to January 1, 1957, may elect to receive benefits under DIC. For more information, see *http://www.vba.va.gov/bln/dependents/spouse.htm*.

Death Compensation
Paid to survivors of those who died in service

Dependency and Indemnity Compensation
Paid to dependents of those who died of service-related cause

Pension

Since 1957, military service pay has been covered by social security. In addition, veterans who are not receiving disability compensation may receive a pension; a veteran eligible for both may choose the higher of pension or disability compensation. The pension is subject to significant eligibility restrictions.

EXHIBIT 15.3
Compensation Table[2]

10%–20% (No Dependents)

Percentage	Rate
10%	$123
20%	$243

30%–60% Without Children

Dependent Status	30%	40%	50%	60%
Veteran Alone	$376	$541	$770	$974
Veteran with Spouse Only	$421	$601	$845	$1064
Veteran with Spouse and One Parent	$457	$649	$905	$1136
Veteran with Spouse and Two Parents	$493	$697	$965	$1208
Veteran with One Parent	$412	$589	$830	$1046
Veteran with Two Parents	$448	$637	$890	$1118
Additional for A/A spouse	$40	$54	$68	$81

70%–100% Without Children

Dependent Status	70%	80%	90%	100%
Veteran Alone	$1,228	$1,427	$1,604	$2,673
Veteran with Spouse Only	$1,333	$1,547	$1,739	$2,823
Veteran with Spouse and One Parent	$1,417	$1,643	$1,847	$2,943
Veteran with Spouse and Two Parents	$1,501	$1,739	$1,955	$3,063
Veteran with One Parent	$1,312	$1,523	$1,712	$2,793
Veteran with Two Parents	$1,396	$1,619	$1,820	$2,913
Additional for A/A spouse	$95	$108	$122	$136

[2]Demonstrates description of disability as percentage—tables for veterans with children not included; see *http://www.vba.va.gov/bln/21/Rates/comp01.htm*.

Veterans of wartime service, age 65 or older, or under age 65 with a disability not caused by their own willful misconduct, may be able to obtain a VA pension benefit (remember, this is not the same as a military retirement pension through the Defense Department, such as the pension received by Greg Duncan see Exhibit 15.4). Eligibility for a VA pension may depend on duration of service, net worth, and family income. A veteran who qualifies for a VA pension may also qualify for **aid and attendance** (A&A). A&A benefits are not available without a VA pension (which is means-based) and are generally available if any of the following are true:

Aid and Attendance
Benefit that may accompany pension

- The veteran requires the aid of another person in order to perform personal functions required in everyday living, such as bathing, feeding, dressing, adjusting prosthetic devices, or protection from the hazards of daily environment.
- The veteran is bedridden.

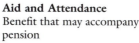

EXHIBIT 15.4
Greg Says

All paralegals need excellent technology skills.

Greg Duncan is a paralegal working in the research department of the Second District Appellate Court of Illinois. He completed two other careers before entering the paralegal field. The first was a 20-year career as an electronics technician in the U.S. Navy submarine nuclear power program. The second was a 15-year career as a technical training supervisor at several Midwestern nuclear power plants. In 1991, Greg earned a master's degree in Technology Education from Bowling Green State University. He completed an ABA-approved paralegal certificate program in 2004.

Being a nontraditional student, Greg was concerned about how he would be perceived by employers in the legal field. To start networking, Greg volunteered his technology skills to a project under the supervision of one of the local trial judges. The judge was trying to put together statistics about outcomes in child custody cases, looking at a number of factors, such as allegations of abuse. The judge did not know how to organize the information so that it could be sorted according to different factors. Greg created a spreadsheet with rows for each factor so that the information could be sorted according to the user's needs. He subsequently created a PowerPoint presentation, with charts and graphs, to share the information with the other judges in the circuit. As a result, Greg conducted his job search armed with a letter of recommendation from a judge. Greg's interest in technology has continued. He developed and taught a class on law office computing for the local community college and is now studying computer forensics.

- The veteran is a patient in a nursing home due to mental or physical incapacity.
- The veteran is blind, or nearly blind.

Housebound
Benefit that may accompany pension

Housebound benefits are also paid in addition to monthly VA pension. Like A&A, housebound benefits may not be paid without eligibility for a VA pension. A veteran may be eligible for housebound benefits under either of these circumstances:

- The veteran has a single permanent disability evaluated as 100 percent disabling and, due to such disability, is permanently and substantially confined to immediate premises.
- The veteran has a single permanent disability evaluated as 100 percent disabling and another disability, or disabilities, evaluated as 60 percent or more disabling.

A veteran cannot receive both A&A and housebound benefits at the same time.

Death and Burial Benefits

Death Pension
Paid to survivors of wartime veterans

Death pension is a benefit paid to eligible spouses and dependent children of deceased veterans who served during war times. Eligibility is means-based. Monthly pension benefits are payable to surviving spouses and children of veterans of the Mexican border period, World War I, World War II, the Korean conflict, and the Vietnam era even if the veteran died of causes not related to service. The veteran must have served at least 90 days unless separated from the service for a service-connected disability.

Five burial benefits are available for all veterans who were honorably discharged:

- United States flag is provided at no cost to drape the casket or accompany the urn of a deceased veteran.
- Families of veterans on VA disability or pension at the time of death may receive a burial and funeral allowance.
- Veterans and dependents may be buried in national cemeteries.
- A Presidential Memorial Certificate expressing the country's thanks is available for families of deceased veterans.
- Upright stones and flat grave markers are available for the veteran regardless of whether internment is in a VA or private cemetery. Spouses and dependents may qualify if burial is in a national cemetery.

Other Benefits

Other benefits and programs available to veterans and surviving dependents include:

- Educational benefits for dependents of deceased/disabled veterans
- Home mortgage and small business administration loans
- Civil service preferences
- Expedited processing of social security disability claims

There are many resources available to assist veterans with respect to all benefits. For example, many members of Congress have assistants assigned to help veterans or have information to assist veterans posted on their Web sites, and the Board of Veterans' Appeals has an online ombudsman: *http://www.bva.va.gov/OMBUDSMAN_CustomerService.asp*.

Assignments

1. Using 38 CFR §14.629, determine how an attorney becomes qualified to represent clients dealing with the VA. Now determine how a non-attorney (paralegal) could qualify.

2. Critical Thinking: Answer the following questions about the *Hite* case at the end of this chapter, using the VA Benefits handbook currently found at: *http://www1.va.gov/opa/publications/benefits_book/benefits_chap13.asp*
   - What is the presumption with respect to chronic conditions?
   - What is the "Board" to which the court refers and, assuming that the initial determination was made by a regional office, how did Mrs. Hite obtain review by that Board and what was the time limit for seeking review?
   - Using the Board's online booklet describing appeals, determine: What is a NOD? What is form 9? Is there any indication that a veteran's representative on appeal must be an attorney?
   - What is the "Veteran's Court" to which the court refers?
   - Visit *http://www.uscourts.cavc.gov* and find the top ten reasons why submissions to the court are rejected.

3. Based on your reading of both cases, discuss:
   - Why do you think the regulation requiring the VA to assist applicants was enacted?
   - Does the assistance requirement shift the burden of proof?
   - Identify two situations in which the burden of proof does shift — in other words, the applicant is not required to prove that an injury or disability is service-related. Why do you think these exceptions were enacted?

4. Write a short report (2–3 pages), citing news media and governmental sources, about the impact that the return of veterans from Iraq and Afghanistan has had on the VA's ability to provide benefits.

Review Questions

1. What are the differences between benefits described as compensation and those described as pension?
2. Why are veterans pursuing VA benefits rarely represented by attorneys?
3. What is a DD214?
4. Who may represent a veteran seeking benefits? What are the limits on attorney fees?
5. How does the VA determine which veterans can receive VA health care?
6. How does a veteran apply for benefits? What can she do if benefits are denied at the first level?
7. Which benefits are available to all veterans?

HITE V. SHINSEKI

United States Court of Appeals for the Federal Circuit (unpublished, 2010)

... Mrs. Hite's husband served on active duty in the United States Army from May 1970 to July 1993. He died in June 1997, of hypertensive cardiovascular disease. Before his death, he had not asserted service connection for any illness or disability. Upon Mrs. Hite's claim, the Board reviewed Mr. Hite's in-service medical records, including records of a 1973 examination, a 1976 examination, a 1988 examination, and a 1991 examination. Records from the 1988 examination noted an abnormal control electrocardiogram ("EKG") manifested after the examining physician administered a treadmill stress test, although the EKG during the stress test was normal. In view of this apparently conflicting test information, the Board in 2002 obtained a medical review of Mr. Hite's service records. The reviewing physician concluded that the normal EKG results during the stress test superseded any abnormal EKG during the control test, and concluded that Mr. Hite's cause of death was unrelated to his service. The Board relied on the reviewing physician's opinion, and stated that "there is no medical evidence to support the contention that the veteran's death was in any way related to service."

On appeal, the Veterans Court found that the Board erred by failing to discuss the issue of hypertension, for Mrs. Hite stated that blood pressure readings throughout her husband's service records and thereafter showed hypertension, including (1) a 1980 reading of 123/82; (2) a 1982 reading of 130/90; (3) a 1983 reading of 126/80; (4) a 1986 reading of 138/76; (5) a 1988 reading of 126/82; (6) a 1992 reading of 136/90; (7) a 1995 reading of 165/101; and (8) a 2000 reading of 132/80. The Veterans Court explained that hypertension is statutorily defined as a reading showing a diastolic pressure of 90 mm or greater, when readings are taken two or more times on three consecutive days, citing 38 C.F.R. §4.104, Diagnostic Code 7101 (2008). The Veterans Court then reviewed Mr. Hite's medical records and found "only the April 1982 reading showing a diastolic pressure of 90 or higher." Veterans Court Decision at 4. The Veterans Court discounted this 1982 reading because it was taken in the emergency room after Mr. Hite sustained an injury during a parachute training jump. The Veterans Court observed that the 1995 reading of 165/101 was taken more than two years after the conclusion of Mr. Hite's service, and was outside of the one-year presumptive period. The court found that the evidence did not support a finding that the veteran suffered from hypertension during service or within one year thereafter. Thus the court concluded that any error by the Board with respect to consideration of hypertension was harmless error. Mrs. Hite moved for reconsideration, which the Veterans Court denied. In this appeal, Mrs. Hite challenges the Veterans Court's factual determinations. ...

Our jurisdiction to review decisions of the Veterans Court is limited by statute and, absent a constitutional issue, we have no authority to review a challenge to a factual determination or a challenge to the application of law to particular facts. 38 U.S.C. §7292(d)(2) (2006). The issues presented are within the proscribed categories. Although Mrs. Hite also contends that the Board erred in failing to apply 38 C.F.R. §3.303(b), which provides a presumption of service connection for a "chronic disease shown as such in service (or within the presumptive period under §3.307)" that is manifested again "at any later date, however remote," "unless clearly attributable to intercurrent causes," the applicability of

§3.303(b) turns on the factual determination of whether a chronic disease was shown during service or within the presumptive one-year period. The Veterans Court's finding that hypertension was not shown during service or within one year thereafter is a factual finding, and review of that finding is not within our appellate jurisdiction.

Mrs. Hite also states that the VA failed to notify her of the information and evidence needed to substantiate her claim, as required by 38 U.S.C. §5103(a). Mrs. Hite disputes that she received a March 2004 notification letter from the VA. However, the Veterans Court affirmed the Board's determination that §5103(a) notice was provided, citing Mrs. Hite's written response in October 2004, which stated "that she had 'no further new evidence to add to her case, and she had exhausted all means to gather any additional information.'" Although failure to notify a claimant of rights or deadlines may be a ground of appropriate relief, the burden of proving that such error occurred, and whether the error was harmful, is on the claimant. . . . Mrs. Hite also states that the Board erred by refusing to give her the benefit of the doubt in accordance with 38 U.S.C. §5107 (b). The benefit-of-the-doubt doctrine applies when the evidence is "nearly equal," thereby creating a "reasonable doubt." . . . It does not apply when the veterans tribunals find that the evidence weighs against the claim, as was found here. As to whether the Board and the Veterans Court erred in any factual findings with respect to Mrs. Hite's claim, we do not have jurisdiction to review these findings. The appeal must be dismissed.

CROMER V. NICHOLSON

455 F.3d 1346 (Fed. Cir. 2006) [internal citations omitted]

. . . Cromer served in the active-duty armed forces from September, 1945, through May, 1947. . . . In 1993, he filed a claim for disability based on service-connected dementia allegedly caused when he "suffered a fever of 108 degrees while assigned at Ft. Sill, Oklahoma, during November 1945 related to consumption of milk contaminated with streptococci agent." The record indicates that Cromer attempted to acquire his service medical records to support his claim, but was told by the National Personnel Records Center that his records were unavailable and "were likely destroyed in a fire in 1973." . . . In the absence of those records, Cromer supported his claim with a physician's statement indicating that his illness dated from his time in service. In addition, the Department of Veterans Affairs ("VA") sought and obtained other records on Cromer's behalf, including "hospital extracts from the Office of the Army Surgeon General . . . showing brief periods of hospitalization for pharyngitis and peritonsillar abscess in 1945." The additional records did not directly support Cromer's claim.

The Veterans Administration Regional Office ("RO") denied the claim on May 25, 1994. Cromer then filed an application seeking to re-open his initial claim; the RO denied that application on April 6, 1996. Subsequently, in 1998, the Board remanded Cromer's case for further development. The RO denied the remanded claim on July 26, 1999, concluding that no "new and material evidence" had been submitted sufficient to justify re-opening Cromer's claim. The Board affirmed that denial. While that decision was on appeal to the Veterans Court, the parties filed a joint motion seeking remand to the Board for further development and adjudication. The Veterans Court granted that motion on December 20, 1999. After further proceedings, the Board once again denied Cromer's claim. Before the Veterans Court, the parties filed another joint motion for remand, stating that Cromer had submitted new and material evidence sufficient to re-open his claim, and asking that the Board be permitted to review Cromer's case on the merits. On December 7, 2001, the Veterans Court granted that motion. After further proceedings, the Board denied Cromer's claim again, concluding that Cromer's "[d]ementia began many years after service and was not caused by any incident of service."

On appeal . . . Cromer did not challenge the Board's finding that "the preponderance of the evidence is against the claim for service connection for dementia." Instead, he raised only a single issue, arguing that the Veterans Court should have applied an "adverse presumption" favoring service connection in circumstances where medical records are lost or destroyed while in possession of the government.

On July 8, 2005, the Veterans Court affirmed the Board's decision. Noting that Cromer raised only the adverse presumption issue, it concluded that "the appellant has not raised any issue contained in the Board's decision," and that therefore "those issues are deemed abandoned." It nevertheless considered Cromer's adverse presumption argument. It noted that the presumption Cromer sought was rooted in no statutory provision or recognized nonstatutory rule, but was grounded "solely on general principles of evidence and equity." It then discussed what it considered the general rule that the "adverse-presumption rule has historically been associated with bad-faith" or negligent destruction of records, and concluded that because Cromer had "not demonstrated that either bad faith or negligent destruction of documents was implicated in the 1973 fire" that destroyed Cromer's records, it "need not decide whether the presumption advanced by the appellant should be adopted." This appeal followed. [standard of review and jurisdictional analysis omitted]

The government argues that Cromer's appeal is nonjusticiable because no relief would be available to him even if he prevailed on the adverse presumption issue. A claim is justiciable if it involves "a real and substantial controversy admitting of specific relief through a decree of a conclusive character." Here, the government argues that Cromer's appeal is nonjusticiable because

> [E]ven if this Court were to grant Mr. Cromer's request and create the presumption that he requests, this presumption would not affect the outcome of his case because: a) the presumption could be overcome by a preponderance of the evidence; b) the board has already concluded that the preponderance of the evidence demonstrated that his dementia is not service connected; and c) Mr. Cromer has not challenged the board's conclusion regarding the preponderance of the evidence.

Although the government's argument carries a certain superficial force, we disagree. Cromer's appeal, by arguing that the adverse presumption should be applied to the determination of service connection, inherently challenges the Board's application of the preponderance standard in making that determination. As we discussed above, evidence that is insufficient to satisfy the preponderance standard in the absence of the presumption is not necessarily insufficient to satisfy the preponderance standard if such a presumption is operative. A contrary ruling would render the presumption superfluous. The better answer, we believe, is that the operation of the adverse presumption would require a reassessment of the evidence by the Board. Thus, Cromer's appeal is susceptible of relief and presents a controversy that is justiciable in this court.

Cromer's claim breaks down into two components. First, he argues that because his medical records were in the custody of the government when they were destroyed by fire, the government should be presumed to have acted negligently in failing to preserve them. Second, he argues that once negligent destruction is presumed, an adverse presumption of service connection should be imposed against the government. Cromer's arguments in support of this double presumption lack merit.

First, neither presumption is rooted in any applicable statute, regulation, or judicial decision. In fact, both presumptions are contrary to the general evidentiary burden in veterans' benefit cases, which requires that "a claimant has the responsibility to present and support a claim for [VA] benefits." 38 U.S.C. §5107 (a). The presumptions, by effectively shifting the burden of proof to the government, conflict with that standard. Second, Congress and the VA have expressly carved out exceptions to the general rule of §5107(a) where they deemed a shift in the burden of proof to be necessary or just — see, for example, 38 U.S. C. §105(a) (creating a presumption that injuries incurred during active military service were incurred in the line of duty), and 38 U.S.C. §1116 (creating a presumption of service connection for diseases associated with Agent Orange) — but have not done so here.

The VA is obligated by statute to "make reasonable efforts to assist a claimant in obtaining evidence necessary to substantiate" a veteran's claim for benefits. 38 U.S.C. §5103A. The VA discharged that obligation here by seeking and obtaining alternative medical records to supplant the records apparently destroyed in the 1973 fire, and Cromer does not contend otherwise. The relief Cromer seeks would amount to a judicial amendment of the statutory duty to assist — a measure beyond the power of this court. In addition, the VA, cognizant of the difficulties faced by veterans whose records have been lost, has enacted several regulations precisely to ease the evidentiary burdens faced by veterans whose records were lost in the 1973 fire. The VA Adjudication Manual provides a procedure for cases affected by the 1973 fire, requiring the VA to "assist the claimant in obtaining [medical] evidence from alternate or collateral sources" and listing ten alternate sources that "might substitute for service medical records in decisions relating to service connection for a disability." Similarly, in cases involving lost records, the Board has a heightened duty to explain its findings. In the absence of a statutory or constitutional imperative, it would be improper for this court to impose a judicial remedy to supplant or supplement the remedies and procedures already provided by Congress and the VA.

Finally, Cromer has identified no decision in which an adverse presumption or inference was drawn in the absence of bad faith or, at a minimum, negligence. Conceding this failure, Cromer asks this court to create a new rule for the admittedly unusual circumstances presented by the "paternalistic" and non-adversarial context of veterans' benefits. This we decline to do. Congress, the VA, and the courts have been aware of the challenges posed by the loss of records in the 1973 fire for more than thirty years, and have enacted procedures intended to ameliorate those challenges for veterans. That Cromer finds the procedures adopted by Congress and the Executive inadequate is not a sufficient basis on which this court can create a new rule that would alter the process for benefits claims. Accordingly, we affirm the decision of the Veterans Court.

www.CrosswordWeaver.com

ACROSS

1. Most benefits require discharge that is not _____
5. Many benefits are calculated from time of _____
7. Aid & _____ may accompany pension
9. Generally refers to payments based on need
10. VONAPP = _____ filing
12. Health benefits allocated by _____
13. VA is required to _____ applicants
14. Benefit, alternative to A&A
15. Veteran generally has burden of proving injury or disability is _____ related

DOWN

1. DIC = _____ and Indemnity Compensation
2. VAROs are _____ offices
3. All vets are eligible for these benefits, if honorably discharged
4. _____ test, takes income into consideration
6. Generally refers to payment for death or injury
8. Disabilities are described in terms of this
11. Some benefits require service during time of _____

INDEX